The Complete Guide to the TOEFL® Test

iBT Edition

Audio Scripts and Answer Key

Bruce Rogers

THOMSON
™

Australia • Canada • Mexico • Singapore • Spain • United Kingdom • United States

The Complete Guide to the TOEFL® Test, iBT Edition
Audio Scripts and Answer Key

Bruce Rogers

Publisher, Academic ESL: *James W. Brown*
Executive Editor, Dictionaries & Adult ESL: *Sherrise Roehr*
Director of Content Development: *Anita Raducanu*
Associate Development Editor: *Jennifer Meldrum*
Director of Product Marketing: *Amy Mabley*
Senior Field Marketing Manager: *Donna Lee Kennedy*
International Marketing Manager: *Ian Martin*
Assistant Marketing Manager: *Heather Soberg*

Senior Print Buyer: *Mary Beth Hennebury*
Production Editor: *Chrystie Hopkins*
Development Editor: *Charlotte Sturdy*
Project Manager: *Merrill Peterson*
Production Services: *Matrix Productions*
Compositor: *Parkwood Composition Service*
Cover Designer: *Studio Montage*
Printer: *West Group*

For permission to use material from this text or product, submit a request online at
http://www.thomsonrights.com

Any additional questions about permissions can be submitted by email to
thomsonrights@thomson.com

ISBN-13: 978-1-4130-2311-4
ISBN-10: 1-4130-2311-8

For more information contact Thomson Heinle,
25 Thomson Place, Boston, Massachusetts 02210 USA, or you can visit our Internet site at elt.thomson.com

TABLE OF CONTENTS

AUDIO SCRIPTS

ANSWER KEY

Audio Script

[CD 1 Track 1]

Narrator: Welcome to the Audio Program for the *Complete Guide to the TOEFL Test: iBT Edition,* by Bruce Rogers. Published by Thomson ELT, Boston, Massachusetts. All rights reserved.

[CD 1 Track 2]

Section 2: Guide to Listening

Preview Test

Listen as the directions are read to you.

Narrator: Directions: This section tests your understanding of conversations and lectures. You will hear each conversation or lecture only once. Your answers should be based on what is stated or implied in the conversations and lectures. You are allowed to take notes as you listen, and you can use these notes to help you answer the questions. In some questions, you will see a headphones icon. This icon tells you that you will hear, but not read, part of the lecture again. Then you will answer a question about the part of the lecture that you heard. Some questions have special directions that are highlighted. During an actual test, you may not skip questions and come back to them later, so try to answer every question that you hear on this test. On an actual test, there are two conversations and four lectures. You will have twenty minutes (not counting the time spent listening) in which to complete this section of the test. On this Preview Test, there is one conversation and three lectures. Most questions are separated by a ten-second pause.

Narrator: Listen to a conversation between a student and a professor.

Student: Professor Dixon? I'm Brenda Pierce. From your Geology 210 class . . . ?

Professor: Yes. I know. That's a big class, but I do recognize you. As a matter of fact, I noticed you weren't in class yesterday morning. Did you oversleep? That's one of the problems with an 8:00 class. I almost overslept myself a couple of times.

Student: Oh, uh, no, I didn't oversleep. In fact, I was up at 5:00—one of my roommates had an early flight and I took her to the airport. I thought I'd make it back here in time, but, uh, well, you know . . . you know how traffic can be out on Airport Road at that time of day. Anyway, uh, I know you were going to tell us . . . give us some information about our research paper in class today. Do you have a few minutes to fill me in?

Professor: Well, umm, a few minutes, I guess. This isn't my regular office hour. I actually just came by my office to pick up a few papers before the faculty meeting.

Student: Okay, well . . . about the research paper . . . how long does it have to be?

Professor: Well, as I told the class, the paper counts for 30% of your grade. It should be at least twelve pages, but no more than twenty-five. And your bibliography should contain at least ten reference sources.

Student: Will you be assigning the topic, or . . .

Professor: I'm leaving the choice of topic up to you. Of course, it should be related to something we've discussed in class.

Student: I, I'm interested in writing about earthquakes . . .

Professor: Hmm. Earthquakes . . . well, I don't know, Brenda . . . that sounds like much too broad a topic for a short research paper.

Student: Oh, well, I'm planning to choose . . . I plan to get more specific than that. I want to write about using animals to predict earthquakes.

Professor: Really? Well, once scientists wondered if maybe . . . if perhaps there was some connection between strange behavior in animals and earthquakes . . . and that maybe animals . . . that you could use them to predict earthquakes. But there have been a lot of studies on this subject, you know, and so far, none of them have shown anything promising . . .

Student: But I thought there was this . . . I saw this show on television about earthquakes, and it said that in, uh, China, I think it was, they did predict an earthquake because of the way animals were acting.

Professor: Oh, right—you're thinking of the Haecheng earthquake about thirty years ago. Well, that's true. There were snakes coming out of the ground in the middle of winter when they should have been hibernating . . . and supposedly horses and other animals were acting frightened. And there were other signs, too, not just from animals. So the government ordered an evacuation of the area, and in fact, there was an earthquake, so thousands of lives were probably saved.

Student: Yeah, that's what I'm thinking of . . . that's what I saw on television.

Professor: The problem is that, unfortunately, no one's been able to duplicate that kind of result . . . in China or anywhere else. There have been lots of earthquakes since then that haven't been predicted, and there have been a couple of false alarms when cities were evacuated for no reason . . . and like I said, none of the studies that have been done have shown that animals are any better at predicting earthquakes than people are.

Student: So that's . . . so you don't think that's a very good idea for a topic, then, I suppose . . .

Professor: I didn't say that . . . just because this theory hasn't been proven doesn't mean you couldn't write a perfectly good paper about this topic . . . on the notion that animals can predict earthquakes. Why not? It could be pretty interesting. But to do a good job, you . . . you'll need to look at some serious studies in the scientific journals, not just some pop-science articles in newspapers, or . . . and you can't get your information from television shows.

Student: You really think it might make a good paper? Well, then, I think if I can get enough information from the library or the Internet . . .

Professor: Okay, why don't you see what you can find? Oh, I forgot to mention . . . you'll need to write up a formal proposal for your paper, and work up a preliminary bibliography, and hand it in to me a week from tomorrow. I'll need to approve it before you get started. Now, if you'll excuse me, Brenda, I've got to get to that faculty meeting.

Narrator: Now get ready to answer the questions. You may use your notes to help you.

Narrator: Question 1: What is this conversation mainly about?

Narrator: Question 2: Listen again to part of the conversation. Then answer the question.

Student: Professor Dixon? I'm Brenda Pierce. From your Geology 210 class . . . ?

Narrator: What can be inferred about the student?

Narrator: Question 3: What assumption does the professor make about the student?

1

Narrator: Question 4: How did the student first get information about the topic she wants to write about?
Narrator: Question 5: What is the professor's attitude toward the topic that the student wants to write about?

Narrator: Now listen to a lecture in a biology class.
Professor: Okay, everyone . . . if you remember, on Wednesday we talked about the general concept of biomes. So, just to review, biomes are large zones, big sections of the planet that have similar conditions and have the same kinds of plants and animals. Last class, we talked about the tundra, remember? This is a strip of land in the far, far north. We said the tundra consists mainly of open, marshy planes with no trees, just some low shrubs.

So, okay, today, we're going to continue our tour of the world's biomes. The next biome you come to, as you head south from the tundra, is the taiga. That's spelled t-a-i-g-a, taiga. It's also called the "boreal forest." The taiga is the largest of all the world's biomes. About 25% of all the world's forests are found in the taiga.

Now, the word *taiga* means "marshy evergreen forest." It comes from the Russian language, and that's not too surprising, really, because there are huge, I mean, really enormous stretches of taiga in Russia. But taiga isn't just found in Russia. Like the tundra, the taiga is a more-or-less continuous belt that circles the North Pole, running through Russia, Scandinavia, Canada, Alaska. Most of this land was—well, it used to be covered by glaciers, and these glaciers left deep gouges and depressions in the land. And not surprisingly, these filled up with water—with melted snow—so you have lots of lakes and ponds and marshes in the taiga.

Within the taiga itself, you'll find three sub-zones. The first of these you come to, as you're going south, is called open forest. The only trees here are needle-leaf trees—you know, evergreen trees, what we call coniferous trees. These trees tend to be small and far apart. This is basically tundra—it looks like tundra, but with a few small trees. Next, you come to what's called closed forest, with bigger needle-leaf trees growing closer together. This feels more like a real forest. This sub-zone—well, if you like variety, you're not going to feel happy here. You can travel for miles and see only half a dozen species of trees. In a few days, we'll be talking about the tropical rain forest; now, that's where you'll see variety. Okay, finally, you come to the mixed zone. The trees are bigger still here, and you'll start seeing some broad-leafed trees, deciduous trees. You'll see larch, aspen, especially along rivers and creeks, in addition to needle-leaf trees. So this sub-zone feels a bit more like the temperate forests we're used to.

So, what are conditions like in the taiga? Well, to start with, you've gotta understand that it's cold there. I mean, very cold. Summers are short, winters long. So the organisms that call the taiga home have to be well adapted to cold. The trees in the taiga, as I already said, are coniferous trees like the pine, fir, and spruce. And these trees, they've adapted to cold weather. How? Well, for one thing, they never lose their leaves—they're "evergreen," right, always green, so in the spring, they don't have to waste time—don't have to waste energy—growing new leaves. They're ready to start photosynthesizing right away. And then, for another thing, these trees are conical—shaped like cones—aren't they? This means that snow doesn't accumulate too much on the branches; it just slides off, and so, well, that means their branches don't break under the weight of the snow. And even their color—that dark, dark green—it's useful because it absorbs the sun's heat.

What about the animals that live up there? You remember I said there were lots of marshes and lakes. These watery places make wonderful breeding grounds for insects. So naturally, in the summer, you get lots of insects. And insects attract birds, right? Plenty of birds migrate to the taiga in the summer to, uh, to feast on insects. Lots of the mammals that live in the taiga migrate to warmer climates once cold weather sets in. But there are some year-round residents. Among the predators—the animals that hunt other animals—there are Arctic foxes, wolves, bears, martens, oh, and ermines. There's one thing all these predators have in common, the ones that live there all year round . . . they all have thick, warm fur coats, don't they? This heavy fur keeps them toasty in the winter. Of course, on the downside, it makes them desirable to hunters and trappers. Some of these predators survive the winter by hibernating, by sleeping right through it . . . bears, for example. And some change colors. You've heard of the ermine, right? In the summer, the ermine is dark brown, but in the winter, it turns white. That makes it hard to spot, so it can sneak up on its prey.

Then, uh, what sorts of herbivores live up there? What do the predators eat to stay alive? There's the moose, of course, but only young moose are at risk of being attacked. The adult moose is the biggest, strongest animal found in the taiga, so a predator would have to be feeling pretty desperate to take on one of these. Mostly, predators hunt smaller prey, like snowshoe rabbits, voles, lemmings . . .

Okay, the next biome we come to is the temperate forest, where broadleaf trees like, oh, maples and oaks are most common, but before we get to this, I'd like to give you an opportunity to ask me some questions about the taiga.
Narrator: Now get ready to answer the questions. You may use your notes to help you.
Narrator: Question 6: What does the professor say about the word *taiga*?
Narrator: Question 7: Why does the speaker say this:
Professor: This sub-zone—well, if you like variety, you're not going to feel happy here. You can travel for miles and see only half a dozen species of trees. In a few days, we'll be talking about the tropical rain forest; now, *that's* where you'll see variety.
Narrator: Question 8: The professor discussed three sub-zones of the taiga. Match each sub-zone with its characteristic.
Narrator: Question 9: When discussing needle-leaf trees, which of these adaptations to cold weather does the professor mention?
Narrator: Question 10: What characteristic do all of the predators of the taiga have in common?
Narrator: Question 11: What does the professor imply about moose?

Narrator: Listen to a discussion in the first class of a business course.
Professor: Well, I guess everyone's here, huh? We may as well get started. Good morning, all. I'm Professor Robert Speed and I'd like you . . . I'd like to welcome you to the Foundations of Business class. The purpose of this class is really to acquaint you with the tools, the various tools, techniques you'll be using in most of your business courses. And we'll concentrate especially on the case study method, because you'll be using that in almost . . . well, in most of the business classes you take.
Student A: The . . . case study method, Professor? Is that a new method of teaching business?

Professor: Oh, no, no, no. I mean . . . it may seem new to you, but, no, in fact, a professor named Christopher Longdell introduced this system at Harvard University back . . . around the 1870's. And he always insisted that it was based on a system used by Chinese philosophers thousands of years ago.

Student B: So then, they've . . . it's been used in business schools ever since the . . . when did you say, the 1870's?

Professor: Well, you see, Professor Longdell, he . . . he in fact taught in the law school at Harvard, not in the business school. So the case method first . . . it was first used to train law students. Then, a couple of years after that, they started using it at Columbia University, at the law school there. It wasn't until . . . When was it? Uh, probably about 1910, 1912, something like that, that it was used . . . first used at Harvard Business School.

Student B: Then, it's used in other fields? Besides law and business?

Professor: Oh sure, over the years, it's been used in all sorts of disciplines. For example, my wife . . . she teaches over at the School of Education . . . she uses cases to train teachers.

Student A: Professor Speed, I get that case study has been around awhile, but I still don't quite understand why we're . . . well, why do we study cases, exactly?

Professor: Okay, before the case method was introduced, the study of law and business was very . . . abstract . . . theoretical. It was just, just lectures about theory. Professor Longdell thought—and a lot of educators thought—that really, the best way to learn law, business, any discipline you can think of, is by studying actual situations and analyzing these situations . . . and learning to make decisions.

Student A: That makes sense, but . . . I mean, what does a case look like, exactly . . . I mean, what does it . . . ?

Professor: What does a case look like? Well, cases are basically descriptions of actual—let me stress that—of real business situations, chunks of reality from the business world. So, you get typically ten to twenty pages of text that describe the problem, some problem that a real business actually faced. And then there will be another five to ten pages of what are called exhibits.

Student B: Exhibits? What are those?

Professor: Exhibits . . . those are documents, statistical documents, that explain the situation. They might be oh, spreadsheets, sales reports, umm, marketing projections, anything like that. But as I said, at the center of every case, at the core of every case, is a problem that you have to solve. So, you have to analyze the situation, the data—and sometimes, you'll see you don't have enough data to work with, and you might have to collect more—say, from the Internet. Then, you have to make decisions about how to solve these problems.

Student B: So that's why we study cases? I mean, because managers need to be able to make decisions . . . and solve problems?

Professor: Exactly . . . well, that's a big part of it, anyway. And doing this, solving the problem, usually involves role-playing, taking on the roles of decision-makers at the firm. One member of the group might play the Chief Executive Officer, one the Chief Financial Officer, and so on. And you . . . you might have a business meeting to decide how your business should solve its problem. Your company might, say, be facing a cash shortage and thinking about selling off one division of the company. So your group has to decide if this is the best way to handle the problem.

Student B: So we work in groups, then?

Professor: Usually in groups of four or five. That's the beauty of this method. It teaches teamwork and cooperation.

Student A: And then what? How are we . . . how do you decide on a grade for us?

Professor: You give a presentation, an oral presentation, I mean, and you explain to the whole class what decision you made and . . . what recommendations you'd make . . . and then you write a report as well. You get a grade, a group grade, on the presentation and the report.

Student B: Professor, is this the only way we'll be studying business, by using cases?

Professor: Oh, no, it's just one important way. Some classes are lecture classes and some are a combination of lectures and case studies and some . . . in some classes you'll also use computer simulations. We have this software called World Marketplace, and using this program, your group starts up your own global corporation and tries to make a profit . . . it's actually a lot of fun.

Narrator: Now get ready to answer the questions. You may use your notes to help you.

Narrator: Question 12: Professor Speed mentions several stages in the history of the case method. Put these steps in the proper order.

Narrator: Question 13: What does Professor Speed say about exhibits?

Narrator: Question 14: What does the professor mean when he says this:

Professor: It wasn't until . . . when was it? Probably about 1910, 1912, something like that, that it was used . . . first used at Harvard Business School.

Narrator: Question 15: Why does Professor Speed mention his wife?

Narrator: Question 16: In this lecture, the professor describes the process of the case study method. Indicate whether each of the following is a step in the process.

Narrator: Question 17: Which of the following reasons does the professor give for using the case study method?

Narrator: Listen to a student giving a presentation in an astronomy class.

Student Presenter: Well, uh, hi, everyone . . . Monday, we heard Don tell us about the Sun, and, uh, Lisa talk about Mercury, the planet closest to the Sun. My . . . my, uh, report, what I'm talking about is the next planet, the second planet, Venus. Okay, to start off, I'm going to tell you what people, well, what they used to think about Venus. First off, back in the really . . . in the really ancient days, people thought Venus was a star, not a planet, and . . . well, actually, you know how you can see Venus in the early morning and in the evening? Well, so they thought it was *two* stars, Phosphorus—that was the morning star . . . and, uh, let's see, Hesperus, the evening star. And then, once they figured out it was just one planet, they named it Venus after the goddess of love—I don't really know why, though.

And then later, people started studying Venus through a telescope, and they found out it was covered by clouds. Not partly covered by clouds, like Earth, but completely wrapped up in clouds. And since it was closer to the Sun than Earth, people imagined it was warm there, like it is in the tropics. In the nineteenth century, there was this belief, a lot of people believed, for some reason, that there were these creatures on Venus who were superior to us, almost perfect beings, like angels or something. Then, uh, in the early part of the twentieth century, people imagined that, uh, under the clouds there were swamps and jungles and monsters. There was this guy, this author, um, Edgar Rice Burroughs, he also wrote the Tarzan books, and, uh, he wrote books in the 1930's about . . . well, the series was called "Carson of Venus," and it was about some explorer from Earth having wild adventures and fighting monsters in the jungles. This idea of a "warm" Venus lasted until the 1950's.

Okay, so . . . Venus is the brightest object in the sky, except for the Sun and the moon, and except for the moon it comes closer to the Earth than any other planet, a lot closer than Mars, the, uh, fourth planet. One of the articles I read about Venus said that Venus is Earth's sister . . . Earth's twin, I guess it said. That's because Venus is about the same size as Earth . . . and uh, it's made out of the same basic materials. And Earth and Venus are about the same age; they, uh, were formed about the same time.

But really, we know nowadays that Earth and Venus are not really much like twins. For one thing, the air, the atmosphere of Venus is made out of carbon dioxide and sulfuric acid—not very nice stuff to breathe. And it's really thick, the atmosphere is. It's so thick, it's like being at the bottom of an ocean on Earth, so if astronauts ever went there, they'd have to have a . . . something like a diving bell to keep from getting crushed. And they'd need really good air conditioning, too, because it's really hot down there, not warm the way people used to think. All those clouds hold in the Sun's heat, you see. It's hotter than an oven, hot enough to melt lead, too hot to have any liquid water. So, guess what that means—no jungles, no swamps, and no weird creatures!

Okay, now here's a really strange fact about Venus. It takes Venus only 225 Earth days to go around the Sun, as opposed to the Earth, which of course takes 365 days— what we call a year. But Venus turns around on its axis really slowly. Really slowly. It takes 243 Earth days to spin around completely. The Earth takes—you guessed it—24 hours. This means that a day on Venus is longer than a year on Venus! In fact, a day on Venus is longer than . . . well, than on any planet in the solar system, longer even than on those big gas planets like Jupiter. And here's something else weird. All the planets of the solar system turn on their axis in the same direction as they orbit the Sun. All except Venus, of course! It has what's called a . . . wait, let's see . . . okay, a "retrograde" spin.

Now, there have been quite a few space probes that have gone to Venus, so I'm only going to mention a few of them, the most important ones. I guess, umm, one of the most important was called Magellan. Magellan was launched in 1990 and spent four years in orbit around Venus. It used, uh, radar, I guess, to map the planet, and it found out that there are all these volcanoes on Venus, just like there are on Earth. The first one to go there, the first probe to go there successfully, was Mariner 2 in, uh, 1962. Mariner 1 was supposed to go there, but it blew up. There was one, it was launched by the Soviet Union back in the, uh, let's see . . . let me find it . . . hang on, no, here it is, Venera 4 in 1967 . . . and it dropped instruments onto the surface. They only lasted a few seconds, because of the conditions, the heat and all, but this probe showed us how really hot it was. Then, there was one called Venus Pioneer 2, in 1978. That was the one that found out that the atmosphere of Venus is made of carbon dioxide, mostly. And, uh, well, as I said . . . there were a lot of other ones too.

Well, that's pretty much it—that's about all I have to say about Venus, unless you have some questions.

Professor: Charlie?

Student Presenter: Yes, Professor?

Professor: First, I just want to say . . . good job on your presentation, Charlie; it was very interesting, and then . . . well, I just want to add this. You said you weren't sure why the planet Venus was named after the goddess of love. It's true Venus was the goddess of love, but she was also the goddess of beauty and . . . well, anyone who's ever seen Venus early in the morning or in the evening knows it's a beautiful sight.

Student Presenter: Okay, so, there you have it, everyone—a mystery solved. Thanks, Professor. Well, I don't have anything to add, so unless anyone has any questions . . . no? Well, Caroline will be giving the next report, which is about the third planet, and since we all live here, that should be pretty interesting.

Narrator: Now get ready to answer the questions. You may use your notes to help you.

Narrator: Question 18: How does the speaker introduce the topic of Venus?

Narrator: Question 19: According to the speaker, which of the following were once common beliefs about Venus?

Narrator: Question 20: In this presentation, the speaker discusses some similarities between Earth and Venus and some of the differences between the two planets. Indicate which of the following is a similarity and which is a difference.

Narrator: Question 21: Which of the following is *not* true about the length of a day on Venus?

Narrator: Question 22: In what order were these space probes sent to Venus?

Narrator: Question 23: It can be inferred that the topic of the next student presentation will be about which of the following?

Narrator: This is the end of the Listening Preview Test.

[CD 1 Track 3]

Lesson 9: Main-Topic and Main-Purpose Questions

Sample Item

Narrator: Listen to a conversation between a student and a professor.

Student: Professor Dixon? I'm Brenda Pierce. From your Geology 210 class . . . ?

Professor: Yes. I know. That's a big class, but I do recognize you. As a matter of fact, I noticed you weren't in class yesterday morning. Did you oversleep? That's one of the problems with an 8:00 class. I almost overslept myself a couple of times.

Student: Oh, uh, no, I didn't oversleep. In fact, I was up at 5:00—one of my roommates had an early flight and I took her to the airport. I thought I'd make it back here in time, but, uh, well, you know . . . you know how traffic can be out on Airport Road at that time of day. Anyway, uh, I know you were going to tell us . . . give us some information about our research paper in class today. Do you have a few minutes to fill me in?

Professor: Well, umm, a few minutes, I guess. This isn't my regular office hour. I actually just came by my office to pick up a few papers before the faculty meeting.

Student: Okay, well . . . about the research paper . . . how long does it have to be?

Professor: Well, as I told the class, the paper counts for 30% of your grade. It should be at least twelve pages . . . but no more than twenty-five. And your bibliography should contain at least ten reference sources.

Student: Will you be assigning the topic, or . . .

Professor: I'm leaving the choice of topic up to you. Of course, it should be related to something we've discussed in class.

Student: I, I'm interested in writing about earthquakes . . .

Professor: Hmm. Earthquakes . . . well, I don't know, Brenda . . . that sounds like much too broad a topic for a short research paper.

Student: Oh, well, I'm planning to choose . . . I plan to get more specific than that. I want to write about using animals to predict earthquakes.

Professor: Really? Well, once scientists wondered if maybe . . . if perhaps there was some connection between strange behavior in animals and earthquakes . . . and that maybe animals . . . that you could use them to predict earthquakes. But there have been a lot of studies on this subject, you know, and so far, none of them have shown anything promising . . .

Student: But I thought there was this . . . I saw this show on television about earthquakes, and it said that in, uh, China, I think it was, they did predict an earthquake because of the way animals were acting.

Professor: Oh, right, you're thinking of the Haecheng earthquake about thirty years ago. Well, that's true. There were snakes coming out of the ground in the middle of winter when they should have been hibernating . . . and supposedly horses and other animals were acting frightened. And there were other signs, too, not just from animals. So the government ordered an evacuation of the area, and in fact, there was an earthquake, so thousands of lives were probably saved.

Student: Yeah, that's what I'm thinking of . . . that's what I saw on television.

Professor: The problem is, that, unfortunately, no one's been able to duplicate that kind of result . . . in China or anywhere. There have been lots of earthquakes since then that haven't been predicted, and there have been a couple of false alarms when cities were evacuated for no reason . . . and like I said, none of the studies that have been done have shown that animals are any better at predicting earthquakes than people are.

Student: So that's . . . so you don't think that's a very good idea for a topic, then, I suppose . . .

Professor: I didn't say that . . . just because this theory hasn't been proved doesn't mean you couldn't write a perfectly good paper about this topic . . . on the notion that animals can predict earthquakes. Why not? It could be pretty interesting. But to do a good job, you . . . you'll need to look at some serious studies in the scientific journals, not just some pop-science articles in newspapers or . . . and you can't get your information from television shows.

Student: You really think it might make a good paper? Well, then, I think if I can get enough information from the library or the Internet . . .

Professor: Okay, why don't you see what you can find? Oh, I forgot to mention . . . you'll need to write up a formal proposal for your paper, and work up a preliminary bibliography, and hand it in to me a week from tomorrow. I'll need to approve it before you get started. Now, if you'll excuse me, Brenda, I've got to get to that faculty meeting.

Narrator: Now get ready to answer the question. You may use your notes to help you.

Narrator: Question 1: What is this conversation mainly about?

[CD 1 Track 4]

Narrator: For the Listening exercises in *The Complete Guide,* the directions will not be read aloud on the tape. Therefore, you must read the directions for each exercise and make sure you understand them before you start the Audio Program.

Exercise 9.1

Narrator: Listen to a conversation between a student and a librarian.

Student: Hi, I'm in Professor Quinn's Political Science class. She, uh, in class today she said that she'd put a journal on reserve . . . We're supposed to read an article from that journal.

Librarian: Okay, well, you're in the right place. This is the reserve desk.

Student: Oh, good—I've never checked out reserve materials before. So what do I need? Do I need a library card, or . . . what do I have to do to . . .

Librarian: You have your student ID card with you, right?

Student: Umm, I think I do . . . I mean, I think it's in my backpack here . . .

Librarian: Okay, well, all you really need to do is leave your student ID here with me, sign this form and the journal is all yours—for—let me see—for two hours anyway.

Student: Two hours? That's all the time I get?

Librarian: Well, when instructors put materials on reserve, they set a time limit on how long you can use them . . . you know, just so all the students in your class can get a chance to read them.

Student: I don't know how long the article is, but . . . I guess I can finish it in two hours.

Librarian: And, one more thing, you, uh, you'll have to read the article in the library. You're not allowed to check reserve material out of the library, or to take it out of the building.

Student: Oh, well, then, . . . maybe I should, uh, maybe I should go back to my dorm and get some dinner . . . before I sit down and read this.

Librarian: That's fine, but . . . I can't guarantee the article will be available right away when you come back . . . some other student from your class might be using it.

Student: Well, I dunno, I . . . I guess I'll just have to take my chances . . .

Narrator: Now get ready to answer the question. You may use your notes to help you.

Narrator: Question 1: What is the main topic of this conversation?

Narrator: Listen to a conversation between two students.

Student A: Tina, hey, how are you?

Student B: Hi, Michael. Hey, how was your summer vacation?

Student A: Oh, not too bad—mostly I was working. How about you? I, uh, I kinda remember you saying that . . . weren't you going to Europe? How was that?

Student B: Oh, that fell through. I was going to travel with my roommate, and she changed her mind about going, so . . . well, my parents own a furniture store, and so instead, I was going to work there. But then . . . well, you know Professor Grant?

Student A: Oh, uh, from the archaeology department? Sure . . . well, I've heard of her, anyway.

Student B: Well, I got a call from her just before the end of the spring semester. She was planning to do this dig in Mexico. So she calls me up and asks if I'd like to be a volunteer, and you know, I've always wanted . . . it's always been a dream of mine to be an archaeologist, so . . . I jumped at the chance.

Student A: So, uh, how was it . . . I mean, was it a good dig . . .

Student B: Do you mean, did we find any artifacts? No, it . . . it was supposed to be a very . . . promising site. But it turned out to be a complete bust! We didn't find anything . . . not even one single piece of broken pottery. Nothing! Just sand!

Student A: Wow, that must have been pretty disappointing.

Student B: No, not really. Oh, sure, I mean, I would've liked to have made some amazing discovery, but, well, I still learned a lot about, about archaeological techniques, you know, and I really enjoyed getting to know the people, the other people on the dig, and it . . . well, it was fun!

Narrator: Now get ready to answer the question. You may use your notes to help you.

Narrator: Question 2: What is the main subject of the speakers' conversation?

Narrator: Listen to a conversation between a student and an administrator.

Administrator: Yes? Come in.

Student: Umm, Ms. Kirchner?

Administrator: Yes?

Student: I'm, uh, Mark Covelli. I live over in Quincy House?

Administrator: Yes, so what can I do for you, Mark?

Student: The woman who's in charge of the cafeteria over at Quincy, I talked to her this morning, you see, and . . . well, she told me that I would have to talk to you . . .

Administrator: Okay, talk to me about . . . ?

Student: Okay, well, I'd like to . . . you see, back at the beginning of the semester, my parents signed me up for Meal Plan 1.You know, the plan where you get three meals a day . . .

Administrator: Okay . . .

Student: So, well, I've decided it's . . . it was kind of a waste of their money because . . . I mean, I almost never eat three meals there in a day. Three days a week I have early classes and I don't have time to eat breakfast at all, and even on days when I do eat breakfast there, I just have coffee and some yogurt so . . . well, I could do that in my room.

Administrator: So what you're saying is, you'd like to be on Meal Plan 2?

Student: Yeah, I guess . . . whatever you call the plan where you only eat two meals a day at the dorm . . .

Administrator: That's Plan 2. We usually don't make that kind of switch in the middle of a semester . . . you know, if I do approve this, we'd have to make the refund directly to your parents. And it could only be a partial refund . . . since you've been on Plan 1 for a month already.

Student: Oh sure, I understand that . . . I just, I just hate to waste my parents' money.

Narrator: Now get ready to answer the question. You may use your notes to help you.

Narrator: Question 3: Why does Mark Covelli want to speak to Ms. Kirchner?

Narrator: Now get ready to listen to a conversation between two students.

Student A: Hey, Larry, how are ya? What're ya up to this weekend?

Student B: Oh, my friends and I are going to be working on our car, the Sunflower II.

Student A: Wait . . . you have a car called . . . the Sunflower?

Student B: Yeah, the Sunflower II. Well, it's not a regular car. It's a solar-powered car.

Student A: Really? That's why you call it the Sunflower then. Oh, wait, are you entering it in that race next month . . . the . . .

Student B: The Solar Derby. Yeah. It's sponsored by the Engineering Department.

Student A: I read a little about that in the campus paper. I'm sorry, but the idea of racing solar cars . . . it just sounds a little . . . . weird.

Student B: I guess, but there are lots of races for solar-powered cars. One of the most famous ones is in Australia. They race all the way from the south coast of Australia to the north coast.

Student A: But your race . . . it's not anywhere near that long, right?

Student B: No, no, our race is only twenty miles long. We entered the Sunflower I in it last year and . . .

Student A: And did you win?

Student B: Uh, well, no . . . . no, we didn't actually win . . . In fact, we didn't even finish last year. We got off to a good start but then we had a major breakdown. But since then we've made a *lot* of improvements to the Sunflower II, and . . . well, I think we have a pretty good chance this year of . . . well, if not of winning, of finishing at least in the top three.

Narrator: Now get ready to answer the question. You may use your notes to help you.

Narrator: Question 4: What are these two people mainly discussing?

Narrator: Listen to a conversation between two students.

Student A: So, Rob, what classes are you taking next semester?

Student B: Let's see, uh, I'm taking the second semester of statistics, calculus, German, and . . . oh, I signed up for a class in the art department, a photography class.

Student A: Oh? Who with?

Student B: Umm, let me think . . . I think her name is . . . I think it's Lyons . . .

Student A: Lyons? I don't think . . . oh, you must mean Professor Lyle, Martha Lyle. She's my advisor, and I've taken a coupla classes from her. She's just great. She's not only a terrific photographer, but she's also a, well, just a wonderful teacher. She can take one look at what you're working on and tell you just what you need to do to take a better photograph. I mean, I learned so much about photography from her. And not only about taking color photographs, but also black-and-white—which I'd never done before. She only takes black-and-white photos herself, you know. So what kinds of photos did you show her?

Student B: Whaddya mean?

Student A: When you got permission to take her class, what kind of photos did you show her? You had to show her your portfolio, didn't you?

Student B: No, I . . . I just registered for her class. The registrar didn't tell me I needed permission . . .

Student A: Well, for any of those advanced classes, if you're not an art major, or if you haven't taken any other photography classes, you have to get the professor's permission, and usually that involves showing your portfolio.

Student B: Oh, see, they didn't tell me that when I registered.

Student A: Well, I think it says so in the course catalog. But, you can always sign up for an introductory level photography class. You wouldn't need the instructor's permission to do that.

Student B: No, I . . . I don't consider myself a . . . well, not a complete beginner, anyway. I took photos for my school newspaper when I was in high school . . . not just news photos but kind of artistic photos too, you know . . . I could show her those. I'd really like to take her class. From what you said about her, I think I could learn a lot.

Narrator: Now get ready to answer the question. You may use your notes to help you.

Narrator: Question 5: What is the main topic of this conversation?

[CD 2 Track 2]

Exercise 9.2

Narrator: Listen to a lecture in a dance class.

Professor: Okay, today we're talking a bit about recording choreography. Let me start with a question for you. Do you know what steps dancers used during the first productions of . . . oh, say, of Swan Lake, or, for that matter, any of the most famous ballets? . . . That's really a trick question because . . . well, in most cases, no one knows, not really. Believe it or not, no written choreography exists for the early performances of most of the world's most famous classical ballets, or, for that matter, even for a lot of modern ballet. So, how did choreographers teach dancers how to perform their dances? Mostly, they demonstrated the steps themselves, or they had one of the dancers model the steps for the other dancers. Sure, systems of written choreography have been around for a long while. Some systems use numbers, some use abstract symbols, some use letters and words, oh, and musical notation, some systems use musical notes. The two most common systems in use are called Labanotation, and, uh, the Benesh system, Benesh Movement Notation it's called. But here's the thing—choreographers don't use these systems all that often. Why not, you ask. Well, because of the time it takes, because . . . Well, because recording three-dimensional dance movements, it's very difficult, very complex, and especially it's very time-consuming. A single minute of dance can take up to maybe, maybe six hours to get down on paper. You can imagine how long recording an entire ballet would take! And choreographers tend to be very busy people. But computer experts came to the choreographers' rescue. Computers have been used since the sixties to record choreography. The first one—well, the first one I know about, anyway, was a program written by Michael Noll . . . and it was . . . oh, I guess by today's standards you'd say it was pretty primitive. The dancers looked like stick figures in a child's drawing. But, uh, since the 1980's, sophisticated programs have been around, programs that . . . uh . . . well, uh, they let choreographers record the dancers' steps and movements quite easily. The only problem with these, these software programs, was that they required very powerful computers to run them . . . and as you no doubt know, not all dance companies have the kind of money you need to buy a mainframe computer. But because personal computers now have more memory, more power, well, now you can choreograph a whole ballet on a good laptop.

Oh, and I meant to mention earlier, we owe a lot of the credit for these improvements in the software for dance choreography to the space program. Back in the sixties and seventies, engineers at NASA needed computerized models . . . three-dimensional, moving models of astronauts' bodies so that the engineers could design spacesuits and

spacecraft, and it turned out that the models they designed could be adapted quite nicely to dancers' bodies. So anyway, I've reserved the computer lab down the hall for the rest of this class. We're going to spend the rest of our time today playing around with some of this choreography software, okay? So let's walk over there . . .

Narrator: Now get ready to answer the question. You may use your notes to help you.

Narrator: Question 1: What is the main point of this lecture?

Narrator: Listen to a discussion in a psychology class.

Student A: Excuse me . . . excuse me, Professor Mitchie, but . . . I'm a little confused about what you just said.

Professor: You're confused? Why is that, Deborah?

Student A: Well, you said that you don't . . . well, that most scientists don't think that ESP really exists.

Professor: Okay, now you're clear what I'm talking about when I say ESP . . .

Student B: It's mind-reading, that kind of stuff. Extrasensory perception.

Professor: Well, that's a pretty good definition. It's . . . well, it can be telepathy . . . that's communicating mind to mind. Or telekinesis . . . that's moving things with your mind . . . . precognition, which is knowing the future, or seeing the future. Other phenomena, too. And the study of ESP is sometimes called parapsychology.

Student A: But you think . . . well, you think all that is nonsense, I guess, right?

Professor: Now, I'm not saying there aren't people who have . . . well, remarkable senses of intuition. But I think that's because they're just very sensitive, very tuned in to their environments, to the people around them. I don't think they have any . . . abnormal mental powers beyond that, no.

Student A: Well, I was just reading an article about ESP, and it said that there were scientific experiments done at some university, I don't remember where, but the experiments were done with cards, and that they proved that some people could read minds.

Student B: She's probably thinking of those experiments at Duke University . . .

Student A: Right, it was at Duke.

Professor: Well, yes, there were a series of experiments at Duke about seventy years ago. Professor J. P. Rhine—who was, interestingly enough, a botanist, not a psychologist—he founded the Department of Parapsychology at Duke, and he and his wife did a lot of experiments, especially involving telepathy.

Student B: He used those cards, didn't he, the ones with, like, stars and crosses?

Professor: Yes. Well, at first he used ordinary playing cards, but then he started using a deck of twenty-five cards. There were five symbols on these cards: a star, a cross, some wavy lines, a circle and, ummm, maybe a square?

Student A: So how did the experiments work?

Professor: Well, basically it went like this. One person turned over the card and looked at it carefully, really trying to focus on it, to . . . to picture it in his mind. This person was called the *sender*. The other person, called the *percipient*, had to guess what symbol the sender was looking at. So . . . if it was just a matter of chance guessing, how many times should the percipient guess correctly?

Student B: Five, I guess? I mean, since there are five types of symbols and . . .

Professor: And twenty-five cards, yes, that's right, the law of averages says that you should get 20% right even if you have absolutely no ESP talent. So if someone—and they tested thousands of people at their lab—if someone on average got more than 20%, they'd get tested more, and some of these individuals went on to get remarkably high scores.

Student A: So, huh, doesn't this prove that some people can . . . that they have powers?

Professor: Well, after Rhine did his experiments at Duke, a lot of similar experiments have been done—at Stanford University, in Scotland, and elsewhere, and the conclusion . . . most researchers have decided that Rhine's results were . . . I guess the kindest word I could use is *questionable.* More recent experiments have been done under more carefully controlled conditions, and those, uh, remarkable results, those really high scores that Rhine got have been rare . . . practically nonexistent. And in science, the trend should be the opposite.

Student B: What do you mean, Professor?

Professor: Well, you know . . . if the phenomenon you're studying is real, and the experiments are improved, are more reliable, then the results you get should be *more* certain, not less certain.

Student A: So that's why you don't believe in ESP?

Professor: To put it in a nutshell—I've just never seen any experimental proof for ESP that stood up to careful examination.

Narrator: Now get ready to answer the question. You may use your notes to help you.

Narrator: Question 2: What are the speakers mainly discussing?

Narrator: Listen to a lecture in an archaeology class.

Guest Speaker: Good afternoon, everyone, I'm Robert Wolf, and I'm president . . . well, I should say past president of the State Archaeological Society. I'd like to thank Professor Kingsly for asking me to, to come in and talk to you all about a subject I'm pretty passionate about: shipwrecks. You see, I'm also a diver, and I'm a member of the International Underwater Archaeology Society, and I've been on a lot of underwater expeditions to investigate shipwrecks.

A lot of times, when someone mentions shipwrecks, you think of pirates and treasures buried under the sea. And in reality, many divers—the ones we call treasure hunters—do try to find shipwrecks with valuables still aboard them. In fact, that's one of the problems we face in this field. Some shipwrecks have literally been torn apart by treasure hunters searching for gold coins or jewelry, even if there wasn't any there, and underwater archaeologists weren't able to get much information from these ships. But, shipwrecks are . . . they can be a lot more than just places to look for treasure. A shipwreck is a time capsule, if you know what I mean, a photograph, a snapshot of what life was like at the moment the ship sank. And unlike sites on land, a shipwreck . . . it's . . . uncontaminated . . . it's not disturbed by the generations of people who live on the site later. Unless, of course, treasure hunters or someone like that has gotten there first. And so, they're valuable tools for archaeologists, for historians. For example, the world's oldest known shipwreck—it sank in about, ummm, 1400 B.C., off the coast of Turkey—the artifacts on that ship completely changed the way we think of Bronze Age civilizations in the Mediterranean.

So, I'm mostly going to stick to shipwrecks that occurred here, that happened off the coast of New England, and I'm going to talk about what we've learned from them, what

archaeologists have learned from them. There have been plenty of shipwrecks in this area. Over the years, fog and storms and rocks and accidents and sometimes even war have sunk a lot of ships around New England. I'm going to be showing you some slides of shipwrecks from trading ships that sank in Colonial days, in the 1600's, to the *Andrea Doria,* which went down in the 1950's. The *Andrea Doria,* that's, uh, I suppose that's the most famous shipwreck in the area, the Italian ocean liner, the *Andrea Doria,* and it's a deep, dangerous dive to get to it, I'll tell you. Oh, and after that we're going to play a little game. I'm going to show you some slides of artifacts that were found on board shipwrecks, show them just the way they looked when they were found, and you have to guess what they are.

Narrator: Now get ready to answer the question. You may use your notes to help you.

Narrator: Question 3: What does this lecture mainly concern?

Narrator: Listen to a discussion in an economics class.

Professor: Okay, good morning, everyone, I trust everyone had a good weekend and that you managed to read Chapter . . . Chapter 7, on taxation. Friday we talked about the difference between progressive and regressive taxes . . . and, today, we're going to talk about two other types of taxation: direct and indirect. What did the text say about direct taxation? Yes, Troy?

Student A: Well, the book . . . according to the chapter that we read, it's, ummm, that's when the person who's being taxed . . .

Professor: Well, it could be a person or it could be an organization.

Student A: Right. The person or organization who's being taxed pays the government directly. Is that it?

Professor: That's great. Now, can you provide an example for us?

Student A: Yeah, uh, how about income tax?

Professor: Why would you consider income tax a form of direct taxation?

Student A: Well, because, um, the person who earns the income pays the taxes directly to the government, right?

Professor: Yes, good, Troy. Okay, so, someone else, what is indirect taxation? Cheryl?

Student B: Well, if I understand the book correctly, it's when the cost of taxes, of taxation, is paid by someone other than the, uh, the person . . . or organization . . . that is responsible for paying the taxes.

Professor: I'd say you understood the book perfectly—that's a good definition. Now, Cheryl, we need an example of indirect taxation.

Student B: Okay, let's see . . . what if someone . . . some company . . . brings, oh, say, perfume into the country from France. And let's say there's an import tax on the perfume that the government collects from the company, and then . . . well, the importer just turns around and charges customers more money for the perfume, to, umm, just to pay the import tax.

Professor: Good example! Anyone think of another one?

Student A: How about this: last year, my landlady raised my rent, and when I asked her why, she said it was because the city raised her property taxes . . . is that an example?

Professor: It certainly is. It . . . yes, Cheryl, you have a question?

Student B: Yes, Professor, what about sales taxes . . . direct or indirect?

Professor: Good question. I'm going to let you all think about it for just a minute—talk it over with the person sitting next to you, if you want—and then . . . then you're going to tell me.

Narrator: Now get ready to answer the question. You may use your notes to help you.

Narrator: Question 4: What is the main purpose of this discussion?

Narrator: Listen to a discussion in an art class.

Professor: Hello, everyone . . . today I'm going to be showing you some slides of . . . well, I'm just going to project a slide on the screen and see if you can tell me who the artist is and what the name of the painting is. This is his most famous painting. Here we go. Anyone know?

Student A: Yeah, I've seen that painting before . . . I don't remember the name of the artist, but I think the painting is called *Nighthawks at the Diner*.

Professor: Yeah, that's . . . well, a lot of people call it that, but the real name of the painting is just *Nighthawks*. Anyone know the artist? Anyone? No? The painter is Edward Hopper. Now tell me . . . what sort of a reaction do you have when you see it?

Student B: It's kind of . . . lonely . . . kind of depressing, and, uh, bleak. It's so dark outside, and inside there are these bright lights but . . . but they're kinda harsh, the lights are, and the people in the diner seem . . . well, to me, they look really lonely.

Professor: A lot of Hopper's works show . . . loneliness, isolation. He was a very realistic painter. One of the reasons he was so realistic, maybe, is that he started off as an illustrator, a commercial artist, and you know, of course, a commercial artist has to be able to paint and draw realistically. In fact, Hopper spent most of his early career doing illustrations and just traveling around. He didn't develop his characteristic style, his mature style, until, I'd say, not until he was in his forties or maybe fifties. Anyway, most of his paintings show empty city streets, country roads, railroad tracks. There are paintings of storefronts, restaurants, and . . . let me show you another, this is the first one of his mature paintings, and the first one that really made him famous. It's called *The House by the Railroad*. It's pretty bleak, too, isn't it? You'll notice as we look at more slides that, uh, well, there aren't many people in the paintings, and the ones that you do see, they look . . . you could almost say impersonal. Melancholy. That's the . . . mood he tried to convey. Wait, let me back up just a second. He, Hopper, always said he was just painting what he saw, that he wasn't trying to show isolation and loneliness but . . . one look at his paintings tells you he wasn't being completely honest about this.

Student A: Some of these paintings remind me of . . . of those old black-and-white movies from, like, the thirties and forties.

Professor: Yeah, I agree. That type of movie, that style of moviemaking is called *film noir*. And yeah, it does have that same feel, doesn't it? And it's interesting that you should say that, because Hopper did have an influence on some moviemakers. On the other hand, he did not have much of an influence on his own generation of painters. Nobody else painted the way Hopper did, at least not until . . . well, until the photorealistic painters in the sixties and seventies. But his contemporaries weren't interested in realism. They were . . . well, we'll see some of their works next week when we talk about abstract expressionism.

Narrator: Now get ready to answer the question. You may use your notes to help you.

Narrator: Question 5: What is the main topic of this discussion?

Narrator: Listen to a discussion in an advertising class.

Professor: Morning, class. In our last class, we were talking about regulation, about regulation in the advertising industry. In fact, you may remember I said that, in the United States, in some European countries, too, advertising is one of the most heavily regulated industries there is. What did, um, what example did I give of regulation, government regulation of advertising?

Student A: Well, you . . . you gave the example of . . . that the United States banned cigarette advertising back in the 1960's . . .

Professor: The early 1970's, actually. That's right. Up until then, tobacco companies and their advertising agencies would portray smoking as part of this . . . oh, this carefree, this oh-so-glamorous lifestyle. And then it came out in these scientific studies done by the government that tobacco smoking was really dangerous, really unsafe, and so . . . no more tobacco advertisements. At least, not on television or radio. You could still advertise in magazines, on billboards, and so on, for a long time after that—don't ask me why, but you could. And some studies showed that . . . the studies seemed to indicate that the advertising ban . . . oh, and I might mention, there was also negative advertising by the government and anti-smoking groups telling people not to smoke . . . anyway, these studies showed that smoking, that the use of tobacco actually went down. Okay, there were also some examples in the article I asked you to read for today, other examples of government regulation . . .

Student: There was the example from Sweden, about how Sweden completely banned advertisements for children.

Professor: Right, for children under twelve. That happened back in 1991. Now . . . not to get too far off track here, but since that article was written, there was a European Court of Justice ruling, and it said that Sweden still has to accept . . . that it has no control over advertisements that target Swedish children, advertisements that come from neighboring countries . . . or from satellite. So this undercuts to a certain extent what the Swedes were trying to do, but still . . . you can see their intent to . . . to protect their children from, uh, from the effects of advertising.

Student A: Don't you think that law was . . . a little extreme, maybe?

Professor: In my opinion? As a matter of fact, yes, yes, I do. Personally, I think advertisements meant for children should be controlled—maybe controlled more carefully than at present—but not necessarily eliminated. And I . . . speaking for myself still, I think they should be controlled by a combination of government regulation and self-regulation. And that's what we're going to be talking about today. Sometimes self-regulation works well enough, but, but if the idea of self-regulation is to create nothing but honest advertisements, advertisements that are in good taste . . . well, you only have to turn on your TV and you'll see that this system of self-regulation has its faults, right?

Narrator: Now get ready to answer the question. You may use your notes to help you.

Narrator: Question 6: What is the class mainly discussing?

Narrator: Listen to a lecture in a world literature class.

Professor: So, for the rest of the class today, we're gonna talk about the two most important poems, epic poems, in Greek literature. And really, not just in Greek literature, but in any literature, anywhere in the world. These are the *Iliad* and the *Odyssey,* written by the blind Greek poet Homer—at least, we think he was blind. Now, if you happen to have a copy of the syllabus that I gave you last week, you'll notice that we're not gonna be able to . . . we just don't have time to read all of these two poems and talk about them. An epic poem . . . I probably don't have to tell you this—is a narrative poem, a really *long* narrative poem. So we're going to read a few passages from the *Iliad,* and we'll read a bit more from the *Odyssey.* What I want to talk about today are some of the . . . the ways these two long poems, especially their main characters, how they're different.

Some people have said that the *Iliad* is the world's greatest war story, and the *Odyssey,* that it's the world's greatest travel story. The *Iliad* tells about the Trojan War, the war between Troy and the various Greek kingdoms. The *Odyssey* tells about a Greek warrior's trip home, and all the amazing adventures he has on the way—and he has some wild ones, too. The warrior's name is Odysseus, hence the name for the poem. I think the reason that I prefer the *Odyssey* to the *Iliad,* myself, is that . . . well, I guess you could say, I just like the main character of the *Odyssey* better than the main characters of the *Iliad.* As I said, the *Iliad* is the story of the Trojan War and about the clash, the personality conflict, between the main characters. The conflict isn't just between warriors from either side—a lot of the story deals with an argument between the two strongest Greek warriors, Achilles and Agamemnon. Anyway, the main characters in the *Iliad,* they're strong, they're great warriors, but you know . . . they're not as clever, not as smart as Odysseus. He's the one who thinks up the plan to end the war—after ten long years—and defeat the Trojans. He's the . . . the mastermind behind the scheme to build the Trojan Horse—you probably know something about that already, the Trojan Horse has been in lots of movies and so on . . . anyway, he helps end the ten-year war, and then he sets off for home and his family. It takes him another ten years to get home, where his wife has been waiting faithfully for him for twenty years, but . . . but like I said, he has plenty of adventures on the way.

Oh, and the other thing about Odysseus that I like is that . . . well, the characters in the *Iliad* are pretty static . . . you know what I mean? They are . . . they don't change much. This is true of most of Homer's characters, in fact. But it's not true of Odysseus. During the course of the epic, on account of the long war and all the, the bizarre experiences he has on the way home . . . he changes. He evolves as a character, just like characters in most modern novels do.

Okay, then, before we go on . . . does anyone have any comments? Comments or questions?

Narrator: Now get ready to answer the question. You may use your notes to help you.

Narrator: Question 7: What is the main point of this lecture?

Narrator: Listen to a lecture in a modern history class.

Professor: All right, then, I want to talk about the founding of the United Nations, but before I do, I want to just mention the League of Nations, which was the predecessor of the United Nations. Last week, we talked about the end of the First World War—it ended in 1918, if you remember. Well, right after the war, several leaders of the countries that had won the war, including Wilson of the United States, and Lloyd George of Britain, Clemenceau of France

. . . oh, and Jan Smuts of South Africa, and, well, there were others too . . . they recognized the need for an international organization, an organization to keep the peace. So when the agreement that ended the war, the Treaty of Versailles, it was called, was signed, it included a provision that . . . that included formation of the League of Nations. Its headquarters were in Geneva, Switzerland.

But, the problem with the League from the beginning was that some of the most powerful nations of the time never joined. As I said, the, ah, the main drive, the main impetus for forming the League came from Woodrow Wilson, president of the United States. But during the 1920's, the United States went through a period of isolationism. In other words, it just basically withdrew from international affairs. Wilson worked and worked to get the U.S. Senate to agree to join the League, but he never could. Other powerful nations joined but then quit—or were kicked out. This included Brazil, Japan, Germany, the Soviet Union . . . The other problem was, ah . . . the League of Nations never had any power, really, no power to enforce its decisions. It had no armed forces. It could only apply economic sanctions, boycotts, and these were pretty easy to get around.

The League of Nations did have a few successes early on. It helped prevent wars between Bulgaria and Greece, Iraq and Turkey, and Poland and Lithuania in the 1920's. And the League also had some success in refugee work and famine relief and so on. Oh, and it brokered some deals, some treaties to get countries to reduce the size of their navies. But . . . the League was completely, totally powerless to stop the buildup to the Second World War in the 1930's.

So, ah, during the war, during World War II, I mean, the League didn't meet. Then, after the war, it was replaced by the United Nations, which, of course, was headquartered in New York City.

Still, the League of Nations was, ah . . . well, I think it served an important role. It developed a new model of Internationalism. In the late nineteenth and early twentieth century, "Internationalism" really just meant alliances of powerful nations, and these alliances often dragged other countries into conflict—that's what happened, really, that's what led to World War I. But the League was at least an attempt to bring all the nations of the world together to work for peace. True, it didn't work, not really, but at least there was an effort made. Oh, and another thing I meant to add, the structure of the League of Nations, the, ah, administrative structure, the "government," if you will—was very similar to that of the United Nations. The secretary-general, the secretariat, the general assembly, the security council, these are all fixtures of the United Nations that came from the League of Nations.

Okay, we're going to have to wait until next class to discuss the United Nations, but . . . I just wanted you to be aware of the League of Nations because of its role, its, ah . . . place in history, which I think has often been misunderstood . . .

Narrator: Now get ready to answer the question. You may use your notes to help you.

Narrator: Question 8: What is the main subject of this lecture?

Narrator: Listen to a lecture in an environmental studies class.

Professor: Let's go ahead and get started. I'd like to finish up our discussion of alternative energy sources this week . . . Remember our definition of an alternative energy source? It has to be environmentally friendly . . . non-polluting, in other words. And what else? Renewable. Not like oil or coal. When you use those, bang, they're gone, they're used up. Renewable sources keep replacing themselves.

Okay, so we discussed solar power and wind power one day . . . and tidal energy, energy from the waves . . . hydro-electric power from waterfalls, we discussed that, too . . . and in our last class we talked about one kind of geo-thermal energy, hydrothermal energy. That's the energy that comes from hot water, from hot springs under the earth. In places like, oh, say, Iceland, parts of New Zealand, where you have these, uh, features, this can be a very good source of heat and power. But unfortunately, hot springs aren't found all over the world. Okay, well, there is *another* source of geothermal power, called "hot dry rock." That's hot dry rock, or HDR. Ever heard of it? No, eh? Well, the chances are, you'll hear a lot about it before long.

How does HDR energy work? Well, in theory, anyway . . . and let me stress, I say in theory . . . it's pretty simple. You use oil-well drilling equipment, big drills, and you punch two holes down into the earth about, oh, maybe two miles—five kilometers, maybe—that's about as far as you can drill into the earth, for now, at least. Down there, deep in the earth, there is this extremely hot cauldron of rock, of granite. So then, you pump water from the surface into the first tube. The water goes down to the hot rock and becomes superheated. Then, the superheated water rises up the second tube—oh, I forgot to mention that these two tubes are interconnected—this hot water rises up the other tube and you use that to heat up a volatile liquid—do I need to go into what I mean by that? No? Okay. So then, this volatile liquid turns into a vapor, a gas, and you use it to turn an electrical turbine, and . . . bingo, you have elec-tricity! And then, when the water has cooled down, you just send it down the first tube again, so that you don't waste water.

So, does HDR technology meet our criteria for alterna-tive energy? Let's see. Is it environmentally friendly? You bet. There are no toxic gases, no greenhouse emissions, no nuclear wastes. Is it renewable? Sure it is, 'cause the earth automatically replaces the heat that is used.

Here's another possibility . . . if you built a big HDR facil-ity by the seacoast, you could pump seawater down one tube. The seawater is heated way past boiling, so you could separate water vapor from the salt and other minerals in the seawater. After you used the hot water vapor to gener-ate electricity, you'd have pure, fresh water for thirsty cities nearby—and as a side effect, you have the salt.

Now, will this work everywhere? No, conditions have to be just right—you have to have really, really hot granite masses no more than about 5 kilometers below the earth. We know there are places like this in Australia, in the south-western United States, in France, a few other places. There are probably a lot of other sites too, that we are not aware of. In fact, there may be a lot of HDR sites, and who knows how important a source of power this may turn out to be. Right now, engineers are building a small, prototype HDR station in southern Australia and one in New Mexico. These could be up and running in a decade or less. Of course, get-ting started will be expensive. Drilling a hole that far into the ground, building generators, all of that will cost lots of money. But, you know, the way oil prices keep going up—HDR energy production could become more and more financially attractive.

Okay, I'm gonna hand out a diagram of what one of these, uh, prototype HDR facilities looks like, the one in

Australia, and then once you've had a chance to take a look at it, we'll talk some more about it.
Narrator: Now get ready to answer the question. You may use your notes to help you.
Narrator: Question 9: What is the main idea of this lecture?

[CD 2 Track 3]

Lesson 10: Factual, Negative Factual, and Inference Questions

Sample Item 1

Narrator: Listen to part of a discussion in a business class.
Professor: What does a case look like? Well, cases are basi-cally descriptions of actual—let me stress that—of real business situations, chunks of reality from the business world. So, you get typically ten to twenty pages of text that describe the problem, some problem that a real business actually faced. And then there will be another five to ten pages of what are called exhibits.
Student B: Exhibits? What are those?
Professor: Exhibits . . . those are documents, statistical doc-uments, that explain the situation. They might be oh, spreadsheets, sales reports, umm, marketing projections, anything like that. But as I said, at the center of every case, at the core of every case, is a problem that you have to solve. So, you have to analyze the situation, the data—and sometimes, you'll see you don't have enough data to work with, and you might have to collect more—say, from the Internet. Then, you have to make decisions about how to solve these problems.
Narrator: What does the professor say about exhibits?

[CD 2 Track 4]

Sample Item 2

Narrator: Listen to part of a lecture in a biology class.
Professor: So, what are conditions like in the taiga? Well, to start with, you've gotta understand that it's cold there. I mean, very cold. Summers are short, winters long. So the organisms that call the taiga home have to be well adapted to cold. The trees in the taiga, as I already said, are conifer-ous trees like the pine, fir, and spruce. And these trees, they've adapted to cold weather. How? Well, for one thing, they never lose their leaves—they're "evergreen," right, always green, so in the spring, they don't have to waste time—don't have to waste energy—growing new leaves. They're ready to start photosynthesizing right away. And then, for another thing, these trees are conical—shaped like cones—aren't they? This means that snow doesn't accumu-late too much on the branches; it just slides off, and so, well, that means their branches don't break under the weight of the snow. And even their color—that dark, dark green—it's useful because it absorbs the sun's heat.
Narrator: When discussing needle-leaf trees, which of these adaptations to cold weather does the professor mention?

[CD 2 Track 5]

Sample Item 3

Narrator: Listen to part of a student presentation in an astronomy class.

Student: Okay, now here's a really strange fact about Venus. It takes Venus only 225 Earth days to go around the Sun, as opposed to the Earth, which of course takes 365 days— what we call a year. But Venus turns around on its axis really slowly. Really slowly. It takes 243 Earth days to spin around completely. The Earth takes—you guessed it—24 hours. This means that a day on Venus is longer than a year on Venus! In fact, a day on Venus is longer than . . . well, than on any planet in the solar system, longer even than on those big gas planets like Jupiter. And here's something else weird. All the planets of the solar system turn on their axis in the same direction as they orbit the Sun. All except Venus, of course! It has what's called a . . . wait, let's see . . . okay, a "retrograde" spin.

Narrator: Which of the following is *not* true about the length of a day on Venus?

[CD 2 Track 6]

Sample Item 4

Narrator: Listen to part of a lecture in a biology class.

Professor: Lots of the mammals that live in the taiga migrate to warmer climates once cold weather sets in. But there are some year-round residents. Among the predators—the animals that hunt other animals—there are Arctic foxes, wolves, bears, martens, oh, and ermines. There's one thing all these predators have in common, the ones that live there all year round . . . they all have thick, warm fur coats, don't they? This heavy fur keeps them toasty in the winter. Of course, on the downside, it makes them desirable to hunters and trappers. Some of these predators survive the winter by hibernating, by sleeping right through it . . . bears, for example. And some change colors. You've heard of the ermine, right? In the summer, the ermine is dark brown, but in the winter, it turns white. That makes it hard to spot, so it can sneak up on its prey.

Then, uh, what sorts of herbivores live up there? What do the predators eat to stay alive? There's the moose, of course, but only young moose are at risk of being attacked. The adult moose is the biggest, strongest animal found in the taiga, so a predator would have to be feeling pretty desperate to take on one of these. Mostly, predators hunt smaller prey, like snowshoe rabbits, voles, lemmings . . .

Narrator: What does the speaker imply about moose?

[CD 2 Track 7]

Exercise 10.1

Narrator: Listen to a conversation between two students.

Student A: I'm glad we could get together for coffee today, Cindy. You know . . . it just seems like forever since I've seen you.

Student B: I know. It seems . . . I just never see anyone from our freshman dorm days. Ever since I, basically ever since I started student-teaching, I've been just *swamped*. I never knew how much work . . . you know, it always seemed to me that teachers had it pretty easy—short work days, summers off, but . . . I never realized how much work you have to take home. Sometimes I'm grading papers until . . . sometimes until after midnight!

Student A: Wow, no wonder we never see you anymore.

Student B: Yeah, and since I'm not taking any classes, any regular classes, on campus this term, I hardly ever get up here. I seem to be spending my whole life at West Platte Middle School—that's where I'm student teaching.

Student A: So how come you're free today?

Student B: Oh, this week is spring break for the middle school, for the . . . the whole school district. So I came to campus to talk to my academic advisor.

Student A: Oh, I didn't realize that—our spring break isn't until next week. So . . . how's it going? With the teaching, I mean? Except for the long hours . . . do you . . . are you enjoying it?

Student B: Well, let me tell you, at first, I thought it was going to be a disaster! A complete disaster! You know, I, I always saw myself teaching in high school, but . . . there were no student-teaching positions open in any of the high schools in the district. I mean zero, except for one for a German teacher! So that's . . . that's how I ended up at West Platte. And that wasn't the only problem. You know I majored in education but I took lots of classes in physics and chemistry, so I figured they'd put me in a science classroom. But noooo! The only available classes for me to teach were a couple of math classes.

Student A: Wow, so you really . . . you really didn't get anything you wanted, did you?

Student B: As a matter of fact, no! But you know, it's actually turned out okay. For one thing, I had a good background in math, and so, really, teaching math was no problem— although I'd still rather teach science. But, it turns out, I like teaching in a middle school, I like it much more than I thought I would. I like working with kids that age. So . . . guess what, I've decided to look for a job at a middle school instead of at a high school after I graduate.

Student A: So, what do you need to talk to your advisor about?

Student B: Oh, I need to talk to her about next fall, to set up my class schedule for then.

Student A: Really? I thought you were all done. I thought you'd finished all your required classes and you were going to graduate when you finished student teaching.

Student B: Well, I have finished all my required classes, I have all the coursework I need in education and in science but . . . I still don't have enough, not quite enough total credits to graduate. So today, I'm . . . my advisor and I . . . are going to decide which electives I should take next semester. I'm thinking of maybe taking a literature class. I've always wanted to take a Shakespeare class, but I've never had time.

Student A: Oh, well, I'm just glad you'll be around next fall—we can get together more often.

Narrator: Now get ready to answer the questions. You may use your notes to help you.

Narrator: Question 1: What is Cindy's major?

Narrator: Question 2: What decision about her future has Cindy recently made?

Narrator: Question 3: What was Cindy's main reason for coming to campus today?

Narrator: Question 4: What will Cindy be doing next semester?

Narrator: Listen to a conversation between a student and a visitor to the campus.

Student A: Uh, excuse me, but, uh, I'm trying to find my way to the Reynolds Building.

Student B: The Reynolds Building? Hmmm. I'm afraid I don't know where that is.

Student A: Really? But I understand that . . . I was told that there's a graduate student exhibit opening today at the Reynolds Art Building.

Student B: Oh, now I know where you mean. I was there earlier today, matter of fact. Yeah, I guess . . . I guess the Reynolds Art Building is its official name, but no one on campus calls it that . . . everyone just calls it the art building.

Student A: The art building, okay. So, uh, how do I get there?

Student B: Well, just go straight ahead and then . . . first you come to the main library, right? Then you see a walkway leading off to the left. Go that way, and walk past the, uh . . . let's see, the chemistry building . . .

Student A: Wait . . . I go to the library, I take the walkway to the right . . .

Student B: No, to the left past the chem building. Then you cross a little service road. You just walk a little bit farther, and you see the art building . . . the Reynolds Building. You can't miss it because there's a big metal . . . *thing* on a platform right in front of it.

Student A: A thing?

Student B: Yeah, there's this . . . this big rusty piece of abstract "art." I guess you'd call it art. Anyway, it's right in front of the doorway.

Student A: A big abstract metal sculpture. Okay, I think I've got it.

Student B: I think you'll like the exhibit. Like I said, I dropped by there this morning and took a quick look around, because—I'm an art major myself, and because, well, grad student exhibits are usually great. My favorite pieces . . . there's this one little room off the main gallery and it's full of sculptures made all . . . they're all made from neon lights. They're just beautiful, the way they glow. I couldn't believe it wasn't the work of some, some professional artist.

Student A: Well, the main reason I'm going is . . . my sister invited me to the opening. She wanted me to see her newest work.

Student B: Your sister's an artist?

Student A: Yeah, she's a painter. She also, well, she just started volunteering to teach art to kids and . . . I think the way her students paint has sort of rubbed off on her. I think her kids have influenced her more than she's influenced them, as a matter of fact. She's using these bright colors, and . . .

Student B: Oh I think I saw her paintings! There was one of a house perched on a hill, and another one of a purple lion. I love the colors she uses!

Narrator: Now get ready to answer the questions. You may use your notes to help you.

Narrator: Question 5: Why was the woman confused at first when the man asked her for directions?

Narrator: Question 6: According to the woman, what is directly in front of the art building?

Narrator: Question 7: What was the woman's favorite exhibit at the art show?

Narrator: Question 8: What can be inferred from the conversation about the man's sister?

Narrator: Listen to a conversation between two students.

Student A: So, Paul, figured out yet where you're gonna live next semester? Are you gonna live in the dorm again or off-campus?

Student B: Well, to tell you the truth, I . . .

Student A: Because, here's the thing . . . I've leased this big three-bedroom apartment . . . it's within walking distance of campus . . . and I only have one other roommate lined up at the moment . . . and so I was just wondering, if you need a place next semester . . .

Student B: It's nice, really nice of you to think of me, Dave, but, I'm not actually going to be living here next fall. I, uh, I'm not going to need a place to live.

Student A: What? You're leaving Rutherford? Are you transferring, or . . .

Student B: No, uh, actually . . . I've decided to do . . . to take part in a Semester Abroad program. I'm going to spend the semester in Athens.

Student A: Really? You mean you're going to be studying in Greece?

Student B: Uh huh . . . I'm really excited about it. It's about all I can think of.

Student A: But, um, you don't speak any Greek, do you?

Student B: No, not a word. But the one and only required course in this program is an intensive language course in modern Greek. So I guess I'll learn some once I get there.

Student A: So what . . . what made you decide on Greece?

Student B: Well, you know, I'm a history major, and eventually I'd like to teach history at the university level, and so I thought I'd like to study history where a lot of it was made. And Professor Carmichael . . . she's my advisor . . . she said we'd be visiting a lot of historical sites all over Greece. She really talked up the idea of signing up for this program. Also, I'm interested in theater, and I'll be taking a course in, uh, Greek drama too.

Student A: You know, I'll bet it's gonna be . . . it's gonna be a real challenge. I mean, it was hard enough for me to find a decent apartment here in town where I've lived for a couple of years and hey, I speak the language. So I can't even imagine looking for an apartment someplace like Athens and not being able to speak Greek . . .

Student B: Okay, well, there are actually two kinds of . . . of Semester Abroad programs. One is called an independent program. If you sign up for that kind of program . . . that's the kind of program you're thinking of, probably—then you have to make your own travel plans, you find your own housing, you make your own arrangements for meals, you're . . . you're basically on your own except for the academic program. But the other type of program—they call it an "island plan"—

Student A: Why do they call it that?

Student B: I dunno. I guess . . . I guess because you're kinda on your own little island even though you're overseas. Anyway, if you go with the island plan, you . . . you stay at a dorm with other students from here at Rutherford College, and you eat with them . . . and the program makes all the airline arrangements, someone meets you at the airport . . . transportation from the dorm to the school—that's all taken care of . . . just about everything is arranged in advance for you. That's the program I . . . that's how I decided to go. I . . .

Student A: Oh, that's the way I'd do it too, if I were going. It just sounds . . . so much easier and you wouldn't feel so . . . so isolated, living alone . . . .

Student B: Well, in a way, I'd rather be in an independent program. It might be a bit tough, but I think I could handle it. And I mean, I think I'd learn more about Greece, and, uh, I'd get to meet more local people. There are some programs, in fact, where they place you with a local family. I'd actually love to live with a family or just out in the community. Plus it's cheaper to go that way.

Student A: So . . . why are you doing that island program, then?

Student B: Well, the main reason is time. My reason for going over there is to concentrate on classes, and I think I would spend all my time taking care of . . . well, just making living arrangements.

Student A: So, will your teachers all be from Greece?

Student B: The Greek language professor is, and some of the other teachers too, but some are from here at Rutherford and from other U.S. universities. Professor Carmichael, my advisor, is going to be teaching over there this year. She's never taught in Greece before, but she taught in a similar program in France a couple of years ago.

Student A: Well, it sounds great . . . I wish I could go myself!

Narrator: Now get ready to answer the questions. You may use your notes to help you.

Narrator: Question 9: Which of these courses is required for students in the Semester Abroad program in Greece?

Narrator: Question 10: Which of these is characteristic of the "island plan" Paul will take part in?

Narrator: Question 11: Why did Paul decide not to take part in the independent plan?

Narrator: Question 12: What does Paul say about Professor Carmichael?

Narrator: Listen to a conversation between two students.

Student A: Morning, Steve . . . boy, you look exhausted!

Student B: Do I? Well, guess that's to be expected. I was up almost all night, trying to get ready for my chemistry mid-term this morning.

Student A: Really? Any idea how you did on it?

Student B: Yeah, as a matter of fact, Doctor Porter's already posted grades on her office door, and I . . . well, I could have done a whole lot better.

Student A: That really surprises me, Steve. You know so much about science.

Student B: Yeah, well, it's not surprising to me. I just . . . I mean, I know the material, but for some reason, when it comes to taking tests . . . I never do well. If a class grade depends on a research paper, I do just fine, but when it comes to taking tests . . . especially multiple-choice tests . . . I just look at the questions and I draw a blank.

Student A: Have you ever considered taking some seminars at the Study Skills Center?

Student B: Uh, I don't really know anything about it.

Student A: Well, the Center's run by some grad students and junior professors that help undergraduates . . . well, help them get organized . . . learn some techniques that help them do better in their classes. When I first got here last year, I took a course from them on . . . on how to do aca-demic research on the Internet, and another one on writing term papers. They were really good, really useful.

Student B: Hmmm . . . so, what . . . what other kinds of courses do they offer?

Student A: Well, I don't know all the courses they offer, but I know they have a class on test-taking skills.

Student B: Wow, that's right up my alley.

Student A: And I know there's one on . . . how to, you know, manage your time . . . how to use time efficiently.

Student B: Yeah, well . . . I guess that's something I need too.

Student A: I should tell you . . . one of the things they're going to tell you is not to stay up all night cramming for a test.

Student B: Yeah, I . . . I already know it's not a great idea, but I . . . I just felt like it was the only way I could get ready . . .

Student A: As a matter of fact, they'll tell you it's the worst thing you can do . . . you need to be fresh and rested for a test.

Student B: Yeah, well . . . I did drink plenty of coffee to keep me alert. So, anyway, where is the Center?

Student A: They have a little office in Staunton Hall, across the quadrangle from the physics tower, you know where I mean? That's where you go to sign up. They actually hold their seminars in the main library. I don't know if they're holding any seminars just now, but, uh, I think they start new ones every six weeks or so.

Student B: I should go by there now and try to talk to someone.

Student A: You know, if I were you, Steve . . . I think I'd go by there tomorrow. Right now, you should go back to your dorm and catch up on your sleep.

Narrator: Now get ready to answer the questions. You may use your notes to help you.

Narrator: Question 13: Why does Steve look tired?

Narrator: Question 14: How does Steve feel about the grade that he received on the chemistry test?

Narrator: Question 15: Who teaches the seminars at the Study Skills Center?

Narrator: Question 16: Which of the courses at the Study Skills Center will Steve probably be most interested in?

Narrator: Question 17: Where is the Study Skills Center?

Narrator: Question 18: What does the woman suggest Steve do now?

Narrator: Listen to a conversation between a student and a campus housing administrator.

Student: Hi, I'm Jeff Bloom. I'm, uh, here to talk to someone about the . . . the Resident Advisor position?

Administrator: Oh, hi, I'm Frances Delfino. You can talk to me about that. Did you see our ad in the campus paper?

Student: No, uh, Mr. Collingswood, down in the off-campus housing office, uh, he suggested I come by and chat with you.

Administrator: Oh, okay, so . . .

Student: Let me tell you what's happening with me. . . . I've been living off-campus, living by myself in an apartment, right, which is great, but my landlord decided to sell the house I'm living in, and the new owner is . . . well, first she's going to remodel, so I have to move out anyway . . . then she's gonna rent the apartments for a lot more money . . . and, well, to make a long story short, I need a place to live just for one more semester.

Administrator: And you're interested in becoming a Resident Advisor?

Student: Well, I . . . I came by the housing office today to see if . . . well, the off-campus housing office has a list of apart-ments available . . . but everything on the list is too expen-sive, or way too far from campus, or you need to sign a year's lease. There just wasn't anything on the list that inter-ested me so . . . so Mr. Collingswood suggested I come up and see you. He said there were some Resident Advisor positions open at one of the men's dorms and that I, I, uh, could get some information about these positions from you.

Administrator: Fine, well, I can tell you a little about the R.A. positions . . . the Resident Advisor positions . . . We do have a couple of openings for grad students or older upper-classmen. If you lived in a dorm yourself, you probably know all about what an R.A. does . . .

Student: Well, actually, I never did live in a dorm. I've always lived off-campus so I . . . I have no idea . . .

Administrator: Well, there's one R.A. per floor . . . we have openings in Donahue Hall and Hogan Hall . . . and you . . . you inform students of . . . oh, you know, university rules, regulations, policies . . . you organize a few social events for residents . . . and, uh, well, there are a lot of other things you may have to do . . . help students who are locked out of their rooms, uh, in general, you're kind of a mentor, you help students solve their problems . . .

Student: Hmmm, that . . . that doesn't sound so bad. And . . . well, my only other option is to share an apartment with a roommate, and I . . . I don't think I want to do that.

Administrator: Well, if you took an R.A. position, you wouldn't have to share. You'd have your own room and . . . in fact, the R.A. rooms are actually a little larger than the typical resident rooms.

Student: So, how much does it pay?

Administrator: Oh, didn't Mr. Collingswood mention that? There's no salary—it's not exactly a paid position. But your room is free and you're entitled to ten meals per week at the cafeteria at Donahue Hall.

Student: Really? Hmmm, well, I guess I'd be saving a lot of money on rent and on meals but . . . I . . . well, here's what I'm most worried about—the noise. I'm just afraid it would be too noisy for me to study, to concentrate. See, like I said, I'm in my last semester here, and I'm taking some pretty tough classes this semester. I just . . . .

Administrator: Well, I'm not going to lie to you and say that the residents will always be quiet and orderly. I mean, come on, they're undergrads, mostly freshmen, so . . . it will probably be noisier than what you're used to, especially on weekends. But during the week, there are quiet hours, from 7 till 10 and then from midnight on . . . in fact, one of your duties is to enforce . . . is to make sure these quiet hours stay quiet.

Student: So, suppose I decide I want to . . . to apply for an R.A. position, what, uh, what would I need to do?

Administrator: I can give you a form to fill out. You'd also need to get two letters of recommendation . . .

Student: Letters? Who from?

Administrator: Oh, teachers, administrators, you know, someone like that. Oh, also, I have a pamphlet that describes the position in more detail. You can look that over. And I could give you e-mail addresses for a couple of R.A.s. You could contact them, see how they like the job, see what kinds of experiences they've had.

Narrator: Now get ready to answer the questions. You may use your notes to help you.

Narrator: Question 19: Why does Jeff have to move out of his apartment?

Narrator: Question 20: How did Jeff find out about the Resident Advisor position?

Narrator: Question 21: What will Jeff receive if he becomes a Resident Advisor?

Narrator: Question 22: What does Ms. Delfino suggest Jeff do to get more information about the position?

[CD 3 Track 2]

Exercise 10.2

Narrator: Listen to a discussion in an anthropology class.

Professor: Morning, class. I want to start off this morning with a question for you. How many of you have ever been to a potluck dinner? Oh, lots of you, I see. Okay, who can describe a potluck dinner for me? Andy?

Student A: It's just a dinner where all the guests bring dishes for . . . well, to share with everyone else. Someone might bring salad, someone might bring dessert . . .

Student B: It's a way you can have a dinner party with your friends and not spend a million dollars, because everyone brings something.

Professor: You're right. Well, today we're gonna be discussing a ceremony called the *potlatch*.

Student A: I'm sorry, the what?

Professor: The *potlatch*. Here, I'll put it on the board for you. This is a ceremony held by Native Americans and Native Canadians in the Pacific Northwest—from Washington state north to British Columbia, all the way up to Alaska. Potlatches were held to . . . well, for all kinds of reasons . . . to celebrate births, weddings, naming ceremonies, even a good catch of salmon. Now, some linguists think that the English word *potluck* might be derived from this word *potlatch*. The word *potlatch* is originally from the Chinook language. The Chinooks were a group of Native Americans who lived along the Columbia River. A form of their language, called Chinook Trade Jargon, became a trade language, a language used by tribes all over the region to communicate with one another. So, ah, the word *potlatch* spread, and . . . and before long, it was used by all the tribes in the Pacific Northwest.

Student B: Professor Burke, were these potlatches . . . were they sort of like the potlucks we have today?

Professor: Well, no, as a matter of fact, they were quite a bit different. I suppose the best way . . . I think the best way to describe a potlatch is as a birthday party in reverse.

Student B: Huh? A . . . birthday party in reverse? What do you mean?

Professor: Well, at a birthday party, what happens? The guests all bring gifts, right? At a potlatch, it's the host who gives the gifts and the guests who receive them.

Student A: Sounds like a pretty good deal for the guests!

Professor: In a way it was, but—but in a way it wasn't. Let me describe a typical potlatch to you. A host—it was often a chief or an important person of some kind—would invite people from his tribe or from other tribes in the area. The guests would arrive and there would be some dancing. Then the guests would be seated, and the host and his family, his relatives would serve the guests a huge, formal feast . . .

Student B: Professor Burke, excuse me . . . I couldn't help wonder . . . what kind of food would be served at these potlatches?

Professor: Well, the tribes that had potlatches all lived near the ocean, so what kind of food do you think they served?

Student B: Ummm . . . I'm guessing fish.

Professor: Right. Mostly salmon, salmon was the staple food of the Northwest tribes, they spent a lot of their time salmon fishing and then preserving salmon . . . They might also serve whale meat, or seal meat, or venison. They'd dip these foods into pots of seal oil to give them more flavor. And . . . the hosts would always serve more than the guests could possibly eat. Okay, then after the feasting, the host would start distributing gifts.

Student B: What kind of gifts would the host give away?

Professor: Well, the most common gift was food: salmon. The host would pack smoked fish in these . . . these elaborately carved boxes. Other gifts they might give . . . goat-hair blankets, jewelry, wooden masks. And, and, ah, after these tribes came in contact with Americans and Canadians of European origin, the gifts became more . . . more varied. There might be sacks of flour, dishes, eating utensils. I even remember seeing a photograph of a potlatch from, oh, around 1900, where a guest is receiving a sewing machine!

Student B: So, what else happened at a potlatch?

Professor: Well, then the host would usually destroy some of his most valuable possessions, such as fishing canoes, and he'd throw coins and . . . and almost anything valuable into the sea . . .

Student A: What?! Excuse me, Professor . . . I just don't get it. It just seems kinda crazy to me. Why would anyone want to host a party like that?

Professor: Okay, well, first off, gift-giving rituals like this are not all that uncommon. I mean, there have been societies all around the world that have gone in for these types of ceremonies, but . . . but having said that, I can't think of any other society where it was such a, such a central part of the culture. See, these tribes . . . to them, status . . . prestige . . . Well, in short, they were highly status conscious. To them, looking good in the eyes of other people was very, very important, and that's what a, a potlatch was all about. It was a means of establishing rank. Status. Power.

Student A: How's that?

Professor: Well, by accepting gifts at a potlatch, the guests . . . they acknowledged the wealth and the generosity of their hosts. And when they were destroying or throwing away valuables, the hosts were really saying, "I'm so important, I'm so wealthy, I can afford to smash up my stuff and throw away my money!"

Student A: Well, I still think it was a much better deal to be a guest than to be a host at these parties.

Professor: Ah, but you see, Andy, there was a catch! In some ways, potlatches were actually a form of . . . of investment.

Student A: Investment?

Professor: Sure. The guests, all the guests at a potlatch were honor-bound to pay the host back by having potlatches of their own and inviting the host.

Student A: Oh, I get it—it was an investment because then the host would be invited to lots of potlatches.

Professor: Right. And the potlatches that the guests held had to be at least as elaborate as the one they'd been invited to. There was this one tribe called the Kwakiutl who lived up on Vancouver Island. Now this group . . . they really turned the potlatch into an art form. They had the most elaborate, most ritualistic potlatches of all the tribes in the Northwest. When the Kwakiutl held potlatches, they would use the ceremony as a . . . as a kind of weapon, a form of revenge against their enemies. They'd throw such extravagant potlatches that their enemies would go broke trying to match them.

Student A: Wow, that was a . . . a clever way to get back at their enemies!

Student B: So, do these tribes still have potlatches?

Professor: That's a really good question. Both the U.S. government and the Canadian government banned potlatches back in the 1880's—although some tribes no doubt held potlatch ceremonies in secret. I suppose government officials just somehow didn't like the idea of people giving away their possessions. At the time, they didn't realize how important potlatches were . . . important culturally, socially, religiously to the tribes. But nowadays—in fact, ever since the 1930's in Canada and the 1950's in the United States— potlatches are legal again. If anything, they're an even more essential element of these societies than they were before.

Narrator: Now get ready to answer the questions. You may use your notes to help you.

Narrator: Question 1: What does the professor say about the word *potlatch*?

Narrator: Question 2: What was the most common gift at a potlatch?

Narrator: Question 3: What purpose did seal oil serve at a potlatch?

Narrator: Question 4: What does Professor Burke imply about the photograph of a potlatch taken in 1900?

Narrator: Question 5: What does Professor Burke say about the Kwakiutl tribe?

Narrator: Question 6: What does Professor Burke say about potlatch ceremonies held today?

Narrator: Listen to a lecture in a space science class.

Professor: As I said at the end of our class on Tuesday, today I'm going to talk about a growing problem in the sky. You can call it . . . call it space junk, space debris, orbital litter, whatever you like—it's basically the leftovers from the thousands of satellites and spacecraft that have been sent into orbit over the last fifty years or so.

The problem started back in the late 1950's. The Soviet Union launched the first satellite—Sputnik, it was called— in 1957. And that's, that's when a tracking network was first set up, too, to monitor bodies in orbit. Today, there's a worldwide network of 21 telescopes and radar stations called the, umm, the Space Surveillance Network, that keeps track of all this stuff, all these items in space.

Almost every launch contributes to the problem, contributes to the amount of junk up there circling the earth. There are non-functioning satellites, food wrappers, an astronaut's glove, the lens cap from a camera, broken tools, bags of unwashed uniforms. Luckily, most of this junk burns up when it re-enters the atmosphere, just like little meteors. And although old pieces fall out of the sky, new pieces are launched. On average, there's a net increase of around 200 pieces per year.

Today there are around 13,000 pieces of . . . 13,000 separate bodies that are monitored from Earth. And of those, only about 400 are still active, still useful pieces of equipment. Most of it is in what is called low-Earth orbit, within . . . well, that's defined as within 1,200 miles of the earth. There are also about a thousand pieces in high orbit. It's in a very thin, very narrow ring, shaped like a bicycle tire, about 22,000 miles above the Equator.

The, uh, Surveillance people can only monitor objects bigger than about a baseball. There are probably, I'd say about half a million pieces of debris that are just too small to be monitored. Most of these small objects are tiny flecks of paint or little pieces of metal, say around the size of a grain of sand. Some orbital debris is huge—big as a bus! The smallest pieces are not that dangerous, not usually. When they hit a spacecraft, they only cause, oh, just some surface damage. Several times outer windows on the space shuttle have had to be replaced because of collisions with micro-objects in space, but there was no real danger. And the really big pieces—those are mostly empty booster rockets or other rocket parts—they're not necessarily all that dangerous either. Why not? Because these large objects can be detected by radar and so . . . so they can be avoided fairly easily. Several times shuttles have had to maneuver to avoid getting close to large pieces of debris. But it's the medium-sized pieces that represent the biggest danger. These objects are so dangerous, of course, because of their tremendous speed. They can be moving up to 12 miles per second. That's way faster than a bullet . . . your typical bullet doesn't even travel 1 mile per second. If one of these flying pieces of debris—say, a lost screwdriver, or a piece of an antenna that broke off a satellite—if one of these hit a space shuttle or the International Space Station—it could puncture the outer hull. Then what would happen? You'd have de-pressurization—all of the air inside would rush out into the vacuum of space, and then, you'd have a disaster on your hands. So far—fortunately—there has never been a major collision involving a manned spacecraft but . . . but space debris has damaged the solar panels on an unmanned communications satellite. And there, there have also been some collisions of these pieces of debris themselves. In January of 2005, the engine from a Thor rocket launched by the United States thirty years ago and a fragment of a Chinese rocket that blew up five years ago met over Antarctica. The event was recorded by a camera on a surveillance satellite. The collision produced even more pieces of space junk.

So, what can we do, what can be done about this problem? Well, a couple of years ago, space engineers came up with an idea, a possible way to solve this, uh, this debris problem. Here's what they suggested. You build a "junk collector," a large cone or group of cones that fits on the front of a spacecraft. The cone is full of sticky plastic fibers that trap debris inside it. This invention is still in its conceptual stage, but . . . there are two ways it might be used. You could launch unmanned satellites equipped with these devices and radar sensors and you could actively hunt down dangerous pieces of space junk. Or you could put one of these on the front of a manned spacecraft and use it as a defensive shield. Oh, and another possible solution . . . you could use laser guns, either on a space-based platform or based here on earth, to shoot some of the smaller pieces out of the sky. Okay, anyone have any questions for me?

Narrator: Now get ready to answer the questions. You may use your notes to help you.

Narrator: Question 7: What happens to most pieces of orbital debris?

Narrator: Question 8: How many orbital bodies are being monitored today?

Narrator: Question 9: Why is it impossible to monitor most pieces of orbital debris?

Narrator: Question 10: Which of the following types of orbital debris would not be particularly dangerous to astronauts on a spacecraft?

Narrator: Question 11: The professor describes a collision in space between which of the following objects?

Narrator: Question 12: What can be inferred about the collector described in this portion of the talk?

Narrator: Listen to a discussion in a pharmacy class.

Professor: Good morning, all. This is our last class before the final, you know, and I told you I'd give you a little more information about the test today, but . . . before I do that, I want to talk about a different class of drugs. This term we've been discussing, mmmm, different types of, of pharmaceutical drugs. Today, though, I'd like to spend a little time discussing another class of drugs. You could lump them all together and call them herbal drugs or herbal remedies.

Student: Oh, I just read a magazine article about herbal drugs. It said that herbal remedies were becoming more and more popular.

Professor: That's probably true. I've heard that, oh, something like 12 million people in the United States use herbal drugs and . . . worldwide—well, there are countries where herbal remedies are as important . . . maybe even more important than pharmaceutical drugs.

Student B: So, Professor Findlay—why do you think—why is it important for pharmacists to know about herbal medicines? I mean, usually patients don't get prescriptions and come to pharmacists for herbal remedies, do they? They just buy them at . . . I don't know, health food stores and so on, right?

Professor: Well, there are several reasons, Thomas. For one thing, pharmaceutical and herbal medicine have a lot . . .

they share a lot of history. I mean, think about it, at one time all drugs came from herbs and other plants. At one time, the "pharmacist" was just some guy, well, usually some woman, who knew what herbs were helpful and knew where to look for them. Also, a lot of pharmaceutical drugs in use today, they, mmm, originally came from herbal sources.

Student B: Really? Which ones?

Professor: Well, the most commonly taken drug of all—good old aspirin—is one example. The active ingredient in aspirin originally came from the bark of a tree—the white willow tree. And anyone remember a drug we talked about last month called digitalis?

Student A: I do. It's used to . . . to treat heart problems, right?

Professor: You're correct. And digitalis originally came from a plant called foxglove. Anyway, to introduce you to alternative medicine, I brought along some samples of plants that are often used in herbal medicines. See this flower that looks like a purple daisy?

Student A: It's a pretty little flower. What is it?

Professor: Well, some people call it the herbal equivalent of a flu shot. It's called Echinacea.

Student A: Oh, I read about that—doesn't it work on the immune system?

Professor: Right. Well, lots of people think it does, anyhow. It's one of the most commonly taken herbal remedies. A lot of people, when they feel a cold or the flu coming on, will take Echinacea.

Student A: What are those yellow flowers with the five petals?

Professor: Those are called St. John's Wort. St. John's Wort. It's used to reduce stress and for mild depression. Now, here's a plant you uh you might find of interest at this time of year, with finals coming on. See this fan-shaped leaf? It's from the Ginkgo Biloba tree.

Student B: What's that one for?

Professor: Ginkgo Biloba is thought to improve memory and to help you be more alert, more focused.

Student A: Is that right? Wow, we really should try some of that! So, Professor, how do you . . . how do most people take these drugs? Do they just . . . swallow them?

Professor: I'd imagine the most common way to take them is in powdered form—the leaves or flowers are crushed and powdered and put in a capsule, and people swallow the capsule. Another way . . . some people make tea from the plants and drink the tea, although I'm told that most of these herbs taste pretty nasty.

Student B: Here's what I don't understand—why would someone use herbal drugs when there are regular drugs, pharmaceutical drugs that do the same thing?

Professor: Well, Thomas, for one thing, a lot of herbal drugs are a form of preventative medicine. In other words, people tend to take these drugs to avoid getting sick. On the other hand, most prescription drugs are used after someone gets sick . . . I mean, to treat some specific problem. Then, for another thing, people—a lot of people that use these drugs, they think that herbs . . . that, umm, herbal remedies have fewer side effects and are generally—well, safer than prescription drugs.

Student B: What do you think, Professor? Do you think that's true? Are they safer?

Professor: Well, I'd have to say, not always. There are some herbs I would never recommend, and then there are definitely some herbal drugs that some people—for example, pregnant women, people with high blood pressure—these folks should definitely not take these drugs.

Student B: But Professor, do you think they work? I mean, are most herbal remedies as effective as prescription drugs?

Professor: I don't really have a simple answer for that question, Thomas. I think that in some cases, they might be. But not all that much research has been done on herbal drugs, so there isn't that much scientific proof.

Student A: Why is that, Professor? Why no research?

Professor: That's easy. Because drug research, most of the research done on drugs is done by pharmaceutical companies that hope to patent the drug and then to make a profit on it. But, guess what, you can't patent an herb, since, well, since it's a natural substance. So . . .

Student B: Professor, as a pharmacist, would you recommend . . . would you ever tell a patient to take herbal medicine instead of a prescription drug?

Professor: Mmm, well, I might, depending on the medical situation, but there are several considerations. Patients need to take a few precautions. First, they should be sure that they get herbs from a reputable company, a dependable company, to make sure the herbs they are taking are pure. They should also talk to their doctors and their pharmacists—*especially* if they are taking any other drugs, because there is always the possibility drugs and herbs . . . well, there could be a serious drug-herb interaction. Finally, I'd remind patients not to, not to expect miracles from herbs. I mean, let's face it, no herbal remedy can take the place of exercise and a healthy diet.

Narrator: Now get ready to answer the questions. You may use your notes to help you.

Narrator: Question 13: What point does Professor Findlay make about the drugs aspirin and digitalis?

Narrator: Question 14: According to Professor Findlay, why do people generally take the herbal remedy Echinacea?

Narrator: Question 15: Which of the following is the best description of St. John's Wort?

Narrator: Question 16: What can be inferred from the professor's remarks about how most herbal medicines are used?

Narrator: Question 17: In what form are herbal remedies most often taken?

Narrator: Question 18: According to the professor, why has research on herbal drugs been limited?

Narrator: Listen to a lecture in a U.S. history class.

Professor: Good afternoon, class. Today I want to talk a little about something that's done more, I think, to shape the landscape of the United States as it is today than, uh, well, probably more that just about any other phenomenon: the Interstate Highway System. The Interstate System has been called the largest public works project in the history of the country—maybe in the history of the world—and it's definitely one of the world's great engineering wonders. When the, uh, the Century Highway in Los Angeles was completed in 1993, it marked the end—well, almost the end, there were still some bits and pieces that weren't finished—but it effectively marked the end of a forty-year project that cost hundreds of billions of dollars.

Okay, let's take a trip back in time; let's go back to the early part of the twentieth century. Let's say you've just bought a brand-new automobile—maybe a shiny new Model A Ford. Here's your problem: you can drive your car around the city, but if you want to go from city to city, there are no roads to speak of. When the weather is bad, well, people joke about losing automobiles in the mud. In fact, in many places, roads are probably worse than they were a hundred years before. Anyone guess why? No? Okay, remember a couple of weeks ago, we talked about how,

after the Civil War, the railroad became dominant, the dominant form of transportation? Does that ring a bell? So, what was one of the side effects of this? The roads meant for horses, for carts, for carriages, these all fell into disrepair because—well, because passengers and goods all moved by railroad. There was no reason to maintain roads. Anyway, you've got these terrible roads, no way to . . . to get from place to place, so what do you motorists do? You organize, you form groups, and then you ask, you demand that the government build roads. These groups of motorists went by a lot of different names, depending on where they were, but collectively, they were known as the Better Roads Movement. And the government responded. It responded slowly, but it responded. Roads were built, but it would be years, many years before there was a comprehensive highway system.

Okay, let's move ahead in time a few years. It's 1919, and a young army officer, whose name is Dwight David Eisenhower, is ordered to lead a military convoy of trucks and motorcycles across the country, from Washington, D.C., to San Francisco, California. He's ordered to get there as soon as possible. It takes him . . . you might find this hard to believe, but it took him sixty-two days. Sixty-two days!

Okay, now it's the 1930's . . . the time of the Great Depression, as I know you'll remember, and there are millions of unemployed workers—millions—and President Roosevelt puts some of them to work on public works projects. These projects include road building. In 1938, the first "superhighway" opens. It's called the Pennsylvania Turnpike. You may have traveled on it yourself and not found it . . . well, not found it all that exciting. However, at the time it opened, it was known as "the dream road." This four-lane highway became a model for the highways of the future.

So . . . after World War II, the United States really and truly enters the automobile age. By 1950, there are over 50 million vehicles on the road. In 1954, Dwight David Eisenhower—he's the president of the United States by now—he proposes a system of superhighways. This system would basically connect all of the major cities in the United States. Of course, Eisenhower has been interested in roads for a long time. There were two events that . . . two major events in his life that influenced the way he thinks about highways. One is his wartime experience. He was commander of the Allied forces in Europe during World War II, and he saw, uh, the advantage that the efficient German autobahn system—the German superhighway system—he saw the advantage this gave Germany during the war. The other event? It's that long, hard trip he took across the country back in 1919.

So, in 1956 Congress passes the Federal Highway Act, and the first section of the Interstate system is built in Kansas—Eisenhower's home state. The system is supposed to be completed by 1972, but it's not finished, as I said, until the 1990's.

The Interstate Highway System has had just a . . . just an enormous impact on life in the United States. It's created millions of jobs. It's provided an incredibly efficient system for moving people and transporting goods around the country—and because of that, it's contributed to the decline of the railroads. Because of the safety factors that were built into the system, it's probably saved thousands of lives. It's helped create the suburbs that surround every U.S. city. Now, it's true, there were suburbs before there were Interstate highways, but the Interstate system has helped accelerate their growth because . . . well, it's just so easy to travel from suburb to central city.

Now don't get me wrong—not all the effects of this superhighway system have been, well, positive, especially in urban areas. There have been whole neighborhoods destroyed to make way for roads. Just in Seattle, for example, thousands of homes were destroyed to make way for Interstate 5. Whole neighborhoods were . . . well, it was like having a river, a concrete river, a river of traffic cut through a neighborhood, or cut off from other neighborhoods. There was opposition, there were protests. In Boston in 1966, an anti-highway group successfully blocked the building of a highway called the Inner Belt. Another group stopped the building of an Interstate highway through San Francisco.

Still, for better or worse, the Interstate Highway System has changed the face of the United States. And remember that trip from Washington to San Francisco in 1919 that took Eisenhower 62 days? Today, you can make that same trip in just 72 hours!

Narrator: Now get ready to answer the questions. You may use your notes to help you.

Narrator: Question 19: Which of the following caused the decline of roads in the United States in the nineteenth century?

Narrator: Question 20: How long did it take Dwight David Eisenhower to drive across the United States in 1919?

Narrator: Question 21: According to the speaker, which of these influenced the way President Eisenhower thought about highways?

Narrator: Question 22: When was the Interstate Highway system originally supposed to have been completed?

Narrator: Question 23: Which of the following is not given as an effect of the Interstate Highway System?

Narrator: Question 24: In which of these cities were Interstate Highway projects blocked by protests?

Narrator: Listen to a discussion among students preparing a presentation for an architecture class.

Student A: Okay, so . . . the presentation on alternative housing in Professor Maxwell's class is going to be . . . what, the 21st?

Student B: Umm, let me check . . . no, it's, uh, not until the 23rd. But we have to hand in a . . . a preliminary outline next Tuesday.

Student C: And this presentation counts for . . . I think it's a fourth of our grade, so we need to do a good job.

Student A: Right. So, either of you do any research, or decide what kind of housing we should talk about?

Student C: Well, I . . . I looked at a couple of Web sites on the Internet, and paged through some journals, but . . . I didn't really come up with much of anything. How about you, Joyce?

Student B: As a matter of fact, ummm, I have some . . . I guess you could call it indirect experience with one type of alternative housing. I think I told you my uncle owns a construction company, and, okay, last year, he had these clients, this couple come to him and say they wanted him to help them build the kind of house called an earthship. They showed him the plans and . . . at first he thought they were nuts, but, well, he needed the business and so . . . he helped them build the house, the earthship . . . and he ended up thinking . . . well, he's actually thinking of building an earthship for himself.

Student C: An earthship! Huh! That sounds like . . . like something from a science fiction movie!

Student B: Yeah, I guess it does!

Student A: So, uh, what's so interesting about earthships?

Student B: Well, for one thing, they're made almost entirely out of recycled materials. In fact, the main building materials are old tires and aluminum cans. The outer walls consist of used tires packed with soil. Then you take the aluminum cans and tuck them between the tires and then . . .you cover the walls with cement.

Student C: You're kidding. I mean, I . . . hate to say this but . . . used tires, old cans, dirt, cement . . . . those aren't the most attractive building materials.

Student B: I know, I know, they don't sound that attractive, not at all, but, uh, you can finish the interior, the inside of the earthship any way you want. You can finish the walls with plaster and paint them, or you can use wood panels . . . I've seen pictures of the one my uncle built, and it's full of plants and art and, and believe me, it looks really nice.

Student A: Well, Maxwell should love them—you know how she feels about building with recycled materials . . .

Student B: Yeah, but that's not all . . . earthships are not only made from recycled materials. They also use . . . very, very little power. They generate their own electricity from solar panels—these are up on the roof . . . and they use, uh, passive solar heating to provide heat in the winter.

Student A: Really? How do they do that?

Student B: Well, earthships are basically shaped like the letter U. The three walls made of tires are on the west, north, and east sides. The open part of the U, which is on the south side, is made of glass windows, and they're . . . they're angled upward to catch the winter sunlight.

Student A: Yeah, this definitely sounds like the kind of house Maxwell would love.

Student C: What about costs? How much does an earthship cost?

Student B: Well, you know . . . dirt, aluminum cans . . . a lot of the materials are either free or almost free . . . and a lot of times, the owners help build the houses themselves. Earthships are a real bargain. My uncle's clients got a small "nest" for . . . well, I'm guessing, but it probably only cost them about $40,000, not counting the land it was built on.

Student C: Umm, what do you mean, a "nest?"

Student B: Oh, that's what . . . that's the most basic form of earthship, the smallest type. Course, you can spend a lot more if you build a big, fancy one.

Student C: Well, I vote we do our presentation on earthships, then, since Joyce already knows a lot about them, and they, uh, they sound pretty interesting to me too.

Student A: I'll go along with that. Like I say, I think Maxwell will love them, and she's the one who gives the grade.

Student C: Joyce, if you can get me some plans, I bet I could build a small model before we give our presentation.

Student B: Well, detailed plans are pretty expensive, but I can probably get you some photos of the earthship that my uncle helped build.

Student C: That's probably all I'd need, as long as they show the house from all sides . . .

Student A: But would you have time to make a model before the presentation?

Student C: Oh, I'm sure I can. I can make a simple architectural model of just about anything in a coupla days.

Narrator: Now get ready to answer the questions. You may use your notes to help you.

Narrator: Question 25: How did Joyce get most of her information about earthships?

Narrator: Question 26: Which of these are not one of the main building materials used to construct earthships?

Narrator: Question 27: Which of the walls of an earthship is made of glass?

Narrator: Question 28: What is meant by the term *nest?*

Narrator: Question 29: Why does Joyce call earthships "a real bargain"?

Narrator: Question 30: What will the students probably bring to the presentation?

Narrator: Listen to a lecture in a political science class.

Professor: Afternoon. How's everyone today? Good. So, we've spent the best part of the last couple weeks going over the structure of the federal government . . . and talking about the document that, that provides the basis for government structure, the U.S. Constitution. Today, as promised, we're going to take a look at the structure of the states, of the individual state governments in the United States.

There are two main types of government . . . two main systems of governing in the world. Under the *unitary* system, the national government, the central government has a great deal of control over the regional and local governments. For example, the central government may completely control the budgets of the provinces, the states, the departments, whatever the political subdivisions are called. The national president may appoint the governors of these regional units. Actually, most of the national governments in the world are of this type: unitary. The other type, the other system of government is the *federal* system. Under this system, the constituent parts of the nation have a great deal of power. Only about twenty-four, twenty-five nations in the world are considered to have federal systems. The oldest one of these is the United States.

The reason that the U.S. has a federal system . . . it's because of our history. Before independence, the thirteen British colonies were ruled separately. People from the colony of Virginia, for example, considered themselves Virginians, really, not Americans. So then, after the Revolutionary War, the former colonies . . . well, as you can imagine, they each jealously guarded their own independence. When the states signed the Constitution, they surrendered some of their sovereign powers but . . . here's the thing: the Constitution says that, whatever powers are not given directly to the federal government belong to the state governments. So . . . compared to other countries . . . well, there may be a few countries that have an equally decentralized system . . . Switzerland comes to mind, the Swiss states, they're actually called cantons there, they have a great deal of power, too . . . and so do the Canadian provinces. But, if you look at other countries . . . France has always had a very centralized system of government. Paris has traditionally controlled everything. Now, this may be becoming less true—there's been some decentralization in recent years—but still, it's a unitary system. And if you look at the United Kingdom, well, local governments there have a fair amount of power, but . . . but there is nothing comparable, really, to state governments. Britain is divided into regions, but these regions have no real governments to speak of. Again, maybe someday soon they will, but for now, we'd have to consider the U.K.'s system of government more or less a unitary system. So anyway, my point here is, compared to most comparable political units around the world, the U.S. states are pretty powerful.

What kind of powers do the states have? They collect taxes . . . they regulate businesses that operate within the state . . . they issue licenses, like drivers' licenses, marriage licenses . . . they build roads. What else? Well, they're involved in education. Mostly with higher education. All the states operate a state university system. Elementary schools, secondary schools, those are mostly controlled by local school boards.

Now, as we said earlier, the structure of the federal government, the rules for operating the federal government, these are determined by the U.S. Constitution. Likewise, each state has its own constitution that determines its structure. Massachusetts has the oldest constitution. In fact, it's older than the national constitution. Granted, it's been changed some since then, but it's, it's really the same document that was adopted in 1780.

We said the federal government was divided into three branches: executive, legislative, and judicial. Same is true of the states. The chief of the executive branch is called the governor, as you no doubt know. The governor—this is true in all the states—is elected for a four-year term. In about half the states, the governor can serve only two terms, in about half he can serve as many as he wants. In one state—Virginia—the governor can only serve one term.

The state legislatures serve the same purpose as the U.S. Congress. Members of the legislature are elected. They make laws, they set tax rates, and in all of the states except Oregon, they can impeach—know what I mean, they can throw out the governor. Like the U.S. Congress, state legislatures have a . . . a bicameral structure. This means they are divided into two bodies, two houses. The upper house is called the state senate, the lower house, well, it has different names, depending on what state you're in . . . Oh, and, uh, when I said every state has a bicameral legislature, I should have said all but one of them do. Nebraska is the exception, Nebraska is unique because it has only one house . . . so its, it has a unicameral system . . . just one house.

State supreme courts . . . those represent the judicial branch . . . their job is to interpret the state constitution . . . . just like the U.S. Supreme Court does . . . and to try various cases. In some states, they are elected, in some states they are appointed by the governor or the legislature. In most states, they serve terms of 8 to 10 years, but in Rhode Island, they're appointed for life.

Next up . . . we're going to take an in-depth look at the structure of our own state government. I'm going to pass out copies of the Ohio State Constitution in just a minute but . . . anyone have any questions first?

Narrator: Now get ready to answer the questions. You may use your notes to help you.

Narrator: Question 31: What does the professor say about the unitary system of government?

Narrator: Question 32: What does the professor say about Switzerland?

Narrator: Question 33: According to the professor, which of the following is mainly responsible for primary and secondary education in the United States?

Narrator: Question 34: Which of these states has the oldest constitution?

Narrator: Question 35: What is the maximum time that a governor of Virginia can serve?

Narrator: Question 36: What is unique about the state legislature of Nebraska?

Narrator: Listen to a discussion in a dance class.

Professor: Okay, everyone. We've been talking about traditional forms of dance. Today, umm, we're going to shift our attention to the islands of Hawaii, and the most famous form of dance that's associated with those beautiful islands. Anyone know what that is? Laura?

Student A: Oh, that's an easy one—it's the hula dance.

AUDIO SCRIPT

Professor: Yeah, you're right, it's the hula—um, you don't have to say hula *dance,* actually, because the word hula means dance in Hawaiian, in the Hawaiian language. Has anyone ever seen this dance performed, or know anything about it? James?

Student B: Well, I've seen a coupla TV shows and movies about Hawaii, and, um, it seems to me, that usually when you see the hula, it's done by women in long grass skirts.

Professor: Laura?

Student A: When I was a little kid, I . . . my parents took me to Hawaii, and there were hula dancers who'd perform at our hotel. I remember being fascinated by . . . by how gracefully they moved their bodies and their hands.

Professor: Yeah, and you know, those body movements and gestures, they all have meaning. The dancers use these to tell stories. But, uh, what I want to emphasize, really emphasize, is the fact that the hula that's performed today for tourists, the one you see at hotels and cultural shows, is very different from the traditional hula, the one that was performed hundreds of years ago. Modern hula is called *hula auane.* The old style, traditional hula, is called *hula kahiko.*

Student A: Hundreds of years ago . . . I didn't realize it was such an old dance!

Professor: Yeah, and as a matter of fact, we don't even know exactly how old the hula is. We do know that when Captain Cook visited the islands in the 1770's—he was the first European to go there . . . , he was allowed to see a hula on the island of Kauai. He wrote in his journal how much he enjoyed it. We also know that one of the queens of Hawaii established a royal school of hula over 500 years ago. Back then, both men and women took part in the dance. There were two types of performers. There were young performers, called *olapa,* which means "graceful ones" in Hawaiian. These were the dancers, the ones that actually performed the dance. Then there were older performers called *h'oa-paa,* which means "steady ones." They chanted and sang, and they also played musical instruments. Apparently back then hula ceremonies could get quite wild! But all that changed in 1820.

Student B: Why? What happened then?

Professor: That was the year that religious missionaries came to Hawaii from the United States–from New England, to be specific. They found the original form of the hula to be a little . . . well, shocking, so they . . . they arranged to have the hula completely banned for around fifty years. Then, when it came back, it was a much tamer version, a much more conservative dance—the *hula auane.*

Student B: So, how was it different?

Professor: Well, remember I told you that the hula tells stories through movements? In the old days, the hula . . . well, probably the most important story was the story of how the islands rose up out of the sea. Also, there were dances about the . . . the Hawaiian gods and goddesses, especially the goddess Laki, who was the special goddess of the hula. Some dances told the stories of brave Hawaiian kings and queens . . . stories of Hawaiian history. But, uh, in the modern version of the dance, the movements of the dance . . . they usually represent some, uh, some natural phenomenon such as palm trees swaying in the wind, or waves crashing on the beach, or birds flying across the sky.

Student B: Professor, what about the music for the hula? It's, uh, a lot of times you hear it played on the ukulele, right? Has that always been true? Is the ukulele a traditional instrument?

Professor: No, no, not at all. There was a group of Portuguese workers who came to Hawaii around 1870, and they brought with them these small guitars that were common in Portugal back then. These little guitars eventually evolved into ukuleles. By the way, in Hawaiian, the word *ukulele* means "jumping flea."

Student B: Jumping flea? Yeah? Why did they call it that?

Professor: Hmmmmm. Probably it was because . . . well, to tell you the truth, I don't have a clue. I'll try to find out for you, though.

Student A: So . . . how did the hula . . . how did it get to be a tourist attraction?

Professor: In the 1950's, tourism became a major industry in Hawaii, and tourists wanted to see . . . to see samples of "authentic" Hawaiian culture. Even though the modern hula is . . . well, it's not really an expression of Hawaiian culture, not the way the traditional hula was, but then, most tourists probably didn't know the difference.

Student B: Well, personally, I think it's too bad that you can't see what the hula was like back in the old days. I'll bet it was a lot more interesting than what you see now.

Professor: Yeah, I have to agree with you on that, but actually, you can. These days, there are several groups of Hawaiian dancers that have gotten together to perform the *hula kahiko* the way it was originally performed. In fact, I have a video of one of their performances, and we'll be taking a look at that next.

Narrator: Now get ready to answer the questions. You may use your notes to help you.

Narrator: Question 37: What does the word *hula* mean in the Hawaiian language?

Narrator: Question 38: What fact about the hula does the professor particularly emphasize?

Narrator: Question 39: What roles did the *h'oa-paa,* or "steady ones," play in the performance of the hula?

Narrator: Question 40: What did the New England missionaries do when they arrived in 1820?

Narrator: Question 41: Which of the following would be the most likely theme of a modern hula?

Narrator: Question 42: What will the members of the class do next?

[CD 3 Track 3]

Lesson 11: Purpose, Method, and Attitude Questions

Sample Item 1

Narrator: Listen to a part of a discussion from the Listening Preview Test.

Professor: Well, you see, Professor Longdell, he, he in fact taught in the law school at Harvard, not in the business school. So the case method first . . . it was first used to train law students. Then, a couple of years after that, they started using it at Columbia University, at the law school there. It wasn't until . . . when was it, probably about 1910, 1912, something like that, it was used, first used at Harvard Business School.

Student B: Then, it's used in other fields? Besides law and business?

Professor: Oh, sure, over the years, it's been used in all sorts of disciplines. For example, my wife, she teaches over at the School of Education, she uses cases to train teachers.

Narrator: Why does Professor Speed mention his wife?

[CD 3 Track 4]

Sample Item 2

Narrator: Listen to a part of a student presentation from an astronomy class.

Student Presenter: Well, uh, hi, everyone . . . Monday, we heard Don tell us about the Sun, and, uh, Lisa talk about Mercury, the planet closest to the Sun. My . . . my, uh, report, what I'm talking about is the next planet, the second planet, Venus. Okay, to start off, I'm going to tell you what people, well, what they used to think about Venus. First off, back in the really . . . in the really ancient days, people thought Venus was a star, not a planet, and . . . well, actually, you know how you can see Venus in the early morning and in the evening? Well, so they thought it was two stars, Phosphorus—that was the morning star . . . and, uh, let's see, Hesperus, the evening star. And then, once they figured out it was just one planet, they named it Venus after the goddess of love—I don't really know why, though.

Narrator: How does the speaker introduce the topic of Venus?

[CD 3 Track 5]

Sample Item 3

Narrator: Listen to part of a conversation from the Listening Preview Test.

Student: So that's . . . so you don't think that's a very good idea for a topic, then, I suppose . . .

Professor: I didn't say that . . . just because this theory hasn't been proven doesn't mean you couldn't write a perfectly good paper about this topic . . . on the notion that animals can predict earthquakes. Why not? It could be pretty interesting. But to do a good job, you . . . you'll need to look at some serious studies in the scientific journals, not just some pop-science articles in newspapers, or . . . and you can't get your information from television shows.

Narrator: What is the professor's attitude toward the topic that the student wants to write about?

[CD 3 Track 6]

Exercise 11.1

Narrator: Listen to a conversation between two students.

Student A: So, Joan, your roommate told me that you had a meeting with Dean Metzger this morning.

Student B: Well, actually, it's later this afternoon—I'm meeting her at four today.

Student A: How come?

Student B: Well, I'm sure you've been hearing and reading about the cuts in the university budget, right? Well, the budget for the university debate team was really slashed. In fact, it was cut more than in half. And it was already a bare-bones budget! To tell you the truth, I don't know if . . . well, I don't really think we'll be able to keep debating.

Student A: Really? So how do you . . . what does the debate team spend its money on? The coach's salary, or . . .

Student B: No, as a matter of fact, my friend Kurt Wyndham is our coach, and he volunteers his time. Kurt's a graduate student now, but when he was an undergrad, he was a debater himself.

Student A: So, then, how do you spend your money?

Student B: Well, mostly, we spend it on travel expenses. We take four or five trips a semester to other campuses, and we need money for bus fares or gas money, hotel rooms, meals, things like that.

Student A: Well, I—I kinda hate to say this, but . . . would it really be the end of the world if the debate team couldn't keep going? I mean, does anyone really care all that much about debate?

Student B: The people on the team do! Most of us have been debating since high school, and it's really important to us. And you know, it can be really good career preparation. You learn research skills, you learn . . . well, to communicate . . . to think on your feet—you learn teamwork. My father's a lawyer, you know, and when he was in college—he went to college over in England—he was involved in debate, and he says it was a wonderful way to train for the courtroom. He's the one who talked me into joining the team.

Student A: Well, I'm just saying . . . except for a few people on the team . . . how does having a debate team really benefit the university?

Student B: Oh, don't even get me started! For one thing, there's the whole matter of school tradition. I mean, did you know that this school has had a debating team for over a hundred years? And over the years, we've won a dozen or more regional tournaments and a couple of national tournaments. Then there's the prestige. We haven't had a good football or basketball team for . . . for years, but our debate team is always one of the best in the region. A good debate team attracts people who debated in high school, and they're always some of the top students. And you know, a lot of famous people were on college debate teams . . . President John F. Kennedy, for one, and . . .

Student A: Okay, okay, you've sold me!

Student B: And we're not even asking for that much. It's like a, like a millionth of what the school spends on football and basketball! I mean, I don't have anything against sports teams, but . . .

Student A: Still, I can't see why you're going to talk to Dean Metzger. She's . . . she's Dean of the School of Arts and Sciences. She's not in charge of the university budget.

Student B: No, I know, you're right. And we tried to get an appointment with President Fisher, but his assistant kept saying he was too busy right now and wasn't able to meet with us. So Kurt came up with the idea of our talking to Dean Metzger. He said Dean Metzger is fair—she has that reputation, anyway—and she's, you know, willing to listen. So, I don't know, maybe if we can convince her, then she can persuade President Fisher and the Board of Chancellors not to cut our budget so much.

Student A: Well, if anyone can convince her, you can! I'll tell you, though . . . if I were you, I'd keep trying to get a meeting with President Fisher. Talking to Dean Metzger won't hurt, but really, President Fisher is the person whose mind you have to change.

Narrator: Now get ready to answer the questions. You may use your notes to help you.

Narrator: Question 1: Why does the woman mention her father?

Narrator: Question 2: How does the man feel about the woman's appointment with Dean Metzger?

Narrator: Listen to a conversation between two students.

Student A: Hey, Julie, want to go see a movie tonight?

Student B: Oh, wish I could, but I'm on my way home to study. I have a mid-term in my math class tomorrow.

Student A: How are your mid-terms going?

Student B: So far, so good . . . the only one I'm at all worried about is the math exam tomorrow. How about you? Don't you have any mid-term exams?

Student A: As a matter of fact, I do have one in geology class tomorrow, but there's nothing I can do tonight to get ready for it.

Student B: What sort of test is it? Multiple-choice or essay?

Student A: Neither, actually. Doctor Fowles gives us a mineral sample and we have an hour to figure out what it is—we work in teams of two.

Student B: How on earth do you do that? I mean, a rock's a rock, isn't it?

Student A: Actually, there are a number of tests you can perform on minerals to, ah, figure out what they are. First off, you just look carefully at the sample.

Student B: Okay . . . what do you look for?

Student A: Well, you check the mineral's color . . . although that's one of the most unreliable tests.

Student B: Why? Why would that be unreliable?

Student A: Because a lot of minerals have impurities that change their color. For example, pure quartz is clear, but then you also have white quartz, rose quartz, smoky quartz—it's all the same, the same mineral, but different colors. Another thing to look for is luster . . .

Student B: You mean, how shiny it is?

Student A: That's right. The way light reflects off the mineral. Most minerals that contain metals tend to have a shiny, metallic luster. Non-metallic rocks often look dull. Then, you can do a taste test . . .

Student B: Ewww, yuck! I wouldn't taste a mineral sample! Who knows where that mineral sample has been!

Student A: Well, it can help you identify certain minerals—for example, halite has a salty taste. Probably the most useful test of all is the hardness test. Have you ever heard of the Mohs scale?

Student B: Huh? The what scale?

Student A: It's a scale that indicates how hard a mineral is. We have a kit that we use that contains samples of minerals, of known minerals that, ah, have a certain hardness. It goes from talc at number 1—talc is so soft you can scratch it with your fingernail—to diamonds at number 10. Diamonds are the hardest . . .

Student B: I know, I know, they're the hardest substance in the world. Do you actually have a diamond in your kit?

Student A: Yeah, sure, a tiny little industrial diamond. So, let's say you can scratch your sample with fluorite, which is number 4 on the scale, but not with, umm, gypsum, that's number 2, then on the Mohs scale, you, ah . . .

Student B: Then the sample must be about 3 on that scale, right?

Student A: Right! So you look on the list that comes with the kit and you know it's one of those minerals that is about 3 on the scale. Another good test is the streak test, which tells you the true color of a mineral . . .

Student B: I thought you said color is unreliable . . .

Student A: Uh, right, I did, but, ah, see, the streak test shows you the true color of the mineral. You take your sample and rub it against a piece of unglazed porcelain, okay, and look at the color of the streak on the porcelain. Remember all those different colors of quartz I mentioned? Well, if you do a streak test on those, the streak on the porcelain looks the same, no matter what color the mineral appears to be. Oh, and my favorite is the acid test. You pour a little bit of acid, of vinegar, say, on the sample, and, sometimes, with a certain kind of mineral, one that contains calcium, it fizzes and foams. It's really cool. And then there's the specific

gravity test, the ultraviolet test—that one's kinda fun too—oh, and the blowpipe test, and then . . . .

Student B: Wait, stop, I get the picture! And after . . . after you've done all these tests, you can identify any mineral?

Student A: Well, usually . . . not always, but usually. My partner and I have done a couple of practice runs, and we didn't have any trouble figuring out what mineral we were looking at. So, I'm pretty sure we can do the same tomorrow.

Narrator: Now get ready to answer the questions. You may use your notes to help you.

Narrator: Question 3: How does the man explain his geology mid-term exam to the woman?

Narrator: Question 4: What is the woman's attitude towards the taste test?

Narrator: Question 5: Why does the man mention quartz?

Narrator: Question 6: What is the man's attitude toward his geology mid-term?

[CD 4 Track 2]

Exercise 11.2

Narrator: Listen to a discussion in a U.S. history class.

Professor: Morning, everyone. We've been discussing the Civil War for the last coupla weeks . . . talking about some of the major battles of the war. So today, I've, uh, invited a guest to come to our class. I'd like all of you to meet Ms. Frances Adams. She's the state coordinator of the Civil War Heritage Society, which is involved in preserving battlefields all over the eastern part of the country. Ms. Adams . . . .

Guest Speaker: Thank you, Professor Nugent, thanks for inviting me. I always appreciate the chance to talk to students . . . to anyone who'll listen, for that matter . . . about our disappearing battlefields. The organization I work with is trying to save battlefields from development. It's an uphill struggle. By one estimate, twenty-five acres of Civil War battlefield are being lost every day. That's like an acre an hour. In fact, we're trying to save one battlefield right here in our state . . . you may have read about it in the newspapers. There's a site, oh, only about 100 miles from here called Ivy Station where a small battle was fought in the closing days of the war, in 1864. A development company wants to build a 300-unit apartment complex where that battle was fought and we—the Society, that is—we're trying to stop them.

Student A: Ms. Adams, I understood . . . I mean, I always assumed, I guess, that battlefields are protected by the government. A few years ago, I went with my family to the battlefield at Gettysburg, and it seemed pretty well protected to me.

Guest Speaker: You're right, the Gettysburg battlefield is well protected. After all, Gettysburg was the largest battle of the whole war, and so . . . well, the sites of most important battles—Gettysburg, Antietam, Shiloh, Vicksburg—they're all national historical sites, and they're under the protection of the National Park Service. But, have you ever heard of, oh, say the Battle of Salt Run in Virginia?

Student A: Ummm, no.

Guest Speaker: Well, that's not too surprising, as it wasn't a turning-point battle, but . . . it involved several thousand Union and Confederate troops . . . Okay, now when I came in I put one of our society's brochures on each of your desks. I want to show you . . . just take a look at the cover of the brochure. What do you see?

Student B: Ummm, a shopping mall?

Guest Speaker: Right. It's called the Salt Run Mall. And it's located right . . . right smack in the middle of what was the Salt Run battlefield. Now, take a look inside the brochure. There's a list of almost 400 Civil War battlefields. As you see, these are classified in, uh, one of three ways. Do you see what I mean? They're classified as "Adequately Protected," "At Risk," or "Lost to Development." Only about 70 are Adequately Protected. About 180 are endangered. You'll find the Ivy Station battlefield on this list. Then there are 150 that have already been developed, that are completely gone. The Salt Run battlefield is on this list, you'll notice.

Professor: David, I see you have a question for Ms. Adams.

Student B: Thanks, Professor. Yeah, Ms. Adams, I'm just wondering—is your organization—is it made up of re-enactors?

Guest Speaker: Of re-enactors? No, not at all. I mean, a few members of the Society may be involved in re-enactment, but not many . . .

Student B: I read somewhere that most of the, ah, pressure to save Civil War battlefields, that it comes from re-enactors.

Student A: Hold on! What are . . . who are . . . re-enactors?

Student B: They're people who pretend the Civil War is still going on . . .

Guest Speaker: Well . . . I don't know if I'd go so far as to say *that,* but . . . they're people who enjoy . . . re-enacting, re-living the Civil War experience. They wear the uniforms of the northern and the southern soldiers—some of them have equipment and wear uniforms that are amazingly authentic—and they . . . well, they fight Civil War battles all over again. Without real bullets, of course. And naturally, they prefer to stage these, umm, re-enactments on authentic—on the actual battlefields where the original battle took place.

Student A: So they're interested in the same thing you are, right?

Guest Speaker: Well, yes, their goals and ours certainly overlap. Now, personally, I have no interest in spending my weekends dressed up as a Civil War nurse and sleeping in a tent on a battlefield. My interest, the Society's interest, is to preserve these battlefields as places of historical . . . of cultural significance. But . . . several of the re-enactment organizations are . . . well, I guess you'd call them our allies . . . yeah, our allies in the fight to save these sites.

Student B: I'm just wondering why it's necessary to save all these sites. The big battlefields, sure, but . . . some of these sites are . . . . well, they weren't all that important to the way the war turned out, and, well—they may have been in the middle of nowhere during the Civil War, but now they're on some pretty valuable suburban real estate, and hey, they're privately owned. Can't we just read about these little battles in history books?

Professor: I'm going to jump in here, Frances, and comment on what David just said. Geography and . . . topography shape a battle. The patterns of uh, hills, valleys, rocks, rivers, streams . . . these are all important. And if future historians, military historians, if they don't have access to these battlefields, they won't be able to understand what really happened back in the 1860's.

Guest Speaker: And I'd just like to add . . . for those of us who are non-historians, who are not professional historians, well, I think it is important for us, too, that these sites be preserved. If you walk around on a Civil War battlefield, and you imagine what happened there, well, you have an emotional, um, connection, an emotional empathy with those who fought there. You can't get that walking around a parking lot! And also, well, I think we owe those soldiers,

the ones who fought and died in these places, I think we owe them a measure of respect for their courage. For their sacrifices. No matter how unimportant the battle was to the outcome of the war.

Student A: So, what does your society do, Ms. Adams, to save battlefields?

Guest Speaker: Well, one of the things we do is what I'm doing today—making people like you aware, educating people about the, uh, the problem of disappearing battlefields. And then, as I said, we work with other groups—re-enactment groups and historical societies and so forth—to coordinate our efforts. We meet with government officials—state, local, federal—and try to persuade them to buy battlefield land in order to preserve it. And, when we can afford it, we buy up land ourselves and keep it free of commercial or industrial development. The Society owns and maintains about 3,000 acres of battlefield land in seven states.

Student B: Well, I'm still of the opinion that . . . that you can't really stop progress. Sometimes you shouldn't even try.

Professor: Well, David, you're certainly entitled to your opinion. But I . . . I can't imagine giving up our own heritage, our own history without a fight. Anyway, if any of you are interested in joining the Society and helping preserve these sites, personally, I think it's a wonderful idea. I've been a member myself for about five years.

Guest Speaker: Inside the brochure I gave you, there's a form you can fill out, if you're interested in joining. There's a special membership for students that's not as expensive as a regular membership.

Narrator: Now get ready to answer the questions. You may use your notes to help you.

Narrator: Question 1: Why does Ms. Adams mention the battle of Ivy Station?

Narrator: Question 2: How does Ms. Adams make the class aware of the current condition of the Salt Run battlefield?

Narrator: Question 3: What is Ms. Adams' attitude toward re-enactors?

Narrator: Question 4: What is David's attitude toward the preservation of Civil War battlefields?

Narrator: Listen to a lecture in an American Literature class.

Professor: Okay, for the last few minutes of class, I'd like to introduce you to the poet Emily Dickinson. A couple of days ago, we were talking about the poet Walt Whitman, and if you recall, I said that he was one of the two great voices in American poetry in the nineteenth century. Today, I'm going to drop the other shoe and talk about the other great poet, Emily Dickinson.

The poetry of Emily Dickinson and the poetry of Walt Whitman couldn't have been more different, as we'll see. Dickinson claimed that she never . . . never even read Whitman's poems. And their lifestyles . . . again, couldn't have been more different. But they were both innovators, important innovators, and they both had a major role in shaping American poetry.

I said Monday that Whitman became famous all over the country and in Europe as well. He was really the first American poet who was read much outside the United States. Dickinson was well known only in her own small town—in those days, it was just a village—Amherst, Massachusetts. But she wasn't known there for her poetry. Oh, no! She was known for her . . . her odd, her mysterious ways. You see, after she finished high school she went to the Mount Holyoke Female Seminary—today, it, uh, it's called Mount Holyoke College—but she only went there for one year. She didn't get along with the headmistress, apparently. After that, she returned to her father's house in Amherst—and she hardly ever left. In fact, she hardly left her own bedroom. And when she did leave the house, she always wore white dresses like a bride. Outside of her family, her only person-to-person contact with others was with the children who lived in her neighborhood. This, uh, may not seem all that odd to us today, but . . . in Amherst, Massachusetts, in the 1800's, this was considered . . . well, pretty strange behavior.

For a woman who lived such an uneventful life—at least, her life was uneventful on the surface—she wrote amazingly perceptive poems about nature, love, and death. Her poems are all quite short and are all untitled. What I like about them the most is their economy. She was able to say so much, to express so much in so few words. She was an extremely prolific poet. Just in one year alone, 1874—that was the year her father died—she wrote, like, 200 poems. But she never wanted her poems to be published. Well, she did engage in a kind of self-publishing. She assembled collections of her poems in packets that were called "fascicles," which she bound herself with needle and thread. There were some forty of these booklets. But she never tried to have these . . . these fascicles published, seldom even showed them to anyone else. She did send a few of her poems to friends and relatives, and somehow, six or seven of these found their way into print in magazines or newspapers during her lifetime. You can imagine, though, how she felt when she heard that her poems had been published.

After Emily Dickinson died in 1886, her family discovered that she had written over 1,700 poems. Her sister Lavinia edited three volumes of Emily's poetry. They were popular as soon as they were published, but it was not until the twentieth century that critics recognized her as one of the top American poets. Martha Dickinson Bianchi, the poet's niece, brought out several more books of poems in the early 1900's. Eventually all of them appeared in print. In 1950, Harvard University bought all of her manuscripts and acquired the publishing rights to all of her poems. Harvard published a complete three-volume collection of her poems and letters five years later.

Okay, for Friday, I'd like you to read all of Dickinson's poems that are in our textbook. There are about twenty, maybe twenty-five of her poems in there. Don't worry, though. That may sound like a lot of reading, but it shouldn't take you long! Friday, we'll take a closer look at her poems.

Before we move on to another topic, I'd just like to say this: These days, a lot of scholars downplay Dickinson's, um, eccentric lifestyle. They point out that she was not as intellectually cut off as people used to think, that she had a lively relationship with others through her letters—and that she was quite learned about other writers, such as John Keats and John Ruskin. But, there's no doubt that she lived in relative isolation and that she did not want to be in the public eye. I'm going to leave you with the first verse of one of her most famous poems:

    I'm nobody! Who are you?
    Are you nobody, too?
    Then there's a pair of us—don't tell!
    They'd banish us, you know.

Narrator: Now get ready to answer the questions. You may use your notes to help you.

Narrator: Question 5: Why does the professor mention the poet Walt Whitman?

Narrator: Question 6: Why does the professor mention Harvard University?

Narrator: Question 7: Which of the following best summarizes the professor's attitude toward Emily Dickinson?

Narrator: Question 8: How does the professor conclude her discussion of Emily Dickinson?

Narrator: Listen to a lecture in an art history class.

Professor: Morning. Today I'm going to take a few minutes to talk about folk art. I, uh, know this isn't on your syllabus, but I saw a wonderful exhibit of folk art from the eighteenth and nineteenth century at the Hotchkiss Museum over the weekend, and I'd like to share my impressions of this exhibit with you.

First off, I should tell you that there's, umm, some disagreement in the art world about what is meant by the term *folk art*. European folklorists, in particular, take the position that folk art must be part of a . . . of some long-standing artistic tradition. They say it must have been created by artists from a distinct group, say, oh, American Indians, Australian aborigines—or that it must have been made by people from some particular occupation—say, uh, sailors on whaling ships. These European folklorists would generally not say . . . . they wouldn't categorize pieces made for commercial reasons as folk art. They would also, um, disqualify pieces made by groups, not by individuals.

Folklorists in the United States, though—not just folklorists, also museums and galleries—don't take such a narrow view—and I must say, I think the European way of looking at folk art is way too restrictive. Among most American folklorists . . . well, they define a folk artist as simply someone who . . . someone who creates art without any formal artistic training. And, uh, in the catalogue for this exhibit, there's a little essay written by the curator of the Hotchkiss, and he says, "A folk artist is someone who would be surprised to find his or her pieces on display in a museum." That's a definition I like! Anyway, lots of pieces on display at the museum would probably be considered crafts by European folklorists. Some pieces were made by groups, some were even made in factories—for example, the wooden animals for carousels.

The exhibit features lots of different kinds of folk art. There are paintings—portraits and landscapes—that were created to be works of art. But most of the pieces have some utilitarian, some commercial purpose. There's furniture, plates and pots, clothing, clocks. There are ships' figureheads, circus carvings, duck decoys, fish lures . . . lots of weathervanes. Then there's a *wonderful* collection of trade signs. You know what I mean, doncha? Signs advertising shops, taverns, hotels, restaurants . . . As a matter of fact, I spent most of my time at the exhibit looking at trade signs. I found them just fascinating . . . charming.

Now, here's something to keep in mind. It wasn't until 1870 that most people in America could read. Signs had to appeal to both readers and non-readers. Sometimes the shape of the sign told you what kind of business was inside. There's a sign in the shape of a tea kettle that was once in front of a tea shop in Boston . . . a sign in the shape of a pocket watch that was in front of a jeweler's shop . . . a boot-shaped sign from a shoe store—you didn't have to be literate to understand these. More often, there were painted images . . . a sign for a blacksmith shop featured a picture of a horseshoe . . . a bookshop sign showed a picture of a man reading a book . . . well, you get the idea.

Sometimes the images weren't so . . . so obvious. For example, there were signs that pictured an American Indian, a Turkish sultan, a, let's see, an exotic Cuban lady, and a race-track gambler. All of these images symbolized the same kind of shop . . . tobacco shops. At the time, people instantly recognized these symbols. Maybe they couldn't read, but they had what's called *visual literacy.* Visual literacy. These symbols were as meaningful to them . . . well, just like today, we know we can get hamburgers and French fries when we see golden arches . . . it was the same sort of thing.

Sometimes signs contained political messages. There was an inn in Philadelphia called King's Inn, and its sign showed a picture of King George III on a horse. Well, this was just before the Revolutionary War and George III wasn't too popular with the colonists . . . they weren't real fond of him. So, the king is pictured on this sign as a clumsy fool practically falling off his horse.

Oh, another thing to keep in mind: back in Colonial times, many streets didn't have names, and most buildings didn't have numbers . . . street addresses. Trade signs served as landmarks. People would say, "Meet me by the sign of the Lion and the Eagle," or "by the sign of the Dancing Bear" . . .

If you go to the exhibit and you look at the trade signs, you'll notice that there are almost no plaques that tell you who painted the signs. There are maybe three, four signed pieces in the show—the sign-painter William Rice of Hartford, Connecticut was one of the few who signed his work. A few of the signs in the exhibit were done by fairly well-known portrait artists . . . Horace Bundy, Rufus Hathaway, who made signs for extra money. Their styles are distinctive, and the signs they made can be easily identified. But most of the sign painters . . . they were mostly itinerant artists, traveling from town to town on horseback, painting a few signs in each town . . . anyway, their names have been long forgotten.

Well, I want to get back to our discussion of Renaissance art, but I do hope all of you get a chance to see the exhibit at the Hotchkiss . . . it will be there another six weeks.

Narrator: Now get ready to answer the questions. You may use your notes to help you.

Narrator: Question 9: How does the professor introduce his discussion of folk art?

Narrator: Question 10: Why does the professor mention wooden carousel horses?

Narrator: Question 11: How does the professor explain the concept of "visual literacy"?

Narrator: Question 12: Why does the professor mention the sign for the King's Inn?

Narrator: Question 13: Why does the professor mention the sign painter William Rice?

[CD 4 Track 3]

Lesson 12: Replay Questions

Narrator: Listen to the following short conversations. Pay special attention to the way the phrase "I'm sorry" is used.

Conversation Number 1

Professor: You know, Donald, that's the, uh, the second or third time you've turned in an assignment after the due date.

Student: I know, Professor Dorn, and I'm sorry, I really am. I won't . . . I'll try not to let it happen again.

Conversation Number 2

Professor: Next, I want to talk about a process that's important, that's of central importance to all living things . . . to all living things that breathe oxygen, anyway. That's the Krebs cycle.

Student: I'm sorry, Professor, the *what* cycle?

Conversation Number 3

Student A: Hey, Laura, you wanna go skiing up at Snowbury this weekend with my roommate and me?

Student B: I'm sorry, I wish I could, but I've gotta hit the books this weekend. I have a big test in my calculus class on Monday.

Conversation Number 4

Employee: University Recreation Center, Jill speaking.

Student: Yeah, hi, I'm calling to reserve a tennis court on Friday morning at 6:30 A.M.

Employee: At 6:30 in the morning? I'm sorry, but we don't even open until 7:30.

[CD 4 Track 4]

Sample Item

Narrator: Why does the speaker say this:

Professor: This sub-zone—well, if you like variety, you're not going to feel happy here. You can travel for miles and see only half a dozen species of trees. In a few days, we'll be talking about the tropical rain forest; now *that's* where you'll see variety.

[CD 4 Track 5]

Exercise 12.1

Narrator: Number 1

Student A: Oh, that statistics course I'm taking is just *loads* of fun!

Student B: Didn't I tell you it would be?

Narrator: Number 2

Student A: So did you and your lab partner get together and write up your experiment?

Student B: No, and wait till you hear his latest excuse. You're going to *love* it!

Narrator: Number 3

Student A: Does Professor White ever change his grades?

Student B: Oh, sure, about once a century!

Narrator: Number 4

Student A: Did you know Greg has changed his major?

Student B: Oh, no, not again.

Narrator: Number 5

Student A: So, you're moving out of your apartment?

Student B: Yeah, I got a place closer to campus. I just hope the landlady here gives me all of my security deposit back.

Student A: Well, you'd better leave the place spic-and-span.

Narrator: Number 6

Student A: Doctor Stansfield, I've decided to drop my physiology class. It just meets too early in the morning for me.

Professor: Do you *really* think that's a good reason, Mark?

Narrator: Number 7
Student: Professor McKee, I know you speak Spanish. I wonder if you could translate this poem for me?
Professor: Let me have a look. Hmmm. Well, I'm afraid this is written in Catalan, not Spanish.

Narrator: Number 8
Professor: Next, next we'll be taking a look at Japanese theater. Kabuki Theater and, uh, Noh Theater . . .
Student: Professor, could you, uh, put those terms on the board?

Narrator: Number 9
Professor: Today we were going to uh, continue to . . . continue our discussion of complex numbers. In our last class, we spent quite a bit of time talking about imaginary numbers, but, uh, I must say, I noticed a few . . . a few puzzled expressions as you filed out. Part of the problem, I think, is the name *imaginary numbers*. They are *not* imaginary, they are as real as any other kind of number. So, here's the thing, we really can't go on to complex numbers until we get this right . . .

Narrator: Number 10
Professor: So, who can tell me who wrote the Brandenburg Concertos?
Student: I *think* . . . umm, was it Bach?

Narrator: Number 11
Professor: Okay, well, uh, I've been digressing . . . no more about my childhood experiments with rockets!

Narrator: Number 12
Professor: Now, I *know* I didn't give you a set number . . . a *maximum* number of words or pages for your term paper . . . I only said it had to be more than ten pages. I didn't really want to discourage anyone from fully exploring the topic you chose. But, uh, I must say, some of these were well, almost ridiculous!

[CD 4 Track 6]

Exercise 12.2
Narrator: Listen again to part of the conversation. Then answer the question.
Student: Oh, well, then, . . . maybe I should, uh, maybe I should go back to my dorm and get some dinner . . . before I sit down and read this.
Librarian: That's fine, but . . . I can't guarantee the article will be available right away when you come back . . . some other student from your class might be using it.
Student: Well, I dunno, I, I guess I'll just have to take my chances . . .
Narrator: Question 1: What does the woman mean when she says this:
Student: I guess I'll just have to take my chances . . .

Narrator: Listen again to part of the conversation. Then answer the question.
Student A: So, uh, how was it . . . I mean, was it a good dig?
Student B: Do you mean, did we find any artifacts? No, it . . . it was supposed to be a very . . . promising site. But it turned out to be a complete bust! We didn't find anything . . . not even one single piece of broken pottery. Nothing! Just sand!
Narrator: Question 2: What does the woman mean when she says this:

Student B: But it turned out to be a complete bust!

Narrator: Listen again to part of the conversation. Then answer the question.
Student B: You just walk a little bit farther, and you'll see the art building . . . the Reynolds Building. You can't miss it because there's a big metal . . . *thing* on a platform right in front of it.
Student A: A thing?
Student B: Yeah, there's this . . . this big rusty piece of abstract "art." I *guess* you'd call it art. Anyway, it's right in front of the doorway.
Narrator: Question 3: What does the woman imply when she says this:
Student B: Yeah, there's this . . . this big rusty piece of abstract "art." I *guess* you'd call it art. Anyway, it's right in front of the doorway.

Narrator: Listen again to part of the conversation. Then answer the question.
Student B: Your sister's an artist?
Student A: Yeah, she's a painter. She also, well she just started volunteering to teach art to kids and . . . I think the way her students paint has sort of rubbed off on her. I think her kids have influenced her more than she's influenced them, as a matter of fact. She's using these bright colors, and . . .
Narrator: Question 4: What does the man mean when he says this:
Student A: I think the way her students paint has sort of rubbed off on her.

Narrator: Listen again to part of the conversation. Then answer the question.
Student B: Hmmm, so, what . . . what other kinds of courses do they offer?
Student A: Well, I don't know all the courses they offer, but I know they have a class on test-taking skills.
Student B: Wow, that's right up my alley.
Narrator: Question 5: What does the man mean when he says this:
Student B: . . . that's right up my alley.

Narrator: Listen again to part of the conversation. Then answer the question.
Student: So, suppose I decide I want to . . . to apply for an R.A. position, what, uh, what would I need to do?
Administrator: I can give you a form to fill out. You'd also need to get two letters of recommendation . . .
Narrator: Question 6: What does the man imply when he says this:
Student: So, suppose I decide I want to . . . to apply for an R.A. position?

Narrator: Listen again to part of the conversation. Then answer the question.
Student A: So then, how do you spend your money?
Student B: Well, mostly, we spend it on travel expenses. We take four or five trips a semester to other campuses and we need money for bus fares or gas money, hotel rooms, meals, things like that.
Student A: Well I—I kinda hate to say this, but . . . would it really be the end of the world if the debate team couldn't keep going?
Narrator: Question 7: What does the man mean when he says this:
Student A: Well, I—I kinda hate to say this . . .

Narrator: Listen again to part of the conversation. Then answer the question.
Student A: Well, I'm just saying . . . except for a few people on the team . . . how does having a debate team really benefit the university?
Student B: Oh, don't even get me started! For one thing, there's the whole matter of school tradition. I mean, did you know that this school has had a debating team for over a hundred years? And over the years, we've won a dozen or more regional tournaments and a couple of national tournaments. Then there's the prestige. We haven't had a good football or basketball team for . . . for *years,* but our debate team is always one of the best in the region. A good debate team attracts people who debated in high school, and they're always some of the top students. And you know, a lot of famous people were on college debate teams . . . President John F. Kennedy, for one, and . . .
Narrator: Question 8: What does the woman mean when she says this:
Student B: Oh, don't even get me started!

Narrator: Listen again to part of the conversation. Then answer the question.
Student A: Well, I'm just saying . . . except for a few people on the team . . . how does having a debate team really benefit the university?
Student B: Oh, don't even get me started! For one thing, there's the whole matter of school tradition. I mean, did you know that this school has had a debating team for over a hundred years? And over the years, we've won a dozen or more regional tournaments and a couple of national tournaments. Then there's the prestige. We haven't had a good football or basketball team for . . . for *years,* but our debate team is always one of the best in the region. A good debate team attracts people who debated in high school, and they're always some of the top students. And you know, a lot of famous people were on college debate teams . . . President John F. Kennedy, for one, and . . .
Student A: Okay, okay, you've sold me!
Narrator: Question 9: What does the man mean when he says this:
Student A: Okay, okay, you've sold me!

Narrator: Listen again to part of the conversation. Then answer the question.
Student B: What sort of test is it? Multiple-choice or essay?
Student A: Neither, actually. Doctor Fowles gives us a mineral sample and we have an hour to figure out what it is—we work in teams of two.
Student B: How on earth do you do that? I mean, a rock's a rock, isn't it?
Narrator: Question 10: Why does the woman say this:
Student B: How on earth do you do that? I mean, a rock's a rock, isn't it?

Narrator: Listen again to part of the conversation. Then answer the question.
Student A: Probably the most useful test of all is the hardness test. Have you ever heard of the Mohs scale?
Student B: Huh? The what scale?
Narrator: Question 11: What does the woman mean when she says this:
Student B: Huh? The what scale?

Narrator: Listen again to part of the conversation. Then answer the question.

Student A: Another good test is the streak test, which tells you the true color of a mineral . . .
Student B: I thought you said color is unreliable . . .
Student A: Uh, right, I did, but, ah, see, the streak test shows you the true color of the mineral.
Narrator: Question 12: What does the man mean when he says this:
Student A: Uh, right, I did, but, ah, see, the streak test shows you the true color of the mineral.

Narrator: Listen again to part of the conversation. Then answer the question.
Student A: And then there's the specific gravity test, the ultraviolet test, that one's kinda fun too . . . oh, and the blowpipe test, and then . . . .
Student B: Wait, stop, I get the picture! And after . . . after you've done all these tests, you can identify any mineral?
Narrator: Question 13: Why does the woman say this:
Student B: Wait, stop, I get the picture!

[CD 4 Track 7]

Exercise 12.3
Narrator: Listen again to the professor's comment. Then answer the question.
Professor: First, I just want to say . . . good job on your presentation, Charlie, it was very interesting, and then . . . well, I just want to add this. You said you weren't sure why the planet Venus was named after the goddess of love. It's true Venus was the goddess of love, but she was also the goddess of beauty and, well, anyone who's ever seen Venus early in the morning or in the evening knows it's a beautiful sight.
Narrator: Question 1: Why does the professor say this:
Professor: . . . well, I just want to add this.

Narrator: Listen again to part of the lecture. Then answer the question.
Professor: Computers have been used since the sixties to record choreography. The first one—well, the first one I know about, anyway, was a program written by Michael Noll . . . and it was . . . Oh, I guess by today's standards you'd say it was pretty primitive. The dancers looked like stick figures in a child's drawing.
Narrator: Question 2: What does the woman mean when she says this:
Professor: The dancers looked like stick figures in a child's drawing.

Narrator: Listen again to part of the discussion. Then answer the question.
Professor: Well, after Rhine did his experiments at Duke, a lot of similar experiments have been done—at Stanford University, in Scotland, and elsewhere, and the conclusion . . . most researchers have decided that Rhine's results were, I guess the kindest word I could use is *questionable.*
Narrator: Question 3: What does the professor mean when he says this:
Professor: . . . most researchers have decided that Rhine's results were, I guess the kindest word I could use is *questionable.*

Narrator: Listen again to part of the discussion. Then answer the question.
Student A: So that's why you don't believe in ESP?

Professor: To put it in a nutshell—I've just never seen any experimental proof for ESP that stood up to careful examination.

Narrator: Question 4: Why does the professor say this:

Professor: To put it in a nutshell . . .

Narrator: Listen again to part of the discussion. Then answer the question.

Student A: Yeah, I've seen that painting before . . . I don't remember the name of the artist, but I think the painting is called *Nighthawks at the Diner.*

Professor: Yeah, that's . . . well, a lot of people call it that, but the real name of the painting is just *Nighthawks.*

Narrator: Question 5: What does the professor mean when she says this:

Professor: . . . a lot of people call it that, but the real name of the painting is just *Nighthawks.*

Narrator: Listen again to part of the lecture. Then answer the question.

Professor: Now, if you happen to have a copy of the syllabus that I gave you last week you'll notice that we're not gonna be able to . . . we just don't have time to read all of these two poems and talk about them. An epic poem—I probably don't have to tell you this—is a narrative poem, a really long narrative poem.

Narrator: Question 6: What does the professor mean when she says this:

Professor: . . . I probably don't have to tell you this . . .

Narrator: Listen again to part of the lecture. Then answer the question.

Professor: Anyway, the main characters in the *Iliad,* they're strong, they're great warriors, but you know . . . they're not as clever, not as smart as Odysseus. He's the one who thinks up the plan to end the war—after ten long years—and defeat the Trojans. He's the . . . the mastermind behind the scheme to build the Trojan Horse.

Narrator: Question 7: What does the professor mean when she says this:

Professor: He's the . . . the mastermind behind the scheme to build the Trojan Horse.

Narrator: Listen again to part of the lecture. Then answer the question.

Professor: How does HDR energy work? Well, in theory, anyway . . . and let me stress, I say in theory . . . it's pretty simple. You use oil-well drilling equipment, big drills, and you punch two holes down into the earth about, oh, maybe two miles—five kilometers, maybe—that's about as far as you can drill into the earth, for now, at least. Down there, deep in the earth, there is this extremely hot cauldron of rock, of granite. So then, you pump water from the surface into the first tube. The water goes down to the hot rock and becomes superheated. Then, the superheated water rises up the second tube—oh, I forgot to mention that these two tubes are interconnected—this hot water rises up the other tube and you use that to heat up a volatile liquid—do I need to go into what I mean by that? No? Okay. So then, this volatile liquid turns into a vapor, a gas, and you use it to turn an electrical turbine, and . . . bingo, you have electricity!

Narrator: Question 8: Why does the professor say this:

Professor: How does HDR energy work? Well, in theory, anyway . . . and let me stress, I say in theory . . . it's pretty simple.

Narrator: Listen again to part of the discussion. Then answer the question.

Student B: So, what else happened at a potlatch?

Professor: Well, then, the host would usually destroy some of his most valuable possessions, such as fishing canoes, and he'd throw coins and . . . and almost anything valuable into the sea . . .

Student B: What?! Excuse me, Professor . . . I just don't get it. It just seems kinda crazy to me. Why would anyone want to host a party like that?

Narrator: Question 9: What does the student mean when he says this:

Student A: Excuse me, Professor . . . I just don't get it.

Narrator: Listen again to part of the discussion. Then answer the question.

Professor: Okay, everyone. We've been talking about traditional forms of dance. Today, umm, we're going to shift our attention to the islands of Hawaii, and the most famous form of dance that's associated with those beautiful islands. Anyone know what that is? Laura?

Student A: Oh, that's an easy one—it's the hula dance.

Narrator: Question 10: What does the student mean when she says this:

Student A: Oh, that's an easy one . . .

Narrator: Listen again to part of the discussion. Then answer the question.

Professor: By the way, in Hawaiian, the word *ukulele* means "jumping flea."

Student B: Jumping flea! Yeah? Why did they call it that?

Professor: Hmmmmm. Probably it was because . . . well, to tell you the truth, I don't have a clue. I'll try to find out for you, though.

Narrator: Question 11: What does the professor mean when she says this:

Professor: . . . to tell you the truth, I don't have a clue.

Narrator: Listen again to part of the discussion. Then answer the question.

Guest Speaker: Thank you, Professor Nugent, thanks for inviting me. I always appreciate the chance to talk to students . . . to anyone who'll listen, for that matter, about our disappearing battlefields. The organization I work with is trying to save battlefields from development. It's an uphill struggle. By one estimate, twenty-five acres of Civil War battlefield are being lost every day. That's like an acre an hour.

Narrator: Question 12: What does the speaker mean when she says this:

Guest Speaker: It's an uphill struggle.

Narrator: Listen again to part of the discussion. Then answer the question.

Student A: Can't we just read about these little battles in history books?

Professor: I'm going to jump in here, Frances, and comment on what David just said.

Narrator: Question 13: What does Professor Nugent mean when he says this:

Professor: I'm going to jump in here, Frances, and comment on what David just said.

Narrator: Listen again to part of the lecture. Then answer the question.

Professor: A couple of days ago, we were talking about the poet Walt Whitman, and if you recall, I said that he was one of the two great voices in American poetry in the nineteenth century. Today, I'm going to drop the other shoe and talk about the other great poet, Emily Dickinson.

Narrator: Question 14: What does the professor mean when she says this:

Professor: Today, I'm going to drop the other shoe . . .

Narrator: Listen again to part of the lecture. Then answer the question.

Professor: Okay, for Friday, I'd like you to read all of Dickinson's poems that are in our textbook. There are about twenty, maybe twenty-five of her poems in there. Don't worry, though. That may sound like a lot of reading, but it shouldn't take you long! Friday, we'll take a closer look at her poems.

Narrator: Question 15: What does the professor mean when she says this:

Professor: Don't worry though, that may sound like a lot of reading, but it shouldn't take you long!

[CD 4 Track 8]

Lesson 13: Ordering and Matching Questions

Sample Item 1

Narrator: Listen to part of a presentation in an astronomy class.

Presenter: Now there have been quite a few space probes that have gone to Venus, so I'm only going to mention a few of them, the most important ones. I guess, umm, one of the most important was called Magellan. Magellan was launched in 1990 and spent four years in orbit around Venus. It used, uh, radar, I guess, to map the planet, and it found out that there are all these volcanoes on Venus, just like there are on Earth. The first probe to go there, the first probe to go there successfully was Mariner 2 in, uh, 1962. Mariner 1 was supposed to go there, but it blew up. There was one, it was launched by the Soviet Union back in, uh, the, let's see . . . let me find it . . . hang on, no, here it is, Venera 4 in 1967 . . . and it dropped instruments onto the surface. They only lasted a few seconds, because of the conditions, the heat and all, but this probe showed us how really hot it was. Then, there was this one called Venus Pioneer 2, in 1978. That was the one that found out that the atmosphere of Venus is made of carbon dioxide, mostly. And, uh, well, as I said . . . there were a lot of other ones too.

Narrator: In what order were these space probes sent to Venus?

[CD 4 Track 9]

Sample Item 2

Narrator: Listen to part of a lecture in a biology class.

Professor: Within the taiga itself, you'll find three sub-zones. The first of these you come to, as you're going south, is called open forest. The only trees here are needle-leaf trees—you know, evergreen trees, what we call coniferous trees. These trees tend to be small and far apart. This is basically tundra—it looks like tundra, but with a few small trees. Next, you come to what's called closed forest, with bigger needle-leaf trees growing closer together. This feels more like a real forest. This sub-zone—well, if you like variety, you're not going to feel happy here. You can travel for miles and see only half a dozen species of trees. In a few

days, we'll be talking about the tropical rain forest; now, that's where you'll see variety. Okay, finally, you come to the mixed zone. The trees are bigger still here, and you'll start seeing some broad-leafed trees, deciduous trees. You'll see larch, aspen, especially along rivers and creeks, in addition to needle-leaf trees. So this sub-zone feels a bit more like the temperate forests we're used to.

Narrator: The professor discussed three sub-zones of the taiga. Match each sub-zone with its characteristic.

[CD 5 TRACK 2]

Exercise 13.1

Narrator: Listen to a lecture in a chemistry class.

Professor: Okay, last class, we were considering various hydrocarbon compounds, and today, we're focusing on the most . . . well, definitely one of the most useful hydrocarbon compounds of all, at least from a commercial . . . an economic point of view. That's right, I'm talking about coal. You know, there probably . . . you probably would never have seen an Industrial Revolution in the eighteenth century without coal. Coal provided the fuel, the power for the Industrial Revolution. And even today, life would be very different if we didn't have coal. You may not know this, but in most countries around the world, electricity is still mostly produced by burning coal.

So, where does coal come from? Well, imagine what the earth was like, oh, say 300 million years ago, give or take a few million years. We call this time the Carboniferous Period. Get the connection? Carboniferous . . . coal forming? Most of the land was covered with . . . with luxuriant vegetation, especially ferns—ferns big as trees. Eventually, these plants died and were submerged in the waters of swamps, where they gradually decomposed. And we've seen what happens when plants decompose—the vegetable matter loses oxygen and hydrogen atoms, leaving a deposit with a high percentage of carbon. When this happens, you get peat bogs—in other words, you, uh, you get wetlands full of this muck, this, umm, partly decayed vegetable matter that's called peat. Okay, so now you've got these great peat bogs and over time, layers of sand and mud from the water settle over this gooey mass of peat. The deposits grow thicker and thicker and this in turn means the pressure gets . . . it increases on the peat. The water is squeezed out, the deposits are compressed and, uh, hardened . . . because of this pressure. And so you have—coal!

There are different grades of coal. Lignite—it's also called brown coal—is the lowest grade. By lowest grade, I mean it has the lowest percentage of carbon. Lignite has a lot of moisture, it can be up to 45% water, and has a fairly high amount of sulfur as well. It's often burned in furnaces to produce heat and to make electricity. Bituminous coal has a higher carbon content—and of course, less moisture. Bituminous coal is usually used for generating electricity. Anthracite is the highest . . . the highest grade of naturally occurring coal. It's used mainly to produce coke. The anthracite is baked and, uh, distilled to make coke. Everyone knows what coke is, right? It's almost pure carbon and is used in the manufacture of steel, mainly. One of the byproducts of . . . of the process of making coke is coal tar. Coal tar is used to make a lot of different types of plastic. It's also used to make some types of soap and shampoo. Oh, and I almost forgot about jet. Jet is a kind of compact lignite, and it's used to make jewelry.

OK, we're going to talk about oil, about petroleum, next, but, uh, any questions about coal first?

Narrator: Now get ready to answer the questions. You may use your notes to help you.

Narrator: Question 1: The lecturer discusses the steps involved in the creation of coal. Summarize this process by putting the steps in the proper order.

Narrator: Question 2: Match the form of coal with the type of industry that primarily uses it.

Narrator: Listen to a discussion in an accounting seminar.

Professor: Hello, everyone. As you can see from our course syllabus, our topic today is something called "GAAP." Anyone have any idea what we mean by that acronym, GAAP? Yes, Jennifer?

Student A: Ummm, I think it means "General Accepted Accounting Practices."

Professor: Almost right. Anyone else? Yeah, Michael?

Student B: Generally Accepted Accounting Principles, I think.

Professor: Bingo, you got it. So, what are these? What do we mean by Generally Accepted Accounting Principles? Well, they are basically a set of rules, of, uh, concepts, assumptions, conventions, whatever you want to call them, for measuring and, um, for reporting information in financial forms.

Student A: What kind of financial forms?

Professor: Almost any kind of form—balance sheets, income statements, cash flow statements, you name it. There are different kinds of GAAP. There are GAAP for government organizations, for non-profit organizations, and for profit-making businesses. The principles we'll be looking at deal with for-profit entities, but they are really general principles that apply to almost any accounting system.

Student A: And so, the purpose of GAAP is to . . .

Professor: It has the same purpose as standards in any field. If every business in one field used different standards—okay, imagine this. You go to the store to get a pound of coffee. Then you go to another store and get another pound of coffee, and it weighs more than the first pound. Or you get a liter bottle of milk from one store, and it's much smaller than the liter bottle from another store. That's what it would be like. There'd be no, uh, no basis for comparison . . .

Student A: That would be pretty confusing!

Professor: You bet. It would be sheer chaos. Now, GAAP includes a lot of concepts, but to get us started, we'll, uh, we'll focus on these three important ones, these three basic ones today. Okay, first off, the business entity principle. Who wants to take a swing at explaining that concept? Jennifer?

Student A: Uh, that means . . . well, a business has to keep its accounts . . . has to keep them separate from its owners' account . . . from their personal accounts.

Professor: Exactly. It means that, for accounting purposes, a business and its owners are separate entities. The assets and liabilities of a business have to be kept separate from the assets and liabilities of any other entity, including the owners and the creditors of the business. This means that if you own a business, and you have a dinner date one night, you can't finance your date with funds from your business. It means that, uh, you can't list your collection of baseball cards as corporate assets—those are your *personal assets*. So, everybody got that? Pretty simple concept . . . the business entity principle. Okay, onward to the next principle, the cost principle. What do you think that might be?

Student B: The cost principle. Hmmm. I don't know, Professor . . . Um, does it just mean that, when your business has a cost, you have to record it in the books?

Professor: Well, not just that you have to record it . . . it means that assets have to be recorded in the company accounts at the price at which they were originally purchased—not at today's perceived market value. Let's say, umm, you bought ten computers five years ago for $1,000 each, and that today they're worth about half that. This principle says that you have to record them on your books at the original price. We'll talk more about that later, but before we do, let's just quickly mention the *matching* principle. Anyone know what that is? Jennifer?

Student A: No idea, Professor.

Professor: Anyone else? No? Well, this principle . . . it simply states that a firm has to record any expenses that it incurs in the period when the sale was made. Say, uh, you own a used car lot, and your books say that you sold ten cars in June. Okay, then you have to record the salespersons' June salaries along with those sales. You have to include the rent you paid for the land that your used car lot is standing on. You have to include the expense of the helium that you used to blow up the balloons that lured the customers onto your car lot, and the money you spent for advertising your wonderful deals on cars on late-night cable television. Okay, now I'm going to give you a handout that explains GAAP in more detail, and we're going to see how these principles actually affect the way you enter information in accounts, but . . . before we go on, anyone have any questions?

Narrator: Now get ready to answer the question. You may use your notes to help you.

Narrator: Question 3: Match the accounting principle with the appropriate description of it.

Narrator: Listen to a guest lecture in an agricultural economics class.

Guest Lecturer: Hi there, I'm Floyd Haney. I'm your U.S. Department of Agriculture's county agent for Harrison County, have been for some twenty-two years. Professor Mackenzie was kind enough to ask me over to the school here today to chat with you about the, uh, agricultural situation in Floyd County today. Now, you probably know, your main crop here in Harrison County has always been wheat, wheat followed by corn. Been that way for, well, likely since the Civil War, I guess . . . maybe even longer. Wheat is still your most important crop here, but, this may come as a bit of a shocker to some of you, in the last few years, soybeans have actually outstripped corn. Soybeans are now more economically important than corn. Imagine.

   Now, down in the southern part of the county, you've got a real interesting phenomenon with your heirloom crops, your heirloom fruit and vegetables. Anyone know what those are? Heirloom crops?

Student A: Well, I've heard of heirloom breeds of animals—breeds of animals that were common a long time ago, but they're really rare today. Some farmers are trying to bring these animals back now.

Guest Lecturer: Right, well, heirloom crops—they're also called heritage crops—they're exactly the same. These are varieties of plants that were grown 20, 40, 100 years ago, but these days, only a few people grow them. Down in the southern part of Harrison County there are, oh, half a dozen small farms—Rainbow Valley, Cloverleaf Farms, Underwood Acres, and a handful of others—that are growing these heirloom crops. They're growing this variety of watermelon, it's called Moon and Star melon—that was popular around 1910. I'll tell you, those melons are so sweet and juicy, you wonder why farmers ever stopped growing them! What else . . . they grow heirloom tomatoes, cucumbers, peppers, squash, just all kinds of fruits and vegetables. These farmers are selling seeds over the Internet and they're selling their vegetables at farmers' markets, mostly. Now, these heirloom crops, they're not as important yet as the other three crops I mentioned, but I'll tell you what, sales of these seeds and veggies are so hot right now that you've got a lot of other farmers in the area thinking about growing some heirlooms themselves.

All right, then, let's talk a bit about our top crop, which is wheat, as I said earlier. Now, according to the Department of Agriculture, there are seven types of wheat, depending on their texture and color. You'll find three or four of those growing here in Harrison County. You get a lot of durum wheat here, that's probably the most common kind you'll see. Durum is used for, mainly used for making pasta—spaghetti, macaroni, linguini, and so on, all your types of pasta. Then there's soft white wheat, which is usually bought up by companies that make breakfast cereals. The next time you're having your Toasty Wheat Squares in the morning, just think, they might be made with Harrison County wheat. And of course, you have hard red wheat, which makes wonderful bread flour.

By the way, I brought some packets of tomato seeds from Rainbow Valley Farms—these are seeds for heirloom tomatoes called Better Boy Tomatoes—you'll notice the seed packages look like they came from around 1910, too. If any of you want to try your hand at growing some of these babies in your backyard, come on up after class and I'll give you a free packet of seeds.

Narrator: Now get ready to answer the questions. You may use your notes to help you.

Narrator: Question 4: The lecturer mentions four types of crops that are grown in Harrison County. Rank these four types of crops in their order of economic importance, beginning with the most important.

Narrator: Question 5: Match the type of wheat with the product that is most often made from it.

Narrator: Listen to a discussion in a modern history class.

Professor: Okay, we're going to continue with "Explorers and Exploration Week." Today we're talking about twentieth-century explorers. Usually, you know, when we, uh, mention twentieth-century exploration, people naturally think about astronauts, cosmonauts. We think about the first man in orbit, the first man to walk on the moon, and so on. And, in fact, we will take a look at space exploration in our next class, but today, we're going to talk about explorers in the early part of the twentieth century. Back then, the place to go if you were an explorer was . . . Antarctica. Tell me, has anyone ever read anything about the early exploration of Antarctica?

Student A: A coupla years ago, I read a book by, umm, Richard Byrd, Admiral Byrd, called *Alone*.

Professor: That's a remarkable book . . . about endurance . . . about courage.

Student A: Oh, I know—it was just incredible how he could survive in that cold, dark place all by himself.

Student B: I've never read that book—what's it about?

Professor: Well, it's about Richard Byrd's second trip to Antarctica, in 1934. He established this advance weather station about 100 miles from his main base. It was basically just a wooden hut, and it was soon completely covered in snow and ice. There were supposed to be three people working there, but because of bad weather, Byrd was cut off from the main base and got stuck there for the whole winter. And at that time of year in Antarctica, it's dark all day long.

Student A: Yeah, and at first he didn't realize it, but his heater . . . it was poisoning him. The, uh, fumes from the heater were toxic . . .

Professor: That's right. It was carbon monoxide poisoning.

Student A: But he kept sending messages back to the main base saying that everything was okay so that they wouldn't try to come rescue him and maybe die themselves in the winter storms. He barely survived.

Student B: So, Professor, was Byrd the first person to go to the South Pole?

Professor: No, no, not by a long shot he wasn't. He was the first person to fly to the South Pole. Well, he didn't actually land there, but he flew over the Pole, he and his pilot Bernt Balchen. That was in 1929. That same year he also established the first permanent . . . the first large-scale camp in Antarctica. Since he was from the United States, he named it Little America. Some people called Byrd "the mayor of Antarctica."

Student B: So then, if it wasn't Byrd, who was it?

Professor: I'm glad you asked that! Years before, about twenty years before Byrd came to Antarctica, there was a race, an international race to see who could get to the South Pole first. The newspapers called it "the race to the bottom of the world." The two main players were Norway and Britain. It was a little like the race to the moon in the 1960's, like the . . . like the space race between the U.S. and the U.S.S.R. The first expedition to get near the South Pole was led by a British explorer, Ernest Shackleton. That was in 1909. He was less than a hundred miles from the Pole when he had to turn around and go back to his base.

Student B: Why did he turn around if he was so close?

Professor: Well, he was running low on supplies, and as happens so often in Antarctica, the weather turned bad. Then, things got really exciting in 1911. Two expeditions left their base camps and headed for the Pole. The race was on. The first one to leave was under the Norwegian explorer Roald Amundsen. The other one was under the British explorer Robert Scott, who had been, um, on Shackleton's expedition a couple of years earlier.

Student A: C'mon, Professor, don't keep us in suspense. Tell us who won!

Professor: Well, in January of 1912—

Student B: January? Wouldn't that be the worst time to travel in Antarctica . . . in the middle of winter?

Professor: You're forgetting, it's in the southern hemisphere, December, January, those are the warmest months, the middle of summer. Of course, anywhere near the South Pole, the middle of summer is hardly tropical. Anyway, the British expedition reached the Pole in January 1912, thinking they were going to be the first. And what do you suppose they found there? The Norwegian flag, planted in the ice. Amundsen's party had reached the Pole about, oh, a few weeks earlier, in late December, 1911.

Student B: Oh, the British team must have been really disappointed, huh?

Professor: No doubt. In fact, there's a picture of the Scott expedition taken at the Pole, and they look exhausted, and terribly disappointed, and dejected, but that was just the beginning of their troubles.

Student A: Oh, no. What else happened?

Professor: Their trip back to their base turned into a—into just a nightmare. The expedition suffered setback after setback. They weren't as well equipped or as well supplied as the Norwegian expedition, either. This being Antarctica, the weather was frightful, there were terrible storms. Then they ran out of food and . . . ironically, they were just 11 miles from where they had left a cache of food, but . . . sadly, none of Scott's men made it back to their base.

Narrator: Now get ready to answer the questions. You may use your notes to help you.

Narrator: Question 6: The professor discusses some of the history of Antarctic exploration. Summarize this history by putting these events in the correct chronological order.

Narrator: Question 7: Match these Antarctic explorers with the countries from which they came.

Narrator: Listen to a lecture in a musical acoustics class.

Professor: Anyone know what this little electronic device is? No? It's a sound-level meter, a digital sound-level meter. It measures intensity of sound . . . what we usually call volume. Loudness. The read-out gives you the decibel level. By the way, I'm lecturing at about 61, 62 decibels. Now, we've been hearing a lot about decibel levels lately. The City Council has been considering a law to regulate the sound levels outside of clubs, and you know, student hangouts along State Street. This law, the one they're thinking about passing, says the decibel level just outside the doorways of these places has to be 70 or below from 10 P.M. until 7 A.M. and 80 or below any other time. If, uh, the police or environmental officers record decibel levels higher than that, they'll give a warning the first time and after that, they could give the business owners a fine. And there's already a law that controls the decibel level for concerts at the stadium. After years of complaining that their window panes rattled during rock concerts, the people who live in the Stone Hill neighborhood over by the stadium, those neighbors got together and got the City Council to limit the sound level just outside the stadium to a maximum of 100 decibels.

And, you know, there are good reasons why we should be concerned about high sound levels. About 10 million people in the United States have some sort of hearing loss due to excessive noise. A lot of this, it's caused by . . . well, there are occupational reasons. People who operate heavy equipment, who work in noisy factories, farmers, miners . . . they all have to deal with high decibel levels. But some of the problem comes from loud, loud music. The thing is, hearing loss is incremental, it, uh, happens bit by bit, so it's . . . well, you don't usually notice it happening, although sometimes . . . have you ever been to a concert and when you came out, your ears were ringing? Or you hear a buzzing sound? This is called tinnitus. Tinnitus. Now, if you are at a really loud concert, or you go to a number of concerts in a short period, you may experience TTS—Temporary Threshold Shift. This means that you, uh, well, it means that you lose the ability to hear low-volume sounds. Everything sounds . . . muffled, like you had cotton in your ears. This can last a couple of hours or it can last all day. And unfortunately, noise exposure over a prolonged period can cause TTS to turn into a permanent condition called NIHL—noise-induced hearing loss.

Anyway, what I wanted to tell you about today is an experiment that a group of students in my class did a couple of years ago. It was their final project for my class. They borrowed this little sound-level meter of mine and took it to all sorts of musical venues. They went to a rock concert at the stadium—this was before the law was passed regulating sound levels there. There was a band called the Creatures playing, I think it was the Creatures. From the

seats they had—they sat pretty close to the stage—they measured a maximum decibel level of about 110 when the band was playing. This level, 110 decibels, is the high end of what is considered "musically useful." Now, 110 decibels is loud, no doubt about it. It's about as loud as a jet taking off when you're 100 meters away. Of course, the sound didn't just come from the music—the meter also measured the crowd noise, too, and rock concert crowds can get pretty loud. Still, I was a little surprised—I mean, given the size of these bands' amplifiers, I was a bit surprised that the sound levels weren't even higher.

The students also took the meter to a classical concert, the University Philharmonic Symphony. I'd estimate that if a full symphony orchestra plays flat-out as loud as they possibly can, you might get levels of about, oh, 95, 100 decibels. The night the students went, though, the loudest level they recorded was only 85 decibels. During a violin solo, the level from their seats was only about 55 decibels. That's at the very low end of the "musically useful" range. At that level, you can barely hear the music over the sound of the ventilating system, and the, uh, the occasional cough. Of course, at a classical concert, you're not going to have the audience noise that you would at a rock concert. Beethoven fans are usually a little more restrained than rock fans.

The loudest music the students recorded in a public place wasn't even live music. It was at a club over on State Street, Club 1010. I think it's closed now. Anyway, as I said, it wasn't live music, it was a disc jockey playing recorded music but . . . well, that club must have had a very powerful sound system, practically a nuclear-powered sound system, because the sound level on the dance floor was 117 decibels. That's not considered "musically useful." That's considered "painfully loud."

One time, the students were on their way to a jazz club downtown, and one of their friends gave them a ride in his van. The friend didn't realize they had their sound-level meter with them. Anyway, he was playing a CD and cranked up the sound system to the maximum volume . . . and guess what? This was the highest reading of all! It was over 125 decibels, which is just this side of being considered "unbearable." It must have been loud enough to shake the fillings out of their teeth!

Okay, well, I'm going to pass out a copy of the students' paper so you can see for yourself just how noisy your favorite places to hear music are . . .

Narrator: Now get ready to answer the questions. You may use your notes to help you.

Narrator: Question 8: The professor mentions several conditions caused by excessively loud music. Match the condition to the correct description of it.

Narrator: Question 9: The professor lists several musical events at which her students recorded sound levels. List these events in the correct order based on volume, beginning with the highest volume.

Narrator: Listen to a lecture in a U.S. literature class.

Professor: Well, I told you at the end of the last class that I thought you would enjoy the reading assignment that I gave you—was I right? . . . Yeah, I thought so . . . most students like reading the works of Edgar Allan Poe—maybe in part because so many of his works have been turned into spooky movies!

Let's, um, take a brief look at Poe's early life. He was born in Boston in 1809. He was an orphan, he was orphaned at an early age. A businessman named John Allan unofficially adopted him. Allan took him to England when he was six, and Poe went to private school there. He came back to the United States in 1820 and in 1826 he went to the University of Virginia in Charlottesville for a year. However, his adoptive father John Allan wasn't happy about the way Poe carried on at the university. He kept hearing stories that Poe was drinking and gambling all his money away. Allan came to Charlottesville and made Poe drop out and go to work as a bank clerk—as a bookkeeper, more or less.

Well, Poe was young and artistic—he already considered himself a poet—and, as you can imagine, he hated this boring bank job. He did everything he could to get himself fired. It didn't take long. After leaving his job, he wrote and published his first book of poems. Right after this, Poe returned to Boston and reconciled with John Allan. Allan decided that all Poe needed was some discipline, so he arranged for Poe to enter the U.S. military academy at West Point. Now, do you think Poe enjoyed the life of a cadet at the academy? You're right, he didn't like it any more than he'd liked working as a bank clerk, and he was tossed out of the school after just a few months for disobeying orders and for, um, generally neglecting his duties. After this . . . well, John Allan was fed up. He figured he'd done everything he could for his adopted son and so Allan completely disowned him. Poe was on his own. He moved to Baltimore—that's the city he's most closely associated with—and devoted himself to his writing.

Now, I'm not going to talk about Poe's later life right now, not until after we've had a chance to talk about some of his works, because . . . well, the tragic events of his later life deeply influenced his writing.

Poe's first love was poetry. He considered himself mainly a poet. In fact, he said that he wrote other works just to make money, money to live on while he wrote his poems. The poem that I asked you to read for this class is "The Raven," and it's definitely one of his most famous pieces. Isn't it amazing how Poe creates such a sad and mysterious and downright scary mood in this poem? Then I also asked you to read Poe's horror story, "The Fall of the House of Usher." Poe wrote a lot of horror stories. Several of them—including this one—are considered classics of that genre. Today's horror writers, like Stephen King, owe Poe quite a debt. Again, in this story, Poe creates a gloomy, haunting mood, but the plot and characterization are outstanding. Finally, I asked you to read the short story "The Gold Bug." This is a detective story, a mystery, a "whodunit." Who do you think invented the detective story? It was none other than Edgar Allan Poe. A lot of people think it was Arthur Conan Doyle, who wrote the Sherlock Holmes stories, but Poe was writing this kind of story years before Doyle.

Okay, I'm going to read Poe's poem "The Raven" aloud. I want you to listen carefully to the rhythm of the poem, the rhymes, the sounds, just the sounds of Poe's words, and see how all these contribute to the meaning of the poem, how he builds this gloomy, almost desperate mood. Okay, ready?

Narrator: Now get ready to answer the questions. You may use your notes to help you.

Narrator: Question 10: The professor gives a brief biography of the writer Edgar Allan Poe. List these events from his life in the order in which they occurred.

Narrator: Question 11: Match these works by Edgar Allan Poe with the type of writing that they represent.

Narrator: Listen to a lecture in an anthropology class.

Professor: All right, today, our class is going to the dogs! Last week, we talked about the process of domesticating

animals in general. Today, we're going to talk about the first animal to be domesticated—man's best friend, the dog!

There's a lot we don't know about the domestication of dogs. For one thing, we don't know when it happened. For a long time, scientists thought that it occurred about 10,000 years ago. Then, some scientists—scientists who study dog DNA, like Robert Wayne of UCLA—they tried to push that date way back in time. They said that domestication occurred about 100,000 years ago. We know now, know for sure that it happened at least 14,000 years ago. A fragment of a bone that has definitely been identified as belonging to a dog was found in a cave in Germany, and it's 14,000 years old. Domestication probably took place around 20,000 years ago.

We don't know where dogs were first domesticated either. By the fifteenth century, the dog was found all over the world—the first domestic animal with a global range. The most likely point of origin is Southwest Asia, but some scientists think that it was in East Asia, while others think maybe Europe or North Africa. We know it wasn't in the Western Hemisphere because the DNA of dogs in the Americas is more closely related to Eurasian wolves than it is to American wolves, so dogs must have followed humans to Alaska across the land bridge from Siberia.

Then we also don't know exactly how humans domesticated dogs, although there are various theories. One theory is that dogs figured out early on that they could feed pretty well just by hanging around humans and eating the scraps of food that were, you know, just thrown out or left sitting around. But, to have access to these morsels, dogs had to get over their natural fear of humans, and so, according to this theory, dogs more or less domesticated themselves. Another theory is that dogs were domesticated from wolves by means of selective breeding. There was an experiment done by a Russian scientist, Dmitri Balyaev, in the 1940's. He bred a group of wild Siberian foxes. The only characteristic he was interested in when he was breeding these foxes was tameness, friendliness towards humans. In only six generations of foxes—only six generations, mind you!—he had bred foxes that weren't afraid of humans, that wagged their tails when they saw their keepers, that even licked their keepers' faces. If he could do this with foxes in six generations, early humans surely could have done it with wolves over thousands of generations.

We do know what animal domestic dogs come from. There are almost 400 breeds of dogs today, but all of them, from Chihuahuas to great Danes, are descendants of the Eurasian grey wolf. Because there are so many differences among types of dogs—size, shape, color, temperament—scientists once wondered if some were related to other types of wild dogs, like African jackals, Australian dingoes, or American coyotes. DNA tests, though, showed that all dogs are related to wolves. But, uh, there are some dogs, like German shepherds, that are closer to wolves than others. This indicates that domestication may have taken place in various stages—you know, some breeds may have been domesticated more recently than others.

Dogs were first domesticated during humankind's earliest stage of development—the hunter-gatherer period. Apparently, umm, their first job was to serve as guards. With their keen sense of smell and hearing, dogs made it almost impossible for strangers to come up to a sleeping village by surprise. Later, humans took advantage of dogs' hunting ability. Dogs helped humans get hold of meat and skins from wild animals. Take a look at this rock painting that was found in the Jaro Mountains in Iraq—it's maybe

8,000 years old. It shows people with spears hunting deer, getting some help from dogs with curly tails. Still later, after humans domesticated herd animals—goats, cattle, sheep—well, dogs helped gather up these animals and move them from place to place by barking and nipping at their heels. Take a look at this fresco. It's from the wall of a sandstone grotto in the desert in Algeria. It's probably 5,000 years old. The herders are driving their oxen home from the fields while their "best friends" are helping them out.

Today, of course, most dogs have taken on another role. Sure, some dogs are still working dogs. They help hunters, they herd animals, they pull loads, they find survivors of natural disasters. Most dogs, though, are not valued so much for the work they do as for the company they provide. But that doesn't mean their ability to perform these earlier roles has been completely bred out of them. My two dogs, Raisin and Cosmo—they still perform guard duty. No way will they let the mail carrier sneak up to my house! And, last weekend, I was at the park with my little nieces and nephew, and the kids were running around the playground. Raisin and Cosmo—they're both border collies, which are herding dogs—they were actually out there herding these kids! I mean, they were barking and jumping around and trying to keep the kids from running off. They still have that herding instinct!

All right, next I'm going to talk a little about horses, about domesticating horses, and what a huge impact that had on humans, but first, any questions about domesticating dogs?

Narrator: Now get ready to answer the questions. You may use your notes to help you.

Narrator: Question 12: The professor mentions a number of archaeological finds that were related to the domestication of dogs. Match these finds with their locations.

Narrator: Question 13: The professor mentions a number of roles that dogs have played since they were first domesticated. List these roles in chronological order, beginning with the earliest role that dogs played.

[CD 5 Track 3]

Lesson 14: Completing Charts

Sample Item

Narrator: Listen to part of a discussion in a business class.

Professor: What does a case look like? Well, cases are basically descriptions of actual—let me stress that, of real business situations, chunks of reality from the business world. So, you get typically ten to twenty pages of text that describe the problem, some problem that a real business actually faced. And then there will be another five to ten pages of what are called exhibits.

Student B: Exhibits? What are those?

Professor: Exhibits . . . those are documents, statistical documents, that explain the situation. They might be oh, spreadsheets, sales reports, umm, marketing projections, anything like that. But as I said, at the center of every case, at the core of every case, is a problem that you have to solve. So, you have to analyze the situation, the data—and sometimes, you'll see you don't have enough data to work with, and you might have to collect more—say, from the Internet. Then, you have to make decisions about how to solve these problems.

Student B: So that's why we study cases? I mean, because managers need to be able to make decisions . . . and solve problems?

Professor: Exactly . . . well, that's a big part of it, anyway. And doing this, solving the problem, usually involves role-playing, taking on the roles of decision-makers at the firm. One member of the group might play the Chief Executive Officer, one the Chief Financial Officer, and so. And you . . . you might have a business meeting to decide how your business should solve its problem. Your company might, say, be facing a cash shortage and thinking about selling off one division of the company. So your group has to decide if this is the best way to handle the problem.

Student B: So we work in groups, then?

Professor: Usually in groups of four or five. That's the beauty of this method. It teaches teamwork and cooperation.

Student A: And then what? How are we . . . how do you decide on a grade for us?

Professor: You give a presentation, an oral presentation, I mean, and you explain to the whole class what decision you made and . . . what recommendations you'd make . . . and then you write a report as well. You get a grade, a group grade, on the presentation and the report.

Student B: Professor, is this the only way we'll be studying business, by using cases?

Professor: Oh no, it's just one important way. Some classes are lecture classes and some are a combination of lectures and case studies and some . . . in some classes you'll also use computer simulations. We have this software called World Marketplace, and, using this program, your group starts up your own global corporation and tries to make a profit . . . it's actually a lot of fun.

Narrator: In this lecture, the professor describes the process of the case study method. Indicate whether each of the following is a step in the process.

[CD 6 Track 2]

Exercise 14.1

Narrator: Listen to a discussion in an urban studies class.

Professor: Okay, I guess most of you are familiar with the, uh, with the commercial section of Harmony Road, right? Who can describe that area for me?

Student A: Well it's . . . there are a couple of big shopping centers and a few strip malls . . . lots of fast food places and motels, uh, big box stores . . . used car lots . . . .

Professor: Right. And, suppose you had to sum up that sort of development, what would you call it?

Student A: I guess you'd call it . . . sprawl. Suburban sprawl.

Professor: Right. And the residential suburbs out in that area, how would you describe them?

Student B: Well, they're fairly nice . . . nice big houses, big yards . . .

Professor: Now, say you lived in one of those neighborhoods and you ran out of bread . . . would you walk to the market?

Student B: No way. Most places there don't even have sidewalks. And . . . everything is so far apart.

Professor: Exactly right. Those suburbs, and that commercial section, represent what we call Conventional Suburban Design, or CSD. Today I want to talk about a theory of urban design, a movement called New Urbanism that challenges CSD. In a New Urban community, you can walk to the store to buy a loaf of bread.

Although this movement, this philosophy is called New Urbanism, in a way, it should be called traditional urbanism because it looks to the past, it models today's communities on the way communities looked in the past. Think about a typical town in the United States a hundred years ago. You had a central business area, a downtown surrounded by residential neighborhoods. That all changed in the fifties and sixties. That's when the "flight to the suburbs" took place. A lot of suburban shopping malls were built. Huge areas of land, usually farmland, were developed. Automobile use soared. Downtowns deteriorated or died, and the old neighborhoods in the city center, mostly they became slums.

Today over 500 "New Urbanist" communities have been built or are being constructed, and most of these feature an old "Main Street" style business center . . . a "downtown," if you will.

Okay, here are some core principles of New Urbanism. First, walkability. Streets are pedestrian friendly and lined with trees. Just as in older cities, streets are laid out on a grid. Actually, New Urbanists generally use a "modified" grid, with "T" intersections and some diagonals to, uh, calm traffic and increase visual interest. There's a mix of narrow streets, wider boulevards, walkways, and alleys between streets. Some streets are designated car-free. You wouldn't get any big surface parking lots. Parking is in underground lots or in garages behind houses, out of sight. And there are some great benefits to this. With more people walking the streets, communities are safer, there's less crime. And fewer cars means less pollution.

Another principle is mixed use. On one block, even in one building, there may be a mix of shops, restaurants, offices, and apartments. A big family house may be right next to a moderately-priced apartment building. Shop owners live upstairs from their shops. This kind of development encourages a diverse population—a mix of ages, classes, cultures, races.

Another principle: increased density. Residences, shops, and services, all of these are closer together than in a CSD, especially around the community center. This helps with the ease of walking I mentioned before—no residences should be more than a ten-minute walk from the community center. But, increased density doesn't mean eliminating open space. New Urban communities are dotted with little parks, pocket parks, and ideally there is a community space, an open plaza, a village green in the center of town where people can gather.

You also want to emphasize smart transportation, and, uh, of course that means de-emphasizing the car. Ideally, there is a train or a light-rail system for transport in and out of the community. Within the community, as I said, you want to encourage walking and bicycling. Of course, this gives you exercise, and it's healthier than driving everywhere.

Student B: Professor, do the, uh, houses, the residences in these New Urban places, ummm, New Urban communities, do they look any different from houses in regular suburbs?

Professor: Well, there's an emphasis on comfort . . . on creating attractive, comfortable houses. I already mentioned that parking spaces, garages are typically behind the house. So, the front of the house is not taken up with two- or three-car garages that are part of the house. Houses are closer to the street. And a common feature is a big front porch, often with a porch swing. This is a, uh, well, an inviting space to get together, to sit around with neighbors. Sometimes, too, you'll get a theme going in a New Urban community. I have some slides that I'm going to show you later. In some East Coast communities, there's a Colonial look to all the buildings. Some communities have a neo-Victorian look. In other communities, all the houses are painted in bright colors.

Student A: You said there were about 500 New Urban communities around the country. Where are they mostly?

Professor: Well, there are some in almost every state. Some are built in undeveloped areas. Those are called "greenfield sites." Others are in run-down urban areas. Those are "grayfield sites." Oh. And some of the most promising sites for future projects are what are called "grayfield malls."

Student A: What are those?

Professor: Well, about 2,000 major shopping malls have been built in the United States. Of these, 8% are closed—and another 11% are in danger of closing. Many of these would make ideal New Urban communities. Well, next I want to show you some slides of some New Urban communities: Seaside in Florida, Kentlands in Maryland, Prospect in Colorado, Plum Creek in Texas. Would someone in the back there dim the lights?

Narrator: Now get ready to answer the questions. You may use your notes to help you.

Narrator: Question 1: In this lecture, the professor describes the New Urbanism Movement. Indicate whether each of the following is a principle of this movement.

Narrator: Question 2: In this lecture, the professor mentions benefits associated with the New Urbanism Movement. Indicate whether each of the following is a benefit mentioned in the lecture.

Narrator: Listen to a lecture in a British History class.

Professor: Good morning. In our last class, we were discussing King Richard. Richard the Lionhearted. We talked, as you'll no doubt recall, about his role in the Third Crusade, how he was kidnapped on his way home to England, how he died fighting in France—although, if he'd just remembered to put his armor on, he probably would have been just fine. Now, after Richard, we have John, John Lackland, the King John. Actually, Richard's nephew Arthur was supposed to become king, he was next in line, but Richard had signed an agreement with John, and so John became king.

Now, there is a tendency, rather an unfortunate tendency, to consider Richard the good king and John the evil one. Frankly, Richard was not all that great although he was a fairly decent military leader. He was more interested in being the subject of songs than he was in ruling England. He was intolerant, and he practically bankrupted the country to pay for his wars. Of course, John was supposedly so wicked that no other British king has ever been named John. It's true, he was no prize, but he was probably no worse than most other medieval rulers.

Like Richard, John spent almost no time in England. The war in France was still going on and John was still bleeding England white to pay for it. England at that time still controlled some odd bits, some dribs and drabs of France—Normandy, Brittany, umm, Anjou—but King Philip of France was trying to take them away. In 1214, at the battle of Bouvines, Philip decisively defeated John. So, defeated and broke, John returned to England hoping to raise some funds. He insisted that the nobles, the barons and dukes and so on, that they pay a kind of tax called *scutage*—this was a payment the barons could make rather than go fight the war in France, a kind of bribe to avoid military service. But the barons, a substantial number of them, anyway, were fed up. They were tired of being taxed whenever John needed some money. There was a Civil War. Barons chose sides, for the king or against him. The anti-John barons were able to capture London. On June 15, 1215, they forced John to meet with them. They confronted him on a green meadow southwest of London. They demanded that their traditional rights be written down and that John sign this document. The result was the Magna Carta—the Great Charter.

Now, one of the great myths about the Magna Carta is that it was some kind of a constitution, that it created a democratic society. There were no democratic societies in Europe in the thirteenth century! Really, it was . . . a feudal document, an agreement between the king and the barons, the aristocracy. It gave rights really to just a few powerful families. In fact, it barely mentions the ordinary people. The, uh, majority of the English population gained little from the Charter and wouldn't have an active voice in government for hundreds of years. Another myth is that the Charter established the parliamentary system of government. It did create a council of twenty-five barons to see that the articles of the Magna Carta were observed, but the first recognizable English Parliament—it was called "the model Parliament"—did not come for almost a hundred years.

Now I said that the Magna Carta didn't have much immediate influence on the ordinary Englishman. That doesn't mean it wasn't a document of great importance. In its own time, the greatest value of the Magna Carta was that it limited royal power . . . and made it clear that even the king had to obey the law. Think about that. Before this time, the King's word was law, but the Magna Carta stated that no one—no one—was above the law. That's pretty revolutionary, eh? And, over time, the charter took on even more significance. Some articles that in 1215 applied only to the powerful barons later applied to the whole nation. For example, one article of the Charter says that no tax can be imposed by the king without the barons' consent. Eventually, this came to be interpreted as "no taxation without the consent of Parliament." Another article says that no freeman can be put in jail, deprived of property, exiled, or executed without the lawful judgment of his *peers,* his equals. Now, in John's time, there was no such thing as trial by jury in criminal cases, but the Magna Carta . . . well, it sort of set this system up.

Now, I'd like everyone to take a look in your textbook, ah, let me see, on page 184. We'll take a quick look at a few more of the most important provisions of the Charter.

Narrator: Now get ready to answer the question. You may use your notes to help you.

Narrator: Question 3: In this lecture, the professor mentions myths (false stories) and realities (true stories) associated with the Magna Carta. Indicate whether each of the following is considered a myth or a reality.

Narrator: Listen to a lecture in a paleontology class.

Professor: In our last class, we were talking about the tar pits at Rancho La Brea in Los Angeles, and, uh, what a great source of fossils, fossil information these, uh, tar pits have been. There have been . . . well, millions, literally millions of fossils, of bones of Ice Age mammals that were, uh, trapped in the asphalt ponds there. It's an ideal place for fossil hunters . . . the sticky asphalt trapped the animals, and then the asphalt helped preserve their bones.

Of course, um, tar pits are not the only place to look for fossil bones. Many are found in stream beds, lake beds, deserts. Another good place for paleontologists to look for remains is in caves.

There are really two types of caves where fossils can be found. One type is the carnivore den, places where carnivores lived. Carnivore dens tend to be small horizontal caves. They're generally about one to three meters in height, and maybe thirty meters in length. They typically have small entrances. These caves often contain the remains of both the herbivores that the, uh, predators dragged into the den and, uh, the remains of the carnivores themselves. Now, with many carnivore dens, you, uh, uh, you often will have multiple occupants of the same den over the centuries. The occupants might not even be the same species. Those dens, they're kinda like dormitory rooms. You get a couple of roommates who live there for a year or two, they move on, then someone else moves in, so sometimes, there's a real jumble of bones in a carnivore's den—the bones of fish, rodents, birds, antelopes, all kinds of creatures. Then, too, most of the time, caves get flooded, and the flood waters wash all the bones and the dirt into one corner of the cave, so you have a pile of sediment-embedded bones. Sorting out these bones of extinct animals—some of which might be from completely unknown species—well, this can be a pretty big challenge for paleontologists.

A good example of a carnivore den was, uh, discovered at Agate National Monument in Nebraska. It was excavated by paleontologists from the University of Nebraska in the 1980's. It's actually a whole complex of dens used by Miocene carnivores about, um, 22 million years ago, more or less. Several types of carnivores used this complex, but the most important was the beardog—a kind of extinct wild dog. There are fragments of the bones of their prey, parts of bones from juvenile camels, woolly rhinoceroses—did you know that there once were camels and rhinos in Nebraska? Pretty hard to picture, isn't it? Giant ground sloths, lots of oreodonts—little raccoon-size mammals that lived in herds. There are the remains of young, mature, and aged beardogs. There's some evidence that they all died off about the same time, possibly because of a prolonged drought. After their death, their skeletons were covered up with sand and silt that blew into the caves.

Now, uh, the second type of cave where you find fossils is called a natural trap. Natural traps are pit caves—holes in the ground, really. Large mammals sometimes fall right into these holes. Generally, natural traps tend to have a lower diversity of fossils than den sites.

One of the most incredible collections of cave fossils was found in a natural trap in the, uh, Naracoote Cave in Australia, in the state of Western Australia. It was found by a group of amateur cave explorers and this site was explored—is still being explored—by paleontologists from a university in Adelaide. This whole area in Australia is riddled with caves, but this is the first time that there's been a major find of fossils there. The hole leading to the cave was covered with vegetation. This is true of most natural traps—vegetation hides the hole and makes it almost invisible. There is a 15-meter drop down to the cave floor. Animals fell in and couldn't get out. Even with that long drop, though, most of the animals that fell into the cave didn't die on impact, apparently. How do we know? Specimens were found in all three rooms of the cave. They probably wandered around for several days, looking for a way out, before eventually dying of dehydration or starvation. If the animals had died on impact, all the bones would have been found in a heap directly below the hole in the ceiling. Now, remember I said that there were usually fewer species in a natural trap than in a den? Not true at the Naracoote Cave. There have been some amazing finds there. Some, uh, ten species of giant kangaroos have been found there. These guys were, like, five meters tall. Then there was a giant wombat. There were Tasmanian tigers. Oh, and one of the most exciting finds was an "Australian lion," a predator about the size of a modern leopard. The Australian lion, though, isn't related to big cats, it's a marsupial, it has a pouch like a kangaroo or a koala.

So, caves. Caves, uh, present a window to the past. Sometimes the view is a . . . a bit murky. Sometimes, like the Naracoote Cave, you get this unbelievably clear look at animal life long ago.

Narrator: Now get ready to answer the questions. You may use your notes to help you.

Narrator: Question 4: In this lecture, the professor describes carnivore dens. Decide if the following are characteristics of carnivore dens.

Narrator: Question 5: In this lecture, the professor describes important fossil finds at Naricoote Cave, a natural trap. Decide if the following are characteristics of Naricoote Cave.

Narrator: Listen to a lecture in an astronomy class.

Professor: Now, ancient Greek astronomers believed that the Earth was the center of the universe. This model is called the *geocentric* model—*geo*, of course, is Greek for *Earth*. Why, you ask, did they think the Earth was at the center of everything? Well, let's think about it a little. Ummm, they were on the Earth and the Earth, obviously, was not moving. I mean, if the Earth moved below our feet, clouds and birds would be "left behind" as we moved, right? If we jumped into the air, we wouldn't land at exactly the same place that we jumped from. We'd feel a constant breeze on our cheeks caused by the Earth's movement. And then, of course, when the Greeks looked up at the sky, it seemed that all the bodies they saw were revolving around the Earth. So you see, this was really a very sensible theory, a theory that was confirmed by observation.

Around the second century, Ptolemy, a Greek astronomer living in Egypt, collected all the ideas of Greek astronomers in a book called *Almagest*, which means "Great Treatise." This Ptolemy, by the way, was quite a genius—he also wrote books about optics and geography. So anyway, he developed, um, an elegant model of a universe that worked like clockwork. This model is so associated with Ptolemy that it's . . . we call it the Ptolemaic model. In this model, the planets are points of light attached to crystal spheres, the "celestial spheres," they're called. These spheres fit one inside another and move in perfect harmony. Their circular movements were believed to create a kind of music called "the music of the spheres." I always liked that idea—heavenly music. So, anyway, in this system, the Earth is immobile and is located at the very heart of things. The moon is attached to the closest sphere, followed by the inner planets, Mercury and Venus. Then came the Sun, followed by the rest of the known planets—Mars, Jupiter, Saturn. The stars are attached to the outermost crystal sphere. All of these heavenly bodies are made out of some glowing substance called "perfect matter."

Now, there were problems with this model. One was the retrograde movement of planets. Sometimes, planets such as Mars seem to slow down and then change direction, they actually seem to go backwards and then loop around and go the other way. That's why the Greeks called them *planets*—*planet* is Greek for *wanderer*. Actually, this is an optical illusion caused by the fact that the various planets don't take the same amount of time to orbit the Sun. Ptolemy theorized that . . . well, he devised a trick to

explain this abnormality. He invented the idea of *epicycles*. I'm not going to bother explaining epicycles because they are very, very complicated. In fact, hardly anyone completely understands this system today. But his system was remarkably accurate. It could predict the future positions of planets and even predict solar and lunar eclipses.

Well, this Earth-centered model was accepted by almost everyone for well, almost 1,500 years. By the Middle Ages, the Ptolemaic system had become part and parcel of the medieval worldview, part of religion, philosophy, science. The planets and stars were believed to have all kinds of powers to influence events on Earth, to shape people's destinies. Then, in the sixteenth century Nicolas Copernicus, a scientist from East Prussia—now part of Poland—came up with a revolutionary theory. It was the heliocentric model—*helios* is Greek for *Sun*. It's also called the Copernican model. In this model, the Sun is the center of the universe, and all the planets circle it, moving in the same direction—first Mercury, then Venus, then Earth. The moon, naturally, circles the Earth. Farther out from the sun are the orbits of Mars and the other planets.

It wasn't until a century later, when Galileo built a telescope and turned it on the planets, that the Ptolemaic model could be definitely proven false. Galileo learned that Venus has phases, just like the moon: crescent, full, crescent, then it disappears. In the Ptolemaic system, Venus should always look like a crescent when viewed from the Earth, but because actually it is lit from the center of its orbit by the Sun, Venus has a complete set of phases. So, Galileo proved Ptolemy was wrong.

Of course, nowadays we know that the Copernican system presents a reasonably accurate picture of our solar system but not of the universe. Copernicus didn't know what to make of the stars. He said they were faraway points of light of an unknown nature. It was impossible for him to know that they were much like our Sun, only unthinkably farther away. Today we know that the Sun is only one of billions of stars in our galaxy. We're not even in the center of that galaxy, but way out in one arm, out in the suburbs. And not only that, we now know that our galaxy is only one of billions, maybe trillions of galaxies. So, in a couple of thousand years, we've moved from being right smack in the center of the universe to living on a rather insignificant piece of real estate.

Narrator: Now get ready to answer the question. You may use your notes to help you.

Narrator: Question 6: In this lecture, the professor describes two ways to look at the universe: the Ptolemaic system and the Copernican system. Decide if the following are characteristics of the Ptolemaic system or the Copernican system.

Narrator: Listen to a lecture in a marketing class.

Professor: All right, then, next topic. I want to talk a bit about attitude, consumer attitude and how it affects consumer behavior. Before we get ahead of ourselves, though, we should define attitude. Attitude is an opinion, or evaluation, of a person, an issue, or—and this is how we'll generally use it—of a product. And anything that you have an attitude towards, that's called an object.

Okay, then, one fairly traditional approach to viewing attitude is called the ABC model. In this model, attitude is made up of three parts, three components. The *A* component, that's the *affective* component, the, shall we say, emotional part of the formula. It reflects the consumer's feelings towards the object. If you look at a product, if you consider a product, how does it make you feel? Does the idea of owning this product give you a warm, happy, glowing feeling or a cold, negative feeling? If you buy it for Aunt Sally, will she be pleased?

The *B* component is the *behavioral* component. This is . . . it's not *just* actual behavior . . . it's both actual behavior and potential behavior . . . . It's . . . it's how you might act and how you do act. For us in marketing, this basically means, do you want to buy something and if you do, do you actually buy it? That's the B in the ABC model.

The C component, now that's the *cognitive* component. That's the consumer's knowledge, intellectual knowledge, ideas, and thoughts about the object. Where does this information come from? How do consumers get knowledge about a product? Well, there are lots of sources. There are consumer magazines that compare products. There's word of mouth . . . your brother-in-law Bob just bought a new digital camera and he tells you how great it is. But of course, these days, most people get product information from advertising, advertising on television, on the radio, in newspapers and magazines . . . on the Internet . . . advertising is everywhere!

So, in marketing, what you are trying to do, obviously, is to influence consumer attitude towards a product. You can do that in an affective way—you can appeal to consumers' emotions—or you can do it in a cognitive way, you can sway consumers' opinion by appealing to their good sense, or you can use a combination of A and C, but what you want to do, bottom line, is to affect behavior. You want consumers to buy your products.

Now, according to the social psychologist Daniel Katz—he did this classic study on attitude in 1960—attitudes are functional. In other words, we have an attitude towards something because it serves some purpose. Katz identified a number of attitude functions. Two of these are especially useful for marketers to understand. The first one is called the value-expressive function. This has to do with how people think about you—or rather, your *perception* of how people think about you. You might not really be able to afford a sleek little sports car, or expensive designer shoes from Italy, or a big flat-screen TV, but perhaps you buy these products anyway. Why? Because you believe that the people you come in contact with will think you look really stylish in those shoes, or they'll think you must be rich if you own that TV, or that you're cool if you drive around in that sports car. Conversely, the value-expression function can work the opposite way. You might *not* buy a perfectly good product because, well, you think it will make you seem . . . what, unsophisticated, unpopular, out of touch, boring.

The second function to consider is the ego-defensive function. These products appeal to your desire to be safe, to minimize threats. You are responding to this function when you buy car insurance, homeowners' insurance, health insurance . . . Also if you buy an alarm system for your house or car . . . if you, if you buy deodorant, you are responding to this function. Again, this function can also cause you not to buy a product. You don't buy it because you think it is dangerous. This could be why you don't buy cigarettes, why you don't buy a car that is known to be unsafe, to roll over. Again, you're responding to this ego-defensive function.

Okay, coming up in our next class, we'll look at some examples of real advertisements and see how they change attitudes and influence behavior. And don't forget to finish reading Chapter 7 before then.

Narrator: Now get ready to answer the questions. You may use your notes to help you.

Narrator: Question 7: The lecturer describes the ABC approach to viewing consumer attitudes. Decide if the following are more closely related to the A component, the B component, or the C component of the ABC approach.

Narrator: Question 8: In this lecture, the professor describes the Katz system of attitude functions. Decide which of the following characteristics is related to which function.

[CD 6 Track 3]

Listening Review Test
Listen as the directions are read to you.

Narrator: This section tests your understanding of conversations and lectures. You will hear each conversation or lecture only once. Your answers should be based on what is stated or implied in the conversations and lectures. You are allowed to take notes as you listen, and you can use these notes to help you answer the questions. In some questions, you will see a headphones icon. This icon tells you that you will hear, but not read, part of the lecture again. Then you will answer a question about the part of the lecture that you heard. Some questions have special directions that are highlighted. During an actual test, you will not be allowed to skip questions and come back to them later, so try to answer every question that you hear on this test. There are two conversations and four lectures. Most questions are separated by a ten-second pause.

Narrator: Listen to a conversation between a student and a professor.
Student: Hi, Professor Calhoun. May I come in?
Professor: Oh, hi, Scott, sure. What's up?
Student: Oh, well, I've decided, uh, I'm going to drop your biochemistry class.
Professor: Oh? Well, we'll just have to see about that! Why ever would you want to do such a thing?
Student: Well, you know, on the last test . . .
Professor: Oh, I know, you blew that last unit test! But you still have a . . . hang on a second, let me take a look on my computer . . . Well, you had a B+ average on your first two unit tests, so, you still have a C average . . .
Student: Well, I talked it over with my advisor, Doctor Delaney, and he said, since I'm taking five classes this semester, he thought it would be a good idea if I dropped this one and concentrated on my four other classes . . .
Professor: Did he now. Well, with all due respect to Doctor Delaney, I couldn't agree with him less. You've already put a lot of work into this class, you're not doing that badly, and . . . well, I'm just not of the opinion that you should drop it. Tell me, what's your major, Scott?
Student: Pre-medicine. But . . .
Professor: There you are! You've got to have a good grade in biochemistry if you're majoring in pre-med, and if you want to be a doctor, you need to know this stuff!
Student: I know, and I know I have to take biochem at some point. It's just that . . . well, for the first few weeks of this class, I felt like I pretty much understood what you were talking about. It was hard, yeah, but I was keeping up. Then we got to that unit on atomic structure, molecular structure, and . . .
Professor: You're right, that's . . . there are some difficult concepts in that unit. But . . . here's the good news! That's as hard as it gets! It's all downhill from there!

Student: Well, my math skills are, um, a little weak, and . . . well, I never realized how much math you need to do biochemistry . . .

Professor: Of course you should have realized that. Trying to understand science without understanding math . . . it's like trying to study music without being able to read notes.

Student: Right. So . . . here's what I'm thinking. I drop biochemistry now, take a couple of math courses, and then I'll retake your class in a year or so . . .

Professor: Listen, Scott, I think all you really need is a little help. Do you know my teaching assistant, Peter Kim? No? Well, he does some tutoring. I think if you spent an hour or two a week working with Peter, he could get you over the rough patches. We still have four more unit tests and a final exam, so there are plenty of opportunities for you to get your grades up.

Student: Well, I . . . the thing is . . . today is the last day I can drop a class and not get a grade . . . I just worry that . . . if I don't do well . . .

Professor: Stop thinking those negative thoughts, Scott! You're going to get a little help and you're going to do just fine!

Narrator: Now get ready to answer the questions. You may use your notes to help you.

Narrator: Question 1: What course does Scott want to drop?

Narrator: Listen again to part of the conversation.

Professor: Did he now? Well, with all due respect to Doctor Delaney, I couldn't agree with him less. You've already put a lot of work into this class, you're not doing that badly, and . . . well, I'm just not of the opinion that you should drop it. Tell me, what's your major, Scott?

Narrator: Question 2: What does Professor Calhoun mean when she says this?

Professor: . . . with all due respect to Doctor Delaney, I couldn't agree with him less.

Narrator: Question 3: What does Professor Calhoun say about her class?

Narrator: Question 4: What does Professor Calhoun suggest that Scott do?

Narrator: Question 5: Which of the following best describes Professor Calhoun's attitude towards Scott?

Narrator: Listen to a conversation between two students.

Student A: Hi, Martha. What brings you up to the library?

Student B: Oh, I've just been using the *Encyclopedia of Art,* looking up some terms for my art history class. What about you, Stanley?

Student A: Well, I've got these two papers due at the end of this term, and I, uh, I've been trying to get an early start on them by collecting some references and getting some data.

Student B: Really? For the end of the term? Wow, you really like to get a jump on things, don't you!

Student A: Yeah, well, I just know how crazy things get at the last moment. Matter of fact, I've spent most of the day here.

Student B: Well, you oughta be ready for a break then. Wanna go get some coffee and grab something to eat?

Student A: Sure, that, uh, that sounds pretty good. I could use some caffeine, actually. Let me just get my stuff together and . . . hey, where are my notes?

Student B: What notes?

Student A: The notes I spent all day working on—I thought they were in my backpack.

Student B: You mean you lost your notebook?

Student A: No, uh, I don't use a notebook—I take notes on index cards. That's really the best way to . . .

Student B: Okay, well, just think about where you could've left them, Stanley. Focus. Retrace your steps in your mind since you came in the library.

Student A: Uhhh, let's see. I think I came in here, first, to the reference room, and I was using one of those computers over against the other wall there . . . but I don't think I made any notes when I was down here. After that . . . let's see, I, uh, think I went up to the stacks . . .

Student B: Stacks? What do you mean, the stacks?

Student A: You know, the, uh, book stacks . . . that's what they call the main part of the library, where most of the books are shelved.

Student B: Okay, well, maybe your cards are up there, then.

Student A: I don't think so. No. After that, I was in the periodicals room up on the third floor. I was sitting in a cubicle up there, looking at some journals, some psychology journals, and . . . well, I definitely remember I was taking notes then . . .

Student B: And you haven't had them since then?

Student A: No, no, I don't think so. Let me run up to the periodicals room and check. I'll bet they're still in that cubicle. When I get back, we can go down to the snack bar in the basement and get some coffee.

Student B: Are you kidding? They have some of the worst coffee on campus—maybe in the world—down there. It tastes like mud! Let's walk over to Williams Street and find some decent coffee.

Student A: All right, wherever. I'll be right back.

Narrator: Now get ready to answer the questions. You may use your notes to help you.

Narrator: Question 6: Why did Martha come to the library?

Narrator: Question 7: What did Stanley misplace?

Narrator: Listen again to part of the conversation:

Student A: Well, I've got these two papers due at the end of this term, and I, uh, I've been trying to get an early start on them by collecting some references and getting data.

Student B: Really? For the end of the term? Wow, you really like to get a jump on things, don't you!

Narrator: Question 8: What does Martha mean when she says this?

Student B: Wow, you really like to get a jump on things, don't you!

Narrator: Question 9: According to Stanley, what does the term "stacks" refer to?

Narrator: Question 10: Where will Stanley go next?

Narrator: Listen to part of a lecture in an elementary education class.

Professor: Okay, in the time we have left today, I wanna talk about the article I asked you to read over the weekend, the one, um, about writing and reading skills. First we'll talk about writing skills, then, uh, later, if we have time, we'll talk about reading too.

One point I want to make before we begin . . . when we talk about stages of writing development, these stages are not associated with grade levels. A child doesn't necessarily enter the first stage in, ummm, say, kindergarten. Children develop these skills at their own pace, in their own way. But, a little encouragement from parents and teachers helps children move through these stages faster.

Well, as you remember, the article first talked about "writing readiness." This is behavior that . . . well, these are ways that children tell us they're almost ready to start writing. There are several signs of this. One early sign is making random marks on the page, sometimes accompanied by drawings. To the child, these marks and drawings may represent a story or a message. Another sign is *mock handwriting.* Mock handwriting. Some children create lines of wavy scribbles, pages and pages of them, sometimes. These look like cursive writing, and children may move their hands from left to right, the way they've seen adults do. The scribbles consist of lots of loopy o's, often, and dashes and, and dots and squiggles. Some kids produce symbols that look more like printing, but with *invented letters,* marks that look like letters but aren't, really. Another sign of writing readiness—the author doesn't mention it, but I remember my own kids did this when they were preschoolers—they ask adults to help them write something by guiding their hands. Oh, and I wanted to mention that one thing you want to do at this stage is to build children's fine motor skills, build up their finger muscles. One good way to do this is to have children use scissors and play with modeling clay—this builds up those muscles.

So, the system that the author uses to describe the stages of learning to write, it's not the only one you'll encounter. Many experts divide the process into more stages, and they use different names for the stages. The system used in this article, though . . . it's pretty clear, don't you think, and it's pretty easy to understand for both teachers and parents.

In this system, the first stage is the symbolic stage. In this stage, children string together pretty much random letters and numbers that they happen to be familiar with. Let's say a child wants to write this sentence. I'll put it on the board.

MY SISTER LIKES TO RIDE HER BIKE.

A child in the symbolic stage may try to write this sentence by writing a series of random letters or numbers. The child may write oh, "PZOL2TX," for example. Children at this stage, they've figured out that letters are symbols for sounds, they just haven't figured out which letters go with which sound. Writing in this stage is, uh, intelligible only to the writer. It doesn't mean anything to anyone else. It could mean "pizza," it could mean "Big Bird." Sometimes it doesn't even make sense to the writers. Sometimes, kids write something like this and then ask an adult, "What did I write?"

The next stage of writing is called the phonemic stage. Children in this stage are beginning to understand letter-sound relationships, so they write the most distinct sounds, the dominant sounds they hear in a word, usually the first consonant sound, and sometimes the final consonant sound in a word. A child in the phonemic stage might write our sentence this way:

MSSRLKRDRBK

After this comes the transitional stage. Children at this stage of writing record every speech sound they hear when they sound out words to themselves. They're often able to distinguish where one word ends and another begins. Children may also use words that are familiar to them from their own reading. I'll put an example of this on the board.

MI STER LIK TO RID HIR BIK

Of course, children who are learning to write English . . . well, they learn basic phonics rules, basic word-attack skills, and they tend to think that those rules work all the time. In fact, they only work about 65% of the time in English. It's easier for kids to learn to write in say, Finnish,

or Spanish, which are more or less phonetic languages. The relationship between written symbols and sounds is closer in those languages. Of course, it's much harder in languages like Chinese, where there is virtually no relationship between written symbols and sounds.

Okay, the fourth stage is called the conventional stage. In this stage, children apply their knowledge of vocabulary, spelling, grammar . . . the basic rules of writing. Children in this stage sometimes make mistakes, but in general their writing is effective and correct. Let me write that on the board and you'll see . . .

MY SISTRE LIKE TO RIDE HER BIKE.

A couple of points I want to make about the teaching of writing skills, and I'll have to make them quickly—one is, communication should be the main focus for writing. If children can express what they're thinking through their writing, then the writing activity is a success. Another point: writing activities should be fun. Most young kids love to write, and the best way to keep them interested in writing over the years is to make writing enjoyable.

Well, obviously I'm not going to have enough time in this class to discuss what the article says about reading skills, so I'm going to save that for our next meeting. I want to give that discussion the time it deserves. Any comments before we stop for the day?

Narrator: Now get ready to answer the questions. You may use your notes to help you.

Narrator: Question 11: Which of the following activities are signs of "writing readiness" in children?

Narrator: Question 12: What does the speaker imply about the system mentioned in the article that the students read, which was used to describe the development of writing skills?

Narrator: Question 13: The speaker mentions four stages in the development of writing skills. Put these stages in the correct order, beginning with the earliest stage.

Narrator: Question 14: Why does the speaker mention Spanish and Finnish?

Narrator: Question 15: Which of the following is the best example of writing done by a child in the transitional stage?

Narrator: Question 16: Which of these statements about writing assignments for young children would the professor probably agree with?

Narrator: Listen to a lecture in an astronomy class.

Professor: Did you know that, when you look up into the night sky, a lot of the stars you see are actually not single stars? To the naked eye, they look like one star, but they're actually double stars.

So, what are double stars? Well, first you should realize that there are two types of double stars. One is called an optical pair, or a line-of-sight double. These are two stars that just seem to be close together when we look at them from Earth. They might really be thousands of light years away from each other. The other type is a true double star, a binary-star system. These consist of two or more stars that are in each other's gravity fields. They, uh, in other words, they orbit each other. Sir William Herschell, in 1803, was the first to discover that some stars were really double stars, and he coined the term "binary star."

There are a lot of double stars out there. A surprising number. Most astronomers think about a quarter of all stars are binary stars, and some astronomers estimate as many as 75% of all stars will turn out to be binary stars. Well, I say binary, but actually, probably 10% of all multiple-star systems have more than two stars. Some have three stars—ternary stars, they're called—and some have four, five, even more.

Some astronomers think that binary stars are more likely to have planets than single-star systems. I've always wondered what it would be like to live on a planet in a solar system around one of these stars. Maybe you'd have two suns in the sky at the same time. Maybe you'd have a sunset and a sunrise at the same time. Imagine that! Or maybe one of the stars would always be in the sky, and there would never be any night on your planet. Aliens from a double-star system who visited Earth would probably find our skies . . . pretty boring.

One of the nice things about double stars is that many are visible with just binoculars or a small telescope. They're among the most interesting objects that an amateur can look at—and . . . uh, I think they're also among the prettiest sights in the night sky. Some binaries, though, are impossible to see as double stars unless you have a powerful telescope. This is either because the two stars are really close together or because one star is much brighter than its companion. By the way, when you have one star brighter than the other, that star's called the *primary,* and the dimmer one is called the *comes,* which means "companion" in Latin.

One of the most famous of all double-star systems is made up of the stars Mizar and Alcor. It's the second-to-the-last star in the handle of the Big Dipper, the one at the bend of the handle. If you get away from city lights, both stars are clearly visible through binoculars, or even with the naked eye. In fact, in ancient times, it was a test of excellent vision to be able to see both stars.

As it turns out, though, Mizar-Alcor is not a true binary-star system at all. It's one of those optical pairs I was talking about. The two stars are quite far apart and don't orbit each other. However, much to astronomers' surprise, when they looked at Mizar-Alcor with a spectroscopic telescope, they discovered that in fact, it was a "double-double" star system. In other words, both Mizar and Alcor, they're . . . uh, actually both binary stars.

One type of binary star is called an eclipsing binary. The star Algol is one of those—don't confuse Algol with the star Alcor in the Big Dipper that we already discussed. Anyway, Algol is usually a fairly bright star, but for a few hours every three days it dims to one-third its normal brightness. That's because the dimmer secondary star—the *comes*—moves between the brighter primary star and the Earth.

One of the reasons I like double stars is because I like to check out the colors. I said before that binary stars are pretty sights. They are particularly pretty, I think, when the pair of stars are of contrasting colors. You often get this when the two stars are of different ages. Think of two jewels of different colors lying on a piece of black velvet! That's what they look like to me. There's a double star named Albireo. One of the stars in this system is gold and the other blue, at least to my eyes. Other people have told me that, to them, the stars appear yellow and green, or even white and purple. Next week, when we visit the observatory again, you'll have a chance to look at Albireo for yourself, and you can let me know what colors you see.

Narrator: Now get ready to answer the questions. You may use your notes to help you.

Narrator: Question 17: What is the main purpose of this lecture?

Narrator: Question 18: According to most astronomers, about what percentage of all stars are double stars?

Narrator: Question 19: According to the speaker, what does the term *comes* mean in astronomy?

Narrator: Question 20: How many stars make up Mizar-Alcor?

Narrator: Question 21: How does the speaker describe double stars of contrasting colors?

Narrator: Question 22: The speaker mentions a number of different double-star systems. Match these systems with their descriptions.

Narrator: Listen to a lecture in a marketing class.

Professor: Okay, next we're going to talk about a process that's important to all marketing managers—it's called product portfolio analysis. First off, what do we mean by a *product portfolio?* Well, a product portfolio is the combination of all the products that a firm sells when considered in terms of their performance. It's a little like, well, like an investment portfolio. You know, investors want a balanced group of stocks: some stocks that are safe but always productive, some that are high-risk but have the chance of making lots of money quickly. So, the marketing manager wants this same kind of balance—some good old standbys, some products that show promise, and some products that may still be under development but have a good payoff potential.

There are a couple of methods used to analyze product portfolios. One's the General Electric/Shell method. Another is the BCG method, which we'll be looking at today. This system was devised by the Boston Consulting Group—that's why it's called the *BCG* method. It's also called the Boston Box or, uh, sometimes the Growth-Share Matrix. This method uses a grid, a box divided into four quadrants. Each quadrant has a rather . . . well, picturesque name: Star, Cash Cow, Problem Child, and Dog.

Okay, to get this into perspective, let's imagine we all work in the marketing department of a big corporation. We want to analyze our product portfolio. Our first step is to identify the various SBUs—those are Strategic Business Units. You can define an SBU as a unit of a company that has its own separate mission, its own . . . goals, if you will. An SBU can be a division of a company, a line of products, even an individual brand—it all depends on how the company is organized. So, now, we can classify our SBUs according to this grid.

Let's say we have four SBUs. SBU #1 makes digital cell phones. The market for this product is hot and SBU #1 has a nice share of this market. SBU #1's product is a *star.* Then let's say that SBU #2 makes chicken soup. There's no growth in the chicken soup market right now, but SBU #2's good old chicken soup is a steady performer. It provides a dependable flow of "milk" for our company, so this SBU is a *cash cow.* Okay, then let's say there is a growing demand for a new kind of athletic shoe, and SBU #3 makes this kind of shoe. Unfortunately, SBU #3's shoes aren't selling all that well. This SBU is called a *problem child.* Finally, let's say SBU #4 makes shaving cream, and there's no growth in that area. SBU #4's shaving cream is not exactly a hot product anyway; it has only a small fraction of the shaving cream market. So SBU #4, it's what's called a *dog.*

Now, once we've classified our SBUs, is the portfolio analysis over? No, it's just starting. We have to decide what to do with this information—whether to commit more of the company's resources into marketing a product, or less, or the same as before. A few years ago, the Australian marketing expert Langfield-Smith identified four basic strategies that companies can adopt to deal with SBUs. We can

build by aggressively trying to increase market share . . . even if it means lower short-term profits. We'd use this strategy to try to turn a cash cow into a star. We can **hold,** preserving our market share. This strategy tries to ensure that cash cows remain cash cows. We can **harvest.** This means that we reduce the amount of investment in an SBU. Why? To maximize short-term profits. This may actually turn stars into cash cows. The last strategy is to **divest.** In other words, the company sells off or kills off dogs, and possibly some problem children.

Of course, all companies want to market stars—who wouldn't? But stars are vulnerable—all competing companies are trying to knock our telephone out of its role as a star and replace it with their own. How do we maintain our product's star status? More advertising? Lower prices? New features? And what do we do to move our athletic shoes from problem child position to star position? How much are we willing to spend to make that happen?

And what about cash cows? Not all SBUs can become stars—but cash cows have value too. Chicken soup may not be an exciting, high-growth market, but it does provide us with a stream of cash. Maybe we can use the cash flow from our cow to finance the development of stars.

Then there are dogs. Now, some marketing experts think a company should get rid of dogs and concentrate on projects that are more profitable. In my opinion, though, dogs may have a place in a portfolio. Products with low share of low-growth markets may appeal to customers who, uh, buy just because of price—bargain-hunters, in other words. And dogs don't cost a company much. There's little or no money spent on advertising dogs or on improving the product. Our SBU #4 can simply place its shaving cream on the shelves of retail stores.

Well, when we meet again—Monday, I guess—I'm going to give you the product portfolios of some real companies. We'll break into small groups and classify SBUs according to the system we talked about today, and make recommendations about how company resources should be spent to market these products.

Narrator: Now get ready to answer the questions. You may use your notes to help you.

Narrator: Question 23: Which of the following is NOT one of the terms for the method the speaker uses for classifying SBUs?

Narrator: Question 24: How does the speaker classify the SBU that makes athletic shoes?

Narrator: Question 25: Why is the term *cash cow* used to describe some SBUs?

Narrator: Question 26: Which of these classification changes would probably most please the marketing manager of the firm that owns this SBU?

Narrator: Question 27: In this lecture, the professor describes the marketing strategies of Langfield- Smith. Indicate whether each of the following is a strategy that Smith lists.

Narrator: Question 28: What is the speaker's opinion of SBUs known as "dogs"?

Narrator: Listen to a discussion in a marine biology class.

Professor: Good afternoon. In today's lecture, we'll be talking about a, umm, a truly remarkable creature, the humpback whale. The humpback, as you may know, is not the largest member of the whale family. That distinction belongs to the blue whale, which is, in fact, the largest animal on earth. But humpbacks *do* have an amazing talent. Anyone know what that is?

Student A: Are they the ones that, uh, sing?

Professor: That's right, they're the opera singers of the animal kingdom. People first became aware of this in the late sixties, in 1968, when a marine biologist by the name of Roger Payne lowered a microphone into the ocean. He really didn't know what to expect. It turns out, the ocean is a very noisy place. He heard all kinds of sounds, sounds from dolphins, from other types of whales, but . . . the weirdest, most complex songs of all came from humpback whales. Hang on a minute . . . okay, um, listen to this: . . . Isn't that haunting, mournful music?

Student B: Professor, how do they do that? How do they make those noises?

Professor: Good question, because, well, we know that whales don't have vocal cords. We know that no air escapes during their songs. We know that their mouths don't move when they sing. But we still aren't exactly sure how they produce the sounds.

Humpbacks actually have two kinds of calls. One is a low-frequency sound, a sound with a relatively simple structure with just a few variations. These low-pitched sounds can be heard from . . . well, at least a few hundred kilometers away, and quite possibly, from much farther than that. These calls probably carry very little information. They probably just mean, "Hey! There's a humpbacked whale here!" It's the other kind of call, the high-frequency sounds that have a lot of variation, that seem to contain a lot of information. These are meant for whales in the . . . well, whales that are right in the neighborhood. This type of call is what we generally think of when we think of humpbacks' songs.

The most basic unit of humpback music is a single sound, or *element*. That might be a low moan, a chirp, a roaring sound, a trill, a grunt, a whistle, a shriek. These elements are arranged into simple repeating patterns called *phrases*, which generally consist of three or four elements. Phrases are repeated several times. A collection of phases are . . . they're called a *theme*. The singer moves from one theme to the next without even pausing. There can be up to seven or eight themes in a song, and they're always sung in exactly the same order. The songs last from ten to twenty minutes. After singing the last theme, the whale surfaces for a breath and then he—it's generally the young males who sing—then he starts all over again. Sometimes they'll do this for up to ten hours at a time!

Student B: So they sing all the time?

Professor: No, you see, whales migrate thousands of miles each year. During the summer they migrate to their cold-water feeding grounds. During their winter breeding season, they travel to the warm waters around Hawaii, in the Caribbean, off the coast of Mexico. They only sing during their four-month breeding season, and then they sing more at night than during the day. The other eight months of the year, when they're migrating or in their feeding grounds . . . they're practically silent then.

Members of the same group of whales always sing the same song. Atlantic whales have one song, northern Pacific whales another, and southern Pacific whales still another. But what's surprising is that these songs evolve from year to year. Isn't that incredible! After eight months of traveling and feeding, the whales return to the warm waters where they mate, and they're all singing a new song. The new song has echoes of the previous year's song, some of the themes are the same, but each year there are also completely new themes. And each whale in the group sings the new song the same way. Within about eight years, the whales create a totally new song. None of the themes are the same as they were eight years previously.

Student A: I'd like to know what these songs mean. Or do they mean anything?

Professor: Well, you're not the only one who would like to know that! Some researchers think the males are singing to attract females. Some think they are singing to warn off other males that get too close.

Student A: Since the humpbacks change their songs every year, well, maybe they're singing about what they've done that year, about where they've been, what they've seen. Do you think that's possible?

Professor: You mean, that their songs are some form of oral history? Well . . . frankly, your guess is as good as anyone else's!

Narrator: Now get ready to answer the questions. You may use your notes to help you.

Narrator: Question 29: What is not known about the songs of the humpback whale?

Narrator: Question 30: In this lecture, the speaker describes two types of calls made by the humpback whale. Indicate whether each of the following is a characteristic of the low-frequency call or of the high-frequency call.

Narrator: Question 31: The speaker analyzes the music of the humpback whale by breaking it down into its component parts. Arrange this list of the parts of the humpback's music, beginning with the simplest and shortest part and moving to the longest and most complex.

Narrator: Question 32: How long does a humpback whale take to sing a complete song?

Narrator: Question 33: When do humpback whales sing the most?

Narrator: Listen again to part of the lecture.

Student A: Since the humpbacks change their songs every year, well, maybe they're singing about what they've done that year, about where they've been, what they've seen. Do you think that's possible?

Professor: You mean, that their songs are some form of oral history? Well . . . frankly, your guess is as good as anyone else's.

Narrator: Question 34: What does the professor mean when she says this?

Professor: Well . . . frankly, your guess is as good as anyone else's!

Narrator: This is the end of the Listening Review Test.

[CD 7 Track 2]

Note-taking Exercise 1

Narrator: Directions: Listen to a list of words and phrases. Write down your own abbreviations of these words in the spaces below. This vocabulary comes from a lecture on business organizations that you will be listening to in order to improve your note-taking skills. When you have finished, compare your notes with those of a classmate. Check for similarities and differences in what you wrote. You can also compare your notes with those in the Answer Key.

Listening Tutorial: Note Taking

1.	business organizations	11.	distinct legal entities
2.	sole proprietorship	12.	artificial persons
3.	partnership	13.	stockholders
4.	corporation	14.	profit
5.	limited liability company	15.	investments
6.	advantage	16.	double taxation
7.	corporate tax	17.	executive
8.	sole agent	18.	board of directors
9.	responsibility	19.	popular
10.	legal documents	20.	hybrid

[CD 7 Track 3]

Note-taking Exercise 3

Narrator: Directions: Listen to the following sentences. Take notes on these sentences using abbreviations and symbols and omitting unimportant words. These sentences come from a lecture on business organizations that you will be listening to in order to improve your note-taking skills. When you have finished taking notes, compare your notes with those of a classmate. Check for similarities and differences in what you wrote. You can also compare your notes with the sample notes in the Answer Key.

1. Today we're going to talk about the most common forms of business structures, of, uh, business organizations.
2. So first, let's, um, discuss the sole proprietorship, the sole proprietorship . . . did you know it's the most common form of business organization? Also the simplest.
3. Basically, there's not much difference between a sole proprietorship and a partnership except that a partnership is owned by more than one person.
4. In some partnerships, there are *silent partners,* partners who invest money in the company but have nothing to do with management decisions.
5. Corporations are . . . this is an important concept . . . distinct legal entities. They're even called "artificial persons."
6. Most shareholders don't bother to attend, and often give their votes . . . uh . . . assign their votes to the top corporate officers. This is called *voting by proxy.*
7. The day-to-day operations of the corporation are performed by the executive officers, and by the corporate bureaucracy.
8. By the way, the CEO is often the chairman of the board as well as being the top executive officer.
9. An LLC, as it's called, it's a . . . a hybrid organization, it combines some of the best features of a partnership and those of a corporation.

[CD 7 Track 4]

Note-taking Exercise 5

Narrator: Directions: Listen to a lecture on business organizations. The lecture will be given in short sections. Take notes on each section. After each section, answer the questions **Yes** or **No** to find out if you are taking notes on the important points in the lecture. (The more **Yes** answers you have, the more complete your notes are.) When you have finished taking notes, compare your notes with those of a classmate. Check for similarities and differences in what you wrote. You can also compare your notes with the sample notes in the Answer Key.

Narrator: Section 1

Professor: Today we're going to talk about the most common forms of business structures, of, uh, business organizations. When I used to give this lecture, oh, just a few years ago, really, I would have said the, uh, the *three* most common forms of businesses: the sole proprietorship, the partnership, and the corporation. Now, though, you . . . uh . . . you really need to add limited liability company to that list. It's . . . it's a new animal, a new way to structure a business that's becoming more and more popular.

Narrator: Section 2
Professor: So first, let's, um, discuss the sole proprietorship, the sole proprietorship . . . did you know it's the most common form of business organization? Also the simplest. As the term *sole proprietorship* implies, there's one owner, and he or she is the boss, period. There may be many employees, but only one boss. You may be wondering, how does someone start up a sole proprietorship? Well, the economist Paul Samuelson, in his textbook, he gives the example of a person who wakes up one morning and says, "I think I'll start making toothpaste in my basement." Samuelson says a sole proprietorship begins with that moment of decision. One advantage of this form of organization is that there is no separate tax on the sole proprietorship, and that's a *huge* advantage. A sole proprietorship is taxed at personal income rates and those . . . those are generally lower than the, uh, the corporate tax rate. Now, the main *dis*advantage of a sole proprietorship is that the owner is legally liable for all the company's debts. If, say, a company gets sued, or, uh, can't pay back a loan, then the owner is liable. The people suing the company can come after the owner's personal assets, like his or her house or car.

Narrator: Section 3
Professor: Now, another type of business organization is the partnership. Basically, there's not much difference between a sole proprietorship and a partnership except that a partnership is owned by more than one person. The tax advantage of operating as a partnership is the same as you'd get as a sole proprietorship.

How about liability? Each partner has the right to act as the sole agent for the partnership. How does this work? Say one partner signs a contract to buy, oh, 500 widgets from company A. He tells his partner what a great deal he got on the widgets, and she says, "Oh no! I just signed a contract to buy 500 widgets from Company B!" Are those contracts legally binding? You bet, because both partners can act as sole agents. So . . . in a partnership, one partner is liable not only for his own actions, but also for the actions of all the other partners.

Who's in charge in a partnership? In most partnerships, partners share responsibility for day-to-day operations. In some partnerships, there are *silent partners,* partners who invest money in the company but have nothing to do with management decisions.

Narrator: Section 4
Professor: Okay, then, that brings us to the corporation. This is the most complex form of business organization, also the most expensive to set up. You need to fill out legal documents called *articles of incorporation* and pay a fee, and it can be . . . well, pretty expensive. Still, almost all large business are organized as corporations.

The most important thing about a corporation is the concept of *limited liability.* Corporations are . . . this is an important concept . . . distinct legal entities. They're even called "artificial persons." What's that mean? Well, a corporation can open a bank account, own property, get sued, all under its own name, just like a person, an individual. The

owners—they're called *stockholders*—share in the company's profits, but their liability is limited to what they invest. See the advantage? If a corporation goes broke, then, sure, stockholders lose their investment, the money they invested in the company's stock—but not their personal property, not their cars or houses.

Now, unlike sole proprietorships and partnerships, corporations have to pay taxes, taxes on their profits. Not only that, but stockholders, they have to pay taxes on dividends, on the money that corporations pay them. This is . . . uh . . . it's really double taxation, and it's one of the disadvantages of organizing your business as a corporation.

Let's, uh, talk about the structure of corporations. There are three important elements. The owners—that is, the shareholders, have ultimate control. There are regular meetings of shareholders, usually once a year, and they vote on important issues. But, in reality, you usually get only the biggest shareholders at these meetings. Most shareholders don't bother to attend, and often give their votes, uh, assign their votes to the top corporate officers. This is called *voting by proxy.* Okay, now, corporations also have a board of directors. This board—oh, and I should mention this, the board is elected by the shareholders—it's responsible for making major decisions. The board appoints the chief executive officer . . . and it, uh, sets policy. However, the day-to-day operations of the corporation are performed by the executive officers and by the corporate bureaucracy. By the way, the CEO is often the chairman of the board as well as being the top executive officer.

Narrator: Section 5
Professor: Now, remember I said that today there are four important forms of business organization. An increasingly popular form of organization for smaller businesses is the limited liability company. An LLC, as it's called, it's a . . . a hybrid organization, it combines some of the best features of a partnership and those of a corporation. It eliminates that double taxation I mentioned. But, uh, I'm afraid I'll have to wait till our next meeting to talk about the LLC because we're out of time today . . .

[CD 7 Track 5]

Note-taking Exercise 6
Narrator: Directions: Listen again to the lecture on business organizations and take notes. After you have listened to the lecture, use your notes to answer the True/False questions and the fill-in-the-blank questions at the end of the lecture. Sample lecture notes appear in the Answer Key.

Professor: Today we're going to talk about the most common forms of business structures, of, uh, business organizations. When I used to give this lecture, oh, just a few years ago, really, I would have said the, uh, the *three* most common forms of businesses: the sole proprietorship, the partnership, and the corporation. Now, though, you, uh, you really need to add limited liability company to that list. It's . . . it's a new animal, a new way to structure a business that's becoming more and more popular.

So first, let's, um, discuss the sole proprietorship, the sole proprietorship . . . did you know it's the most common form of business organization? Also the simplest. As the term *sole proprietorship* implies, there's one owner, and he or she is the boss, period. There may be many employees, but only one boss. You may be wondering, how does someone start up a sole proprietorship? Well, the economist Paul

Samuelson, in his textbook, he gives the example of a person who wakes up one morning and says, "I think I'll start making toothpaste in my basement." Samuelson says a sole proprietorship begins with that moment of decision. One advantage of this form of organization is that there is no separate tax on the sole proprietorship, and that's a huge advantage. A sole proprietorship is taxed at personal income rates and those . . . those are generally lower than the, uh, the corporate tax rate. Now, the main disadvantage of a sole proprietorship is that the owner is legally liable for all the company's debts. If, say, a company gets sued, or, uh, can't pay back a loan, then the owner is liable. The people suing the company can come after the owner's personal assets, like his or her house or car.

Now, another type of business organization is the partnership. Basically, there's not much difference between a sole proprietorship and a partnership except that a partnership is owned by more than one person. The tax advantage of operating as a partnership is the same as you'd get as a sole proprietorship.

How about liability? Each partner has the right to act as the sole agent for the partnership. How does this work? Say one partner signs a contract to buy, oh, 500 widgets from company A. He tells his partner what a great deal he got on the widgets, and she says, "Oh no! I just signed a contract to buy 500 widgets from Company B!" Are those contracts legally binding? You bet, because both partners can act as sole agents. So . . . in a partnership, one partner is liable not only for his own actions, but also for the actions of all the other partners.

Who's in charge in a partnership? In most partnerships, partners share responsibility for day-to-day operations. In some partnerships, there are *silent partners*, partners who invest money in the company but have nothing to do with management decisions.

Okay, then, that brings us to the corporation. This is the most complex form of business organization, also the most expensive to set up. You need to fill out legal documents called *articles of incorporation* and pay a fee, and it can be . . . well, pretty expensive. Still, almost all large business are organized as corporations.

The most important thing about a corporation is the concept of *limited liability*. Corporations are . . . this is an important concept . . . distinct legal entities. They're even called "artificial persons." What's that mean? Well, a corporation can open a bank account, own property, get sued, all under its own name, just like a person, an individual. The owners—they're called *stockholders*—share in the company's profits, but their liability is limited to what they invest. See the advantage? If a corporation goes broke, then, sure, stockholders lose their investment, the money they invested in the company's stock—but not their personal property, not their cars or houses.

Now, unlike sole proprietorships and partnerships, corporations have to pay taxes, taxes on their profits. Not only that, but stockholders, they have to pay taxes on dividends, on the money that corporations pay them. This is, uh, it's really double taxation, and it's one of the disadvantages of organizing your business as a corporation.

Let's, uh, talk about the structure of corporations. There are three important elements. The owners, that is, the shareholders, have ultimate control. There are regular meetings of shareholders, usually once a year, and they vote on important issues. But, in reality, you usually get only the biggest shareholders at these meetings. Most shareholders don't bother to attend, and often give their votes . . . uh . . . assign their votes to the top corporate officers. This is called *voting by proxy*. Okay, now, corporations also have a board of directors. This board—oh, and I should mention this, the board is elected by the shareholders—it's responsible for making major decisions. The board appoints the chief executive officer . . . and it, uh, sets policy. However, the day-to-day operations of the corporation are performed by the executive officers and by the corporate bureaucracy. By the way, the CEO is often the chairman of the board as well as being the top executive officer.

Now, remember I said that today there are *four* important forms of business organization. An increasingly popular form of organization for smaller businesses is the limited liability company. An LLC, as it's called, it's a . . . a hybrid organization, it combines some of the best features of a partnership and those of a corporation. It eliminates that double taxation I mentioned. But, uh, I'm afraid I'll have to wait till our next meeting to talk about the LLC because we're out of time today . . .

Narrator: This is the end of the Guide to Listening.

[CD 7 Track 6]

Section 3: Guide to Speaking

The Independent Speaking Task

Sample Responses for Independent Speaking

Narrator: Sample Response 1
Speaker: When I was young, I used to play rugby. I was a member of the . . . of our national team . . . the junior team from my republic in the Soviet Union. My team, uh, we became the junior champions of rugby of the Soviet Union. It was the most important and happiest time in my life. I . . . it was most important event in my life because I made my first big steps in rugby. Also, because at that time I was only fourteen years and it was . . . well, you could say the biggest success in my life. I was happy and I was proud of my success . . . of our team success. These events will . . . uh, always be a pleasure to remember in my life as the best time I ever had. Even the success I have had in science and business cannot compare to this moment.

Narrator: Sample Response 2
Speaker: For me the most important day in my love, in my life was a day when I . . . um . . . got accepted to Simmons College. Um . . . um . . . I got accepted to the . . . um . . . teaching program and it was very exciting . . . um . . . during the symposium important for me because it took almost two years for me . . . um . . . to get accepted to the program and during this two years I had to take the tests and I had challenges because I had to take the tests two times . . . um . . . because of various reasons . . . um . . . so . . . um having seen that I got this . . . um . . . test (posital) (?) and I got accepted it was worthwhile and on top of that . . . ah . . . during this two years I worked hard on getting a job and I was eligible enough to be offered the job and the great thing also for financial reason is . . . um . . . to be eligible for . . . um . . . scholarship, which was a rare scholarship offered to . . . ah (foreigner?). So it was . . . um . . . all over . . . um . . . a great day for me.

Narrator: Sample Response 3
Speaker: The most important day in my life . . . um . . . I think . . . um . . . the day I . . . I got married to my wife. Um

. . . because . . . um before I met her I was thinking a lot a thing about how different between us and . . . um . . . um . . . I was thinking about . . . ah . . . culture, country, religions . . . uh . . . a lot of thing even though indi . . . indication and . . . ah . . . made me think just . . . um . . . like a . . . what a . . . was gonna happen . . . just don't expect too much about . . . about life and . . . um . . . the first time that I have trying to move to the university . . . to the U.S., I . . . ah . . . changed my mind a little bit about . . . ahmmm . . . how to expect something about between us and finally I had a chance to married to her and made me more . . . um . . . happy and I think the day that most important days in my . . . ah . . . my marriage day to her and . . . um . . . make me so happy . . . and . . . and . . .

Narrator: Sample Response 4
Speaker: Most important day I . . . especially . . . when have my first baby borned. It was . . . amazed. . . . For the, uh . . . is um, beginning for . . . the . . . uh . . . for big . . . promise? Many time ago, uh, several more or less important day of the, of the life, uhhhh . . . other day I go my, uhhh, my first work, I was . . . And uh, most important . . . for example, as holiday . . . holiday? . . . the people go . . . the people umm . . . to the house . . .

[CD 7 TRACK 7]

Exercise: Scoring the Response
Narrator: Response 1
Speaker: The most important day of my life was last . . . last . . . April . . . eh . . . fifteenth when Nicol and I got married. We got married here in the U.S. and, ah, it was a very . . . eh . . . special day. Eh . . . we were very . . . (emotionated?) and excited and . . . eh . . . we were alone because our families were in . . . eh . . . our countries but we invited our friends, best friends, here and . . . ah . . . it was very . . . eh . . . it was very . . . I mean, very . . . um . . . special and . . . and . . . very . . . eh . . . intimate and . . . eh . . . we got married in our place and then . . . we had, we organized a little party with . . . ah . . . Italian food and . . . and wine and an Italian cake and we were happy and all of our friends were happy with us so it was very pretty special day for us.

Narrator: Response 2
Speaker: About most important day . . . uh, that's the day I test the examination . . . for . . . uh, go . . . to go university. It decide our future. If you pass this, this . . . you can go to university and . . . uh, can continue study, so . . . uh, in that day, is . . . very important. So ummm in my country, the education is very different from here . . . when we are in school, there is . . . we have only one, one main exam to pass . . . and so, I . . . for Vietnamese youth, in our life is . . . uh . . . such important day.

Narrator: Response 3
Student: The day . . . a most important in my life was when . . . ah . . . I received the letter from the university in Montreal and . . . ah . . . they accepted me to do my master's degree but not just that, they also . . . ah gave me . . . ah . . . scholarship so that made a big difference in my life because I really wanted to go to a foreign country to study international law and I didn't know if . . . ah . . . I would have been able to do it without all the help and my . . . obviously my brains helped too. So I think . . . um . . . the fact that they accepted me at the university that I really

wanted to go was . . . ah . . . was . . . ah . . . very exciting and made my life very happy because I always dreamt about going and doing a master's degree, living in different country, and I really wanted to do this master's 'cause I thought that coming back to my country with a master's degree from a different country with all the experiences living in and . . . ah . . . writing and speaking in different languages, sharing . . . ah . . . different cultures, could . . . ah . . . benefit a lot my country and . . . ah . . . my professional life.

[CD 7 Track 8]

Independent Speaking Preview Test
Narrator: Directions: The first two tasks in the Speaking Section are Independent Speaking tasks. You have fifteen seconds in which to prepare your responses. When you hear a beep on the Audio Program, you will have forty-five seconds in which to answer the questions. During actual tests, a clock on the screen will tell you how much preparation time or how much response time (speaking time) remains for each question. It is important that you time yourself accurately when you take this preview test. If possible, speak into a microphone and record your response. On an actual test your responses will be recorded and evaluated by trained raters.

Narrator: Task 1. . . . Please listen carefully
Narrator: Describe the person who has had the greatest influence on your life. Explain why this person has had such an important influence on you. Give specific details and examples to support your explanation. Please begin speaking after the beep. [15-second pause, then beep] [45-second pause, then beep] Now please stop speaking.

Narrator: Task 2. . . . Please listen carefully
Narrator: In some university classes, students are graded according to a Pass/Fail system. In other words, the only possible grades that you may receive are P (Pass) or F (Fail). In most classes, however, students are graded according to a more traditional system in which many letter grades can be given (A+, A, A–, B+, etc.). Explain which of these two systems you prefer and why. Include details and examples in your explanation. Please begin speaking after the beep. [15-second pause, then beep] [45-second pause, then beep] Now please stop speaking.

Narrator: This is the end of the Independent Speaking Preview Test.

[CD 7 Track 9]

Lesson 15: Personal Preference Task
Sample
Narrator: Describe the person who has had the greatest influence on your life. Explain why this person has had such an important influence on you. Give specific details and examples to support your explanation.

Speaker: I think the person who has influenced me the most is my brother, my older brother. He's six years older than me and has always been . . . a kind of model. Everyone in my family—actually, everyone who has met my brother—thinks he's the . . . ah, the kindest person who they know.

Why I say that my brother is my most influential person? . . . Well, he's had a big role in . . . in shaping my life. For example, my brother is very good golfer, and when I was quite young, he started taking me to the golf course. He taught me to play. Today, playing golf and watching golf is the way . . . ah, how I relax. Also, after he . . . ah, finished university, my brother studied international law in the United States. Because of him, I've . . . ah, decided to go to university in the United States too.

[CD 7 Track 10]

Exercise 15.4

Narrator: Question 1
Speaker: I'd say that the . . . the most important trip I've ever taken was a trip to Italy. It was a two-week trip, and it was sponsored by my university. We went to Rome, to . . . uh . . . Florence, and then to the Italian Alps, the mountains in the north of Italy. I enjoyed this trip because I have always been interested in Renaissance art, and Florence has some of the best examples of this kind of art, such as Michelangelo's statue *David*. I also enjoyed this trip because of the beautiful scenery, especially the mountain scenery. Oh, and . . . uh, another reason why this was a great trip was the food. I love Italian food!

[CD 7 Track 11]

Exercise 15.5

Narrator: Question 1
Narrator: You are going to give a gift to a friend and you want it to be symbolic of your country. Describe the gift that you would give. Include details and examples to support your explanation. Please begin speaking after the beep. [15-second pause, then beep] [45-second pause, then beep] Now please stop speaking.

Narrator: Question 2
Narrator: Describe your ideal job. Explain why you would like to have this job. Include details and examples to support your explanation. Please begin speaking after the beep. [15-second pause, then beep] [45-second pause, then beep] Now please stop speaking.

Narrator: Question 3
Narrator: Imagine that you have the ability to solve any one problem in the world. Describe which problem you would choose to solve, and explain how you would solve it. Include details and examples to support your explanation. Please begin speaking after the beep. [15-second pause, then beep] [45-second pause, then beep] Now please stop speaking.

[CD 7 Track 12]

Lesson 16: Paired Choice Task

Sample

Narrator: In some university classes, students are graded according to a Pass/Fail system. In other words, the only possible grades that you may receive are P (Pass) or F (Fail). In most classes, however, students are graded according to a more traditional system in which many letter grades can be given (A+, A, A−, B+, etc.). Explain which of these two systems you prefer and why. Include details and examples in your explanation.

Speaker: In my opinion, the letter grades system is the better. I see some advantage in the Pass/Fail system. For example, there is less stress on students, less pressure to try to get good grades. But, uh, personally I like the challenge of grades, of working to get grades. A grade of A+ or A is . . . it's something to aim for, like a goal. Uh, also, grades are a way to compare students, uh, to compare their performances. This can be important in ranking students and later, when students are . . . are looking out for jobs. For example, some businesses and, uh, some government agencies only hire people who are in the tops of their class—if everyone had a *Pass* grade, they couldn't make good decisions about who to hire. So, all in all, I like the letter grades system.

[CD 7 Track 13]

Exercise 16.4

Narrator: Question 1
Speaker: I think I'd rather work in the . . . uh, in the library than in the . . . . than on the Internet. Why do I say this? Well, it's pretty convenient to work at home, on a home computer, and find information on the Web. However, from my experience, not all academic books and journals are available online now, at least not for free, not in my field, anyway—you might have to pay to use some of these journals, subscribe, you know. Also, a lot of the information that is online, it is not really appropriate for university research, it's not really academic. Finally, I just like to go to the library because I see a lot of people that I know there, it's, you know, just more social.

[CD 7 Track 14]

Exercise 16.5

Narrator: Question 1
Narrator: Some students prefer to go to a small college or university, while others prefer to go to a large university. Explain which view you prefer, and why. Include details and examples in your explanation. Please begin speaking after the beep. [15-second pause, then beep] [45-second pause, then beep] Now please stop speaking.

Narrator: Question 2
Narrator: Some people believe that technology has improved life, while other people believe it has not. Explain which view you prefer, and why. Include details and examples in your explanation. Please begin speaking after the beep. [15-second pause, then beep] [45-second pause, then beep] Now please stop speaking.

Narrator: Question 3
Narrator: Because of computers and telephones, it is now possible for many people to work at home. Some people enjoy this, while others would rather work in an office. Explain which of these you prefer. Include details and examples in your explanation. Please begin speaking after the beep. [15-second pause, then beep] [45-second pause, then beep] Now please stop speaking.

[CD 7 Track 15]

The Integrated Speaking Task

Narrator: Now listen to two students discussing the new parking policy.

Student A: So, Brad, are you still going to be parking your car at the stadium next semester?

Student B: Huh? Oh, you mean because of the new parking rules? I dunno. I'm pretty upset about them. I mean, I always parked over at the stadium lot, and . . .

Student A: Me, too . . . why not, it was free? But still, it's not going to cost that much. Just $25 a semester. That's pretty cheap.

Student B: Yeah, but now, you've gotta register your car . . .

Student A: Yeah, so? That's only $10.

Student B: Well, maybe for you that's all it will be, but I have to pay my outstanding parking tickets first. That could be . . . I don't know, a lot, maybe over a hundred bucks. But it's not just the money. That parking lot at the stadium . . . . it's never more than half full anyway. I don't know why the university should suddenly start charging us to park there. I just don't think it's fair . . .

Student A: Oh, I don't really agree. For one thing, it costs the university money to maintain those lots. They have to fix the cracks in the concrete . . . they have to paint lines . . . . plow snow . . .

Student B: Well, sometimes they plow the snow . . . the other thing is, students who used to park at the stadium, now they're gonna park in the neighborhood near campus. That's gonna cause a problem for people who live there.

Student A: I don't know, I don't really think so . . . I think most people will just pay the fees and keep parking at the stadium. And the university has to raise money for the new parking structure somehow.

Narrator: The woman expresses her opinion of the new parking policy. State her opinion and explain the reasons she gives for having that opinion.

[CD 7 Track 16]

Sample Responses for Integrated Speaking

Narrator: Sample Response 1

Speaker: The man is upset because of the parking rules, the . . . uh . . . new parking rules. He . . . he always parks at the stadium but now, uh, he must pay $25. Also, he must register his car and . . . um, pay his parking tickets. He doesn't think that the new rules are fair.

The woman doesn't . . . she doesn't think . . . she doesn't agree with what the man says. She . . . uh, she thinks that this is not . . . not so much money to pay for parking. The university will use the money for repairing the parking lot, for plowing the snow, for painting the lines in the parking lot. They will also use it for building new parking structure. So . . . uh, unlike the man, she doesn't think . . . she thinks that the policy is fair.

Narrator: Sample Response 2

Speaker: The woman . . . eh, um . . . usually parks her car at the stadium and for her . . . eh . . . the new . . . eh . . . Minnesota policy about parking is not . . . ah, so bad and she just will have another . . . eh . . . eh . . . opinion and . . . eh . . . for . . . for the man . . . eh . . . it this is not a good . . . eh . . . policy . . . eh . . . because . . . eh . . . twenty-five dollar per semesters and more, ten dollars . . . eh . . . for just . . . registering the car. It's too much and the . . . maybe people . . . eh . . . will park . . . eh . . . their car in the . . . um . . . neighborhood around the university and . . . eh . . . eh . . . so . . . eh . . . the two people have different opinions . . . eh . . . the woman agrees with day . . . eh . . . university's policy while the man don't.

Narrator: Sample Response 3

Speaker: First, uh, she's not . . . uh . . . she agree, she's not upset to university decision because . . . uh . . . she felt that the fee for parking and the registration is not expensive, only twenty-five dollars for semester and she thought university also have to pay to maintain the parking area it costs . . . it costs . . . mmmmm . . . it, it may cost high, the cost for . . . mmmmm . . . paving or painting and clean snow during the winter so she, she thought that it fair that university . . . uh . . . made a rule for parking.

Narrator: Sample Response 4

Speaker: The ladies seemed like a . . . um . . . she more agree with the new policy because she realized she didn't have, she doesn't have the problem with the parking, the new parking rules . . . um . . . she really seem like she ready to pay twenty-five dollars, personally there, but the guy Brad he's kinda like a little bit upset and . . . um . . . upset and he have some money situation and . . . um . . . he doesn't really want to . . . to pay more money . . . um . . . . The lady, she . . . um . . . she gave a good reason about why the university have to . . . um, ah . . . cause the money for the parking and . . . um . . . she also . . . ah . . . say that if the . . . they collect the money for fixing the stadium . . .

[CD 7 Track 17]

Exercise: Scoring the Response

Narrator: Response 1

Speaker: The woman is in favor of the new . . . um . . . rule for parking . . . um . . . at the . . . um . . . stadium. Um . . . she thinks that . . . um it's (very) reasonable, it's only just ten dollars . . . um, it's affordable . . . um . . . to park in the stadium and um . . . she thinks that . . . um . . . you would just . . . um . . . you'll pay for it . . . um . . . so that also . . . um . . . the fee that will be raised from parking . . . um . . . will be used . . . um . . . by the . . . um . . . school . . . um . . . because . . . um . . . she thinks that . . . um . . . there's . . . um . . . there . . . the school has some money to take care of the parking lot . . . um . . . at the . . . um . . . stadium. There are times, . . . um . . . especially in the . . . um . . . in the winter when they need to plow . . . um . . . clean up . . . um . . . shovel, um . . . and other things . . . um . . . so that this . . . um . . . fee . . . um . . . raised . . . together from parking . . . from the . . . um . . . new rule . . . um . . . policy . . . um . . . will go . . . um . . . towards that, and . . . um . . . she thinks . . . um . . . that . . . um . . . these . . . um . . . shouldn't be a big deal. And . . . um . . . if there not cause . . . um . . . problems . . . um . . . this way . . . um . . . and . . . um . . . and there will be enough so . . . um . . . the parking lot . . . ah . . . will be taken care of.

Narrator: Response 2

Speaker: There no longer is . . . uh, free parking and they, the student must . . . um, must pay $10. There two opinions . . . two options . . . can pay . . . uh . . . $75 or $25 to the . . . for the university parking. I . . . uh, I don't think is . . . is too much for the students pay for the parking.

Narrator: Response 3

Speaker: She . . . she kind of liked . . . ah, ah . . . the new policy because . . . a, um . . . eventually it's gonna be the good thing for the students . . . ah . . . and actually the cost isn't . . . ah . . . very much, it's only twenty-five dollars for the parking outlying lots and also the registration fee is like ten dollars, it's not very expensive for students, and also the . . .

ah . . . the . . . ah . . . the, the school needs some money for maintain parking lots so and then they gonna have more spaces for parking eventually . . . that's why she like the idea and she support that idea.

[CD 8 Track 2]

Integrated Speaking Preview Test

Narrator: Directions: The last four tasks of the Speaking Section are Integrated Speaking tasks. The third and fourth questions involve a reading text and a listening passage. You will have forty-five seconds in which to read a short text. You will then hear a short conversation or part of a lecture on the same topic. You may take notes on both the reading and listening passage. You will then see a question on the screen asking about the information that you have just read and heard, and you will have thirty seconds in which to plan a response. When you hear a beep on the Audio Program, you will have sixty seconds in which to answer the question. The fifth and sixth questions involve a short listening passage. You may take notes as you listen. After listening to the conversation or lecture, you will see a question, and you will have twenty seconds in which to plan your response. When you hear a beep on the Audio Program, you will have sixty seconds in which to answer the question. During actual tests, a clock on the screen will tell you how much preparation time or how much response time (speaking time) remains for each question. It is important that you time yourself accurately when you take this practice test. If possible, record your response. On an actual test your responses will be recorded and evaluated by trained raters.

Narrator: Task 3
Narrator: Beginning this semester, all faculty members at Monroe University are required to hand out copies of the university's plagiarism policy. You will have forty-five seconds in which to read the policy. Begin reading now. [45-second pause]
Narrator: Now listen to two students discussing this notice.
Student A: So it looks like they're serious about stopping plagiarism. I've gotten a copy of this in every class.
Student B: Yeah, well, in general, I don't have any argument with the policy . . . I'm just glad they're finally making this policy . . . making it a little more public, passing it out in every class. If I'd known about this policy a coupla years ago, I wouldn't have gotten in trouble . . .
Student A: Wait a minute, you got in trouble for plagiarism?
Student B: It . . . uh, well, it wasn't exactly plagiarism . . . . at least, I didn't consider it plagiarism, but it did . . . uh, violate the policy. See that part about using the same research paper for more than one class? Well, I was writing a paper for a geology class and one for a chemistry class. They were both about hydrocarbon compounds, and I used one section of my geology paper in my chemistry paper. I didn't know I couldn't do that. I'll tell you one thing—that software for detecting plagiarism really works. Or at least it did for my paper!
Student A: So, what happened? Did you just get a warning?
Student B: No, at the time, I was in my second year here, and so the grade on both my papers was lowered by a whole letter grade. That's another thing about this policy . . . I don't understand why a first-year student gets a warning and a second-year student gets a lower grade. That doesn't seem right to me.

Student A: Yeah, I know, that seems strange to me, too. I suppose the idea is, the longer you've been a student here, the more aware of the policy you should be. I guess you should be glad that it didn't happen when you were an upperclassman or you would've failed both classes.
Narrator: Now get ready to answer the question.
Narrator: Question 3: The man expresses his opinion of the policy. State his opinion and explain the reasons he gives for having that opinion. [30-second pause] Please start talking now. [60-second pause] Please stop talking now.

Narrator: Task 4
Narrator: Read these paragraphs from a textbook describing animal camouflage. Begin reading now. [45-second pause]
Narrator: Now listen to part of a lecture in a zoology class.
Professor: So, um, we've been talking about ways animals avoid predators, especially how animals use camouflage to stay safe, to hide from their predators. Let's consider an animal called the sloth. The sloth is a mammal that lives in the forests of Central America, South America. They hang from trees and they're lazy, very slow-moving, they sleep fifteen hours a day. Anyway, sloths are a very dull color, their fur is a dull brown and it has dull green streaks in it. Know what these green streaks are? They're algae—a kind of plant. This animal moves around so slowly that plants grow on it! Anyway, this dull green and brown color camouflages the sloth when it's hanging from trees.

Then there's a butterfly, you may have heard of it, it's called the blue morpho. It also lives in Central and South America. It has beautiful, shiny blue wings. It's so pretty its nickname is "the living jewel." You look at a blue morpho, you think, "Now this creature is not camouflaged!" But in fact, it is. Blue morphos' wings are only bright blue when viewed from the top. The bottoms of its wings are dark brown. When it flaps its wings and flies, there are alternating flashes of bright blue and brown. When birds see this, they think they're seeing flashes of blue sky between trees. So, although blue morphos sure don't seem camouflaged to us, they are basically invisible to predators.
Narrator: Now get ready to answer the question.
Narrator: Question 4: The professor describes how camouflage protects two types of animals. Explain how this is related to the concepts of camouflage described in the reading. [30-second pause] Please start talking now. [60-second pause] Please stop talking now.

Narrator: Task 5
Narrator: Listen to a conversation between two students.
Student A: Hey, Lucy, how are things?
Student B: Hi, Rick. Oh, I don't know. Okay, I suppose . . . I'm just . . . I'm just exhausted!
Student A: Yeah, you do look kinda tired . . . how come?
Student B: Well, I just never get enough sleep . . . my classes are really hard this term, especially my physiology class, so I'm in the library until it closes at eleven, and then I study for a couple of hours or so when I get back to my dorm room.
Student A: Yeah, I've had a couple of semesters like that myself . . .
Student B: I feel especially dead in the afternoon, and I have a one o'clock and a three o'clock class. Yesterday, the most incredibly embarrassing thing happened in my physi-

ology class—I actually fell asleep! I've never done that before . . . And Doctor Daniels was like, "Am I boring you, Ms. Jenkins?"

Student A: That's embarrassing! You should do what I do . . . just get yourself some coffee.

Student B: Yeah, I bought a cup of coffee from the vending machine the other day—it was terrible!

Student A: Vending machine coffee's usually pretty awful—you could walk up to College Avenue—there are a coupla coffee shops up there.

Student B: Yeah, but it's pretty expensive . . . and . . . I don't know, sometimes coffee just makes me really nervous . . . I don't feel that awake, I just feel nervous!

Student A: Hey, here's an idea. What buildings are your afternoon classes in?

Student B: One's in Old Main and one's in Castleton.

Student A: Those aren't far from your dorm. Here's what you should do. Go by your dorm and lie down for fifteen or twenty minutes between your two classes.

Student B: I don't know . . . I haven't taken a nap during the day . . . probably since I was in kindergarten.

Student A: Yeah, but, you don't have to sleep. Just lie down and completely relax. If you sleep, that's fine, if not . . . I still think you'll find yourself refreshed.

Narrator: Now get ready to answer the question.

Narrator: Question 5: The man offers Lucy two possible solutions to her problem. Discuss her problem and then explain which of the two solutions you think is better and why you think so. [20-second pause] Please start talking now. [60-second pause] Please stop talking now.

Narrator: Task 6

Narrator: Listen to part of a lecture in a linguistics class.

Professor: You know, Wednesday after class, a student came up to me and said, "Professor, you're constantly using the terms *language* and *dialect* in class, but you've never really defined these words." Fair enough; I guess I haven't. And there's a good reason why not—I'm afraid to. Because, in my opinion, there's no good way to distinguish between these two terms. The standard definition of dialect is this . . . they're forms of one language that are mutually intelligible to speakers of other forms of the same language. If you have someone from Jamaica, say, and uh, someone from India, and they're seated next to each other on an airplane, they'll be able to have a conversation, they'll more or less understand each other, even though those are two very different dialects of English. But consider the various forms of Chinese. A person from southern China can't understand a person from Beijing. Yet these forms of Chinese are usually considered dialects, not separate languages. Now, people who speak different languages are not supposed to be intelligible to those who cannot speak that language. But what about Danish and Norwegian? Danish speakers and Norwegian speakers can understand each other perfectly well, but Danish and Norwegian are considered separate languages, not dialects of the same language. Why? Who knows. I suppose part of it is national pride—countries are proud of "owning" a language. In fact, there's an old joke among linguists that a language is a dialect with an army and a navy. Anyway, these questions—What is a language? What is a dialect?—they're difficult to answer, and, uh, I guess that's why I've avoided them up until now.

Narrator: Now get ready to answer the question.

Narrator: Question 6: Using specific examples and points from the lecture, explain the professor's concept of dialects

and languages. [20-second pause] Please start talking now. [60-second pause] Please stop talking now.

Narrator: This is the end of the Integrated Speaking Preview Test.

[CD 8 Track 3]

Lesson 17: Announcement/Discussion Task
Sample

Student A: So it looks like they're serious about stopping plagiarism. I've gotten a copy of this in every class.

Student B: Yeah, well, in general, I don't have any argument with the policy . . . I'm just glad they're finally making this policy . . . making it a little more public, passing it out in every class. If I'd known about this policy a coupla years ago, I wouldn't have gotten in trouble . . .

Student A: Wait a minute, you got in trouble for plagiarism?

Student B: It . . . uh, well, it wasn't exactly plagiarism . . . . at least, I didn't consider it plagiarism, but it did . . . uh, violate the policy. See that part about using the same research paper for more than one class? Well, I was writing a paper for a geology class and one for a chemistry class. They were both about hydrocarbon compounds, and I used one section of my geology paper in my chemistry paper. I didn't know I couldn't do that. I'll tell you one thing—that software for detecting plagiarism really works. Or at least it did for my paper!

Student A: So, what happened? Did you just get a warning?

Student B: No, at the time, I was in my second year here, and so the grade on both my papers was lowered by a whole letter grade. That's another thing about this policy . . . I don't understand why a first-year student gets a warning and a second-year student gets a lower grade. That doesn't seem right to me.

Student A: Yeah, I know, that seems strange to me, too. I suppose the idea is, the longer you've been a student here, the more aware of the policy you should be. I guess you should be glad that it didn't happen when you were an upperclassman or you would have failed both classes.

Narrator: The man expresses his opinion of the policy. State his opinion and explain the reasons he gives for having that opinion.

Narrator: Sample Response

Speaker: The notice tells about the plagiarism policy and . . . uh, defines plagiarisms. It says plagiarism is using someone else's words, um, like your own words. It can be a little bit, just a sentence, or a whole paper. It can be from other students or from books, Web sites, it doesn't matter where. It can also be that you use the same paper for more than one class, um, you hand in one paper for more than one class. The announcement also lists the . . . uh, punishments for plagiarism. These are worse for the older students than for the new students. It says that they, that there is software used to find a plagiarism.

   The man says that he, uh, generally agrees with the plagiarism policy. But he says that he just wishes that they published it more in the past, because he didn't know about it. The reason for that is . . . he, uh, violated the policy by using part of one paper in two classes, for geology and chemistry. His grades were lowered for his two classes. He also says he doesn't understand why there are different punishments for different students. The woman says it's maybe because students who have been at Monroe University for longer times, they should know this policy.

[CD 8 Track 4]

Exercise 17.1

Narrator: Task A

Narrator: Listen to two students discuss the announcement.

Student A: Wow, I guess Professor Ribaudo was pretty upset about those cell phones going off in his class last week.

Student B: Well, yeah, I guess so . . . it happened, what, four times?

Student A: Maybe five. I can't believe people were so thoughtless that they left their phones turned on and set to ring.

Student B: I know, that's just rude.

Student A: But, don't you think it's kinda harsh that you can't turn off the ring and set the phone to vibrate? I mean, what if there's a family emergency?

Student B: I don't agree. The professor's right, it's distracting to see people messing with their phones in class. As far as I'm concerned, students can go an hour without their cell phones.

Narrator: Task B

Narrator: Listen to two students discuss the announcement.

Student A: Wow, this is great—this is a break for me.

Student B: Really? Why's that? Do you . . . ?

Student A: Yeah, I do. I have five way overdue books from the science library. I checked them out when I was writing a paper last spring, and then I never got around to returning them before I left for the summer. So, uh, by the time I got back here in September—well, I couldn't afford to return them.

Student B: How much is the fine a day?

Student A: It's twenty-five cents a day per book . . . so $1.25 a day for six months . . . I owe a lot on them!

Student B: Well, you better hurry—the last day for the amnesty program is Friday—you only have two days left.

Student A: I'm gonna take those books over there this evening. Wow, I've really been worried about this. You know, they won't let you graduate if you don't return the library materials and pay all your fines.

Narrator: Task C

Narrator: Listen to two students discuss the announcement.

Student A: Hey, this isn't good. I just put a message up on that bulletin board saying I was looking for a roommate.

Student B: Well, there are plenty of other bulletin boards around campus where you can put that up. Or you could put an ad in the campus paper.

Student A: Yeah, but I wanted to room with another computer science major. I mean, when I talk to most people about computers, they just look at me. I wanted to live with someone who understood me.

Student B: Well, just say in your ad you're looking for another person who's obsessed with computers. But you have to admit, that bulletin board is so crowded with notices about roommates and potlucks and study groups that you can't find any real bulletins from the Department.

Student A: Yeah, that's true—there are messages on there from months ago, maybe years ago.

Narrator: Task D

Narrator: Listen to two students discuss the announcement.

Student A: So, did you go to this film festival last year?

Student B: Yeah, I thought it sounded pretty good, so I bought a weekend pass. And I hated every movie I saw. I mean, they didn't make any sense, and they were really boring.

Student A: Yeah, some independent films don't make sense, and some of them are boring, I guess, but not all. I mean, I've seen some independent films that . . .

Student B: Well, I saw three or four movies last year, and they were all like that—confusing and boring!

Student A: So, uh, I'm guessing you don't want to go to the festival with me this year . . .

[CD 8 Track 5]

Exercise 17.2

Narrator: Task A

Narrator: Listen to two students discuss the announcement.

Student A: Oh, good! Another experiment!

Student B: What, you'd take part in a psychology experiment? I dunno if I would. I'd feel like a . . . a lab rat or something. I dunno . . . I just think it would be dangerous.

Student A: Well, I wouldn't . . . I wouldn't volunteer for any medical experiments or any experiment where I had to take any kinda drug or anything but . . . these psychology experiments, they're pretty harmless . . . I've already taken part in two or three.

Student B: Really, you have?

Student A: Well, you know, it's a good way to pick up a little spending money. And I've earned credits towards graduation as well.

Student B: But . . . you have trouble sleeping?

Student A: Yeah, and not just once a week. Three or four nights a week, I'm tossing and turning and not able to get to sleep until way after midnight. That's one of the good things about this experiment—according to this notice, I might learn how to fall asleep more easily.

Narrator: Task B

Narrator: Listen to two students discuss the announcement.

Student B: What are you doing this weekend?

Student A: I think I'm going to this Internship Fair on Saturday.

Student B: You're going to that? Why? You want to spend your summer doing volunteer work?

Student A: No, but . . . these aren't all volunteer positions. Some of them are internships. Most internships are paid positions.

Student B: Yeah, but I bet you don't get paid much.

Student A: I don't know. My sister was an intern at an advertising agency. She was paid pretty well. And besides, being an intern, it's good experience. It looks good on your résumé, especially if you find a position in your own field. My sister found a job at a New York ad agency right after she graduated, mainly because she had that experience as an intern.

Student B: Well, I've already found a summer job. I'm going to be working as a lifeguard again at Gold Beach. I admit, it doesn't look that great on my résumé, but it's a lot of fun.

Narrator: Task C

Narrator: Listen to two students discuss the announcement.

Student A: This is interesting—you know, I always thought you had to be a Theater Arts major to even try out for a play.

Student B: I guess not. Why—are you thinking about trying out for a part in this play?

Student A: Well, you know—I think I am! I was in a play when I was in high school, it was just a small role, but, uh, I guess I caught the acting bug! And guess what, that high school play I was in, it was one of George Bernard Shaw's plays too. I really like Shaw!

Student B: But . . . you only have a little bit of acting experience.
Student A: Yeah, but that's why I'm so excited about this. It says right here, "no prior acting experience is required," so I guess it won't matter that I haven't had a lot of experience.
Student B: Well, good luck.
Student A: You know, even if I don't get a part, I might see if there's something else I could do—you know, work on costumes or the sets or lighting or something.

Narrator: Task D
Narrator: Listen to two students discuss the announcement.
Student A: So you're signing up for one of these finals workshops?
Student B: Yeah, I figure, it can't hurt to try. I mean, maybe it will help.
Student A: You know, you don't seem . . . well, I mean, you seem to cope with stress really well.
Student B: Well, you know what they say. It's the people who hold it in who are most affected by stress. But you know what? When I was taking my chemistry mid-term test, I uh, I had such bad text anxiety that I could barely finish my exam. My palms were sweating, and I felt like my stomach was tied up in knots.
Student A: Well, in that case, maybe you should go to one of these workshops. But you know, this notice says that they're gonna teach you how to eat and exercise to release stress. I already know I should exercise and eat healthy, but . . . there's no time to do that when you're in the middle of finals week. You don't have time to go work out and you sure don't have time to be cooking healthy meals.
Student B: Yeah, I guess you're right but . . . I'm mostly interested in learning how to deal with stress during an exam . . . how to deal with test anxiety, you know . . . so, if I learn a few techniques for doing that, I'll be happy.

[CD 8 Track 6]

Exercise 17.3
Narrator: Task A
Narrator: The woman expresses her opinion of the announcement about the psychology experiment. State her opinion, and explain the reasons she gives for having that opinion. [30-second pause, then beep] Please start talking now. [60-second pause, then beep] Please stop talking now.

Narrator: Task B
Narrator: The man expresses his opinion of the Summer Internship Fair. State his opinion, and explain the reasons he gives for having that opinion. [30-second pause, then beep] Please start talking now. [60-second pause, then beep] Please stop talking now.

Narrator: Task C
Narrator: The woman expresses her opinion of the announcement about the audition. State her opinion, and explain the reasons she gives for having that opinion. [30-second pause, then beep] Please start talking now. [60-second pause, then beep] Please stop talking now.

Narrator: Task D
Narrator: The man expresses his opinion of the Stress Management Workshop. State his opinion, and explain the reasons he gives for having that opinion. [30-second pause, then beep] Please start talking now. [60-second pause, then beep] Please stop talking now.

[CD 8 Track 7]

Lesson 18: General/Specific Task
Sample
Narrator: Listen and read along as you hear a lecture in a zoology class.
Professor: So, um, we've been talking about ways animals avoid predators, especially how animals use camouflage to stay safe, to hide from their predators. Let's consider an animal called the sloth. The sloth is a mammal that lives in the forests of Central America, South America. They hang from trees and they're lazy, very slow-moving, they sleep fifteen hours a day. Anyway, sloths are a very dull color, their fur is a dull brown and it has dull green streaks in it. Know what these green streaks are? They're algae—a kind of plant. This animal moves around so slowly that plants grow on it! Anyway, this dull green and brown color camouflages the sloth when it's hanging from trees.
Then there's a butterfly, you may have heard of it, it's called the blue morpho. It also lives in Central and South America. It has beautiful, shiny blue wings. It's so pretty its nickname is "the living jewel." You look at a blue morpho, you think, "Now this creature is not camouflaged!" But in fact it is. Blue morphos' wings are only bright blue when viewed from the top. The bottoms of its wings are dark brown. When it flaps its wings and flies, there are alternating flashes of bright blue and brown. When birds see this, they think they're seeing flashes of blue sky between trees. So, although blue morphos sure don't seem camouflaged to us, they are basically invisible to predators.
Narrator: The professor describes how camouflage protects two types of animals. Explain how this is related to the concepts of camouflage described in the reading.

Narrator: Sample response
Speaker: The reading discusses, uh, . . . it says that all animals are in danger, that they can be eaten by predators. And, uh, one way animals can be safe from predators is with camouflage. Camouflage—this means that an animal is hard to see by other animals. This animal doesn't look visible. The reading says some animals that use camouflage, they look dull and it's hard to notice them. But . . . uh, some don't look that way, they are easy to see. I mean, ummm, it is easy for us to see them, but not for the predators to see them.
The professor talks about two examples of animals that use camouflage. One example of these is the sloth. Sloth is a lazy animal. It is brown and has green color from an algae plant that grows in the fur because it moves so slow. So the sloth is an example of an animal that is hard to see because its colors are dull. The other example is the blue morpho butterfly. Like the reading said, some animals, umm . . . they don't look camouflage because they are bright colors—the blue morpho is really bright blue. But, uh, when birds see this flying butterfly, they see flashes of the sky through trees, that is . . . that's what the butterfly looks like to them. So . . . blue morphos are camouflage too.

[CD 8 Track 8]

Exercise 18.1
Narrator: Task A
Narrator: Listen to a lecture in a mathematics class.
Professor: Now, we've been talking about numeral systems. As our textbook says, most numeral systems have been

base-10. But before we move on, I wanted to mention that not all numeral systems are base-10. One system, used by the Yuki Indians of California, is base 8. That's because the Yukis counted the spaces between their fingers rather than their fingers themselves. So, if the Yukis used our number words, they would count like this: one, two, three, four, five, six, seven, ten—eleven, twelve, thirteen, fourteen, fifteen, twenty, and so on.

Another system that still has a major impact on us today is the system used by the Sumerian people, the Sumerians. They lived in West Asia about, um, 3,000 years ago. They used a very complex base-60 system. There were sixty separate symbols for numbers. Now, the reason I say this system had a big impact . . . well, how many seconds are there in a minute? Sixty, right? How many minutes in an hour? Sixty again. So, as you can see, the Sumerian system has a big impact on the way we measure time, and in a few other situations. But the Sumerian system isn't used otherwise. It's very difficult to do calculations in a . . . in a base-60 system. It's not impossible, mind you; it's merely very difficult.

Narrator: Task B
Narrator: Listen to a lecture in an anthropology class.
Professor: So, anyone know what kind of dolls these are?
Student A: Umm, I'm not sure what they're called, but they're from the Southwest, aren't they?
Professor: Right, from the Hopi people who live in the Southwest—in New Mexico.
Student B: Aren't they called kachina dolls?
Professor: Yeah, kachina dolls. And what are they used for?
Student A: I don't know. Just to play with, I guess.
Professor: Umm, kachina dolls are not just toys. They're . . . I guess you'd call them educational toys. They provide a kind of, uh, religious training. The dolls represent kachina spirits, spirits that are important to the Hopi in their day-to-day life. These dolls teach the Hopi children what the spirits' names are and what they look like.
Student B: Are there a lot of these spirits? I mean, is it hard to keep them straight?
Professor: As a matter of fact, there are over 200 kachina spirits. So, uh, that's why the Hopi children need these dolls.

Narrator: Task C
Narrator: Listen to a lecture in a chemistry class.
Professor: Rust is the, uh, the common name for a common chemical—iron oxide. So, uh, in other words, rust is formed by the oxidation of iron. You need three things to get rust: iron, of course, and air, and finally water. And, uh, rust is worse when the water contains salt . . . that's why you see so much rust near the seacoast.

Rust is a type of corrosion. It causes lots of problems. Rust can make iron and steel—of course, steel is just a mixture of iron with other metals—it can make iron and steel fragile, make it break easily. It, uh, it affects all kinds of stuff—cars, ships, industrial equipment, farming equipment, military hardware, almost anything made of steel. People spend millions of dollars every year trying to protect metal from rust, or . . . uh, replacing equipment that's too rusted to use.

Narrator: Task D

Narrator: Listen to a lecture in a psychology class.
Student A: So, professor, what kinds of experiments were done on these twins?
Professor: Well, lots of experiments have been done. Many of them were medical, they had to do with illnesses . . .
Student B: But what about the psychological experiments?
Professor: Well, there have been quite a few, but one of the most famous was an investigation of happiness . . .
Student B: Happiness? How can you inherit happiness? That . . .
Professor: Well, I guess I should say the capacity for happiness . . . the ability to be happy.
Student A: So what did they find out? About happiness?
Professor: Well, one study showed that, among the subjects of the experiment, happiness has nothing to do with how much money you have, with your job, with your marital status. According to one study, for 80% of the subjects, it all has to do with genetics.
Student B: I don't know—that just doesn't seem to make sense to me.
Professor: Well, you're not the only one who feels that way. A lot of psychologists don't think much of twin research. For one thing, many of the separated twins have actually had various degrees of contact. Some of them spent a year or more together as infants. Some of them got in touch with each other as teenagers or as adults. Anyway, as the textbook points out, there won't be many more experiments like this in the future.

[CD 8 Track 9]

Exercise 18.2
Narrator: Task A
Narrator: Now listen to a lecture in a zoology class.
Professor: Now, in southern Africa, there's a bird that's, uh, called the hamerkop—its name means "hammerhead" in the Afrikaans language. The hamerkop builds an absolutely huge nest in the forks of trees. You can see this nest from over a kilometer away. It's made of, I don't know, maybe 8,000 sticks. The nest sometimes holds several generations of hamerkops. There are at least three rooms. The highest is the sleeping room. This is where the female lays her eggs. When the babies grow up, they move into a middle room. Then there's a room which serves as a lookout post.

Once, uh, people had a pretty interesting belief about hamerkops. People thought that they, that hamerkops carried baby snakes to their nests and then brought food to these snakes. It was thought that, when they grew up, the snakes would protect the hamerkops, like faithful family dogs. This story originated, probably, because people saw snakes that had moved into hamerkop nests after they'd been abandoned by the birds.

Narrator: Task B
Narrator: Now listen to a lecture in a geology class.
Professor: Well, then, let me talk about marble for a few minutes. Marble . . . it's a type of metamorphic rock. . . . Marble is formed from limestone. Now, limestone is a kind of sedimentary rock—but limestone is much softer, much more easily broken than marble. It is formed deep in the Earth's crust over millions of years. Marble formed from pure limestone is almost pure white. Impurities—you know, different types of minerals mixed in with the lime-

stone—these give marble its different colors—green, yellow, tan, pink, and so on.

Marble is valued for its beauty, and, uh, its strength. It's been used for temples, monuments, statues. It's still used for building today, especially for public buildings.

Narrator: Task C
Narrator: Now listen to a lecture in a journalism class.
Professor: Today, uh, I want to start off by focusing on one of the more influential journalists of the early twentieth century, Ida Tarbell. She began reporting for a magazine in 1894. She was interested in writing about corporations, especially about the Standard Oil Company, so she became an investigative reporter. She was one of the famous "muckrakers" that we read about last week.

Now, uh, Ida Tarbell spent two years studying Standard Oil's corporate records, interviewing company officials—she even met with the director of the corporation. For some reason, he trusted her, and told her all kinds of things. In 1904, she published a series of articles about Standard Oil. Her articles gave details about all kinds of corporate scandals, abuses of power, unfair practices. These articles made her readers angry—and not just angry at Standard Oil but at trusts in general. And it was probably Tarbell's writings that caused Congress to break up Standard Oil in 1911.

Narrator: Task D
Narrator: Now listen to a discussion in a photography class.
Professor: Okay, everyone, last class, we were talking about some of the advantages of taking monochromatic photos rather than color photos. Today I'm going to start by showing you two monochromatic photos of the same street scene in Boston. Here's one—take a good look—okay, now here's the other. What can you tell me about these two photos?
Student A: Well, the second one is obviously much older . . .
Professor: Oh? And why do you say that?
Student A: Well, it . . . I dunno, it just looks older . . .
Professor: Okay. Actually, they're both the same age.
Student A: Really?
Professor: Yeah, really. I took them both myself a year or so ago. But you're right—the second photograph does look older. What else did you notice?
Student B: The first one seems . . . the light seems different. It seems harsher, somehow. There's a lot more contrast between the shadow and the lit portions of the picture.
Professor: Good point. What else?
Student B: Well, the second one has, umm, a kind of brownish look to it, a brownish tint.
Professor: Okay, very good. Actually, these two photos were just developed using two different processes. Today in the darkroom, we'll develop some black-and-white film, and I'll show you the difference between the two processes.

[CD 8 Track 10]

Exercise 18.3
Narrator: Task A
Narrator: The professor's lecture is about the nest of the hamerkop bird. Describe the hamerkop's nest, and explain why it is a good example of an enclosed nest. [30-second pause, then beep] Please start talking now. [60-second pause, then beep] Please stop talking now.

Narrator: Task B
Narrator: The professor lectures about marble. Describe this type of rock, and explain why it is a typical metamorphic rock. [30-second pause, then beep] Please start talking now. [60-second pause, then beep] Please stop talking now.

Narrator: Task C
Narrator: The professor lectures about the journalist Ida Tarbell. Describe her accomplishments, and explain why she is considered a "muckraker." [30-second pause, then beep] Please start talking now. [60-second pause, then beep] Please stop talking now.

Narrator: Task D
Narrator: The professor and the students discuss two photographs. Describe the photographs using information from the discussion and the reading passage. [30-second pause, then beep] Please start talking now. [60-second pause, then beep] Please stop talking now.

[CD 8 Track 11]

Lesson 19: Problem/Solution Task
Sample Item
Narrator: Listen to a conversation between two students.
Student A: Hey, Lucy, how are things?
Student B: Hi, Rick. Oh, I don't know. Okay, I suppose . . . I'm just . . . I'm just exhausted!
Student A: Yeah, you do look kinda tired . . . how come?
Student B: Well, I just never get enough sleep . . . my classes are really hard this term, especially my physiology class, so I'm in the library until it closes at eleven, and then I study for a couple of hours or so when I get back to my dorm room.
Student A: Yeah, I've had a couple of semesters like that myself . . .
Student B: I feel especially dead in the afternoon, and I have a one o'clock and a three o'clock class. Yesterday, the most incredibly embarrassing thing happened in my physiology class—I actually fell asleep! I've never done that before . . . And Doctor Daniels was like, "Am I boring you, Ms. Jenkins?"
Student A: That's embarrassing! Hey, you should do what I do . . . just get yourself some coffee.
Student B: Yeah, I bought a cup of coffee from the vending machine the other day—it was terrible!
Student A: Vending machine coffee's usually pretty awful. You could walk up to College Avenue—there are a coupla coffee shops up there.
Student B: Yeah, but it's pretty expensive, and . . . I don't know, sometimes coffee just makes me really nervous . . . I don't feel that awake, I just feel nervous!
Student A: Hey, here's an idea. What buildings are your afternoon classes in?
Student B: One's in Old Main and one's in Castleton.
Student A: Those aren't far from your dorm. Here's what you should do. Go by your dorm and lie down for fifteen or twenty minutes between your two classes.
Student B: I don't know . . . I haven't taken a nap during the day . . . probably since I was in kindergarten.
Student A: Yeah, but, you don't have to sleep. Just lie down and completely relax. If you sleep, that's fine, if not . . . I still think you'll find yourself refreshed.
Narrator: Now listen to a question about the conversation:

Narrator: The man offers Lucy two possible solutions to her problem. Discuss her problem and then explain which of the two solutions you think is better and why you think so.

Narrator: Sample response.

Speaker: Well, this conversation about a problem that this woman, mmm, Lucy, that she have. Her main problem is with not so much sleep. She has very difficult class and has to study too much, for eleven hours at, at library. Mmmm, so she is exhausting, and felt asleep in her class.

The man tell her drink some coffee, but she doesn't like taste of coffee, especially from vending machine. He suggest she get coffee from the people who sell on the street, but she say is too expensive. She say coffee sometime make her nervous.

Then he suggest she go to her dormitory and sleep a short time. Lucy say not sleep during day for long time, since she a kid, but he tell her not have to feel asleep. Just relaxing.

Mmmmm . . . I suggest she, Lucy, get a nap too, I think is better for her than coffee, because coffee make her nervous, but if she rest in her bed maybe feel not so tired, feel refreshing. Uh, sometimes in afternoon I take a little rest, I feel much more awake, so I think she should go to her dormitory and take it easy.

[CD 8 Track 12]

Exercise 19.3

Narrator: Task A

Narrator: Listen to a conversation between a nurse and a student.

Nurse: Hi, I'm Nurse Greenwell. What can I do for you?

Student: Hi. Well, first off, I'm a smoker . . .

Nurse: Okay . . .

Student: I've been smoking since I was in, I don't know, maybe my third year of high school. I smoke about . . . well, nearly a pack a day.

Nurse: That's, uh, that's quite a lot.

Student: Yeah, I know. Anyway, about six months ago, I got interested in speed-skating. I've been playing hockey and skating off and on for years, but . . . I don't know, I just all of a sudden got interested in competitive speed-skating.

Nurse: Gotcha. And that's a pretty . . . pretty energetic sport, isn't it?

Student: You bet. So, you probably see where I'm going with this. I don't have nearly as much endurance as I should have, I get out of breath pretty easily because . . . because of the smoking.

Nurse: I see . . . I can see where that would be a problem for you.

Student: Yeah, so anyway, I've tried to quit on my own a few times, but . . . no luck.

Nurse: Did you try to quit all at once?

Student: Yeah, but . . . one time I lasted about three days. The next time I tried to quit, I had this really stressful day and well, by 2 in the afternoon, I was smoking again.

Nurse: I'm not surprised—95% of people who try to quit on their own, who don't, uh, take part in a program, they end up going back to smoking.

Student: Really? I guess I'm not that surprised. It's *hard*. Well, anyway, I stopped by here because my girlfriend told me that the Health Center had some programs . . . you know, some programs to help people kick the habit . . .

Nurse: Yeah, she's right, we do. The Health Center sponsors weekly Smoke Stoppers programs.

Student: So, do you use hypnosis?

Nurse: Umm, no, hypnosis isn't part of our treatment program.

Student: 'Cause I've always heard that's the easiest way to quit. You just get hypnotized and then you don't have any more desire to smoke.

Nurse: Well, some people have had success with hypnosis. I don't think it's quite as painless, quite as simple as you make it sound, but . . . you still might want to give our program a try.

Student: So, what do you . . . what does your program consist of?

Nurse: Well, nicotine is the addictive chemical in cigarettes, so we provide you with what's called a nicotine replacement system. Some people use nicotine gum, some people use an inhaler, some people use a patch. We, uh, also teach you a lot of techniques to help you get through those first few weeks, that's a tough time, and we provide a support group of other people who are going through the process of trying to quit as well.

Student: Well, I was thinking I'd really like to try hypnosis . . .

Nurse: Well, you can try it, of course. There are several trained hypnotherapists in town. But their treatments are fairly expensive. If you're a student here, our Smoke Stoppers programs are free.

Narrator: Task B

Narrator: Listen to a conversation between two students.

Student A: Hey, Dennis, did you get tickets for the play Saturday night?

Student B: No, I couldn't. I went by the box office but they wouldn't take my check.

Student A: Why not?

Student B: I didn't have the right ID.

Student A: Really? Couldn't you just have shown them your student ID card?

Student B: I did, but, for some reason, they wanted two forms of picture ID.

Student A: So . . . why didn't you show them your driver's license?

Student B: Believe it or not . . . I don't have one.

Student A: You don't? Really?

Student B: Well, I got one when I turned 16, but . . . since I've been a student here, I haven't had a car on campus and I really haven't needed a license . . . I walk or ride my bike everywhere I need to go.

Student A: You know, you can get an official state ID card—it's less expensive than getting a driver's license, and you don't have to take the written test or the driving test.

Student B: Oh, yeah? Where do I get one of those?

Student A: Same place as you get your driver's license—the Department of Motor Vehicles.

Student B: I should probably look into that.

Student A: If it were me, though, I think I'd just renew your driver's license. I mean, you don't have a car now, but who knows when some situation will come up when you want to drive . . . and it's good for . . . I think it's good for five years.

Student B: I guess I could give it some thought. Right now I need to go to an ATM and get some cash to get those tickets.

Narrator: Task C

Narrator: Listen to a conversation between a student and her chemistry professor.

Professor: So, Tina, I asked you to stop by because . . . well, your grades on the unit tests have been fine, quite good, but . . . your lab reports have . . . have been a little disappointing. And they are an important part of your grade.

Student: Well, yeah, uh, things aren't going so well in the lab.

Professor: Really? And why's that?

Student: Well, I hate to say this . . . I really do . . . but it's kinda Robert's fault . . . he's my lab partner, and . . .

Professor: Robert Lewis?

Student: Yeah, he and I went to the same high school, and . . . well, he asked me to be his lab partner on the first day of class, and uh, I didn't really know how to say no . . .

Professor: And so he, uh, he's not so good in the lab?

Student: No, professor, he, uh, he doesn't have much talent for lab work, to say the least! For one thing, he's not careful when he measures chemicals . . . and then, um, he breaks test tubes and glass beakers . . . and he's burned himself twice . . .

Professor: Really? I had no idea . . .

Student: The worst thing, though, is that I'm the one who has to do almost all of the write-up, the lab report. He doesn't take notes while we're doing the experiments, and then afterwards, he just expects me to write up the results, and . . . well, I guess I've been so discouraged by his lack of help that I haven't done a great job. Is there any way you could assign me another lab partner?

Professor: Hmm, I just don't know, Tina. Maybe I could do that, but . . . all the other students are used to working with the lab partners that they have now.

Student: Yeah, that's true . . . and I guess it's not fair for anyone else to have to work with Robert.

Professor: Well, if you want, I'll talk to Robert. I could tell him that he's got to be more careful in lab and share the work when it comes to doing the report. I mean, you both get a grade on your report, so you both should work on it. He's taking advantage of you.

Student: Yeah, something needs to be done. This really can't go on.

Narrator: Task D

Narrator: Listen to a conversation between two students.

Student A: Well, uh, I've been trying to decide what to do about, uh, well, I have this uh, situation . . .

Student B: What's the matter?

Student A: Well, uh, you know my friend Jack . . .

Student B: Sure. Well, I know him a little.

Student A: Well, he's down in Mexico on spring break . . . and, uh, you see, Jack has this pet . . . a uh, pet rat . . .

Student B: Jack has a rat?

Student A: Yeah, uh, I guess it's not actually a rat, it's a mouse . . . a white mouse. Its name is Samson. And Jack asked me to take care of Samson while he's gone.

Student B: Okay . . .

Student A: So anyway, last night, I was trying to sleep, and you know how mice and little rodents like that have those wheels in their cages . . .

Student B: Right . . . so they can get some exercise.

Student A: Uh huh, so this wheel in Samson's cage was really squeaky, really noisy, and Samson was running on it all night long and . . . I can't tell you how annoying the noise was. After a couple of hours of this, I got up and I put the mouse in an old shoebox. Uh, I didn't realize that mice could . . . could chew right through cardboard. So . . . so when I woke up this morning . . . no mouse! Samson'd vanished!

Student B: Oh no! So, you've searched your apartment?

Student A: Yeah, he's not here. I have a tiny apartment, you know, and there aren't many places for even a mouse to hide. I guess he escaped under the door.

Student B: What are you gonna do then?

Student A: Well . . . I thought I'd go down to a pet store and buy another mouse that looks just like Samson . . .

Student B: Wait, you can't do that! You can't just substitute one mouse for Jack's pet and not tell him . . .

Student A: It's a mouse! You can't tell one mouse from another!

Student B: Still, it's just not honest, it's not fair to your friend Jack. You've got to call Jack in Mexico and tell him what happened . . .

Student A: Well, I guess you're right. It'll ruin his whole trip though. You don't know how much that mouse means to Jack. He's really attached to Samson!

[CD 9 Track 2]

Exercise 19.4

Narrator: Task A

Narrator: Listen to a conversation between a student and his advisor.

Advisor: So, Stan, thanks for coming by.

Student: No problem, Professor.

Advisor: I'm going to get right to the point, Stan. I've been meeting with all the students majoring in Classical Languages . . . you've probably heard the rumors that . . .

Student: That the department is going to be shut down?

Advisor: Right. Well, I'm afraid the rumors are all true. The dean let me know last week that, as of next September, Central State's Classical Languages department will no longer exist.

Student: I can't believe they're slashing the whole department . . .

Advisor: Well, we're down to about twenty students. I guess the university is just trying to save some money. They're eliminating two or three departments, and we're one of them.

Student: So, what are you going to do, Professor?

Advisor: I'm taking a position teaching at Winston College. They have a pretty strong Classical Languages program down there.

Student: Well . . . I'm not really sure what my options are . . . I . . .

Advisor: Well, of course, you could change majors. I know you've been taking Spanish classes. Maybe you could transfer to the Modern Languages Department.

Student: The thing is, I'm planning to go to graduate school, and I want to get my master's degree in archaeology. I think Classical Languages would be a much more useful major if I want to get into a good graduate program in archaeology.

Advisor: Yeah, I think you're right about that. Well, here's another possibility I thought I'd bring up . . . you could transfer down to Winston College.

Student: Wow . . . I've never even considered leaving Central State.

Advisor: I could make sure that all your credits transfer down there, and help you make the transition.

Student: It's just that . . . that'd be a pretty big change . . . I have a lot of friends here . . .

Advisor: I know, I understand . . . but Winston is only about forty miles from here . . . you could still see your mates, especially on weekends.

Student: Yeah, true. Well, you've . . . you've certainly given me something to think about.

Narrator: Task B
Narrator: Listen to a conversation between two students.
Student A: Hey, Margaret, have you found a place to live for next semester yet?
Student B: Yeah, I . . . uh, just signed a lease on an apartment last week.
Student A: You don't sound that excited about it—isn't it a nice place?
Student B: Actually, it's really a nice place. I love it. It has this wonderful sunny front room . . .
Student A: And let me guess, you're planning to use that room for your art studio.
Student B: Yeah, it's a perfect place to paint. It's a great apartment for an artist.
Student A: Yeah, well, it sounds great. So, uh, what's the matter with it?
Student B: It's just too expensive! The rent is way more than I can afford. Y' know, I saw that front room, and I imagined myself painting there in the morning sunlight and I . . . well, I told the landlord I'd take it. I must have been out of my mind!
Student A: Well, you could go back to the landlord and tell him you've changed your mind. Just tell him you can't afford it.
Student B: But I already gave him a deposit. If I break the lease and don't move in, he'll keep my deposit.
Student A: Hmmm. So how big is this apartment?
Student B: Well, it has that huge room I'd use as a studio; it has a bedroom, a small kitchen, a living room . . .
Student A: Okay, so why don't you get a roommate? Your roommate can have the bedroom and you can sleep in the studio.
Student B: Well, I don't know about living with someone else. I like my privacy.
Student A: Well, if you can't get your deposit back, let's face it, you're going to have to share with a roommate.

Narrator: Task C
Narrator: Listen to a conversation between a clerk and a student.
Clerk: That comes to $352.68. Would you like to charge that?
Student: Umm, yeah, I guess. I can't believe how expensive textbooks have gotten. That's not even all the books that I need for this semester, either.
Clerk: Yeah, just in the two years I've been working here, it seems like they've gone up quite a bit.
Student: So, what's your buy-back policy here? I mean, at the end of the semester, if I return these books, how much do I get back?
Clerk: Okay, the bookstore buys back books for 50% of their new value. So . . . you'd get back about $175 on these books.
Student: Really. That's all, huh? Just half the purchase price . . .
Clerk: Yeah, that doesn't sound like much, does it? But that's the policy. Oh, and if you mark up the books heavily, you get only 25% back.
Student: Yeah? So, what does "heavily" mean?
Clerk: You know, if you do a lot of underlining, if you write a lot of notes in the margin, if you highlight a lot of the text.
Student: That's how I study, though. I . . . When I read a textbook, I mark the important parts with yellow highlighter. Then before an exam, I just go back and look at what I've highlighted.
Clerk: Well, I dunno, maybe you could mark stuff in the books with a pencil, and that way, at the end of the course, you could erase all your marks . . .

Student: It would be a lot to erase and . . . I'd just rather use a highlighter. It makes the important ideas really stand out and it's easier to get ready for exams.
Clerk: Yeah, well, some students just mark up their books as much as they like and then just hang on to their textbooks . . . they don't sell them back at all.
Student: Yeah, some of these texts would make pretty good reference books, I guess . . . but at the end of this semester, right before summer break, I'm probably gonna need some cash.

Narrator: Task D
Narrator: Listen to a conversation between two students.
Student A: What's the matter, Jim? You're a nervous wreck today! That's not like you.
Student B: Yeah, I am a bit nervous. I'm worried about the concert tomorrow.
Student A: You told me yesterday that everything was all set.
Student B: Everything's ready, yeah, but did you watch the weather report this morning? There's a fifty-fifty chance of thunderstorms tomorrow. You can't have an outdoor concert in a thunderstorm.
Student A: No. No, you can't. So you'll have to move it indoors.
Student B: Yeah, I've thought of that. I talked to someone at the university, and she told me I could use the Women's Gymnasium.
Student A: Well, there you go. Just have the concert in the gym.
Student B: But . . . this is supposed to be an old-fashioned concert and ice cream social. The Commons is such a great location for that kind of concert. It just won't be the same indoors. And the whole idea of the concert is to raise money for the university orchestra. I'm afraid if we move it indoors, into an old gymnasium, hardly anyone will come and we won't make much money.
Student A: Well, don't move the concert until tomorrow . . . wait and see what the weather looks like then.
Student B: I can't wait that long. If I decide to use the gym, I need to put up posters this evening and get the word out that the location has been changed.
Student A: Well, you can either move it this evening, I guess, or cross your fingers and hope that the skies are clear tomorrow evening.

[CD 9 Track 3]

Exercise 19.5
Narrator: Task A
Narrator: Stan's advisor offers him two possible solutions to his problem. Discuss his problem, and then explain which of the two solutions you think is better and why. [20-second pause, then beep] Please start talking now. [60-second pause, then beep] Please stop talking now.

Narrator: Task B
Narrator: The man offers Margaret two possible solutions to her problem. Explain her problem, and then explain which of the two solutions you think is better and why. [20-second pause, then beep] Please start talking now. [60-second pause, then beep] Please stop talking now.

Narrator: Task C
Narrator: The clerk offers the student two possible solutions to his problem. Explain his problem, and then explain

which of the two solutions you think is better and why. [20-second pause, then beep] Please start talking now. [60-second pause, then beep] Please stop talking now.

Narrator: Task D
Narrator: The woman offers Jim two possible solutions to his problem. Discuss his problem, and then explain which of the two solutions you think is better and why. [20-second pause, then beep] Please start talking now. [60-second pause, then beep] Please stop talking now.

[CD 9 Track 4]

Lesson 20: Summary Task

Sample

Narrator: Listen to a lecture in a linguistics class.
Professor: You know, Wednesday after class, a student came up to me and said, "Professor, you're constantly using the terms *language* and *dialect* in class, but you've never really defined these words." Fair enough; I guess I haven't. And there's a good reason why not—I'm afraid to. Because, in my opinion, there's no good way to distinguish between these two terms. The standard definition of dialect is this . . . they're forms of one language that are mutually intelligible to speakers of other forms of the same language. If you have someone from Jamaica, say, and uh, someone from India, and they're seated next to each other on an airplane, they'll be able to have a conversation, they'll more or less understand each other, even though those are two very different dialects of English. But consider the various forms of Chinese. A person from southern China can't understand a person from Beijing. Yet these forms of Chinese are usually considered dialects, not separate languages. Now, people who speak different languages are not supposed to be intelligible to those who cannot speak that language. But what about Danish and Norwegian? Danish speakers and Norwegian speakers can understand each other perfectly well, but Danish and Norwegian are considered separate languages, not dialects of the same language. Why? Who knows. I suppose part of it is national pride—countries are proud of "owning" a language. In fact, there's an old joke among linguists that a language is a dialect with an army and a navy. Anyway, these questions—What is a language? What is a dialect?—they're difficult to answer, and, uh, I guess that's why I've avoided them up until now.
Narrator: Now listen to a question about the lecture: Using specific examples and points from the lecture, explain the professor's concept of dialects and languages.

Narrator: Sample response.
Speaker: This lecture is about the difference, um, the difference between dialect and language. It's, uh, the main idea is that this difference is difficult to define. The professor says basically . . . the basic definition of dialect is a form of the language that, uh, that other people can understand—that other people who speak the language can understand each other. For example, people from Jamaica and India. These people speak different dialect but they understand each another. But, sometimes this definition is not true. For example, dialect of Chinese language. These are called as dialects but, um, very difficult to understand. In the other hand, people who speak other languages, they can't understand each another, but then, uh, some languages, different languages, the people can understand them. For example, Denmark people and Norway people. They have different

languages but can understand each other. Maybe because of national pride—some people want their own country to have its own language. So—very difficult to answer this question about dialect and language.

[CD 9 Track 5]

Exercise 20.1

Narrator: Task A
Narrator: Listen to a lecture in a business class.
Professor: Okay, today we're going to talk about a form of retailing, a form we're all familiar with . . . the supermarket. Supermarkets appeared in the United States in the 1930's, but they didn't really take off until the 1950's. Now, before this time, most people shopped at small, neighborhood grocery stores, usually family owned. After supermarkets appeared, many of these small stores disappeared. They couldn't compete with supermarkets. Why not?

Well, there are two main reasons. The most important reason is low costs. Most supermarkets are part of large regional chains involving hundreds of stores. They pay low prices for the goods they sell because they buy them in huge volumes. We call this economy of scale. Also, supermarkets have low personnel costs. They're completely self-service: customers select products from the shelves, put them in carts, and bring them to a check-out area at the front of the store. And these days, there are self-service check-out areas where customers even serve as their own cashiers; they ring up their own purchases and put them in bags. Another reason is product variety. Supermarkets offer a much greater variety of canned goods, fruits and vegetables, meats, all kinds of food than a neighborhood market ever could. And not just food; you can get health and beauty products, magazines, automotive supplies, housewares . . .

Now, in the last few decades, supermarkets have been challenged by what are called "hypermarkets" or "megamarts." These giant stores—they're usually part of a national chain—are a combination supermarket and discount department store. They not only sell food, they sell toys, tools, clothes, furniture—almost anything! And not only do they have a greater choice of products, they usually offer cheaper prices than supermarkets because they have an even greater economy of scale.

Narrator: Task B
Narrator: Listen to a lecture in an astronomy class.
Professor: We've been talking about stars in general. Today I'm going to talk about the star we know best—our Sun. We mentioned several different types of stars last week, remember? Our Sun today is what's called a yellow dwarf star. A yellow dwarf. It basically consists of exploding gases, a huge sphere of exploding gases. The explosions, they're really thermonuclear explosions, so it's like thousands of hydrogen bombs going off all at once. So—what keeps the Sun from flying apart, from blowing up? It's the fact that the Sun is so big, so huge that it has an incredibly powerful field of gravity. Then, what keeps these gases from collapsing because of this gravity? It's the explosions—there's this balance, see, between the force that is pulling the Sun apart and the force that is holding it together. Isn't that lucky for us?

Now, by studying other stars, we can predict what the rest of the Sun's life will be like. There are some big changes coming—but don't panic, they're a long way off. The Sun is about halfway through its life as a yellow dwarf. In about 5 billion years, the center of the Sun will start getting hotter and hotter. The rate of interior explosions will increase. The Sun will start to grow in size. In fact, it will expand as far as the orbit of Mercury, the closest planet to the Sun. It will then be a . . . what's called a red giant . . . . a red giant. Temperatures on the Earth will be too hot for life to exist at this point. We have to hope that, if any of our descendants are still around, they've picked out a nice planet around another star and relocated there.

Once the Sun has used up most of its fuel, it will shrink. It'll become a white dwarf star. After a billion years, all the fuel will be gone and it will lose its heat. This kind of star is called a black dwarf. If the Earth still exists at this time, it will be cold, dark, lifeless—not a good place for a vacation home.

Narrator: Task C
Narrator: Listen to a lecture in a telecommunications class.
Professor: It was in the late 1940's, the early 1950's, when television first began to . . . to seriously compete with radio and movies. At the time a lot of people predicted that television would make movie houses and radio sets obsolete. Why would you want to go out to see a movie when you could sit in the comfort of your living room and be entertained? And why would you want to just listen to a program on radio when you could see pictures on your television screen?

Well, uh, as you know . . . it didn't work out that way. Somehow audiences found time to do all these activities— and today these media exist perfectly well side by side. What did change was the way audiences used the old media. There was a, uh, you could say a change in audience habits. Let me give you an example. At one time, people gathered around the radio every evening and listened to dramas and comedies—there were dozens of these serials. These nightly radio programs pretty much disappeared once home audiences started watching prime-time television shows in the evening. However, people continued to listen to music and news on the radio, particularly when they weren't able to . . . to give their full attention to television—when they were getting ready for work, when they were driving to work—you can't drive and watch TV—when they were at work.

Same is true of movies. Habits changed, but movies didn't disappear. Back in the 1930's and 40's, people went to the movies a lot more often than they do these days—three, four times a week, maybe more. But these days, a night at the movies is more of a special occasion, a night out rather than part of a weekly routine. 'Course, many people enjoy watching films as part of an audience rather than watching alone or in a small group. And they like seeing the action on a big screen and listening to a great sound system. So movies have remained popular even in the television age.

Who knows, maybe ten years, twenty years from now, people may be talking about the next big thing, about how some new form of communication and entertainment technology will replace television, CDs, and the Internet. Well, that's always possible, but as we've seen in the past, it's also possible that this new technology will exist alongside of older technologies rather than replace them.

Narrator: Task D
Narrator: Listen to a lecture in a biology class.
Professor: Okay, you've all seen TV shows about scientists who solve mysteries—today we're going to talk about a murder mystery, the biggest murder case of all times, and what scientists have learned about it.

This event is called the Great Dying. Now, don't confuse this with the extinction of the dinosaurs 65 million years ago. The Great Dying was 250 million years ago and was much worse. It involved the death of 90% of the ocean species and 75% of the land species on Earth.

What caused this terrible event? For a long time, scientists have thought it was caused by a huge meteor hitting the earth—that's what probably caused the extinction of the dinosaurs much later. Now there's new evidence for that. Scientists have looked at rocks from that period in Hungary, Japan, and Antarctica, and they've found molecules of minerals that are usually found only in meteors. This means that these molecules came from space. They've also found a crater in Australia that might be the meteor impact site—hard to say after 250 million years.

Around the time that the meteor hit, there was also, uh, a huge volcanic eruption in what's now Siberia. This wasn't like today's volcanoes. No, it was basically a sea of lava, millions of times bigger than a regular volcano. Now, between the dust created by the meteor and the ash thrown up from the super-volcano, the earth was cut off from sunlight. Plants died and no oxygen was being created. That's probably the direct cause of the deaths of all these species—not enough oxygen. The oxygen level dropped from 30% of the atmosphere to 12%. Twelve percent—about what you get on top of a 6,000 meter mountaintop. Just moving around to look for food and water must have been difficult for animals. The lack of oxygen and the stress proved to be too much, and most species died off. It was almost the end of life on Earth.

[CD 9 Track 6]

Exercise 20.2
Narrator: Task A
Narrator: Now listen to a lecture in a psychology class.
Professor: Today, I'm going to talk about a psychological condition, a form of depression that's called Seasonal Affective Disorder, usually abbreviated SAD. SAD hasn't been recognized as a medical condition very long—the term first appeared in medical journals in 1985. This type of depression occurs every year as the days grow shorter during the autumn, and becomes worst in the darkest days of the year, in December and January, at least in the Northern Hemisphere. Symptoms disappear in the spring. It's, mmm, it's thought that the decreasing amounts of light somehow affect brain chemistry, triggering this condition, although the exact causes of this problem are still unknown. So, mmm, the incidence of this disorder, and the severity of this disorder, increases with distance from the equator. Its, mmm, its symptoms include not just depression but also fatigue, irritability, headaches, weight gain. It's more common in women than in men . . . it usually appears when people are in their early twenties.

The treatment for SAD is pretty simple, really—people are treated with bright light. Patients sit a few feet away from a special lamp—about twenty times brighter than an ordinary lamp—and this light essentially duplicates the light of the Sun. Patients do this for thirty minutes every day in the morning and in the evening. They can do other things, they can read or eat breakfast or watch TV while they're sitting in the light. Of course, for those who can afford it, a trip to the tropics in the dead of winter is also a pretty good cure for this condition.

Narrator: Task B
Narrator: Now listen to a lecture in a chemistry class.

Professor: Okay, in lab today, we're going to do a pretty simple little experiment. It involves a process called fractional distillation. Whenever you have a mixture of liquids with different boiling points, you can use this method to separate the two types of liquids. Okay, we're going to start by mixing water and ethanol alcohol in a flask, and then we're going to heat it, as you see if you take a look at the diagram in your lab manual. Now, the alcohol boils at a lower temperature than water. It, uh, boils at about 78 degrees centigrade, and water boils at 100 degrees centigrade, of course. So, you want to heat this mixture higher than 78 degrees but lower than 100 degrees. How do you figure that out? You keep checking the thermometer to keep track of your temperature. So then what happens? The alcohol boils and turns to vapor, to gas. It goes up the column and then passes into the condenser. We have cold water running around the condenser, and this cools down the alcohol vapor inside the condenser. The gas becomes liquid alcohol again, and drips into the other container. After awhile, you have pure water in the first container, the round flask, and pure alcohol in the other container.

Now, uh, this is a simple experiment, as I said, but the process of fractional distillation is an extremely important one. On a much larger scale, on an industrial scale, engineers use this same process to distill crude oil in order to get gasoline and other petroleum products. It's a bit more complicated, because crude oil has many different compounds, each with a different boiling point, but it's basically the same process. Okay, so let's get to work. Let's assemble our equipment and give this experiment a go.

Narrator: Task C
Narrator: Listen to a lecture in a history class.
Professor: Okay, imagine that the year is 1900. The date is November 3. We're in New York City for the opening day of the first National Automobile Show. In fact, this is the first automobile show ever held. There are some forty car manufacturers here. About 8,000 people show up to see the "horseless carriages"—that's what a lot of people call them. People are all dressed up in formal evening wear—they're treating the show more like a formal social occasion than as a sales event. Lots of important people are looking at the cars. Even the president of the United States, William McKinley, is here. In fact, he's the first U.S. president to ever ride in a car.

Now, the automobile wasn't invented in the United States. It was invented in Germany back in the 1880's. But the U.S. pioneered the merchandising, the selling of the automobile. The auto show turned out to be a good way to get the public interested in cars.

These early model cars were . . . well, they were practically handmade, and not very dependable. They were basically toys for rich people. Some were powered by steam, but people worried that these might explode. Some burned gasoline. These were not popular because they were noisy and smelled bad. Electric cars were the most popular because they were safe and almost silent. Some of the cars at the show didn't even have steering wheels. The Gasmobile, for example, was steered with a tiller like a boat.

In the next few years, the number of car manufacturers attending the National Auto Show would explode. In 1905, there'd be 247. Auto shows provided a, . . . a good opportunity for car makers to learn from one another, to learn how to make vehicles more reliable, more comfortable. Who knows? Maybe without the New York Auto Show of 1900

and other auto shows, the United States would never have surpassed France as the world's leading automaker in 1904.

Narrator: Task D
Narrator: Listen to a lecture in a statistics class.
Professor: Okay, has anyone ever heard this before? "If you seat an infinite number of monkeys in front of typewriters"—these days I guess we'd say computer keyboards—"and the monkeys type at random, one of them will eventually create a perfect copy of Shakespeare's *Hamlet*." Yeah, it's quite a famous theorem, isn't it? It's called the Infinite Monkey Theorem. This theorem is mentioned in books about astronomy, computer science, math, statistics. I've seen a mention of it in novels, poems, movies, blogs—even on the cartoon show *The Simpsons*.

Sometimes people use this theorem to . . . umm, to illustrate a very unlikely event. Let's say, uh, Harry isn't much of a student. One day he gets a score of 98% on a multiple-choice test. Harry's friends say, "Well, you know what they say about monkeys . . . "

But the theorem is a good way to get people thinking about some difficult concepts: really large numbers, unlikely events, coincidences, randomness, infinity.

Just how unlikely is it that monkeys would type out Hamlet? Let's say a typewriter has fifty keys—not quite accurate, but close enough. The odds that a monkey will type the first letter of Hamlet are 1 in 50, right? The odds that a monkey will type two correct letters goes up to one in 2,500. Three correct? One in 125,000. How likely is it that a monkey will type the first page of *Hamlet*? Well, suppose you have ten billion planets, and each planet has ten billion monkeys. It would take ten billion years for one monkey to type a page perfectly. Now, there are about 150,000 characters in *Hamlet*. The probability of monkeys typing out the whole play perfectly . . . well, it's beyond comprehension.

[CD 9 Track 7]

Exercise 20.3
Narrator: Task A
Narrator: Using specific examples and points from the lecture, explain Seasonal Affective Disorder (SAD) and its treatment. [20-second pause, then beep] Please start talking now. [60-second pause, then beep] Please stop talking now.

Narrator: Task B
Narrator: Using specific examples and points from the lecture, explain the process of fractional distillation and its importance. [20-second pause, then beep] Please start talking now. [60-second pause, then beep] Please stop talking now.

Narrator: Task C
Narrator: Using specific examples and points from the lecture, describe the 1900 National Automobile Show and its importance. [20-second pause, then beep] Please start talking now. [60-second pause, then beep] Please stop talking now.

Narrator: Task D
Narrator: Using specific examples and points from the lecture, explain the Infinite Monkey Theorem and its importance. [20-second pause, then beep] Please start talking now. [60-second pause, then beep] Please stop talking now.

[CD 9 Track 8]

Speaking Review Test

Narrator: Directions: This section tests your ability to speak about various subjects. There are six tasks in this section. Listen carefully to the directions, and read the questions on the screen. The first two tasks are Independent Speaking tasks. You will have fifteen seconds in which to prepare your response. When you hear a beep on the Audio Program, you will have forty-five seconds in which to answer the question. The last four tasks are Integrated Speaking tasks. The third and fourth questions involve a reading text and a listening passage. You will have forty-five seconds in which to read a short text. You will then hear a short conversation or part of a lecture on the same topic. You may take notes on both the reading and listening passage. You will then see a question on the screen asking about the information that you have just read and heard, and you will have thirty seconds in which to plan a response. When you hear a beep on the Audio Program, you will have sixty seconds in which to answer the question. The fifth and sixth questions involve a short listening passage. You may take notes as you listen. After listening to the conversation or lecture, you will see a question, and you will have twenty seconds in which to plan your response. When you hear a beep on the Audio Program, you will have sixty seconds in which to answer the question. During actual tests, a clock on the screen will tell you how much preparation time or how much response time (speaking time) remains for each question. It is important that you time yourself accurately when you take this practice test. On an actual test your responses will be recorded and evaluated by trained raters.

Narrator: Task 1. . . . Please listen carefully
Narrator: Describe an event in the history of your country and explain why you think it is important. Include details and examples to support your explanation. Please begin speaking after the beep. [15-second pause, then beep] [45-second pause, then beep] Now please stop speaking.

Narrator: Task 2. . . . Please listen carefully
Narrator: Imagine that you have a time machine and can take one trip through time. Would you visit the past or the future? Explain your choice. Include details and examples in your explanation. Please begin speaking after the beep. [15-second pause, then beep] [45-second pause, then beep] Now please stop speaking.

Narrator: Task 3. . . . Please listen carefully
Narrator: Colton College gives an annual prize to a member of the faculty. Read the following announcement in the campus newspaper about this prize. You will have forty-five seconds in which to read the announcement. Begin reading now. [45-second pause]
Narrator: Now listen to two students discussing this announcement.
Student A: So, did you see our microbiology teacher from last semester won that big award?
Student B: Yeah, that . . . I guess that's great for her.
Student A: You don't sound like you mean that.
Student B: Well, I liked the class I took from her, but I was hoping that Dr. Pottinger would win it again. He's such a great lecturer. I mean, when I was in his class, I'd close my eyes, and it seemed like I was back in the Middle Ages or the Renaissance.

Student A: I've always heard he's a good teacher, but hey, so is Professor Weng. Besides, she's gone to Africa and I don't know where else trying to find ways to fight malaria and diseases like that . . . I mean, you have to admit, that's . . . that's pretty important research.
Student B: Yeah, but . . . Pottinger is just . . . he's like an institution here at Colton. I mean, my mom took his world history class, so did my brother, and . . .
Student A: The thing is, he's already won the prize a couple of times, hasn't he?
Student B: Yeah, I know, he has . . . but I just thought . . . well, since he's retiring at the end of this year, I hoped he'd win one last time. You know, kinda like a goodbye gift for all his years at Colton . . .
Student A: See, that's another thing . . . I mean, the prize is . . . it's mainly time off from teaching to do research, right? So, really, Professor Pottinger doesn't need time off. He's not going to be teaching next year anyway.
Narrator: Now get ready to answer the question. The woman expresses her opinion of the announcement. State her opinion, and explain the reasons she gives for having that opinion. Please begin speaking after the beep. [30-second pause, then beep] [60-second pause, then beep] Now stop speaking.

Narrator: Task 4. . . . Please listen carefully . . .
Narrator: Read this passage about a type of American film. You will have forty-five seconds in which to read the passage. Begin reading now. [45-second pause, then beep]
Narrator: Now listen to a lecture on two movies, *The Maltese Falcon* and *Chinatown*.
Professor: Okay, today we're going to watch parts of two movies, two examples of *film noir*. The first one is the 1941 murder mystery *The Maltese Falcon*. It has the dark, shadowy look of a typical *film noir*, it has classical *film noir* characters. It, uh, well, it has all the elements of *film noir*. This movie stars the famous actor Humphrey Bogart as a San Francisco private detective. He's tough, he's cynical, he has a biting sense of humor. Like lots of *noir* films, it has a complicated plot, but it's the gloomy atmosphere, not the story, really, that makes the movie interesting.

We're also gonna take a look at some clips from the 1974 movie *Chinatown*. I know, I know, the book says *noir* movies were all made in the 40's and 50's. And I also know that the book says that *noir* films were always filmed in black and white, not in color. Still, critics usually call *Chinatown* a *noir* movie. The private eye in this movie is played by Jack Nicholson. He's as tough and cynical as Humphrey Bogart in *The Maltese Falcon*, although, deep down, he's a little more caring, a little more sympathetic than the typical *noir* character. However, it's because of the atmosphere that this movie is also considered part of the *film noir* genre. Although the movie is filmed in color, the atmosphere of the film is as dark, gloomy, and violent as that in *The Maltese Falcon*, as you'll soon see.
Narrator: Now get ready to answer the question. The professor's lecture is about two movies: *The Maltese Falcon* and *Chinatown*. Describe these movies, and explain why they are considered examples of *film noir*. Please begin speaking after the beep. [30-second pause, then beep] [60-second pause, then beep] Now stop speaking.

Narrator: Task 5. . . . Please listen carefully
Narrator: Listen to a conversation between two students.
Student A: Hey, Mark, do you know anything about designing Web sites?
Student B: Um, not that much, really. In fact, almost nothing. Why do you ask?

Student A: Well, I'm working part-time at the campus museum, and the museum director wants to re-design the Web site, and I said I'd be interested in doing that . . .

Student B: Michelle, why would you say that if you don't know anything about designing Web pages?

Student A: Well . . . I think it would be a useful skill to have, you know? It's something I'd like to learn . . .

Student B: I imagine if you went online, you could find some Internet site . . . some tutorial that teaches you the basics . . .

Student A: Yeah, I thought of that, and maybe I should take a look at some sites but . . . I learn by asking questions . . . I'd rather have a real, live person give me some hints, get me started, answer my dumb questions . . . do you know any Internet geniuses?

Student B: I . . . I dunno, I don't think I do. But hey, why don't you just drop by the Computer Science department. Maybe put up a note on the bulletin board asking for someone to give you a few hours of their time. Maybe one of the Computer Science students would be willing to help you out.

Student A: Yeah, that's an idea. I might drop by there on the way back from class . . .

Narrator: Now get ready to answer the question. The man discusses two possible solutions to Michelle's problem. Discuss her problem and then explain which of the two solutions you think is better and why you think so. Please begin speaking after the beep. [20-second pause, then beep] [60-second pause, then beep] Now stop speaking.

Narrator: Task 6. . . . Please listen carefully

Narrator: Listen to part of a lecture in an economics class.

Professor: All right, today our topic is *externalities*. Externalities are one of the most important concepts in economics.

Okay, so what do we mean by this term? An externality happens when one organization or an individual is producing a good or service and does something to affect the well-being of another person or organization. The, uh, benefit of this or the cost of this is not reflected in market prices.

Externalities can be negative or positive. A classic example of a negative externality is pollution. Let's say Company X owns a factory that manufactures plastic plates. This factory is located on a river. During the process of manufacturing these plates, the company releases toxic wastes into the river. Now, there's a community, a town, right down the river from the factory. This town has to spend a lot of its money to clean its water so people can drink it. And some people get sick anyway and they have to go to the doctor. So then, when Company X sells its plates, do they charge extra to pay for the cost of cleaning up the water? To pay for the doctor bills? No, because this is an externality.

Now, here's a standard example of a positive externality—a man keeps bees on his land, he raises bees to get honey to sell it. His bees pollinate the fruit trees on his neighbor's farm. Without his bees, in fact, his neighbor would have no fruit to sell. So, when the beekeeper sells his bees' honey, does he get extra money because of the good deed his bees have done? Nope. Once again, we're talking about an externality.

Some economists believe that the government should step in to correct externalities. When a company produces a negative externality, such as pollution, the company should be taxed or their activities should be regulated. If a company produces positive externalities, it should receive an award, a subsidy, from the government. Of course . . . even if you think this is a good idea, calculating the costs of externalities can be very difficult.

Narrator: Now get ready to answer the question. Using specific examples and points from the lecture, explain the concept of externalities. Please begin speaking after the beep. [20-second pause, then beep] [60-second pause, then beep] Now stop speaking.

Narrator: This is the end of the Speaking Review Test.

[CD 9 Track 9]

Speaking Tutorial: Building Pronunciation Skills

Exercise 1: Number of Syllables

1. basic
2. home
3. Brazil
4. decide
5. decided
6. understand
7. authority
8. Korea
9. president
10. information

1. basic
2. home
3. Brazil
4. decide
5. decided
6. understand
7. authority
8. Korea
9. president
10. information

[CD 9 Track 10]

Exercise 2: Syllable Stress

1. lecture
2. problem
3. discuss
4. solution
5. possibility
6. important
7. compare
8. situation

[CD 9 Track 11]

Exercise 3: Stress in Academic Vocabulary

1. minor   minority
2. valid   validity
3. stable   stability
4. strategy   strategic
5. philosophy philosophical
6. economy   economic
7. distribute distribution
8. apply   application

[CD 9 Track 12]

Exercise 4: Find the Stressed Syllable

define	airport	credit	produce	produce
obtain	software	outcome	progress	progress
prefer	math test	concept	conduct	conduct
select	health care	office	insult	insult
compare	stock market	factor	record	record
assume	supermarket	input	present	present

[CD 10 Track 2]

Exercise 5: Identify the Stress

secure	security	classic	classical
legal	legality	democracy	democratic
diverse	diversity	history	historic
electric	electricity	geology	geological
personal	personality	photography	photographic
notify	notification	fourteen	forty
graduate	graduation	eighteen	eighty
define	definition	nineteen	ninety
register	registration	seventeen	seventy
congratulate	congratulation	fifteen	fifty

[CD 10 Track 3]

Exercise 6: Producing Word Stress in Context
"Well, *education* is important to my family and me so . . . I guess . . . the most important day in my life . . . was my *graduation* from Seoul *National University*. I'd always dreamed . . . of becoming a *medical* doctor and my degree in *biology* was my first step toward that . . . that goal. On my *graduation*, it was a hot day and the *humidity* was high but nobody seemed to . . . notice. Everybody was so excited that they paid no *attention* to the weather . . . even though it took hours to call everyone's name. When the ceremony was over, my family and friends from my *community* . . . *we* all went to a restaurant for a *celebration*."

[CD 10 TRACK 4]

Exercise 7: Listening to Word Stress in a Lecture
Well then, let me talk about *marble* for a few minutes. Marble . . . it's a type of *metamorphic* rock. . . . Marble is formed from *limestone*. Now, limestone is a kind of *sedimentary* rock—but limestone is much softer, much more easily broken than marble. It is formed deep in the earth's crust over millions of years. Marble formed from pure limestone is almost pure white. Impurities—different types of minerals mixed in with the limestone—these give marble its different colors—green, yellow, tan, pink, and so on.

Marble is valued for its beauty, and . . . its strength. It's been used for temples, monuments, statues. It's still used for building today, especially for public buildings.

[CD 10 TRACK 5]

Exercise 8: Identifying Stressed and Unstressed Words
1. The problem is her neighbors are noisy.
2. Participants can earn credit and also make money.
3. I'd prefer to work for a company.
4. The announcement is about regulations for parking at the university.
5. Her choices are to talk to her neighbors or to move.

[CD 10 Track 6]

Exercise 9: Matching English Rhythm
Stan's trying to make a decision about college . . . about where to attend his last semester of college. The problem is . . . that . . . well, his major is classical languages . . . and his university is going to close that department at the end of the term.

[CD 10 Track 7]

Exercise 10: English Rhythm in Context
Listen to the conversation.
Speaker A: Hey, Lucy, how are things?
Speaker B: Hi, Rick. Oh, I don't know. Okay, I suppose . . . I'm just . . . I'm just exhausted!
Speaker A: Yeah, you do look kinda tired . . . how come?
Speaker B: Well, I just never get enough sleep . . . my classes are really hard this term, especially my physiology class, so I'm in the library until it closes at eleven, and then I study for a couple of hours or so when I get back to my dorm room.
Speaker A: Yeah, I've had a couple of semesters like that myself . . .
Speaker B: I feel especially dead in the afternoon, and I have a one o'clock and a three o'clock class. Yesterday, the most incredibly embarrassing thing happened in my physiology class—I actually fell asleep! I've *never* done that before . . . And Doctor Daniels was like, "Am I boring you, Ms. Jenkins?"

[CD 10 Track 8]

Exercise 11: Reduced Forms
1. I thought <u>uh</u> calling the cops.
2. She'll pay the fees <u>'n'</u> keep parking at the stadium.
3. Stan, <u>'ve</u> you decided what classes you're taking?
4. He should <u>uh</u> listened to the nurse's advice.
5. They more <u>uh</u> less understand each other.
6. We <u>hafta</u> register our cars.
7. He's <u>gotta</u> get another form of ID.
8. He's not <u>gonna</u> change his major.
9. She doesn't <u>wanna</u> call the police on her neighbors.
10. The man has a <u>coupla</u> solutions for Lucy's problem.
11. Tina <u>oughta</u> talk to her lab partner.

[CD 10 Track 9]

Exercise 12: Can or Can't?
1. You can't park there with a student permit.
2. She can't study in her building.
3. Letter grades can be used to rank students.
4. Today, couples can't adopt twin babies separately.
5. English speakers from Jamaica and India can understand each other.
6. I can't believe some students don't turn off their phones in class.
7. You can always use another bulletin board on campus.
8. The blue morpho is brightly colored, but its predators can hardly see it.

[CD 10 Track 10]

Exercise 13: Predicting Thought Groups
To describe marble, / first you have to define metamorphic rock. / Metamorphic rock / is rock that's, uh, changed, / from one kind of rock / to another. / umm, marble comes from a softer rock / that's called limestone, / which is a sedimentary rock. / Marble is a hard rock. / Marble comes in various colors. / Like other metamorphic rocks, / it is so strong / that it is often used for building.

Supermarkets have been successful / for two main reasons. / The first reason / is that costs are low. / One reason the costs are low / is . . . uh, that supermarkets buy / in huge quantities. / This is called / . . . let's see . . . / economy of scale.

[CD 10 Track 11]

Exercise 14: Listening for Thought Groups
She wants to take part ⬈
in the experiment. ⬊
One reason is ⬈
that she can make some extra money. ⬊
Another reason is ⬈
that she has lots of problems ⬈
going to sleep at night. ⬊

His sister ⬈
got a position as an intern ⬈
at an advertising agency ⬊
The pay was pretty good, ⬈
and besides, ⬈
it was good experience for her. ⬊
It looks good ⬈
on her résumé. ⬊

AUDIO SCRIPT

There was a numeral system ↗
that was used by the Yuki Indians ↗
of California ↗
that was base 8. ↘
The Yukis ↗
counted the spaces between their fingers ↗
rather than their fingers themselves. ↘

The announcement is about plagiarism. ↘
What is plagiarism? ↗
According to the announcement, ↗
it is using someone else's words or ideas ↗
as your own ↗
without crediting the other person. ↘

[CD 10 Track 12]

Exercise 15: Listening for the Focus Words

She <u>wants</u> to take part ↗
in the ex<u>peri</u>ment. ↘
<u>One</u> reason is ↗
that she can make some extra <u>money.</u> ↘
A<u>nother</u> reason is ↗
that she has lots of <u>problems</u> ↗
going to <u>sleep</u> at night. ↘

His <u>sister</u> ↗
got a position as an <u>intern</u> ↗
at an <u>a</u>dvertising agency. ↘
The <u>pay</u> was pretty good, ↗
and be<u>sides,</u> ↗
it was good ex<u>peri</u>ence for her. ↘
It looks <u>good</u> ↗
on her <u>ré</u>sumé. ↘

There was a <u>numeral</u> system ↗
that was <u>used</u> by the Yuki <u>Indians</u> ↗
of Cali<u>for</u>nia ↗
that was base <u>8.</u> ↘
The <u>Yukis</u> ↗
counted the spaces be<u>tween</u> their fingers ↗
rather than their fingers them<u>selves.</u> ↘

The announcement is about <u>plagiarism.</u> ↘
What is <u>plagiarism?</u> ↗
According to the an<u>nouncement,</u> ↗
it is using someone <u>else's</u> words or ideas ↗
as your <u>own</u> ↗
without <u>cre</u>diting the other person. ↘

[CD 10 Track 13]

Exercise 16: Finding the Focus

My <u>sister</u>—
my <u>older</u> sister—
got a job with an <u>ad</u> agency.
It was a <u>New York</u> ad agency.

He got in trouble for <u>plagiarism.</u>
Well, it wasn't ex<u>actly</u> plagiarism.
At <u>least,</u> <u>he</u> didn't consider it plagiarism.

The nest of the <u>hamerkop</u>
has at least three <u>rooms.</u>
the <u>highest</u> room
is the <u>sleeping</u> room
where the female lays her <u>eggs.</u>
When the babies grow <u>up</u>
they move to the <u>middle</u> room.

[CD 10 Track 14]

Exercise 17: Putting Thought Groups, Intonation, and Focus Together

I think I'd prefer living in a <u>dorm</u> ↗/ to living in an a<u>part</u>ment ↘./ It's <u>true</u> ↗/ that many apartments are <u>roomy</u> ↗,/ and most <u>dorm</u> rooms ↗/ are kind of <u>cramped</u> ↘,/ but there are <u>other</u> reasons why dorm rooms are better ↘./ The <u>first</u> ↗ / is trans-portation ↘./ If I lived off-<u>campus</u> ↗,/ I'd have to <u>drive</u> ↗/ and owning a car is ex<u>pen</u>sive. ↘ / So is <u>parking.</u> ↘./ I have heard it can <u>cost</u> ↗   / . . . $100 a se<u>mes</u>ter ↘./ A<u>nother</u> reason living in a dorm is better ↗ / is that it is easier to make <u>friends</u> ↘. / In <u>a</u>partments buildings, ↗ / people may say he<u>llo</u> ↗ / but they aren't very <u>friendly</u> ↘. / In <u>dorms,</u> ↗ / people stop and <u>talk</u> ↗ /and are much more <u>sociable</u> ↘./ Finally, what about <u>meals?</u> / If I lived in an a<u>part</u>ment ↗, / I'd have to <u>cook</u> ↘. / On the other hand, in a <u>dorm</u> ↗ /meals are pro<u>vided</u> ↘./ And that's a re<u>lief</u> ↗,/ because <u>frankly,</u> ↗ / I'm a <u>terrible</u> cook ↘."

[CD 10 Track 15]

Exercise 19: Added Sound or Added Syllable?

1. add - added
2. park - parked
3. plan - planned
4. wait - waited
5. intend - intended
6. apply - applied
7. decide – decided
8. believe - believed

[CD 10 Track 16]

Exercise 20: Listening to Present and Past Tense

1. A lot of students park at the stadium.
2. People believed that hamerkops carried snakes to their nests.
3. They want to have control of their time.
4. The students appreciated her assistance.
5. Those two individuals caused all of the problems in the department.
6. Not enough students majored in classical languages.

[CD 10 Track 17]

Exercise 22: Saying the -s Ending

1. takes
2. causes
3. credits
4. expresses
5. dislikes
6. explains
7. fixes
8. thinks
9. Nancy's
10. discusses
11. reasons
12. changes
13. gives

[CD 10 Track 18]

Exercise 23: Listening to –s Endings in Context

The two students are discussing preferences in housing. They both prefer living in a dorm to living in an apartment. They agree that many apartments are roomy, and most dorm rooms are kind of cramped, but they give some uh, good rea-sons why they think that dorm rooms are better. The first one is that it is easier to make friends. People are more sociable. Also, a dorm usually provides meals. This is good, because they are both awful cooks.

[CD 10 Track 19]

Examples of initial voiced and voiceless consonants.

1. pay   bay
2. time   dime
3. cold   gold
4. few   view
5. sip   zip
6. cheap   jeep

[CD 10 Track 20]
Examples of final voiced and voiceless consonants.
1. cop   cob
2. neat   need
3. back   bag
4. proof   prove
5. price   prize
6. rich   ridge

[CD 10 Track 21]

Exercise 24: Identifying Voiced and Voiceless Consonants
1. The audience was cheering the actors.
2. This is a vast network.
3. She gave her son a little pat.
4. There was a mob in the lobby.
5. Don't you hear that buzz?
6. Eugene's acting a little tense this morning.
7. You have a lot of fans.
8. What a nice bear!
9. She has lovely little girls.
10. Sam, who put that dent in your car?
11. What was the prize?
12. He burned his bridges behind him.

[CD 10 Track 22]

The professor talked about the success of supermarkets. They took off in the 50's for several reasons. One was the good selection of products—food, beauty products, magazines, and so on. Another reason was cost. Neighborhood groceries couldn't compete with their low prices.

[CD 10 Track 23]

Listening Test:
1. it's through – it's true
2. a lot of math – a lot of mass
3. pilot software – pirate software
4. copy machine – coffee machine
5. cash it – catch it
6. in a vial – in a while

[CD 10 Track 24]

Exercise 25: /p/ as in past vs. /f/ as in fast
peel   feel   copy   coffee   pin   fin   pact fact

1. peel peel 2. copy coffee 3. pin fin 4. fact fact

1. Can we agree on this fact?
2. Sometimes you have to pace yourself.
3. I saw Amy driving past.
4. Where's the new copy machine?
5. He feels fine.
6. Toss that letter in this pile.
7. Is this is a new fad?
8. He had to face his fears.

[CD 10 Track 25]

Exercise 26: /ʃ/ as in wash vs. /tʃ/ as in watch
shop   chop   shoes   choose
wish   which   much   mush

1. shop   chop   2. shoes   choose
3. wish   wish   4. much   much

1. This is a good block for shopping.
2. Don't wash that pot.
3. He tried to catch it.
4. He chose his paintings.
5. He just wants his proper share.
6. Hey! There's a chip in that bottle!
7. My dog hates leashes.
8. She bumped her shin.
9. There were so many toppings that there wasn't much room on the pizza.
10. I had a dream about three witches.

[CD 10 Track 26]

Exercise 27: /v/ as in verse vs. /w/ as in worse
verse   worse   vial   while   vest   west   very   wary

1. worse worse 2. vial vial 3. vest west 4. very wary

1. This type of _vine_ was brought to California from Italy.
2. You call this _verse_?
3. He'll bring the money _in a while_.
4. He was pointing to the _west_.
5. I was talking with my cousin _Vinnie_.

[CD 10 Track 27]

Exercise 28: /l/ as in light vs. /r / as in right
late   rate   locks   rocks
long   wrong   collect correct

1. late   late   2. rate   rate
3. long   wrong   4. collect correct

1. The teaching assistant was correcting the tests.
2. He wants to make the right choice, not the wrong one.
3. The lecture was about the locks in Panama.
4. In the late afternoon, clouds began to form
5. The huge nests have three rooms.
6. She put the clock on the shelf.
7. They tried to free the wild animals.
8. Can you fry this?

[CD 10 Track 28]

Exercise 29: /θ/ as in thin vs. /s / in sin, /f / in fin, and /t / in tin
think   sink   math   mass   three tree
both   boat   thought fought

1. think sink   2. math   math   3. tree tree
4. both   boat   5. thought thought

1. Suddenly, Tony started to sink.
2. The council fought about that issue all afternoon.
3. They found the pass through the mountains.
4. They had to call in three surgeons to solve the problem.
5. A physicist must understand math.
6. The general offered his thanks.
7. That's a nice boot.
8. He didn't pick the right team.
9. That's a thick tree.
10. Will Dorothy be free on Saturday?

[CD 10 Track 29]
Examples of glided and simple vowels.
She's leaving there.   She's living there.
He's worried about the date. He's worried about the debt.
They pooled it.   They pulled it.

[CD 10 Track 30]

Listening Test
1. don't hit it – don't heat it
2. test it – taste it

[CD 10 Track 31]

Exercise 30: /iʸ/ as in h<u>ea</u>t vs. /ɪ/ as in h<u>i</u>t

seen sin	leave live	steal still	feel fill
1. seen seen	**2.** leave live	**3.** still still	**4.** feel fill

1. That was a chip shot.
2. I keep trying to fill the empty space.
3. The students want to leave here.
4. They need better heaters.
5. When the men came around the bend, they saw the ship.

[CD 10 Track 32]

Exercise 31: /eʸ/ as in l<u>a</u>te vs. /ɛ/ as in l<u>e</u>t

wait wet	late let	main men	date debt
1. wait wet	**2.** late let	**3.** men men	**4.** date debt

1. She sure has a lot of _debts_.
2. Don't you think that there's too much _pepper_?
3. Gus had a _pen_ behind his ear.
4. Give that sauce a _taste test_ to see if it needs more salt.
5. Cynthia likes to wear _lace_ in the summer.

Narrator: This is the end of the Speaking Tutorial.

[CD 10 Track 33]

Section 4: Guide to Writing

The Integrated Writing Task

Narrator: Listen to a lecture in a secondary education class.

Professor: Now, as your textbook points out, there are two types of tests: objective and essay. Your textbook author takes a pretty strong stand in favor of essay tests, doesn't he? Well, I happen to agree with some of his ideas. I have nothing against essay tests, and they do get at different things than . . . objective tests do. They test students' ability to think critically, to . . . solve problems. That's why I generally include a couple of essay questions in every test I give. But I also use multiple-choice items.

It's true that objective tests check your memorization skills—but what's wrong with that? Sometimes, in some classes at least, you need to memorize basic facts and information!

And it's also true that . . . that essay tests emphasize writing skills. It's true—and it's part of the problem! Good writers can get good grades on essay tests even if they don't know very much about the topic.

And as far as saving time—sure, it may take less time to write essay tests. But . . . it takes a lot more time to grade them. Not only that, but you really should grade all the essays at the same time, because . . . well, studies show that the same teacher will grade the same essay differently at different times. To be fair, you've got to grade all the tests at one sitting. Now, with a small class, this isn't a big problem, but if you have a large class . . . well, it's a lot easier to grade objective tests, and lots of times, you can have them machine graded.

So, when you start teaching, and giving tests yourself . . . by all means, use essay tests, but for some classes, for some material, for some situations . . . objective tests, or combinations of objective and essay tests, may be best.

[CD 10 Track 34]

Integrated Writing Preview Test

Narrator: This Writing Section tests your ability to write academic English. It consists of two writing tasks. The first writing task is an "integrated" task. It involves reading a short passage and listening to a short lecture on the same topic. You will then have twenty minutes in which to write a response based on the information in the passage and the lecture. Now read the directions for the first writing task.

Narrator: Directions: Take three minutes to read the short passage on the following page. You may take notes as you read. After three minutes, start the Audio Program. You will hear a lecture on the same topic as the reading. Again, you may take notes as you listen. You will have twenty minutes to write your response. Your response should include information from both the reading and the lecture. Your essay will be rated on the completeness and accuracy of your response as well as on the correctness and quality of your writing. A typical response should be 150 to 225 words. You may use your notes and look at the reading passage as you write. (During the actual exam, you can view the reading passage on the computer screen after the lecture is over.) You will have twenty minutes in which to finish the Integrated Writing Task. If possible, you should write your response on the computer. Begin reading now. [3-minute pause]

Narrator: Now listen to part of a lecture in a biology class.

Professor: Now, most of you in the class know how I feel about medical research done on animals. I oppose it, no matter why . . . no matter what the justification. But . . . for the sake of fairness, I wanted you to see this article that my colleague in the biology department, Professor White, wrote for our departmental journal.

At the heart of his argument is the professor's claim that animal experimentation has led to the discovery of some important drugs, useful drugs, like penicillin. Well, that may be true, but who knows if these drugs wouldn't have been discovered without animal testing? And, you know, here's the thing—there are plenty of important drugs that were discovered without the benefit of animal testing. Quinine, used to treat malaria, ether, used as an anesthesia, and of course aspirin, they were all discovered without harming any animals. In fact, if some drugs had been tested on certain animals, well, they probably wouldn't be used today. Morphine, for example, kills pain in people but it stimulates cats. And large doses of aspirin poison cats and dogs and have no effect on horses.

And Professor White says that there are no substitutes for animal testing. There are plenty! For example, now we can cultivate human tissues and test the effects of drugs on these tissues. There are clinical studies, and . . . most important of all, these days, computer simulations. There are lots of other ways too.

People in favor of animal research always say that animals in labs are treated as humanely as possible. Don't believe that! It may be true some of the time, but I've spent a lot of time in biology labs and I've seen many animals undergoing tests with terrible diseases and toxic chemicals. Many times these animals were not adequately anesthetized or they were routinely abused by handlers or experimenters.

No, I believe that no one should be forced to undergo experimentation without giving their . . . their consent, their agreement. Since animals can never do that, I believe it is immoral to experiment on them, no matter what the benefits might be.

Narrator: Now get ready to answer the question. Remember you may look back at the reading passage. You may also use your notes to help you. You have twenty minutes to prepare and write your response.

Question: Summarize the main points made in the lecture that you just read, discussing how they cast doubt on points made in the reading. You can refer to the reading passage as you write.

[CD 10 TRACK 35]

Lesson 21: Taking Notes and Planning the Integrated Response

Sample

Narrator: Now listen to part of a lecture in a biology class.

Professor: Now, most of you in the class know how I feel about medical research done on animals. I oppose it, no matter why . . . no matter what the justification. But . . . for the sake of fairness, I wanted you to see this article that my colleague in the biology department, Professor White, wrote for our departmental journal.

At the heart of his argument is the professor's claim that animal experimentation has led to the discovery of some important drugs, useful drugs, like penicillin. Well, that may be true, but who knows if these drugs wouldn't have been discovered *without* animal testing? And, you know, here's the thing—there are *plenty* of important drugs that were discovered without the benefit of animal testing. Quinine, used to treat malaria, ether, used as an anesthesia, and of course aspirin, they were all discovered without harming any animals. In fact, if some drugs had been tested on certain animals, well, they probably wouldn't be used today. Morphine, for example, kills pain in people but it stimulates cats. And large doses of aspirin poison cats and dogs and have no effect on horses.

And Professor White says that there are no substitutes for animal testing. There are plenty! For example, now we can cultivate human tissues and test the effects of drugs on these tissues. There are clinical studies, and . . . most important of all, these days, computer simulations. There are lots of other ways too.

People in favor of animal research always say that animals in labs are treated as humanely as possible. Don't believe that! It may be true some of the time, but I've spent a lot of time in biology labs and I've seen many animals undergoing tests with terrible diseases and toxic chemicals. Many times these animals were not adequately anesthetized or they were routinely abused by handlers or experimenters.

No, I believe that no one should be forced to undergo experimentation without giving their . . . their consent, their agreement. Since animals can never do that, I believe it is immoral to experiment on them, no matter what the benefits might be.

[CD 10 Track 36]

Exercise 21.1

Narrator: Task 1

Listen to part of a lecture in an ecology class.

Professor: Okay, that article I gave you to read—I just want you to know, it makes me really angry! I mean . . . well, I've told you this before, but I spent a year at McMurdo Station, at the Antarctic research station. I had a chance to experience what a beautiful . . . incredible . . . but unforgiving place Antarctica is.

It's true, Antarctica is a huge continent, and it is largely lifeless. However, like the Arctic regions, like high mountaintops, it's a very fragile region, very easily damaged. The article mentions that only the coastline supports life. But isn't it from these coastal areas that oil or gas would have to be shipped? The southern oceans are some of the most dangerous waters anywhere. Imagine . . . imagine a supertanker hitting an iceberg. I mean, imagine, if there were a big oil spill, what effects that would have on the penguins, the whales, the seals, the sea birds . . . terrible!

Besides, people who haven't been to Antarctica—and I'll bet the author hasn't set foot there—they just can't imagine how harsh conditions there are. He compares Antarctica with Alaska and the North Sea, but it would be much more difficult to drill for oil in Antarctica, or in the seas nearby. And it would be unbelievably expensive, prohibitively expensive, no matter how much a barrel of oil is selling for. Here's what I think—I think it would be better, much better, to invest all that money in alternative fuel sources like, uh, say, hydrogen.

The 1993 treaty wasn't just agreed to by scientists. It was agreed to by . . . by government representatives from all over the world. Putting the southern continent into the care of scientists and . . . and out of the reach of politicians, of multinational corporations, well, it was a wise decision, it . . . it made sure Antarctica will remain undeveloped for generations to come.

Narrator: Task 2

Listen to part of a lecture in an astronomy class.

Professor: Okay, class, I want you to imagine something. Imagine a little lake in the middle of a forest, far from any other lakes. This lake is full of fish. One day, one of the fish says this: "We've never seen any other lakes and we've never seen any other fish. Therefore, we must be the only fish in the world."

We know, just in our own galaxy—our Milky Way galaxy—there are over 400 billion—that's right, four hundred billion stars. Now, our star, the Sun, has one habitable planet. Suppose our star is really unusual. Suppose only one in a thousand stars has planets that have ideal conditions for life. That means that there are 400,000,000 planets with life on them just in our galaxy. And remember, life on Earth, at least, has developed under some pretty harsh conditions, so really, you don't even need ideal conditions.

Of course, that doesn't mean that this life is intelligent life. But, according to the famous scientist Carl Sagan . . . Carl Sagan . . . "smart is better." According to his theory, some species like sharks and tigers become strong and fast because these qualities help them hunt, help them survive. Some species, like man, become intelligent, because this quality helps them survive. Anyway—suppose only one in a thousand worlds with life developed intelligence. That means there are 400,000 intelligent species just in our galaxy.

Now, why haven't we heard from these species? For one thing, their interests and ours may not be the same. They may not be interested in technology, in developing radio transmitters—maybe they're interested in philosophy, or religion, or . . . who knows, maybe in basket weaving. Maybe they have no interest in communicating with other worlds.

Anyway, I think we are being very self-centered if we don't at least admit the possibility of intelligent life on other planets. We're just like those fish I mentioned—the ones who think they are the only fish living in the only lake in the world.

Narrator: Task 3

Listen to part of a lecture in a political science class.

Professor: Everyone read the article I gave you about mandatory voting? Okay, good. Well, in recent general elections in both the U.S. and the U.K., voter turnout has been quite low, and so, there have been editorials in newspapers and commentators on TV talking about . . . about forcing people to come out and vote, about making them vote if they want to or not.

Now I know, as it says in the journal article that I gave you, that Australia and a number of other countries have this mandatory voting system. And . . . I'm sure that in these places, that they have a, a really good turnout. I mean, it's the law, you gotta vote. But personally, I think it's better to have a smaller number of people who vote really well, who vote smart, than to have a really big turnout. If there's no compulsion to vote, no law that says you have to vote, then the people who *do* vote really want to vote, and they're the ones who are well informed about the candidates, about the issues and so on . . .

To me, there's a huge difference between voting and paying taxes. If, say, 40% of citizens don't pay taxes, what happens? The government runs out of funds, it stops functioning. What happens if 40% of the people don't vote? Think about it. Nothing. Nothing happens. Officials are still elected, and the government goes along just fine.

Now, it may be true that, if you don't vote, you're not giving your active consent to your choice of government, but you are exercising a freedom, your freedom *not* to vote. In fact, some people use not voting as a way to make a statement. You may be saying, for example, that you don't agree with any of the candidates, or that you feel the political process has nothing to offer you.

In a democracy, you have lots of rights. You have the right to, say, open your own business if you want. That doesn't mean that you should have to open your own business. It should be the same way with voting. Because you have the right to do something shouldn't mean that you have the obligation, the duty to do it.

Narrator: Task 4
Listen to part of a lecture in a geo-science class.
Professor: All right, now, we're going to continue our discussion of extinction, extinction at the end of the Ice Ages. I gave you a couple of articles to read over the weekend. I'd like to talk about . . . let's see, let's talk about the wooly mammoth article first. Everyone pull that one out, okay?

Now, the article seems to imply that one of these three theories about the mammoths is probably the right one, but in fact, there are some problems with . . . well, with all three theories. First off, there's the idea that humans directly killed off the mammoths by hunting them to death. Sure, it's tempting to blame humans because mammoths were doing just fine until people showed up in North America. But think about this: mammoths were huge, strong, dangerous, well-armed creatures—look at those tusks! They had thick, thick skin and thick layers of fat—hard to pierce with any spear, no matter how sharp. Why should humans hunt these giants when there were other animals around that were smaller, easier to kill? The Clovis People were few in number and they were widely scattered. A computer study shows that they could've eaten only 10% of the mammoths that they supposedly killed. Why would they have killed so many if they weren't going to eat them?

Then, there's the theory that humans killed off mammoths indirectly, by bringing disease to the New World. This is an interesting theory, but a theory needs evidence. Scientists have examined the remains of many dead mammoths and found no sign, none, of any infectious disease.

Then there's the climate-change theory, that mammoths died because it got warmer. The thing is, mammoths endured much more violent climate changes in the past and survived them just fine. Besides, their relatives in the Old World, the ancestors of the African and Indian elephants, managed to survive this climate change without any problems.

So, maybe one of these theories is correct. Maybe a combination of these factors doomed the mammoths, killed them all off. But . . . maybe, just maybe, none of these theories is true, and we still don't know the true cause of the mammoths' extinction.

Narrator: Task 5
Listen to part of a lecture in an art class.
Professor: Now, um, it may surprise you to hear this, because I don't just teach art, I'm a working artist myself, as you know, but . . . I don't agree with the idea of government support for individual artists. Why not, you ask?

Well, plumbing is an important occupation. Where would we be without plumbers, huh? But are there special grants for plumbers? Plumbers can't take a year off at taxpayers' expense to . . . to finish a special plumbing project, now can they? To me, it's not fair to treat artists as any different from plumbers or from anyone else. There were great American artists before there were government grants. How did they make it? Well, they sold their works of art on the marketplace.

Okay, you say, what about the unpopular artists, the controversial artists that the author mentions? Well, no one is saying these artists can't produce what they like, but . . . if they can't sell their works . . . they can always . . . gasp! . . . get jobs! There are jobs for artists—they can work as commercial artists, they can teach art . . .

Sure, artists once had wealthy patrons. Of course, these were private sponsors, not government sponsors. What I object to is giving public money to one special group. Some artists today have corporate sponsors. Personally, I wouldn't take money from a corporation. But if that's what an artist wants to do, that's fine with me . . .

The author mentions a study exploring how the arts generate economic activity. I'd like to point out that this study was done on groups of performing artists, on art organizations like ballet companies or theater groups. Giving grants, giving money to art organizations may be a good investment, but I don't think that spending money on individual artists generates much economic activity. And there's always the possibility that government programs meant to help artists may end up wasting money, wasting huge amounts of money. Let me give you an example: There was a program in France which provided certain artists grants to make their lives better, to make them more secure financially. Everyone connected with arts applied for this program—I mean everyone, even people who cut actors' hair, applied for these grants. This program generated a deficit approaching one billion—that's one *billion*—euros. So, you see, investments in the arts are *not* always good investments.

Narrator: Task 6
Listen to part of a lecture in a psychology class.
Professor: All of you know I'm no big fan of television, especially of commercial TV . . . . still, I have to disagree with the author's view of children's TV and especially with her assessment of the study that she refers to. For one thing, I'm a mom myself, and I know how difficult it is to ban television altogether from your house, to prevent kids from watching. Anything that's forbidden . . . that just makes it more attractive to kids! Kids'll just go watch TV at their friends' houses if you don't let them watch at home. So . . .

yeah, parents do need to monitor their children's TV watching, but it's gonna be very, very difficult to unplug the TV until your kids are 18.

Now, I took a look at the study the author mentions. Yeah, the study says kids 6 to 7 who watch a lot of TV get lower test scores. But there's something the author doesn't mention in her article. According to this same study, kids aged 3 to 5 who watch a lot of television every day score higher on reading recognition tests than kids who don't!

What I think is important, is monitoring how much TV children watch. For children 2 and under, most psychologists suggest *no* television, and I agree. For kids over 2, I'd set strict limits. I'd limit children to two hours a day. That leaves plenty of time for play and study. I'd mostly let young children watch only educational shows . . . shows that are designed to teach children things they need to know, like how to count, how to recognize the letters of the alphabet. I wouldn't let younger kids watch much entertainment TV. And I'd only let kids watch Public Television, where there are no commercials.

And sure, physical fitness is a problem, a lot of kids are overweight these days, but we can't blame this problem entirely on television. If you limit kids to no more than two hours a day in front of the tube, there's plenty of time for them to get outside and get some exercise, get some fresh air. And of course, you need to teach kids about good nutrition.

So . . . like a lot of things, television is not purely good or purely bad, it just depends on how it's used. If television is used wisely, it's not such a bad thing.

[CD 11 TRACK 2]

Lesson 22: Summarizing, Paraphrasing, Citing, and Synthesizing for the Integrated Writing Response
Sample
Narrator: Listen to part of a lecture in a biology class.
Professor: At the heart of his argument is the professor's claim that animal experimentation has led to the discovery of some important drugs, useful drugs, like penicillin. Well, that may be true, but who knows if these drugs wouldn't have been discovered without animal testing? And, you know, here's the thing—there are plenty of important drugs that were discovered without the benefit of animal testing. Quinine, used to treat malaria, ether, used as an anesthesia, and of course aspirin, they were all discovered without harming any animals. In fact, if these drugs had been tested on certain animals, well, they probably wouldn't be used today. Morphine, for example, kills pain in people but it stimulates cats. And large doses of aspirin poison cats and dogs and have no effect on horses.

[CD 11 TRACK 3]

Exercise 22.1
Narrator: Task 1
Listen to part of a lecture in an astronomy class.
Professor: Most astronomers agree that asteroids pose some danger to Earth, but they . . . they don't really agree as to just how much of a danger they pose. Large asteroids, you know, the kind that can cause global problems, probably only hit Earth about every 100,000 years. Right now, our technology is not able to detect all asteroids coming in our direction. For example, if . . . uh . . . well, if asteroids approach us from the direction of the Sun, they're invisible, invisible until after they've already passed us by. Besides, unless we develop some way to destroy an asteroid in

space before it reaches the planet, it won't help us to be able to detect it in space.

Narrator: Task 2
Listen to part of a lecture in a political science class.
Professor: Today I'm gonna talk about the presidential system . . . which is the system used in the United States—as compared to the parliamentary system, which is the British system, the system used in the U.K. Now, uh, under the presidential system, there is a strict separation of powers. In other words, all three branches of government—the executive, legislative, and judicial branches—they're all very much independent of each other. They all have their own powers. The chief executive, who is called, unsurprisingly, the president—is not part of the assembly—which of course is called the Congress in the United States. Neither are the members of his or her cabinet. So . . . that's one major difference . . .

Narrator: Task 3
Listen to part of a lecture in a linguistics class.
Professor: Very well, I'd next like to talk about the journal article I showed you, the one that calls English a so-called "killer language." Now it's true, certainly, that languages are disappearing at an increasingly rapid rate, and, let's face it, when a language disappears, that's, er, it's tragic, there's no doubt about it. But I don't think . . . well, it's not entirely fair to put all the blame on the English language. Regional languages play a big role too in destroying languages. As a regional language, English has done its share of damage to smaller languages in the British Isles. Same in North America, Australia, other places. But other regional languages have been every bit as destructive. A 1992 study showed that it was the Hindi language—not English—that was replacing smaller languages in India. In West Africa, Hausa has weakened minority languages. Swahili has done the same in East Africa. The same is true for Russian, Spanish, Arabic. It's ten or so regional languages, not one global language . . . these are the real killer languages.

Narrator: Task 4
Listen to part of a lecture in an ecology class.
Professor: Now, uh, this article is perfectly correct: wind generators do pose a danger to birds at the Altamont Pass Wind Farm. That particular site was chosen because the wind blows almost constantly through that mountain pass, and at the time, the engineers building it didn't realize that they were locating the plant in the middle of a major migration route for birds. However, the Altamont Pass site—well, it's an exception. No other wind farm has resulted in so many bird kills. In some places, like Denmark, wind energy is already generating a big percentage of energy needs. A Danish study showed that a wind farm in Denmark killed only a few birds a year, less than the average housecat. Now definitely, we should make sure that we're not putting a wind farm in a place that endangers birds. The Altamont plant probably needs some kind of screening to protect birds, or it needs to be relocated. However, we should not stop building wind farms! Wind power is a much cleaner, much safer source of power than fossil fuels or nuclear energy. We should be building more wind farms, and as quickly as possible.

Narrator: Task 5
Listen to part of a lecture in an astronomy class.
Professor: Okay, I'm going to give you part of an article that was written to defend the use of nighttime lighting. Now,

we've already talked about how difficult this "light pollution" makes things for astronomers, so I'm not going to say any more about that. But to address the question of lighting as a crime deterrent . . . well, there are just as many studies showing that increased lighting has no effect on crime. That's right, zero effect. But the letter that I wrote to the editor of the campus newspaper, and the ones that my colleagues wrote, did not ask the university to get rid of outdoor lighting, it simply asked the university to get smarter lights. The typical unshielded street lamp, the kind that is in use on the campus now, it sends 20% of its light upwards and 20% out to the side—only 60% goes downward! By shielding these streetlamps, you direct light where it's needed—on the ground—and keep it out of the sky. By just taking this step and a few other simple steps, we can still have well-lit streets and a well-lit campus but, uh, everyone—not just astronomers, but everyone—can see the stars at night.

Narrator: Task 6
Listen to part of a lecture in a biology class.
Professor: Now this little paragraph in your book illustrates a basic problem. Of course, as . . . uh, as I've said, the system we use for classifying organisms, the Linnaean system, it used the two-kingdom system of classification for over 200 years. It was hard for biologists to think outside this basic two-part model for classifying living things. Organisms had to be plants or animals 'cause . . . well, those were the only two possibilities. Protozoa, as our book points out, weren't much like fish or horses or any other animals, but they had to be classified as something, so they were called animals. Bacteria weren't much like oak trees, but they had to be classified as something too, so they were called plants. It was like putting square pegs in round holes. Finally, in the late 1950's, someone got a brilliant idea: let's change the classification system! At first, one new kingdom was added. Protozoa and other microorganisms were put in this kingdom. Later, there was a five-kingdom model. Today there is an even more complicated model. There are now three domains divided up into from eight to fifteen kingdoms, depending on who's doing the classifying. So anyway . . . the lesson to be learned here is—if you're classifying something, and it doesn't fit into the system—take another look at the classification system—maybe the problem is there!

[CD 11 TRACK 4]

Writing Review Test

This Writing Section tests your ability to write academic English. It consists of two writing tasks. The first writing task is an "integrated" task. It involves reading a short passage and listening to a short lecture on the same topic. You will then have twenty minutes in which to write a response based on the information in the passage and the lecture. Now read the directions for the first writing task.
Narrator: Directions: Take three minutes to read the short passage on the following page. You may take notes as you read. After three minutes have passed, start the Audio Program. You will hear a lecture on the same topic as the reading. Again, you may take notes as you listen. You will have twenty minutes to write your response. Your response should include information from both the reading and the lecture. Your essay will be rated on the completeness and accuracy of your response as well as on the correctness and quality of your writing. A typical response should be 150 to 225 words. You may use your notes and look at the reading passage as you write. (During the actual exam, you can view the reading passage on the left side of the computer

screen after the lecture is over.) You will have twenty minutes in which to finish the Integrated Writing Task. Begin reading now. [3-minute pause]

Narrator: Now listen to part of a lecture in an economics class.
Professor: Morning, everyone. Hope you had a chance to look at the articles I gave you Friday. I want to start by talking about one of the articles, the . . . uh, the one by Professor Woodall that . . . that takes a stand against Free Trade, and in favor of Protectionism. The thing is, in a global economy, the concept of Protectionism . . . it just doesn't work. It's not effective. Look at those developing countries whose economies have been the most successful; they're the countries that have been most open to Free Trade. And those countries whose economic growth has stalled or died, they're the ones that have closed themselves off to international trade.

Now, it's true, international competition can cause problems for local businesses. Some local companies will go bankrupt when you invite in the global big boys, the multinational corporations. Workers will lose their jobs, and labor groups will get upset. But the companies that do survive, the ones that learn to compete with global companies, they'll be stronger than ever. And global companies always hire local people. These local people have well-paying jobs and they learn how international corporations work. That's what's called a transfer of technology, and that's a good thing for local economies.

It's also true that governments that throw open their borders to trade no longer have income from tariffs. But . . . governments that collect tariffs on foreign goods are often the same ones that spend lots of money subsidizing local farmers, or steel manufacturers. A truly free-market country will not subsidize inefficient sectors of the economy, and so the government saves money that way.

The author says that Free Trade doesn't always lead to peace between nations. Perhaps not, but just look at Europe. For centuries, the great powers of Europe fought wars among themselves. Then, after World War II, the European Common Market was set up, and for once there was truly Free Trade among the members. Today, a war between, say, France and Germany or France and Britain is unimaginable. When you're engaged in a trading relationship that helps both your country and other countries, there's no reason to . . . to risk this relationship with war or aggression.
Narrator: Now get ready to answer the question. Remember, you may look back at the reading passage. You may also use your notes to help you. You have twenty minutes to prepare and write your response. Summarize the main points made in the lecture that you just heard, discussing how they differ from the points made in the reading. You can refer to the reading passage as you write.

Narrator: This is the end of the Review Test and the end of Section 4, Writing.

[CD 12 Track 1]

Practice Test 1

Listening Section

Narrator: Directions: This section tests your understanding of conversations and lectures. You will hear each conversation or lecture only once. Your answers should be based on what is stated or implied in the conversations and lectures. You are allowed to take notes as you listen, and you can use these notes to help you answer the questions. In some questions, you will see a headphones icon. This icon tells you that you will hear, but not read, part of the lecture again. Then you will answer a question about the part of the lecture that you heard. Some questions have special directions that are highlighted. During an actual listening test, you will *not* be able to skip items and come back to them later, so try to answer every question that you hear on this practice test. This test includes two conversations and four lectures. Most questions are separated by a ten-second pause.

Narrator: Listen to a conversation between a student and a professor.

Professor: Ted, did you get my e-mail?

Student: Umm, no, I, actually I haven't had a chance to check my e-mail yet today, sorry.

Professor: Well, I just wanted to see if I could have a quick word with you after this class.

Student: Well, the thing is, professor, I'm working on the campus newspaper and . . . and I need to get over there right after class for a meeting . . .

Professor: Well, this won't take long . . . let's just chat now before class starts . . .

Student: Sure, what's up, Professor Jacobs?

Professor: Well, next week, the students in my graduate Creative Writing seminar are going to be reading aloud from their works at the Student Union . . .

Student: Yeah, I saw a poster about that on the bulletin board down the hall.

Professor: Yes, well, anyway, Ted, I'm also inviting a few students from my undergraduate class to take part, and I'd like one of them to be you, if you're willing.

Student: Me? Seriously? I don't know what to say . . .

Professor: Well, just say you'll do it, then. The reading will be in the ballroom of the Student Union at noon next Friday.

Student: You know . . . I'd really like to read the first two or three chapters of this novel I've been working on . . .

Professor: I was thinking that you could read some of your poems. In fact, I didn't even realize that you were writing a novel. What's it about?

Student: Umm, well, I . . . it's about the commercial fishing business, about working on a fishing boat . . .

Professor: Really? Do you know a lot about that topic?

Student: Well, I grew up in Alaska, and my grandfather owned a fishing boat, and I worked on it one summer. Plus my grandfather told me a million stories about fishing. Of course, I've changed the stories some and fictionalized all the characters.

Professor: I was hoping you'd read that poem about spending the night alone in the forest . . . what was it called? *Northern Lights,* I think . . .

Student: That poem? Huh! When I read it in class, you didn't say much about it at all, so I figured . . . I figured you didn't much like it.

Professor: Well, I wanted to hear what the other students in class thought of it . . . but, yes, I quite liked it. The language was very strong and in particular I found the imagery . . . powerful. Almost a little frightening.

Student: How about this, then . . . I'll read just one chapter from the novel, the first one's pretty short, and then a couple of poems as well. Will that be okay?

Professor: I think that should work. Drop by my office sometime this week and we'll figure out which poems you should read.

Student: Okay, and Professor Jacobs, thanks . . . I'm really flattered that you'd ask me to take part.

Narrator: Now get ready to answer some questions about the conversation. You may use your notes to help you.

Narrator: Question 1: Why is Ted unable to meet with Professor Jacobs after class?

Narrator: Listen again to part of the conversation.

Professor: Yes, well, anyway, Ted, I'm also inviting a few students from my undergraduate class to take part, and I'd like one of them to be you, if you're willing.

Student: Me? Seriously? I don't know what to say . . .

Narrator: Question 2: What does Ted mean when he says this?

Student: Me? Seriously? I don't know what to say . . .

Narrator: Question 3: What is Ted most interested in reading aloud next Friday?

Narrator: Question 4: Which of the following can be inferred about Professor Jacobs?

Narrator: Question 5: Why does Professor Jacobs ask Ted to come to his office?

Narrator: Listen to a conversation between a university administrator and a student.

Administrator: Hello, Financial Aid Office, Connie Fong speaking.

Student: Hi, Ms. Fong. My name's Dana Hart and I'm a second-year student. I'm, uh, just calling to see if I can get some information on your . . . on the work-study program?

Administrator: Sure, happy to help you. What would you like to know?

Student: Well, what do you . . . what are the requirements for . . .

Administrator: The eligibility requirements? Okay, first off, are you taking at least 60% of a full-time academic load?

Student: Yeah, a hundred percent—I'm a full-time student.

Administrator: Okay, that's fine. Then, let me ask you this, are you qualified to receive financial aid?

Student: Ummm, I have no idea. I'm not getting any financial aid now. See, I have a personal bank loan to pay for my tuition, and my parents are helping me out with my room-and-board expenses. But I really have no money for living expenses, so, uh, that's why I'm hoping to land a part-time job . . .

Administrator: Well, you'd need to fill out some financial aid forms to see if you qualify . . . it depends on your level of income and on your parents' level of income . . . .

Student: So, if I fill out these forms and . . . and I don't qualify for financial aid, then . . . then there's no way I could get a work-study job?

Administrator: No, uh, no, that's not necessarily true. You see, there are two kinds of work-study positions. There are needs-based positions—those are the ones funded by the government, and for those, yes, you have to qualify for financial aid, but there are also what we call merit-based work-study positions. These positions are available regardless, uh, regardless of financial need, as long the financial aid office determines that a work-study position helps you meet your educational goals, if it's a . . . a . . . you know, useful supplement for your formal classes. It's even possible that you could earn academic credit for some of these positions.

Student: So, what sorts of positions do you have open right now?

Administrator: Well, it depends on your interests, your experience . . .

Student: The only job I've ever had, I worked in a restaurant but . . . I don't want anything in food service, food preparation . . . no cafeteria job . . .

Administrator: Well, we try to find you jobs related to your educational goals. Say, for example, if you're studying biology, we might try to place you as a technician in a biology lab . . .

Student: I'm an art major, and I was wondering . . . are there any jobs in the art gallery at the Student Union?

Administrator: Hang on a sec. No, no positions at all at the Student Union . . . but, uh, okay, here's a position at the Metropolitan Art Museum . . . it's as a tour guide there.

Student: Really? Wow, that sounds fabulous. But, uh, I thought work-study jobs were all on campus.

Administrator: Oh, no, about 25% of all our positions are off-campus . . . they're positions with foundations or organizations that we think perform some worthwhile community service.

Student: So, how many hours a week is this job?

Administrator: I'll check . . . it looks like they want someone there for around twenty to twenty-five hours a week.

Student: Really? I don't know if I could put in that much time and still . . . still do okay in my classes.

Administrator: Well, don't give up on the position for that reason. Y' know, we really encourage job-sharing—two students working one position. It's possible that we could arrange something where you'd only work about half that much time.

Student: That sounds more like what I had in mind: ten, twelve hours a week or so. So what do I do to apply for this job?

Administrator: Well, the first step is to fill out the Financial Aid forms I mentioned. You can come down and get them from the receptionist at the front desk, or you can fill them out online if you like. Then I'll call the contact person at the museum. Let's see . . . okay, it's, uh, it's a Doctor Ferrarra, he's the personnel director at the museum. I'll call him and set up an interview for you. And you understand that he's the one . . . the one who makes the hiring decision, not anyone in our office, right?

Student: Sure. Okay, then, thanks a lot for all the information. I'll get those forms from your Web site and send them back to you this afternoon or tomorrow.

Narrator: Now get ready to answer some questions about the conversation. You may use your notes to help you.

Narrator: Question 6: Why does Dana want a work-study position?

Narrator: Question 7: What can be inferred about merit-based work-study jobs?

Narrator: Question 8: Which of these work-study positions does Dana express the most enthusiasm for?

Narrator: Question 9: What must Dana do first to apply for the position that she is interested in?

Narrator: Question 10: Why does Ms. Fong say this?

Administrator: Well, don't give up on the position for that reason.

Narrator: Listen to a lecture in an anthropology class.

Professor: Okay, class, we've been talking about traditional types of shelters . . . about the, uh, styles of houses used by traditional people, and today . . . today I'd like to talk a bit about the homes of the Inuit people, the Eskimos, the people who live in the far north, in the Arctic regions of North America. Now, *all* the Inuit used to have two types of houses, summer houses and winter houses. Their summer houses were called *tupiq,* and they were originally made of animal skins and, later, canvas. There were various types of winter houses, though. The Inuit who lived in northern Alaska, where there was plenty of driftwood, built their winter houses from wood they found on the shore. The Inuit who lived in Labrador—that's in Northeastern Canada—now, they built their winter houses from stone and earth and supported them with whalebones. It was only in the north central part of Canada and in one place in Greenland that the Inuit built their winter houses from snow. Oh, and by the way, the Inuit who lived up in Greenland, in a place called Thule, they were some of the most isolated people in the world. Until sometime in the early nineteenth century, in fact, they thought they were the only people in the world. Imagine how surprised they were the first time they met outsiders!

Anyway, when the first Canadians of European descent arrived in northern Canada, and they saw these houses made of snow, they asked what they were called. The Inuit replied, "Igloos," and so that's what we call them now. In English, the word *igloo* means a dome-shaped house made of snow. However, it turns out, the word *igloo* in Inuit just means *house,* any sort of house—a house of wood, a house of snow, whatever.

How did the Inuit make these snow houses? They used knives made of bone or ivory to cut wind-packed snow into blocks. They arranged these in a circle and then kept adding smaller and smaller blocks in a rising spiral until a dome was formed. Then they'd pack the cracks between the blocks with loose snow. A skilled igloo-builder could put up a simple igloo in a couple of hours, and you know what? He could do it in a blizzard!

The igloo was the only dome-shaped traditional housing that was built without internal support. It didn't need any interior support because, well, because it was so strong. The bitter Arctic winds caused the outside of the igloo to freeze solid. Then, the interior was "set" with a seal-oil lamp. What I mean is, they used these lamps to melt a little bit of the snow blocks, and then the water refroze into ice. So you had a layer of ice on the outside of the dome and one on the inside, and like I say, it was strong. In fact, it would support the weight of a man standing on top of it.

Igloos were remarkably warm inside. I mean, given that they were made out of snow, they were surprisingly cozy. Snow is actually a good insulator, believe it or not, and it keeps the intense cold out. Igloos were usually small enough so that body heat warmed them up pretty quickly. The Inuit slept on platforms of packed snow covered with furs. Oh, and the entrance tunnel to the igloo was dug out so that it was lower than the igloo floor, and cold air got trapped in the tunnel. Seal-oil lamps were usually used to heat igloos, so there had to be a hole at the top of the dome to let out stale air and smoke.

If igloos were to be used for a fairly long time, they, uh, they naturally tended to be more elaborate. Sometimes circular walls of snow were built around igloos to shield them from the wind. Sometimes these walls were even built into a second dome around the first one, and the layer of air between the two domes provided even more insulation. These semi-permanent igloos had windows and skylights made of freshwater ice or translucent seal gut. And sometimes you'd have clusters of igloos. They were connected by tunnels. Sometimes five or more Inuit families lived in these clusters. And, uh, sometimes the Inuit built larger snow domes that could be used more or less as . . . uh, community centers. You know, the nights are long up there in the Arctic, so they needed some entertainment. They held dances and wrestling matches and their famous singing competitions in these larger igloos.

In the early 1950's, the Inuit began living in permanent, year-round housing. They only used igloos when they went on overnight hunting trips. Today, they don't use these wonderful snow-domes for shelter at all, not even as temporary housing. But, uh, sometimes they'll build igloos for special exhibits, and sometimes you'll see little igloos in their yards that they build as playhouses for their children.

Narrator: Now get ready to answer some questions about the lecture. You may use your notes to help you.

Narrator: Question 11: The professor mentions three types of winter houses used by the Inuit. Match these three types of houses with the locations where they were used.

Narrator: Question 12: Why does the professor say this?

Professor: Oh, and by the way, the Inuit who lived up in Greenland, in a place called Thule, they were some of the most isolated people in the world. Until sometime in the early nineteenth century, in fact, they thought they were the only people in the world. Imagine how surprised they were the first time they met outsiders!

Narrator: Question 13: What can be inferred about the word *igloo*?

Narrator: Question 14: In this lecture, the professor describes the process the Inuit used to build a simple igloo. Indicate whether each of the following is a step in the igloo-building process.

Narrator: Question 15: The professor did *not* mention that larger igloos were used in which of these ways?

Narrator: Question 16: According to the professor, what did the Inuit do in the early 1950's?

Narrator: Listen to a discussion in an astrophysics class.

Student A: Ah, excuse me, Professor Fuller . . . ?

Professor: Yes, Mark?

Student A: You just said . . . you just told us that it's impossible to travel faster than light . . .

Professor: Well, that's according to the theories of Albert Einstein, as I said. And who am I to argue with Einstein?

Student A: So that means . . . well, doesn't that mean people can never travel to other stars in spaceships?

Professor: Well, let's think about it . . . how fast does light travel?

Student A: Wait, you just told us . . . let me find it in my notes . . . . Okay, 186,000 miles an hour.

Professor: That's miles per *second*, Mark—186,000 miles per second. Almost 6 *trillion* miles per hour! And how far is it to the nearest star?

Student A: I think you told us it's four light years . . .

Professor: It's a little more, but that's close enough . . . so, think about that. Moving at 6 trillion miles per hour, it takes about four years to get to the closest star. And of course, we can't travel anywhere near as fast as light. A couple of years ago, the Voyager spacecraft left our solar system, and it was traveling faster than any man-made object ever. And you know what? It would take Voyager 80,000 years at that speed to get to the closest star.

Student A: Wow. If you brought along sandwiches for the trip, they'd get pretty stale before you arrived, wouldn't they?

Professor: No doubt they would! Now, of course, Voyager isn't accelerating, it's just coasting; it's traveling through space like a bullet that was shot from a gun. What you need is a ship that can constantly accelerate and keep increasing its speed. Clearly, rockets won't work . . .

Student A: What's wrong with rockets?

Student B: I think I know . . . they couldn't carry enough fuel, right?

Professor: Right. It takes an enormous rocket full of fuel just to lift one of the shuttles into Earth orbit. You could *never* carry enough to get to another star. Even if you used nuclear-powered engines, you just couldn't bring enough mass.

Student B: Professor, I read an article about a space ship that used sails to propel itself through space.

Student A: You couldn't use sails in space, it's a vacuum . . . no air . . .

Professor: No, Liza's right. These aren't conventional sails, of course. A scientist named Robert Forward came up with this idea. He said you could launch a ship with rockets, and then unfurl these *giant* sails made of thin plastic—I mean, many square kilometers of thin plastic sails. Then you fire intense bursts of laser beams at the sails, and since lasers travel at light speed, pretty soon, you're scooting along at close to the speed of light.

Student B: I thought it was a brilliant idea . . .

Professor: There's a catch, though . . .

Student A: What's the catch?

Professor: Well, you'd still need huge amounts of fuel to power the lasers—more than you could carry. No, to reach the stars, you need some revolutionary drive system that requires little or no fuel.

Student B: Is anyone even working on something like that?

Professor: As a matter of fact, yeah, there are teams of some cutting-edge physicists who are looking at things like anti-gravity, anti-matter, artificial wormholes, things called negative mass and zero-point energy—as possible ways to power ships. But these concepts are all in the speculation phase . . .

Student B: What do you mean, they're in the speculation phase?

Professor: Well, any workable technology goes through at least four phases of development. There's the speculation phase—that's where you figure out what your need is and dream up a system or a device that can fill that need. Next is the science phase, where you basically do experiments and see if the technology you dreamed up might possibly work. After this comes the technology phase. You bring in the engineers, tell them what you need, and they build it for you. Finally, you put the technology to work. That's the application phase. But all these technologies that I mentioned, they're just in the speculation phase.

Student A: Okay, professor, let's say, for the sake of argument, that scientists dream up a way to travel *half* as fast as light, and engineers manage to build it . . . then it would only take about eight years to get to the nearest star and eight years to get back That's . . . isn't that just a sixteen-year trip?

Professor: Well, possibly. But 4.2 light years is the distance to the *nearest* star, *not* to the nearest star with planets. We don't know if any of the stars in our immediate neighborhood have planets. Suppose you went all that way and just found empty space! The closest star with planets—at least with earthlike planets—may be *much* farther away.

Student B: Professor, I thought you said that, these days, scientists could detect planets around other stars.

Professor: Well, yes, that's true, I did say that . . . there have been hundreds of what are called "extra-solar" planets discovered, but if you remember, I said that almost all of them are huge planets, gas giants, a lot like Jupiter, probably. And a few that were discovered recently are smaller, rocky planets but they are *very* close to their stars, closer than the planet Mercury. We still don't have the know-how to detect earth-like planets. Maybe the closest earth-like planet is dozens, even hundred of light years away.

Student A: Well, professor, I guess you're saying that we'll never be able to visit other stars. I just think that's too bad. I love science fiction books and movies, and I always hoped that people would one day be able to whiz around the galaxy the way people travel around our planet today.

Professor: You know, Mark, I don't think that trips to the stars will be practical unless we develop a way to travel faster than light, or close to that, and I don't think that will ever happen. So . . . I don't want to rule out anything . . . who knows what kind of scientific breakthroughs we might have in the future. But Mark, I don't think I'd pack my bags and head for the spaceport any time soon.

Narrator: Now get ready to answer some questions about the discussion. You may use your notes to help you.

Narrator: Question 17: What is Professor Fuller's opinion of Albert Einstein?

Narrator: Question 18: What powers the "sails" on the ship that the class discusses?

Narrator: Question 19: According to Professor Fuller, what must be developed before ships can travel to the stars?

Narrator: Question 20: Professor Fuller discusses the process by which a new technology evolves. Summarize this discussion by putting these four steps in the proper order.

Narrator: Question 21: What does Professor Fuller say about the planets that have so far been discovered around other stars?

Narrator: Listen again to part of the discussion.

Professor: You know, Mark, I don't think that trips to the stars will be practical unless we develop a way to travel faster than light, or close to that, and I don't think that will ever happen. So . . . I don't want to rule out anything . . . who knows what kind of scientific breakthroughs we might have in the future. But Mark, I don't think I'd pack my bags and head for the spaceport any time soon.

Narrator: Question 22: What does Professor Fuller imply about travel to other stars when she says this?

Professor: But Mark, I don't think I'd pack my bags and head for the spaceport any time soon.

Narrator: Listen to a lecture in an art class.

Professor: Morning, class. Okay, so today we're gonna continue our study of twentieth-century art with a discussion of photorealism. This, ah, style of art—it was also called hyperrealism or superrealism—it was popular in the late 1960's and the 1970's. Painters who worked in this style, they . . . they portrayed their subjects down to the smallest detail, and so their paintings look like photographs, they resemble photographs in many respects.

Now, you have to keep in mind that at this time, in the 60's and 70's, art was dominated by Minimalism and Conceptual Art, which were very *non*-representational types of art, very abstract, and so this was . . . this incredible realism was kind of a reaction to that.

Okay, I'm going to show you a slide of a painting by the photorealist Audrey Flack. It's called *The Farb Family Portrait*. When she painted this, she used the same techniques that a lot of Photorealists used. First, she took a photo of the family. Next she drew a grid on her canvas, dividing the whole surface of the canvas into little squares. Then she made a slide from the photo and projected the picture onto her canvas. One by one, she systematically painted what was projected onto each of the little squares. Each square was really its own tiny work of art. Audrey worked with an airbrush, and she used acrylic paints. The acrylic paints account for the bright, luminous colors that you see in most of her works. In fact, most Photorealist paintings tend to be bright and colorful.

So, ah, where did this style of painting come from? You might say, what's the big deal, people have been painting realistically for hundreds of years. The Dutch Masters were obsessed with getting details right. And in the eighteenth century there was a European school of painting called *trompe l'oeil*, and painters who worked in this style were as interested as Photorealists in . . . in capturing every detail of what they saw, in . . . ah, making their subjects look real. However, these painters were . . . they were also interested in creating optical illusions, three-dimensional optical illusions—the phrase *trompe l'oeil* means "trick of the eye." For example, one of the paintings from this school pictures a boy who appears to be climbing out of the painting, climbing right out of the frame. That's not . . . not one of the interests of Photorealism, creating optical illusions.

Anyway. What sort of subjects did the Photorealists paint? Photorealists painted still-lifes, portraits, landscapes—although there are not many paintings of rural scenes, mostly they show urban scenes. The subjects of Photorealist paintings are interesting only because they are so . . . just so ordinary. One Photorealist, the painter Chuck Close, once said the subjects of his paintings were "so normal that they are shocking." Another one, a painter named Richard Estes, said, "I don't enjoy looking at the things I paint, so why should you enjoy it?" What he meant there, I think, is that the *technique* of painting is the important thing, that the subject itself means little. *How* one painted was much more important than *what* one painted. In a little while, when we look at some more of the slides I brought, you'll see typical Photorealist subjects. There's one of a gas station . . . one of an elderly man waiting at a bus stop . . . let's see, there's one of an old, closed-down drive-in movie. Weeds are growing up between the speaker stands and the screen is practically falling down.

Some painters specialized in painting one type of subject. Richard Estes, for example, liked to paint urban scenes, ordinary city sights, reflected in sheets of window glass. For example, he might paint a parking lot reflected in glass, or a drug store reflected in big plate-glass windows. There was one Photorealist who only painted neon signs and one who painted only trucks. The point is, Photorealists never chose grand, inspiring subjects to paint. They always painted ordinary, everyday, banal subjects.

Now I'm going to show you another slide. This picture was taken at the museum where Duane Hanson's works were on display. Looks like a photo of the museum security guard, doesn't it? That's ah, what a lot of the visitors to the museum thought too. They would come up to the "guard" and ask him questions. But this isn't a photo of a flesh-and-blood person; it's a photo of one of Hanson's sculptures. Hanson was a Photorealist sculptor. He fashioned human-size statues of people from plastic. He then painted them to make the plastic look like human skin, and he added hair, clothing, shoes, jewelry, sometimes props—one of his sculptures features a man riding on a lawn mower. Again, his subjects were ordinary people—a car salesman, a homeless person, a student, a child putting together a puzzle. As you'll see in a couple of minutes, all of these statues are as realistic as this one of the security guard.

Okay, as promised, I'm, uh, going to have a little slide show for you. While you're viewing these works of Photorealistic art, I'd like you to take notes on what you think of them. Then, over the weekend, I'd like you to write a short paper—really short, just a page or two—that describes your reactions to these works.

Narrator: Now get ready to answer some questions about the lecture. You may use your notes to help you.

Narrator: Question 23: What does the professor say about Minimalism and Conceptualism?

Narrator: Question 24: Which of the following did Audrey Flack *not* use when painting *The Farb Family Portrait*?

Narrator: Question 25: How does the professor explain the subjects that Photorealists painted?

Narrator: Question 26: Which of the following would Richard Estes most likely choose to paint?

Narrator: Question 27: According to the speaker, why are the sculptures of Duane Hanson so remarkable?

Narrator: Question 28: In this lecture, the professor gives a number of characteristics of the Photorealistic school of painting. Indicate whether each of the following is a typical characteristic of paintings of that school of art.

Narrator: Listen to a discussion in a meteorology class.

Professor: Afternoon, everyone. So, um, in our last class, we talked about thunderstorms. Today, I want to talk about a similar phenomenon: hailstorms. Anyone here ever been caught in a hailstorm?

Student A: As a matter of fact, last year, I was driving home from the university one weekend—my parents live about seventy miles from here—and the sky got really dark, and it started to rain. And then, all of a sudden—it, well, it was like . . . like little pebbles were pounding on the car, and there were balls of ice as big as marbles bouncing around on the highway.

Student B: So what did you do, Mike?

Student A: Well, as soon as I could, I pulled off the road and parked under a highway bridge until the storm was over. But it was too late—I had lots of little dents in my car.

Student B: I remember when I was in high school, there was a bad hailstorm, and it wiped out my parents' garden. They were really upset, because they love gardening.

Professor: Well, that's interesting, those two examples you gave—because every year, hailstorms cause more than a billion dollars worth of damage, and you know what? By far the most damage is done to vehicles and plants—not gardens, really, but farmers' crops.

Student A: There's nothing farmers can do? Can't they cover their crops with plastic sheets or . . .

Professor: No, there's no . . . no practical way to protect crops, although farmers can buy insurance against hail damage. Now, back in the fourteenth century in Europe, farmers tried to ward off hail by ringing church bells, banging on pots and pans, and firing cannons. Hail cannons were common in wine-producing regions, at least through the nineteenth century. And . . . uh, in the Soviet Union, as late as the 1950's, the government used cannons to shoot silver iodide crystals into clouds. This . . . uh, was supposed to make the hailstones smaller so they wouldn't do as much damage, but it didn't really work too well.

Student B: Professor, are people . . . do they get hurt by hailstorms very often?

Professor: Hurt? Hmmm, well, it doesn't . . . it doesn't really seem like it to me. Sometimes you'll hear about a person stuck up in a Ferris wheel or some other ride at an amusement park being injured, or something like that, but . . . uh, it doesn't seem to happen very often, does it? And that's . . . well, it's kind of surprising, isn't it, considering that hailstones can be as big as baseballs—sometimes even bigger—and can travel like, a hundred miles an hour. So, uh, I don't really have any statistics about that, but I'll try to get some information. Okay, now, another question—has anyone ever cut a hailstone in half to see what it looks like? No? No one? Well, what do you *think* it would look like? Penny?

Student B: Well, I dunno. I suppose . . . it must look like a little snowball cut in half . . .

Professor: No, as a matter of fact, it looks more like an onion cut in half—lots of layers. And what does it usually mean when you find layers in something? Mike?

Student A: Um, well . . . I guess that it wasn't formed all at once.

Professor: Exactly. Here's how you get hailstones. A hailstone starts off as a droplet of water in a cumulonimbus cloud—that's a thundercloud. Then—remember, last class, we said there were a lot of strong updrafts of warm air and strong downdrafts of cold air inside a thunderstorm? Well, one of these updrafts picks up the droplet and lifts it high into the cloud, where the air is cold, and it freezes. Then, because of gravity and cold downdrafts, it falls.

Student B: Professor? Wouldn't it melt when it falls . . . I mean when it gets into the warmer air?

Professor: Yeah, when it hits the warmer air at the bottom of the thundercloud, it might start to thaw—but then, our little half-frozen droplet gets picked up by another updraft, carrying it back into very cold air and refreezing it. This happens again and again. With each trip above and below the freezing level, the hailstone adds another layer of ice. Eventually, the hailstone gets so heavy that the updrafts can't lift it anymore, so it drops out of the cloud and . . . bingo, you've got hail!

Student A: So, Professor, you said that you only get hail when there's a thunderstorm—is that right?

Professor: Well, hail only forms in cumulonimbus clouds, which are the only kind of clouds that generate thunderstorms—though you don't always get thunder and lightning when you have hail.

Student B: Sometimes, I've seen on weather reports, you get a lot of hail just before tornadoes.

Professor: Well, that's true. But hail isn't always associated with tornadoes, and . . . uh, not all tornadoes are accompanied by hail.

Student A: So if you just look at a thundercloud from the ground, can you tell if you're going to have hail?

Professor: No, not just by looking. But a meteorologist can tell by using Doppler radar. Doppler radar can "look" inside a cloud. Okay, we said thunderstorms are most common in summer. How about hailstorms? When are they most common?

Student B: I'd guess in the winter.

Professor: Nope, afraid not.

Student A: The hailstorm I was caught in was in April, maybe early May, so I'd guess spring.

Professor: You're right. And the part of the United States where they're most common is along the Rocky Mountains . . . in Colorado, Wyoming, Montana . . . . In fact, the most costly hailstorm in U.S. history was in Denver, Colorado. Just that one storm caused over . . . I believe it was about $750 million dollars' worth of damage.

Narrator: Now get ready to answer some questions about the discussion. You may use your notes to help you.

Narrator: Question 29: According to the professor, which of the following are most often damaged by hail?

Narrator: Question 30: According to the professor, which of these methods of preventing damage from hail was used most recently?

Narrator: Listen again to part of the discussion.

Student B: Professor, are people . . . do they get hurt by hailstorms very often?

Professor: Hurt? Hmmm, well, it doesn't . . . it doesn't really seem like it to me. Sometimes you'll hear about a person stuck up in a Ferris wheel or some other ride at an amusement park being injured, or something like that, but, uh, it doesn't seem to happen very often, does it?

Narrator: Question 31: What does the professor mean when he says this?

Professor: Hurt? Hmmm, well, it doesn't . . . it doesn't really seem like it to me.

Narrator: Question 32: Why does the professor compare a hailstone to an onion?

Narrator: Question 33: At what time of year are hailstorms most common?

Narrator: Question 34: In this lecture, the professor describes the process by which hail is formed. Indicate whether each of the following is a step in that process.

Narrator: This is the end of the Listening Section of Practice Test 1. You may take a ten-minute break before beginning work on the Speaking Section.

[CD 12 Track 2]

Speaking Section

Narrator: Directions: This section tests your ability to speak about various subjects. There are six tasks in this section. Listen carefully to the directions and read the questions on the screen. The first two tasks are Independent Speaking tasks. You have fifteen seconds in which to prepare your response. When you hear a beep on the Audio Program, you will have forty-five seconds in which to answer the question. The last four tasks are Integrated Speaking tasks. The third and fourth questions involve a reading text and a listening passage. You have forty-five seconds in which to read a short text. You will then hear a short conversation or part of a lecture on the same topic. You may take notes on both the reading and listening passage. You will then see a question on the screen asking about the information that you have just read and heard, and you will have thirty seconds in which to plan a response. When you hear a beep on the Audio Program, you have sixty seconds in which to answer the question. The fifth and sixth questions involve a short listening passage. You may take notes as you listen. After listening to the conversation or lecture, you will see a question, and you have twenty seconds in which to plan your response. When you hear a beep on the Audio Program, you have sixty seconds in which to answer the question. During actual tests, a clock on the screen will tell you how much preparation time or how much response time (speaking time) remains for each question. It is important that you time yourself accurately when you take this practice test. On an actual test your responses will be recorded and evaluated by trained raters.

Narrator: Question 1. . . . Please listen carefully . . .

Narrator: What is the most important decision that you have ever made? Give specific details and examples to support your explanation. Please begin speaking after the beep. [15-second pause, then beep] [45-second pause, then beep] Now stop speaking.

Narrator: Question 2. . . . Please listen carefully . . .

Narrator: In some university classes, grades depend mainly on tests, such as quizzes and final exams. In other classes, grades depend primarily on academic papers that the students write. Which type of class would you prefer to take? Give specific details and examples to support your explanation. Please begin speaking after the beep. [15-second pause, then beep] [45-second pause, then beep] Now stop speaking.

Narrator: Question 3. . . . Please listen carefully . . .

Narrator: Lincoln University is instituting a new policy regarding requirements for graduation. Read the following notice from the Dean of Education. You will have forty-five seconds in which to read the notice. Begin reading now.

Narrator: Now listen to two students discussing this notice.

Student A: So I guess it's back to the language classroom for us! Have you . . . uh, given any thought about what language you're going to study?

Student B: Well, I *think* I could probably get at least an 85 on the placement test for Japanese, because . . .

Student A: Oh, that's right, you used to live in Japan, didn't you?

Student B: Yeah, my dad worked for a Japanese company and my family spent a year and a half there when I was in high school. I took classes and I had a lot of Japanese friends, so I got to be fairly fluent.

Student A: Lucky for you. I studied Spanish in high school but, well, my teacher wasn't a native Spanish speaker and . . . all we did was memorize grammar rules. I didn't really learn much of the language, to tell you the truth. No real point to my trying to take a test; I'm just going to start over.

Student B: Well, I am too. I kinda agree with what the regents are saying—you gotta be able to speak another language these days. I don't think you can understand another culture without speaking at least a bit of the language. And if you want to work abroad or even just travel, you need some fluency in another language.

Student A: So . . . what language are you going to study?

Student B: Well, I think I should learn a European language, just for balance. Probably French or Italian.

Narrator: The woman gives her opinion of the notice written by the Dean of Education. Explain her opinion and discuss the reasons she gives for having this opinion. Please begin speaking after the beep. [30-second pause, then beep] [60-second pause] Now stop speaking.

Narrator: Question 4. . . . Please listen carefully . . . Read the following passage about airships. You will have forty-five seconds in which to read the passage. Begin reading now.

Narrator: Now listen to a discussion about airships.

Professor: So, how many of you were at the football game on Saturday night? Quite a few of you, huh? Did you happen to look up and see something in the sky? Yeah? What did you see?

Students: A blimp!

Professor: Right, a blimp—it was the Blimp *Columbia.* You'll see the *Columbia* and other blimps at sporting events and other big gatherings. What are they used for, mostly?

Student A: To, uh, carry television cameras so they can show what things look like from above, I guess.

Professor: Right, aerial photography, and . . .

Student B: And advertising. A lot of times they'll have electric signs on them advertising something.

Professor: Right. Now, these, uh, blimps you see today, they're descendants of the zeppelins that were built in the first part of the twentieth century. Most of them were built in Germany—not all, but most. These zeppelins were *huge*—over 250 meters long. What were *these* airships used for?

Student B: I don't know. Didn't they carry passengers?

Professor: Right, there was regular passenger service on zeppelins—even transatlantic service. They could travel amazingly long distances. They were also used for military purposes in World War I. Okay, I'm going to show you a picture, a very famous picture—what's happening in this picture?

Student A: That's the . . . uh, what's it called, the Hindenburg disaster.

Professor: That's right—this happened in 1937, in Lakehurst, New Jersey. There was an explosion and a terrible fire on the German zeppelin *Hindenburg* and thirty-five passengers and crew members lost their lives . . .

Student B: What caused it, Professor?

Professor: No one knows for sure, although there've been lots of theories. Anyway, this tragedy pretty much ended the age of the giant zeppelins. At least, until about ten years ago. That's when a German company started building zeppelins again. We'll talk about that in our next class . . .

Narrator: The professor and the students discuss two airships, the blimp *Columbia* and the zeppelin *Hindenburg*. Using information from the passage and the discussion, compare these two airships. Please begin speaking after the beep. [30-second pause, then beep] [60-second pause] Now stop speaking.

Narrator: Question 5. . . . Please listen carefully . . .

Narrator: Listen to a conversation between two students.

Student A: Hi, Diane. Gettin' ready to go somewhere for spring break?

Student B: Hey, Mike. Uh, no, this year I guess I'll just hang out on campus. I was going to go see my sister in Boston, but . . . well, I waited too long to make an airline reservation. The only tickets available are way too expensive for me.

Student A: Why don't you just drive to Boston?

Student B: I thought about that, but it's at least a 20-hour drive, so I'd have to stop somewhere and get a hotel room. And gas is so expensive these days. Driving there would be almost as expensive as flying, and I'd be exhausted when I got there.

Student A: Hey, you should go check the Ride Board over at the Student Union building.

Student B: What are you talking about?

Student A: You've probably seen it, you just didn't realize what it was. It's, well, basically it's a map of the United Sates divided up into regions. And for each region there's an envelope hanging on the wall. If you have a car, you fill out a blue card saying where you're going, when you're leaving, how many riders you can take, and so on. You put it in the envelope for the region where you want to go—for New England, in your case. If you don't have a car, if you're just looking for a ride, you fill out a white card. Usually riders share the gas expenses and sometimes the driving. I used the Ride Board and found a guy who wanted a ride to San Francisco last summer. It was a lot cheaper and easier than traveling alone.

Student B: Okay, so I should fill out a blue card since I have a car . . .

Student A: Right. Well, you could fill out both. That way if someone else was driving there, you could go with him or her.

Student B: Well, I guess I should give it a shot. A lot of students are traveling at this time of year.

Student A: Hey, you know, I just had another idea—you might also think about taking a train.

Student B: A train. I never think about taking trains—it seems kinda—I don't know, old-fashioned somehow, although in Europe I rode some of those high-speed trains, and those were great . . .

Student A: Yeah, well, the train to Boston won't be high-speed. It will take quite awhile to get there. But you can sleep and study or whatever on the way. And taking a train, I dunno for sure, but I think it's usually a little cheaper than flying. Probably not all that much cheaper, though.

Student B: Okay, well, I suppose I could look into that, too. Thanks for the suggestions, Mike.

Narrator: Mike offers Diane two possible solutions to her problem. Discuss her problem and then explain which of the two solutions you think is better and why you think so.

Please begin speaking after the beep. [20-second pause, then beep] [60-second pause, then beep] Now stop speaking.

Narrator: Question 6. . . . Please listen carefully . . .

Narrator: Listen to part of a lecture in a botany class.

Professor: Okay, we, uh, we were speaking in our last class about pollination, about how all flowering plants have to

be pollinated. I said then that, uh, the most common method of pollination was by bees, butterflies, and other insects. These insects visit flowers to get a sweet liquid called nectar that the flowers produce. This is their source of food. It just so happens that these flowers, these nectar-rich flowers, are also fertile and are ready to pass on their pollen to other plants by means of these insects . . . or, uh, they could also receive pollen the insect has picked up from another plant.

Now, for most plants, this process is pretty much hit or miss; it's pretty random. Insects have no way of knowing which flowers contain nectar and pollen, so . . . they have to visit a lot of flowers to find the right ones. However, there are some plants that have a system that tells the insects which flowers to visit. It's based on a color code, believe it or not. For example, there's a plant, a shrub called the lantana, and on the first day it blossoms, its flowers are yellow. That day, the flower is full of pollen and nectar. The next day, the flower turns orange. There's less nectar, less pollen. On the third day it turns red and it's no longer fertile. It has no pollen, no nectar. Only about 10% of the lantana's flowers are yellow at any one time, but insects are ten times more likely to visit a super fertile yellow flower than a less fertile orange one and nearly 100 times more likely to visit a yellow one than an infertile red one. And this system, it's a good deal for both plants and insects. Insects have to visit fewer flowers, and plants do not have to expend energy trying to keep all their flowers full of nectar and pollen all the time.

Now, you might say, maybe it's something else, maybe it's the smell of the nectar and not the colors that provide the signal to the insect. But no. There were experiments done with flowers made of yellow paper, and insects were as likely to visit these as . . . . as real flowers. So . . . no, it's the color. Any questions about this?

Narrator: Using specific examples and points from the lecture, explain the relationship between the lantana plants and insects and discuss how it benefits both of them. Please begin speaking after the beep. [20-second pause, then beep] [60-second pause, then beep] Now stop speaking.

Narrator: This is the end of the Speaking Section. Go directly to the Writing Section.

[CD 12 Track 3]

Writing Section

Narrator: Directions: Take three minutes to read the short passage that follows. You may take notes as you read. After three minutes, turn the page and start the Audio Program. You will hear a lecture on the same topic as the reading. Again, you may take notes as you listen. You will have twenty minutes to write your response. Your response should include information from both the reading and the lecture. Your essay will be rated on the completeness and accuracy of your response as well as on the correctness and quality of your writing. A typical response should be 150 to 225 words.

Narrator: Listen to part of a lecture in a psychology class on the same topic that you just read about.

Professor: Okay, everyone have a chance to read that little piece I gave you about risk-taking personalities? It comes from an article in a journal published . . . I don't know, maybe seventy years ago.

The author takes a pretty harsh view of risk-taking, doesn't he? Today, most psychologists take a somewhat

AUDIO SCRIPT

more tolerant view of many types of risk-taking than psychologists did then.

Sure, some people are natural risk-takers. And others are risk-averse. But I can't go along with this article when it says there's a . . . a "universal risk-taking personality." Some people take risks in one part of their lives but not in others. An investment banker might always buy safe stocks, but then he might race motorcycles on weekends.

The article discusses the connection between risk-taking and suicidal tendencies. Well, I'd argue that most risk-takers tend to be pretty confident that nothing bad will happen to them. They recognize that their activities are dangerous, sure, but because of their skill, their . . . their positive attitude . . . their experience, they will succeed. Motorcycle racers don't think they will have accidents, no matter how fast they drive.

The article suggests that there's no reward for people who take unnecessary risks. Actually, there are rewards. For one thing, there's a physical reward, a *chemical* reward. What I mean is, when people take risks, when skydivers, say, jump from airplanes, their bodies pump chemicals like adrenaline into their bloodstreams. For some people, this is pleasurable, something to repeat over and over. There are also psychological benefits. Studies have shown that risk-takers have higher self-esteem, higher levels of confidence, more, uh, social and financial success than those who don't.

Now, I don't want to make any blanket statements about taking risks. There are some risks that people shouldn't take. Smoking is a health risk, one that's just foolish to take. But we psychologists have changed our opinion since this article was written. We realize that sometimes it's important to take risks, and that risk-takers aren't mentally ill.

Narrator: Now get ready to answer the question. Remember, you may turn the page and look back at the reading passage. You may also use your notes to help you. You have twenty minutes to prepare and write your response.

Question: Summarize the main points made in the lecture that you just heard, discussing how they cast doubt on the main points of the reading. You can refer to the reading passage as you write.

Narrator: This is the end of the Integrated Skills Writing Section and of the Audio Program for Practice Test 1.

[CD 13 Track 1]

Practice Test 2

Listening Section

Narrator: Directions: This section tests your understanding of conversations and lectures. You will hear each conversation or lecture only once. Your answers should be based on what is stated or implied in the conversations and lectures. You are allowed to take notes as you listen, and you can use these notes to help you answer the questions. In some questions, you will see a headphones icon. This icon tells you that you will hear, but not read, part of the lecture again. Then you will answer a question about the part of the lecture that you heard. Some questions have special directions that are highlighted. During an actual listening test, you will not be able to skip items and come back to them later, so try to answer every question that you hear on this practice test. This test includes two conversations and four lectures. Most questions are separated by a ten-second pause.

Narrator: Listen to a conversation between two students.

Student A: Hey, Allen, have you decided who you're going to vote for tomorrow? In the student government election?

Student B: Oh, that's tomorrow?

Student A: Yeah, haven't you seen the posters all over campus?

Student B: Tell you the truth, there're always a lot of posters around campus, and I never pay much attention to any of them. So are you running for office again, Janet?

Student A: As a matter of fact, yeah, I am, I'm running for re-election for the seat on the Student Council that belongs to the School of Business. But you can't vote for me, because you're in the School of Engineering.

Student B: Oh, that's how it works? You can only vote for someone from your own school?

Student A: Right. Each of the ten schools on campus—the Engineering School, the Law School, the School of Arts and Sciences, the Business School, all ten of them—has one representative on the Student Council, and you can only vote for someone from your own school. Except for the Student Council President and Vice President. All the students at the university get to vote for those two offices. So you'll be voting for council member, president, and V.P. tomorrow.

Student B: Oh, I thought I read somewhere that first the council was elected and that then they voted for president and vice president.

Student A: Uh, well, you're right, it *used* to be that way. But last year the Student Council voted to change the student government charter. We decided it was more . . . well, more democratic if all the students could directly elect the president and vice president.

Student B: Why didn't you run for president then? Almost everyone on campus knows you, and . . .

Student A: I want to serve one more year on the council . . . and then, well, I'm thinking that next year, I'll try to get elected president.

Student B: Well, if I can't vote for you tomorrow, Janet, I don't think there's much point in voting. I don't know anything about any of the other candidates.

Student A: You should vote anyway, Allen. You may not think so, but student government's important.

Student B: Why? Why should it matter to me who's on the Student Council?

Student A: Well, the most important thing is—the Council gets to decide how to spend your money. Fifteen dollars from each student's fees goes into the Student Council's general fund. That's a budget of, like, a hundred and fifty thousand dollars. The Council decides how much each campus organization can spend, it decides what concerts we're going to have.

Student B: Tell you the truth, Janet, I'm too busy to join any organizations or go to any concerts—most engineering students are. Besides, everyone knows that student government doesn't have any real power. Real power on this campus belongs to the Board of Trustees.

Student A: Yeah, but the president of the Student Council goes to the Trustees' Meetings. Now it's true, he or she doesn't get to vote, but that doesn't mean that the Trustees don't listen to the Council President's concerns sometimes. Just last year . . .

Student B: Well, I have my doubts—I think the Trustees do what they want to do. But I'll tell you what, Janet—since you asked me, I'll vote in the election tomorrow.

Student A: Great! Then you should also go to the debate tonight, to figure out who's the best candidate for you to vote for.

Student B: Don't push your luck! I have a quiz tomorrow that I have to study for.

Narrator: Now get ready to answer some questions about the conversation. You may use your notes to help you.

Narrator: Question 1: Why can't Allen vote for Janet?

Narrator: Question 2: How many members of the council is each student allowed to vote for?

Narrator: Question 3: What is learned about Janet from this conversation?

Narrator: Question 4: According to Janet, what is the most important responsibility of the Student Council?

Narrator: Listen again to part of the conversation.

Student B: Well, I have my doubts—I think the Trustees do what they want to do. But I'll tell you what, Janet—since you asked me, I'll vote in the election tomorrow.

Student A: Great! Then you should also go to the debate tonight, to figure out who's the best candidate for you to vote for.

Student B: Don't push your luck! I have a quiz tomorrow that I have to study for.

Narrator: Question 5: What does Allen imply when he says this?

Student B: Don't push your luck!

Narrator: Listen to a conversation between two students.

Student A: Hi, Tony. Hey . . . I wonder if you could . . . uh, do me a little favor tomorrow afternoon?

Student B: Oh, hi, Alison. Well . . . depends on what the favor is.

Student A: Okay, you know that class I'm taking with Professor Marquez? Well, she's asked us to try to find some volunteers to . . . uh, well, to take part in a role play . . .

Student B: And so what sort of a role would I have to play?

Student A: Well, you won't find out until tomorrow. See, we're learning about focus groups and how they work and how to be a moderator of a focus group. You and the other volunteers from outside our class will be members of the focus groups. The students in my class will take turns being moderators. In real life, there's only one moderator for each focus group, usually, but Professor Marquez wants everyone to have a chance to play the role of moderator. Now, since a good focus group has people from different backgrounds, uh, when you come in the classroom tomorrow, Professor Marquez will give you a little card that tells you your vital information: your age, your occupation, how much education you have, that sort of thing . . . and that's the role you play when you're pretending to be in this focus group.

Student B: Tell me a little about focus groups. I mean, I've heard of them, but . . .

Student A: All right. Well, according to Professor Marquez, there are two basic types. There's . . . uh, the exploratory group . . . the moderator asks the focus group if a company should market a new product at all, if there would be any demand for it. Then there's the experiential group—you'll be in an experiential group tomorrow. Experiential groups, they try out several versions of a product. People in the group tell the moderator which version of the product they like better. This helps the company decide which one of these versions of the product to market.

Student B: Don't they use focus groups a lot in Hollywood? To make movies?

Student A: Yeah, they do. I mean, a movie's a product, too, and film companies want to know which version of a movie to market. So a lot of times, a director will make several different versions of a movie. Usually each version has a different ending. The focus group watches them all and then says which one they like best.

Student B: So, what product will the groups in your class be testing?

Student A: Well, different teams will have different products. My team, the three students I'm working with, we're . . . uh, pretending that a client company, an imaginary food company came to our marketing agency and said, "We're thinking about adding a new flavor of ice cream to our product mix, and we've come up with a half-dozen recipes for this ice cream flavor, and we want you to help us figure out which of these we should market."

Student B: Ice cream, huh. So where are you getting the ice cream?

Student A: We're just gonna buy different brands of the same flavor of ice cream at the supermarket.

Student B: So, you get a grade for this project?

Student A: Yeah, and it's actually a fairly important part of our total grade. Professor Marquez says that . . . that the chemistry, the uh, interaction between the moderator and the focus group, is key in making sure a focus group goes well. You have to be sure that the people in the group feel free to give their opinions, but you have to keep them on topic. And you want to help the group develop a . . . a group identity, a group spirit, you know? But at the same time you don't want them to fall into the "group think" trap, where the members say things just to be going along with the group . . . being a moderator's not all that easy, I guess.

Student B: Well, I'm pretty sure I'm free tomorrow afternoon. Oh, and . . . uh, what flavor ice cream are we going to be tasting?

Student A: Umm, mint chocolate chip.

Student B: Okay, that settles it . . . I'm in!

Narrator: Now get ready to answer some questions about the conversation. You may use your notes to help you.

Narrator: Question 6: What subject does Professor Marquez probably teach?

Narrator: Question 7: What will Professor Marquez give the man if he comes to her class the next day?

Narrator: Question 8: What does the woman imply about focus groups that test Hollywood films?

Narrator: Question 9: What will Professor Marquez probably pay most attention to during the focus group activity?

Narrator: Listen again to part of the conversation.

Student B: Well, I'm pretty sure I'm free tomorrow afternoon. Oh, and . . . uh, what flavor ice cream are we going to be tasting?

Student A: Umm, mint chocolate chip.

Student B: Okay, that settles it . . . I'm in!

Narrator: Question 10: What does Tony imply when he says this?

Student B: Okay, that settles it . . . I'm in!

Narrator: Listen to a lecture in an American Literature class.

Professor: Today I'd like to continue our discussion of nineteenth-century literature by talking about the novelist Harriet Beecher Stowe. She was born Harriet Beecher in Connecticut in 1811. When she was 21, she moved to Cincinnati, Ohio. Now, Cincinnati's on the border between the Northern states and the Southern states. In those days, before the Civil War, Ohio was one of the free states—slavery wasn't permitted there—but right across the river is Kentucky, where slavery *was* permitted. Stowe said that when she lived in Cincinnati, she met people who gave her ideas and she heard stories that she used in her book. However, she never really lived *in* the South, and that's one of the criticisms that Southerners directed at her—that she had no firsthand knowledge of slavery, of life in the South, because she'd never spent time there.

Okay, Harriet Beecher was what we call an Abolitionist—a person who was utterly opposed to slavery . . . uh, to the whole idea of owning slaves. In Cincinnati, she met another Abolitionist, a man named Calvin Stowe. They got married, and she became Harriet Beecher Stowe. After a while, Stowe and her husband moved back to New England, to Brunswick, Maine. He encouraged her to write a book that showed the evils of slavery. So, Stowe wrote *Uncle Tom's Cabin,* by far her most famous work. This novel was first published in an Abolitionist newspaper, the *National Era,* in 1851. It didn't attract a lot of attention at first. Then in 1852, *Uncle Tom's Cabin* was published in book form. It became extremely popular in the United States—at least in the Northern half of the United States—and also in Britain. Harriet Stowe became a celebrity and gave readings all over the North. If she were writing today, no doubt we'd see her all the time as a guest on television talk shows.

Uncle Tom's Cabin's true historical impact has been debated. Southerners hated it and said it presented an unfair, overly negative view of slavery. On the other hand, some Northern Abolitionists thought that it didn't go far enough, that it painted too soft a picture of slavery. But there's no doubt that it, uh, stirred up lots of opposition to slavery and played a role in causing the Civil War. Supposedly, when Abraham Lincoln met Stowe during the Civil War, he said to her, "So you're the little lady whose book started this great war."

Basically, *Uncle Tom's Cabin* is the story of a group of slaves. When the book opens, they're owned by a fairly humane, kind farmer, but for business reasons, he has to sell them to new masters. Some—like the character Eliza—escape and, even though they are chased by hired slave hunters, they make their way with the help of Abolitionists to Canada, where they're safe. Other slaves from this group—including kindly old Uncle Tom, whom the book is named for—are taken to the Deep South and are treated miserably, horribly, and come to tragic endings.

One strange thing about *Uncle Tom's Cabin* is that some of the most famous scenes aren't in the original book. Soon after the book was published, it began to inspire theatrical versions, little dramatic plays called "Tom Shows." These were mostly of pretty bad quality and didn't follow the plot of the book very carefully. Anyway, one of most famous of these Tom Shows was directed by George Aiken. It featured a scene where the slave Eliza is chased by men with dogs, with bloodhounds, across the ice of a frozen river. This scene was also featured in the movie *Uncle Tom's Cabin,* which was made later, in, like 1927. That's probably why this scene sticks in people's minds, but it wasn't in the book at all.

Now, uh, the novel has come in for its share of criticism since it was written. I've already mentioned a few of these criticisms. Another criticism is that Stowe's treatment of her characters is overly sentimental, overly emotional. But remember, Stowe lived in a sentimental age. Even some great writers of the time, like the British author Charles Dickens, treated his characters sentimentally—think about Little Nell in his book *The Old Curiosity Shop.*

Anyway, sentimental or not, *Uncle Tom's Cabin* is still an important book. I don't think you can understand the pre–Civil War era in the U.S. without reading it. Now, our textbook has some short selections from the novel, but I really suggest you go to the library and get a copy and read it cover to cover.

Narrator: Now get ready to answer some questions about the lecture. You may use your notes to help you.

Narrator: Question 11: Where did Harriet Stowe live when she wrote *Uncle Tom's Cabin?*

Narrator: Question 12: The professor mentions a number of versions of *Uncle Tom's Cabin.* List these in the order in which they were produced, beginning with the earliest.

Narrator: Question 13: Why does the professor mention Charles Dickens?

Narrator: Question 14: What does the professor say about the scene in which Eliza is chased across the icy river by men with dogs?

Narrator: Question 15: In this lecture, the professor mentions a number of criticisms of Harriet Beecher Stowe's novel *Uncle Tom's Cabin.* Indicate whether each of the following is a criticism that was mentioned in the lecture.

Narrator: Listen again to part of the lecture. Then answer the question.

Professor: Anyway, sentimental or not, *Uncle Tom's Cabin* is still an important book. I don't think you can understand the pre–Civil War era in the U.S. without reading it. Now, our textbook has some short selections from the novel, but I really suggest you go to the library and get a copy and read it cover to cover.

Narrator: Question 16: What does the professor suggest to the students when she says this?

Professor: But, I really suggest you go to the library and get a copy and read it cover to cover.

Narrator: Listen to a lecture in a geology class.

Professor: Morning, everyone. Everyone have a good weekend? As I said on Friday, I want to talk some about glaciers today. Now, glaciers just start with ordinary snow, but in some parts of the world—in . . . uh, polar and mountainous regions—snow builds up, it accumulates faster than it is removed by melting in the summer. Now, ordinary snow is about 80% air and about 20% solids. This snow melts and refreezes several times, and becomes a dense, more compact form of snow. There's less air and more solids. It's then called *névé.* Now, um, when névé doesn't melt for a whole year, when it goes all summer without melting, it becomes what's called *firn.* Firn is a type of ice, a granular ice that looks a lot like wet sugar. It's even more compressed, even denser than *névé.* Then, every year, more and more snow falls, and the most deeply buried firn becomes even more tightly compressed, it becomes about 90% solid. This type of ice is called *glacial ice.* As the weight of accumulated snow and ice builds, the ice on the underside becomes pliable, it becomes elastic enough to flow, and a glacier is born. The glacier flows just like a river, but a glacier moves only about three centimeters a day.

There are two main types of glaciers, the valley glacier and the continental glacier, plus a couple of minor types. Valley glaciers usually form near the top of a mountain. They flow down the mountainside. Valley glaciers follow a V-shaped valley carved by an old stream of water or else they, um, well, they cut their own path. The glacier is gonna pick up rocks as it moves downhill, and carry them along with it. These rocks that the glacier drags along round out the bottom of the valley, and the V-shaped stream bed becomes U-shaped. Because they're rigid, glaciers don't take sharp corners very well, so their downhill paths are generally gonna be a series of gentle curves. In some cases, valley glaciers are fed by little glaciers, called tributary glaciers, that form in smaller valleys that lead into the main valley. And sometimes, you get one or more valley glaciers that flow together, forming what are called piedmont glaciers.

Now, uh, the second major type of glacier is called the continental glacier. It's a lot larger than a valley glacier. The average continental glacier is about the size of the state of West Virginia. Today, continental glaciers are found only on the island of Greenland and on the continent of Antarctica, but still, they cover almost 10% of the world's land area.

During the Ice Ages—and remember, we said the last one of those was only about eleven thousand years ago—an additional 20% of the world was buried under these giant continental glaciers. Most of North America—most of the northern hemisphere, for that matter—was covered by continental glaciers.

Now, a continental glacier moves, too, but not down a slope the way a valley glacier does. In fact, most continental glaciers were on relatively flat land. Still, they move at a . . . uh—well, you can measure their movement. As ice piles up to a greater and greater thickness—it can be 1,000 meters deep or more—you get a tremendous amount of pressure inside the ice sheet. This force is so powerful that it causes the interior ice to practically liquefy, and so a continental glacier moves out in all directions from the glacier's central point.

At some point, glaciers, all types of glaciers, become stationary. In other words, they appear to stop growing. That's because they're melting at the same rate at which new ice is being added. Then they begin to recede. When they recede, valley glaciers seem to be moving uphill. Continental glaciers seem to be retreating towards their central point. What's really happening is that they are melting faster than they are adding new materials.

A lot of glaciers around the world these days are receding—the glaciers in the high mountains of Africa, Mt. Kenya, Mt. Kilimanjaro, for example, are noticeably smaller every year. A lot of scientists are afraid that the reason behind this is global warming. If glaciers melt—especially the continental glaciers in Greenland and Antarctica—the level of the sea will rise. A lot of great beaches around the world will disappear, some cities will be underwater—some low-lying island nations like those in the Indian Ocean may completely disappear.

Now, I'm gonna talk about the effects of glaciers on the landscape, about some of the geological features that are a result of glaciers, but first, questions or comments, anyone?

Narrator: Now get ready to answer some questions about the lecture. You may use your notes to help you.

Narrator: Question 17: The professor discusses four types of materials involved in the formation of a glacier. Give the order in which these materials appear.

Narrator: Question 18: Where can continental glaciers be found today?

Narrator: Question 19: Which of the following describe a valley formed by a valley glacier?

Narrator: Question 20: It can be inferred from the lecture that which of the following is the smallest type of glacier?

Narrator: Question 21: In this lecture, the professor gives a number of characteristics of valley glaciers and continental glaciers. Indicate which type of glacier each of the following is typical of.

Narrator: Question 22: What danger does the professor mention?

Narrator: Listen to a discussion in an economics class.

Student A: Professor Martin, you said that there would be an essay question on the mid-term exam about the business cycle. I wonder if we can go over the . . . ah, well, the whole concept of the business cycle again . . .

Professor: Umm, well, Donald, we only have a few minutes left, but we can do a quick review, sure. Let's see what you remember from that lecture. Who knows what the names of the four stages of the business cycle are?

Student B: Umm, let's see . . . I think it's . . . expansion, downturn, contraction, upturn, right?

Professor: Yes, those are the most common names for the four stages these days. And the highest point of the expansion is . . .

Student A: The peak. And, uh, the lowest part, the lowest point of the, uh, contraction is called the trough, I believe.

Professor: Yes, you're right. And as I said, we measure a cycle from the peak of one cycle to the peak of the next. Now, what's going on during the expansion phase of the business cycle?

Student B: Uh, that's when things are going pretty good, when the economy is just humming along.

Professor: Exactly. Business profits are up . . . wages are high . . . economic output is growing . . . then what happens?

Student A: Well, you have a downturn . . . there are economic problems . . . uh, the economy stops growing.

Professor: Right, and eventually the economy enters a contraction. Usually, during a contraction, you have a recession. Demand for goods is down, and . . . well, you know what a recession is like. Businesses close, people are laid off. It's a painful period for many people. After a while, though, things start to improve. Sometimes the government steps in. Or sometimes this just happens on its own. Demand picks up again, and businesses' inventories shrink, so manufacturers have to hire people to produce more goods . . .

Student A: Professor? What can a government do to stop a recession?

Professor: Well, there may not be *anything* a government can do to completely prevent recessions. What they usually do is, the government . . . the Central Bank, really . . . manipulates the money supply. This doesn't really stop recessions from occurring, but it may make these dips in business activity less severe. Anyway, as I said, after a while, the economy starts to improve. The recovery is usually slow at first, then it picks up speed, it improves, and you have an upturn. Pretty soon the economy is back in the expansion phase and the cycle starts all over.

Student B: Professor, what I'd like to know is . . . is this oversimplified? I mean, is the business cycle really this regular?

Professor: That's a good question. It's a useful model, but you're right, no business cycle is exactly the same. They vary in length, for example. In fact, they are so irregular in length that some economists prefer to talk about business *fluctuations* rather than a business cycle.

Student A: So how long does the typical cycle last?

Professor: Well, since the end of World War II, there've been ten cycles. That averages out to six years a cycle. But some were quite a bit longer than others. For example, the U.S. economy was in an expansion phase throughout most of the 1990's. Some economists even said that, because of globalization, recessions were a thing of the past. Then, sadly, along came the recession of 2001 to prove them wrong.

Student A: Don't they also vary by . . . uh, how bad they are? How bad the recession is?

Professor: That's right, they do vary in intensity. For example, the downturn in the early 90's was quite mild, but some recessions have been so serious that they were called *depressions*. We haven't had a depression recently, though. The last one was in the 1930's—that one was so bad we call it the *Great Depression*. There was another one in the 1870's.

Student B: Professor Martin, I never really understood—what causes business cycles anyway?

Professor: Well, if I could answer that, I'd probably win a Nobel Prize in economics. There are a lot of theories—there are several in your book. I always thought one of the most interesting theories was the one that the economist William Jevons came up with back in the nineteenth century. The way he explained it, business cycles were caused by sunspots.

Student B: Sunspots? How could something happening on the sun cause business cycles?

Professor: Well, he thought that sunspots affected the climate. A lot of sunspots cause the weather to be cooler, and this affects both the quality and the quantity of agricultural production, and this in turn causes a drop in economic activity.

Student A: And this theory . . . a lot of people believed it?

Professor: Yeah, at the time, it was widely accepted. And as a matter of fact, there were a lot of statistics that seemed to back it up. Today, though, it's no longer considered a valid theory. Still, you have to admit, it's an interesting one!

Narrator: Now get ready to answer some questions about the discussion. You may use your notes to help you.

Narrator: Question 23: What is the main topic of this discussion?

Narrator: Listen again to part of the discussion.

Professor: Who knows what the names of the four stages of the business cycle are?

Student B: Umm, let's see . . . I think it's . . . expansion, downturn, contraction, upturn, right?

Professor: Yes, those are the most common names for the four stages these days.

Narrator: Question 24: What does Professor Martin imply when he says this?

Professor: Yes, those are the most common names for the four stages these days.

Narrator: Question 25: In this lecture, the professor describes the business cycle. Indicate whether each of the following is a characteristic of the cycle mentioned by the professor.

Narrator: Question 26: In which of these decades did economic depressions occur?

Narrator: Question 27: In what ways do governments usually try to affect business cycles?

Narrator: Question 28: Which of the following statements about William Jevons's theory would Professor Martin probably agree with?

Narrator: Listen to a lecture in a film studies class.

Professor: OK, settle down, everyone, let's get started, lots to do today. If you remember, in our last class, we were discussing movies about the American West, and we saw some scenes from some classic westerns. Today we're going to shift our attention to another genre of film, science fiction, or "sci-fi" as a lot of people call it. Sci-fi movies are about aliens from outer space, they're about people from Earth traveling to other planets, they can be about time travel, about robots. They're often set in the future—sometimes the far future, sometime the near future, but sometimes they're set in the present and sometimes even in the distant past—like the *Star Wars* films.

Now, most people think of sci-fi as being a fairly recent phenomenon, a contemporary kind of film, but . . . uh, in fact, some of the very first movies ever made were science fiction films. The very first one was probably *Voyage to the Moon,* made way back in 1902 by the pioneering French director Georges Méliès—who, by the way, was also a magician. It's . . . uh, it's loosely based on a novel by the French science fiction novelist Jules Verne, and given that it was made over a hundred years ago, it has some pretty amazing special effects. There . . . uh, there's this bullet-shaped rocket that's shot to the moon by a giant cannon. In fact, it hits the Man in the Moon right in the eye!

Probably the first really great science fiction film was the 1926 film *Metropolis*. It involves a sinister, industrialized city of the future—it was set a hundred years in the future, in the year 2026. It features a beautiful but evil robot named Maria—the first robot to ever appear in a movie. It has these wonderful futuristic sets. The themes this movie explores—well, they seem as up-to-date now as they did then. In fact—this is kinda interesting—it was re-released in 1984 with a rock-and-roll music soundtrack.

The 1950's—that's the . . . the so-called Golden Age of sci-fi movies. Hundreds, maybe thousands of sci-fi movies were made then. Most of them, frankly, were pretty awful. About the only reason to watch them today is that they can be unintentionally funny because of their terrible dialogue, bad acting, and really low-budget special effects. Now, the 1950's was the height of the Cold War between the Soviet Union and the United States. It was a really anxious time, there was the danger of nuclear war, and both the U.S. and the Soviet Union were testing nuclear weapons. So, uh, Hollywood responded to this fear of atomic energy by making a lot of movies about the, about . . . ummm, about the mutations atomic energy could cause. One of the first of these was the movie *Them!,* which was about ordinary ants that are exposed to atomic radiation during a test in the desert. These ants grow into giant ants and they attack the city of Los Angeles. There were movies about lots of big bugs—about giant scorpions, about huge spiders, crabs, grasshoppers. The famous Japanese movie *Godzilla* was about a bad-tempered, prehistoric lizard who's brought back to life by an atom bomb test.

Of course, there *were* a few good sci-fi movies made during the Golden Age. My favorite science fiction movie of all time is *Forbidden Planet,* which is, interestingly enough, based on William Shakespeare's play *The Tempest.* It also makes use of ideas from the theories of the famous psychologist Sigmund Freud.

Now, most sci-fi movies of the 50's were seen by small audiences and were either ignored or attacked by critics. The first science fiction movie that was a hit with both the public and with critics came along in 1969. It was the brilliant movie *2001: A Space Odyssey.* Then, in 1977, came the most popular science fiction movie of all time, the first *Star Wars* movie—eventually there would be a series of six of these. The director got his ideas for this film from . . . from everywhere: from western movies, Japanese samurai movies, 1930's serials, Greek mythology, you name it. This first *Star Wars* movie had awesome special effects, and people fell in love with the characters, like Luke Skywalker, the evil Darth Vader . . . and especially those robots.

Another important sci-fi movie was 1982's *ET*. Think about most of the movies you've seen about visitors from space: there's *Independence Day*, and *War of the Worlds*, and *Predator*, and oh, of course, *Alien*. These visitors are horrible invaders that want to kill us or enslave us or . . . or eat us. But in *ET*, the space creature is cute, he's cuddly, he's smart, he makes friends with a young Earth boy—he's much nicer than most Earth people!

Okay, well, for the rest of the class, let's look at some clips from science fiction films. Today I brought along some scenes from the really early sci-fi moves I mentioned: *A Trip to the Moon* and *Metropolis*. Then, uh, unfortunately, we just have time for a few quick scenes from my favorite, *Forbidden Planet*, then we'll look at some bits from some slightly more recent movies, like the latest *Star Wars* film.

Narrator: Now get ready to answer some questions about the lecture. You may use your notes to help you.

Narrator: Question 29: Why does the professor mention the work of the French director Georges Méliès?

Narrator: Question 30: When does the action in the movie *Metropolis* supposedly take place?

Narrator: Question 31: What topic does the movie *Them!* and many other 1950's science fiction movies deal with?

Narrator: Question 32: Which of the following influenced the movie *Forbidden Planet*?

Narrator: Question 33: What does the speaker think is remarkable about the movie *ET*?

Narrator: Question 34: What does the professor imply when she says this?

Professor: Then, uh, unfortunately, we just have time for a few quick scenes from my favorite, *Forbidden Planet*, then we'll look at some bits from some slightly more recent movies, like the latest *Star Wars* film.

Narrator: This is the end of the Listening Section of Practice Test 2. You may take a ten-minute break before beginning work on the Speaking Section.

[CD 13 Track 2]

Speaking Section

Narrator: Directions: This section tests your ability to speak about various subjects. There are six tasks in this section. Listen carefully to the directions and read the questions on the screen. The first two tasks are Independent Speaking tasks. You have fifteen seconds in which to prepare your response. When you hear a beep on the Audio Program, you will have forty-five seconds in which to answer the question. The last four tasks are Integrated Speaking tasks. The third and fourth questions involve a reading text and a listening passage. You have forty-five seconds in which to read a short text. You will then hear a short conversation or part of a lecture on the same topic. You may take notes on both the reading and listening passage. You will then see a question on the screen asking about the information that you have just read and heard, and you will have thirty seconds in which to plan a response. When you hear a beep on the Audio Program, you have sixty seconds in which to answer the question. The fifth and sixth questions involve a short listening passage. You may take notes as you listen. After listening to the conversation or lecture, you will see a question, and you have twenty seconds in which to plan your response. When you hear a beep on the Audio Program, you have sixty seconds in which to answer the question. During actual tests, a clock on the screen will tell you how much preparation time or how much response

time (speaking time) remains for each question. It is important that you time yourself accurately when you take this practice test. On an actual test your responses will be recorded and evaluated by trained raters.

Narrator: Question 1. . . . Please listen carefully . . .

Narrator: Describe the most interesting book that you have ever read. Explain why it was important to you. Include details and examples to support your explanation. Please begin speaking after the beep. [15-second pause, then beep] [45-second pause, then beep] Now stop speaking.

Narrator: Question 2. . . . Please listen carefully . . .

Narrator: Because of computers, telephones, and other technology, it is now possible for many people to work at home. Some people prefer working at home, while others would rather work in an office. Which of these do you prefer and why? Please begin speaking after the beep. [15-second pause, then beep] [45-second pause, then beep] Now stop speaking.

Narrator: Question 3. . . . Please listen carefully . . .

Narrator: Linslade University has begun a new program involving free laptop computers. Read the following notice from the university. You will have forty-five seconds in which to read the notice. Begin reading now.

Narrator: Now listen to two students discussing this notice.

Student A: Wow, this is a great program.

Student B: Well, yeah, I guess—it's great for you, anyway.

Student A: What do you mean?

Student B: You're a first-year student. I went here last year, so . . . no laptop for me!

Student A: Oh, that's right. Well, you can pick one up cheaply, anyway.

Student B: Don't need one. I found it impossible to get by without a laptop last year, so I went out and bought one.

Student A: Oh. Well, so you agree that a student here needs a laptop!

Student B: Absolutely! I use mine every day. I just wish this program had been in place a year ago.

Narrator: The man expresses his opinion of the new program. State his opinion and explain the reasons he gives for having that opinion. Please begin speaking after the beep. [30-second pause, then beep] [60-second pause] Now stop speaking.

Narrator: Question 4. . . . Please listen carefully . . .

Narrator: Now listen to a lecture on the utopian community Brook Farm.

Professor: Brook Farm is, I'd say, the most famous utopian community ever established in the United States. It was founded in West Roxbury, Massachusetts, in 1841 by George Ripley. Today, West Roxbury is a suburb of Boston, but back then it was way out in the country. It consisted of 200 acres of land and half a dozen buildings to house the 120 or so residents.

Brook Farm had an unusual economic structure. Residents received one year's room and board in return for working for the community for 300 days a year. Residents could work in the fields, in crafts shops, in the kitchen. And . . . uh, although they worked hard, the residents also spent time attending lectures, dancing, taking walks. The farm practiced complete equality of the sexes—a radical idea back then. It had the support of some of the most famous writers and thinkers of the time, many of whom visited the farm.

But Brook Farm never did well, not financially. The land wasn't much good for farming. In 1846 there was an outbreak of disease, and in 1847 a fire destroyed the main building, which had never even been finished. That year the farm closed. It lasted six years, longer than most utopian societies, but like all of them it failed to produce a permanent community.

Narrator: The professor's lecture is about Brook Farm community. Describe this community and explain why it is a typical utopian community. Please begin speaking after the beep. [30-second pause, then beep] [60-second pause] Now stop speaking.

Narrator: Question 5. . . . Please listen carefully . . .
Narrator: Now listen to a conversation between two students.
Student A: Hey, Nancy—what brings you to the library?
Student B: I just needed a quiet place to study—you remember that problem I told you about with my neighbors?
Student A: With those two guys who live upstairs from you? Are they still being loud?
Student B: All the time, practically. I can't study at home, I can hardly hear my own music, I can't get to sleep at night . . .
Student A: You really need to talk to those guys, Nancy.
Student B: I *have* talked to them, three or four times. And every time I do, they act really apologetic, they say that they'll try to be quieter . . . but, the next day, the noise is back as bad as ever.
Student A: Well, if I were you, I'd call the police. It's against the law to make that much noise, especially late at night.
Student B: I know, I've thought of calling the cops, but . . . the thing is, they're really nice guys, it's that they're in a band and . . . well, they told me they don't have any other place to practice their music.
Student A: Well, that's not your problem. You shouldn't have to put up with that kind of noise.
Student B: I know, but . . . for one thing, it's not just them. The people in the next apartment always have their television on too loud, and there's a guy up on the third floor who's always having parties. It's just a noisy building, and there doesn't seem to be much sound-proofing.
Student A: Well, I know it wouldn't be any fun to move in the middle of a semester, but . . . maybe you should consider it. I live in Ormond Towers. I think there are some vacancies in my building. It's not as close to campus as your place, but I bet it's a lot quieter. There are a few grad students there, but mostly there are couples in their late twenties and thirties. It's not exactly party central.
Student B: Yeah, I hate to be driven out of the place I live— it's such a convenient location and all, but I'm at the point where I . . . well, I should probably at least consider moving.
Narrator: The man discusses two possible solutions to Nancy's problem. Discuss her problem and then explain which of the two solutions you think is better and why you think so. Please begin speaking after the beep. [30-second pause, then beep] [60-second pause] Now stop speaking.
Narrator: Question 6. . . . Please listen carefully . . .
Narrator: Now listen to a lecture in a meteorology class.
Professor: Someone asked me last week if I'd talk about how hurricanes get their names . . . . up until 1953, hurricanes didn't have names. Beginning that year, hurricanes in the Atlantic Basin—which includes the North Atlantic, the Caribbean, and the Gulf of Mexico—they were given names by the World Meteorological Organization. The first hurricane of the season starts with the letter A, the second with B, and so on. At first, hurricanes were all given female names, but in

1979, I guess people decided that it was sexist to name these storms after women, so now names alternate—male, female, male, and so on. So you get Alison, Brian, Charlotte, Dean, Ellen—sounds like the guest list for a party, doesn't it? There are no names beginning with the letters Q, U, X, Y, and Z, though, so there are only twenty-one names on each list. Now, there are six lists of names for storms and these are used in rotation. So, the 2007 list, for example, will be used again in 2013. The only exception to this is when there's a particularly bad storm, a particularly deadly or costly one. Then that name is retired, it's never used again, and it's replaced with another name. For example, in 1992, the name Andrew was retired—in '98, the name Mitch was retired—in 2005, the name Katrina was retired. All in all, there have been over sixty names retired. Now, what happens if there are more than twenty-one named storms in one year? That first happened during the hurricane season of 2005. Then, hurricanes are named after the letters of the Greek alphabet: Alpha, Beta, Gamma, Delta, Epsilon, and so on.
Narrator: Using specific examples and points from the lecture, explain the naming process for hurricanes. Please begin speaking after the beep. [20-second pause, then beep] [60-second pause] Now stop speaking.

Narrator: This is the end of the Speaking Section. Go directly to the Writing Section.

[CD 13 Track 3]

Writing Section

Narrator: Directions: Take three minutes to read the short passage that follows. You may take notes as you read. After three minutes, turn the page and start the Audio Program. You will hear a lecture on the same topic as the reading. Again, you may take notes as you listen. You will have twenty minutes to write your response. Your response should include information from both the reading and the lecture. Your essay will be rated on the completeness and accuracy of your response as well as on the correctness and quality of your writing. A typical response should be 150 to 225 words.

Narrator: Listen to part of a lecture in an economics class on the same topic that you just read about.
Professor: Good morning, class. Today I'd like to continue our discussion of tourism and its impact on the economy. Now, I know I've said some negative things about tourism—like most industries, tourism has its good points and bad points. One of you brought me an article about what's called "eco-tourism" or sometimes "green tourism." I made some copies of this and gave them to you Monday. The author of this article would have you believe that eco-tourism is an entirely good thing. Well, don't you believe it. One of the points I've made over and over in this class is that *all* development has its positive and its negative sides.

Now, eco-tourism may have less impact than ordinary tourism—it's better to build a few small lodges in the jungle than a 25-story beach hotel, two swimming pools, and a golf course. But eco-tourism *does* require infrastructure, especially roads, since tourists have to be able to get to these areas somehow, and building this infrastructure is going to stress delicate environments. There's going to be more air pollution, water pollution. And, while eco-tourists are supposed to be more environmentally conscious, there's still going to be problems of litter and so on.

The author says that, if an area is bringing in tourists, the government is going to protect it. Unfortunately, just

...ing

protected, that doesn't mean
...ources of that area. You can hire
...urces but they can be corrupted,
...rket for the parts of some endan-
...al hardwoods, for the artifacts of
...ve got a lot of illegal hunting, of . . .
...of stealing, and the roads just make
...et there and to get those illegal
goous ...

And what a... ...le local people who are supposed to
benefit so much from this influx of eco-tourist revenue? It's
true; there are usually more jobs than before. But often the
local people have the most menial, the lowest-paying jobs
available. Not only that, many of the jobs are filled by people from other areas who come there looking for work. And
then, there's cultural pollution, which happens when an
isolated society suddenly comes in contact with Western
civilization. You have people who were poor farmers or
hunter-gatherers one day and the next, they're talking on
cell-phones, they're surfing the Internet. Societies are
changed, customs are lost.

So, once again, eco-tourism and in fact, *all* tourism has
its benefits, but it is not the perfect solution to development.

Narrator: Now get ready to answer the question. Remember,
you may turn the page and look back at the reading passage. You may also use your notes to help you. You have
twenty minutes to prepare and write your response.

Question: Summarize the main points made in the lecture that you just heard, discussing how they cast doubt on
the main points of the reading. You can refer to the reading
passage as you write.

Narrator: This is the end of the Integrated Skills Writing
Section and of the Audio Program for Practice Test **2.** This is
also the end of the Audio Program for *The Complete Guide
to the TOEFL Test: iBT Edition.*

ANSWER KEY

Section 1: Guide to Reading

(The TOEFL iBT does not use the letters A, B, C, and D for the
multiple-choice items. However, in these answer keys, *A* corresponds to the first answer choice, *B* to the second, *C* to the
third, and *D* to the fourth.)

Preview Test

Biological Barriers

Answer	Explanation
1. A	The word *cosmopolitan* means "found in most places in the world" rather than in a limited range. It is often used about people to mean "worldly and sophisticated," but here it is used to describe animals that live all over the world. The example of the housefly provides a clue to the meaning of the word.
2. C	The author compares the concept of biological barriers with a fence, a familiar type of man-made barrier: "Just as barbed wire fences prevent cattle from leaving their pasture, biological barriers prevent the dispersal of many species."

3. C   The author says, "the American bison spread
throughout the open grasslands of North America,
but in the southern part of the continent there are
deserts, so the bison could not spread there." We
can infer from this sentence that bison can live
only in open grasslands.

4. D   The author says that "Most places that are suitable
for the growth of dandelions are already occupied
by other plants that are well adapted to the area.
The dandelion seedling must compete with these
plants for space, water, light, and nutrients. Facing
such stiff competition, the chances of survival are
slim." Clearly, it is the competition with other
species of plants that causes so few dandelion
seedlings to survive.

5. B   The author *does* give an example of A in paragraph
4 (the Kirkland's warbler). There is an example of C
in paragraph 4 (the blue spotted salamander) and
of D in paragraph 5 (the Engelmann spruce).
However, there is no example of B, an aquatic animal that is stopped by physical barriers.

6. D   In many cases, the word *slim* means "thin," but in
this case it is used with the word *chances* to mean
"unlikely possibilities."

7. D   The two locations that the Kirkland's warbler is
restricted to by behavioral borders are "a few
places in Michigan in the summer and . . . the
Bahamas in winter."

8. C   The author states, "Brazil's Amazon River serves as
a northern or southern boundary for many species
of birds. They could freely fly over the river, but
they seldom do." This indicates that the Amazon is
an example of a behavioral barrier rather than a
physical one.

9. A   In paragraph 6, the author says, "The greatest difference between a corridor and a filter route is that
a corridor consists of one type of habitat, while a
filter consists of several similar types."

10. A   The New Zealand mud snail is an example of an
invasive species that was carried unintentionally
to its new environment. ("An example is the New
Zealand mud snail, which was accidentally
brought to North America . . .")

11. B   This choice best restates the original sentence.
Although this choice does not give the examples
mentioned in the original sentence (predators,
parasites, and competitors) and although it uses
different grammar and vocabulary, this choice is
closest in meaning to the sentence from the passage. Choice A leaves out some important information from the original sentence, and choices C
and D are not accurate.

12. You should circle the second square. The word *they* in the
new sentence refers back to *birds,* and the sentence
explains why birds appear in places far from their homes.

The third type of natural pathway is called a
sweepstakes route. This is dispersal caused by the
chance combination of favorable conditions. ■
Bird watchers are familiar with "accidentals,"
which are birds that appear in places far from their
native areas.■**They may be blown off course by
storms or may be escaping population pressures
in their home areas.** Sometimes they may find a
habitat with favorable conditions and "colonize" it.
■ Gardeners are familiar with "volunteers," culti-
vated plants that grow in their gardens although

they never planted the seeds for these plants.
■ Besides birds and plants, insects, fish, and mammals also colonize new areas. Sweepstakes routes are unlike either corridors or filter routes in that organisms that travel these routes would not be able to spend their entire lives in the habitats that they pass through.

13. B, C, E   Choice B summarizes the information in paragraphs 2, 3, and 4 of the passage. Choice C summarizes the information in paragraphs 5 and 6, and choice E summarizes the information in paragraph 7. Choices A and F are only details in the passage. There is nothing in the passage to indicate that behavioral boundaries are not as effective as physical or climatic barriers, so choice D is not a valid answer.

Mysteries of Easter Island

14. A   *Immense* means "large," "huge."

15. C   All of the statues were carved from volcanic stone (A) and all of them portrayed human heads (D). "Some of them" had red stone hats, but only "a few" had white coral eyes. The statues with white coral eyes must therefore be the least common.

16. A   Paragraph 2 says that "The statues were moved on a network of roads on rollers made of palm logs and were then placed on stone bases called *ahu.*"

17. B   The author says in paragraph 3 that when the first westerner visited Easter Island in 1722, there were hundreds of statues standing, but when Captain Cook visited in 1774, there were only nine standing. The author then says "Obviously, something dramatic had occurred during those years." The phrase *something dramatic* refers to the toppling (knocking over) of the statues.

18. A   Paragraph 4 says, "Any commentary about Easter Island would be incomplete without mentioning the theories of the Norwegian explorer and scientist Thor Heyerdahl . . ." This means that the author finds Heyerdahl's theories important. However, the author also mentions evidence (such as the fact that all Easter Islanders are descended from Polynesians) that contradict Heyerdahl's theory. Therefore, "important but incorrect" best sums up the author's opinion of the theories.

19. D   The author says that the *Hanau Momoko* and *Hanau Eepe* were "once mistranslated as 'Short Ears' and 'Long Ears.'" Since they were "mistranslated," they must have different meanings.

20. C   The author says that "The Hanau Eepe used heavy earrings to extend the length of their ears." He also points out that the ears of the statues resembled those of the Hanau Eepe. Therefore, the statues must have had long ears.

21. B   *Intricate* means "complex, complicated, involved."

22. D   In paragraph 6, the author says, "As for the sweet potato, most scientists now believe that sweet potato seeds came to the island in the stomachs of sea birds."

23. B   The author's main point in paragraph 7 is that dangers such as "overpopulation and overuse of resources" can destroy societies.

24. C   *Thriving* means "successful, flourishing, prospering."

25. You should circle the fourth square. The word *they* in the missing sentence links to the word *Archaeologists* in the previous sentence, and the sentence explains why archaeologists think the resemblance between the expert stonework of the Easter Islanders and that of the Inca was coincidental.

DNA testing has proven that all Easter Islanders were in fact descended from Polynesians. ■ The current theory is that the Hanau Momoko and Hanau Eepe were two of perhaps twelve clans of islanders, all of whom built statues. ■ The "statue toppling wars" broke out among the clans as the island became overpopulated. When one group won a victory over another, they toppled their enemies' statues. ■ Archaeologists say that the resemblance between the stonework of the Easter Islanders and that of the Inca is coincidental. ⊙ **After all, they say, the statues themselves show that the islanders were skilled stone workers.** As for the sweet potato, most scientists now believe that sweet potato seeds came to the island in the stomachs of sea birds.

26. Hanau Momoko: B, D, I; Hanau Eepe: A, E, F, H. Choice A refers to the Hanau Eepe. In paragraph 4, the author says, "The Hanau Eepe used heavy earrings to extend the length of their ears." Choice B refers to the Hanau Momoko: "Heyerdahl theorized that the Hanau Momoko were Polynesians from other Pacific islands, but that the Hanau Eepe came later in rafts from South America." Choice C does not refer to either group. Heyerdahl believed there were only two groups of Easter Islanders. (Current theory believes there were twelve.) Choice D refers to the Hanua Momoko. The author says, "He (Heyerdahl) believed that the Hanau Momoko became the servants of the Hanau Eepe and forced them to build the statues." Choice E refers to the Hanau Eepe. In paragraph 5, the author says, "Another piece of evidence Heyerdahl presented was the fact that the staple of the Easter Islanders, the sweet potato, is not found in Polynesia. He believed that it came with the Hanau Eepe from South America." Choice F refers to the Hanau Eepe as well. The author says in paragraph 4, "Because the Hanau Eepe were the masters, the statues resembled them." Choice G does not refer to either group. There is no mention in the passage that other Pacific Islanders taught anyone on Easter Island how to make statues. Choice H refers to the Hanau Eepe. In paragraph 4, the author says, "According to Heyerdahl's theory, the Hanau Momoko eventually rose up in revolt . . . killing off all but a few Hanau Eepe." Choice I refers to the Hanau Momoko. The author says, "According to Heyerdahl's theory, the Hanau Momoko eventually rose up in revolt, overturning most of the statues . . ."

Lesson 1: Factual and Negative Factual Questions

Exercise 1.1
Passage 1
The first known dentist to practice in the North American colonies was William Dinly, who came to Plymouth Colony from England in 1630. According to legend, he became lost in a snowstorm while riding to see a patient and was never seen again. **(1)** In most colonial settlements, however, dentistry was a rare and unusual practice. In emergencies, barbers, jewelers, and blacksmiths all probably extracted teeth. **(2)**

One of the first native-born dentists was Paul Revere, the famous silversmith and patriot. Revere, who began practicing in Boston in 1768, made false teeth from African ivory. **(3)** One of his patients was the Revolutionary War general Joseph Warren. When the general died at the battle of Breeds Hill,

Revere identified him by examining his teeth. This was the first known case of identification by means of dental records. Today, of course, dental records are commonly used as a means of identification.

By the early nineteenth century, most communities in the United States had one or more dentists, although not all of them had much training. In 1840, dentistry became a true profession. That's when the first dental school was opened in Baltimore, Maryland. The course lasted sixteen weeks. There were only five students in the first class, and only two of these graduated. **(4)** This school has recently been restored as a museum of dental history. **(5)**

The most common cure for toothaches was simply to pull out the offending tooth. Many dentists advertised "painless" extraction methods in the newspapers of the times. "Negative Spray" and "Vitalized Air" were two methods of reducing pain. **(6)** It is not known today how these mysterious processes worked, but it is unlikely that they worked very well. In 1844, dentist Horace Wills had patients inhale the gas nitrous oxide just before having a tooth pulled. The tooth could then be painlessly removed. Nitrous oxide, mixed with oxygen, is still used today to reduce pain during dental procedures. Two years later, in 1846, the dentist William Morton gave a public demonstration of the effects of ether, which could be used as anesthesia not only during dental operations but for surgeries of all kinds. **(7)**

Another important development in dentistry was the discovery of X rays in 1895. X rays allow dentists to look inside teeth to discover defects. Early decay, impacted teeth, abscesses, and bone loss are all things that dental X rays reveal. **(8)**

The first dental drills appeared in the 1870's. They were powered by foot pedals like the sewing machines of the time. Drills were given electric power in the late 1890's. These power drills, which were at first called "dental engines," could be used for more than drilling cavities. **(9)** They could also be used to shape and polish teeth. Quieter, faster drilling equipment aimed at reducing the discomfort of drilling was developed by John V. Borden in the 1950's. These drills work at high speeds to reduce the pressure and vibration caused by older drills, and are cooled by air or water to reduce the pain caused by the heat that drilling produces. **(10)**

Passage 2

A deer's antlers grow from knob-like bones on the deer's skull. Antlers are made of bone, not horn, and are live, growing tissue. **(11)** They have a constant blood and nerve supply. Deer use their antlers to fight for mates during the breeding season or to gain leadership of a herd. **(12)** Among most species, only the bucks (male deer) have antlers, but both male and female caribou and reindeer (which are domesticated caribou) have antlers. **(13)** Musk deer and Chinese water deer do not have antlers at all.

Unlike animals with horns, such as cattle and bison, deer lose their antlers every year. Those that live in mild or cold climates lose their antlers in the winter, after the breeding season. **(14)** New ones begin to grow out in the early spring. Deer that live in tropical climates may lose their antlers and grow new ones at any time of year.

New antlers are soft and tender. Thin skin grows over the antlers as they develop. The short, fine hair on the skin looks like velvet. **(15)** When the antlers stop growing, in early fall, this velvety skin dries up. Deer scrape their antlers against trees and shrubs to rub the skin off, an activity called a buck rub. **(16)** The full-grown antlers are hard and strong. The antlers fall off several months later.

Young male deer—called button bucks—develop only small bumps for antlers during their first winter of life. For the next few years, the deer's antlers are small and straight. **(17)** As deer mature, their antlers grow larger and form intricate branches. However, contrary to popular belief, it is not possible to accurately determine ages of deer by counting their "points" (the branches of their antlers). The size and shape of a buck's antlers depend on diet and general health as well as on genetic factors. **(18)**

Deer antlers can grow up to one inch (2.5 centimeters) in a single day. **(19)** That is the fastest growth rate in the animal kingdom. Scientists doing cancer research are studying deer antlers to try to learn how they can grow so rapidly. They hope that if they can answer that question, they may learn how cancer cells grow so quickly. **(20)**

Passage 3

Henry Schoolcraft was a pioneer in the study of Native American cultures. He studied chemistry and geology at Middlebury College in Vermont. As a young man, he managed his family's glassmaking business, and his first book was a treatise on glassmaking. **(21)** However, when the family business failed he decided to head west to explore unknown territory and write about it in hopes of making a profit. **(22)**

In 1803 the United Sates purchased the Louisiana Territory from France. President Thomas Jefferson immediately authorized the exploration of the vast territory. Meriwether Lewis and William Clark were chosen to find a pathway to the Pacific Ocean. Steven Long was sent to explore the Rocky Mountain region. Zebulon Pike went to the Southwest. **(23)** Henry Schoolcraft was chosen to lead an expedition to the Ozark Mountain region of Missouri. In his book *Journal*, Schoolcraft wrote about the minerals, the plants, the animals, and the people, both Native Americans and white frontiersmen of the Ozarks. **(24)**

Later, Schoolcraft was made the chief naturalist for an exploration party that went to the upper Mississippi River Valley and the Great Lakes district. **(25)** He became a negotiator with the Native Americans of the area and was appointed Indian Agent to the Ojibwa tribe. He married the daughter of an Ojibwa man and a white woman. He learned to speak the Ojibwa language. With the help of his wife, he collected a great deal of authentic folklore of the Ojibwa and other tribes. **(26)** He wrote many books on Native Americans and their history and culture. The famous American poet Henry Longfellow based his epic poem *Hiawatha* in part on the writings of Schoolcraft. **(27)**

Schoolcraft has his critics, who point out that Schoolcraft's research was incomplete and sometimes inaccurate. But he lived in a romantic age. There is no doubt that he changed his materials to make them more appealing to his readers. **(28)** He invented some of his stories completely and he mixed the traditions of the Ojibwa with those of other tribes. Despite his failings, he did succeed in bringing the culture of Native Americans to the attention of the public.

Schoolcraft's work contrasted sharply with that of the ethnographers who worked in the last decade of the nineteenth century and the first decade of the twentieth. Their aim was to achieve complete accuracy in creating a record of Native American life, which at that time appeared to be in danger of completely vanishing within a few decades. **(29)** Unlike Schoolcraft, they tended to take notes in the original language. With the development of the phonograph, it became possible to preserve not just words but also the tone and emphasis of oral delivery. **(30)**

Exercise 1.2

1. B	12. D	23. A	34. C
2. A	13. D	24. C	35. C
3. C	14. C	25. C	36. B
4. B	15. A	26. D	37. D
5. C	16. B	27. D	38. C
6. B	17. A	28. A	39. B
7. D	18. C	29. C	40. A
8. C	19. A	30. B	41. D
9. A	20. C	31. A	42. B
10. B	21. D	32. C	43. D
11. C	22. B	33. B	

Lesson 2: Vocabulary Questions

Exercise 2.1

(Any of the words listed for each item may be considered correct, and other correct definitions or synonyms are possible.)

1. uninteresting, dull, boring, dreary
2. endless, continuous, unending, continual
3. twilight, evening, sunset, early evening, night
4. basic, simple
5. dim, weak, pale
6. garbage, trash, rubbish
7. wander, travel freely, stray
8. took control, assumed control, took charge
9. course of study, academic program, syllabus
10. optional, voluntary, non-required
11. emphasized
12. group, mass
13. haze, fog, cloud
14. bright, shining, brilliant, radiant
15. fragments, remains, waste, junk
16. a few, a small number
17. grieving, lamenting, weeping, showing sorrow
18. single, lone, sole
19. conspicuous, noticeable, prominent, dramatic
20. clear, see-through
21. searched, hunted, looked
22. fearful, wary, easily frightened
23. avoiding, escaping, evading, getting away from
24. disadvantages, problems, weaknesses, shortcomings
25. responsible, accountable
26. disagreements, arguments, clashes, disputes
27. afflict, upset, bother, trouble, cause problems
28. end, finish, stop, conclude, put an end to, cease
29. cut, carve, divide
30. final, last, eventual
31. tiny, very small, minute, minuscule, very little
32. understand, comprehend
33. magnify, enlarge, expand, increase
34. blurry, unclear, indistinct, hazy, misty

Exercise 2.2

1. B	12. D	23. B	34. A
2. C	13. C	24. D	35. C
3. C	14. A	25. D	36. C
4. D	15. B	26. B	37. C
5. A	16. D	27. A	38. A
6. D	17. B	28. A	39. D
7. B	18. A	29. D	40. B
8. B	19. C	30. C	41. C
9. A	20. B	31. A	
10. A	21. C	32. D	
11. A	22. A	33. B	

Lesson 3: Inference Questions

Exercise 3.1

1. B	5. A	9. B	13. C
2. C	6. B	10. A	14. C
3. C	7. A	11. B	15. A
4. C	8. C	12. A	

Exercise 3.2

1. D	12. A	23. D	34. D
2. A	13. D	24. A	35. C
3. D	14. A	25. C	36. D
4. B	15. C	26. C	37. B
5. B	16. B	27. A	38. B
6. B	17. A	28. B	39. A
7. C	18. A	29. C	40. C
8. A	19. D	30. A	41. D
9. A	20. C	31. D	42. C
10. B	21. B	32. B	
11. B	22. A	33. C	

Lesson 4: Purpose, Method, and Opinion Questions

Exercise 4.1

1. T	9. F	17. F	25. F
2. F	10. T	18. F	26. T
3. F	11. F	19. T	27. T
4. F	12. F	20. T	28. T
5. T	13. T	21. T	29. F
6. T	14. F	22. F	30. F
7. F	15. T	23. T	31. T
8. T	16. F	24. T	

Exercise 4.2

1. B	8. A	15. C	22. A
2. A	9. B	16. A	23. A
3. A	10. D	17. D	24. B
4. B	11. A	18. A	25. A
5. C	12. C	19. C	26. D
6. A	13. D	20. C	27. D
7. D	14. B	21. B	

Lesson 5: Sentence Restatement Questions

Exercise 5.1

1. I
2. C
3. X (Note: The original sentence is about the town of *Muncie*, not *Middleton*.)

4. X	8. I	12. X	15. I
5. C	9. X	13. X	16. X
6. X	10. C	14. X	
7. C	11. C		

Exercise 5.2

1. C	4. C	7. D	9. C
2. A	5. B	8. A	10. B
3. B	6. D		

Lesson 6: Reference Questions

Exercise 6.1

1. paintings
2. cut flowers
3. water's
4. principles used in air conditioning; the human body
5. strands
6. smaller pieces

7. leaves
8. ancient Minoans; archaeological sites
9. mushrooms and other fungi
10. machines based on wheels and gears
11. glaciers in Olympia National Park; altitudes
12. satellite photography
13. American importers
14. New York City; the 1920's; Paris
15. anemone; its nest
16. Hamlin Garland's; William Dean Howells
17. fats; three basic types of nutrients; the fat soluble vitamins A, D, E, and K; fats
18. The Wisconsin Dells (*or* a region along the Wisconsin River); the strange formations

Exercise 6.2

1. D	12. A	22. A	32. D
2. B	13. D	23. D	33. C
3. D	14. B	24. A	34. D
4. C	15. B	25. A	35. B
5. C	16. C	26. C	36. B
6. D	17. C	27. C	37. C
7. B	18. D	28. A	38. A
8. A	19. A	29. B	39. C
9. C	20. B	30. B	40. A
10. C	21. D	31. A	41. A
11. A			

Lesson 7: Sentence Addition Questions

Exercise 7.1

1. Until the nineteenth century, when steamships and transcontinental trains made long-distance travel practical for large numbers of people, only a few adventurers, mainly sailors and traders, ever traveled out of their own countries. ■ In fact, most people never traveled more than a few miles from the place where they were born. ■ "Abroad" was a truly foreign place that the vast majority of people knew very little about indeed.●**Early mapmakers, therefore, had little danger of being accused of mistakes even though they were wildly inaccurate.** ■ When mapmakers drew maps, imagination was as important as geographic reality. ■ Nowhere is this more evident than in old maps illustrated with mythical creatures and strange humans.

2. Throughout the centuries, the dream of medieval alchemists was to discover how to turn lead and other "base" metals into gold. Some alchemists were fakes, but many were learned men with philosophical goals. Their quest was based on the ancient idea that all matter consists of different proportions of just four substances: earth, water, fire, and air. ■ They believed that it was possible to adjust the proportions of the elements that made up lead by chemical means so that it turned into gold, a process that they called *transmutation.* ■ Their experiments were concerned with finding the substance, which they called the *philosopher's stone,* that would cause this astonishing change to take place.●**In addition, they searched for the elixir of life, a substance that could cure disease and prolong life.** They failed to achieve either of their goals. ■ However, their techniques for preparing and studying chemicals helped lay the foundation for the modern science of chemistry.

3. When a small gray square is placed on a larger white square, the small square appears much darker than when the same square of gray is placed on a larger black square. ■ A gray square placed on a colored square—bright blue or yellow, for instance—tends to take on the color of the background. ■ To a viewer, the gray square actually seems to have a blue or yellow tinge. ■ The tinge of color is easier to see if a thin piece of tissue paper is placed over the squares.●**When a patch of color is placed on a background that is approximately complementary—say red on green—both colors appear brighter and more vibrant.** ■ For this reason, many flags, pennants, and advertising banners are red and green or bright blue and yellow.

4. The process of miniaturization began in earnest with the transistor, which was invented in 1947. This was perhaps the most important electronics event of the twentieth century, as it later made possible the integrated circuits and microprocessors that are the basis of modern electronics. The transistor was far smaller than the smallest vacuum tube it replaced and, not needing a filament, it consumed much less power and generated virtually no wasted heat. There was almost no limit to how small the transistor could be made once engineers learned to etch electronic circuits onto a substrate of silicon. ■ In the 1950's the standard radio had five vacuum tubes and dozens of resistors and capacitors, all hardwired and attached to a chassis about the size of a hardbound book. ●**Today all that circuitry and much more can fit into a microprocessor smaller than a postage stamp.** In fact, the limiting factor in making electronic devices smaller is not the size of the electronic components but the human interface. ■ There is no point in making a palm-held computer much smaller unless humans can evolve smaller fingers. ■

5. When drawing human figures, children often make the head too large for the rest of the body. ■ A recent study offers some insight into this common disproportion in children's drawings. ■ As part of the study, researchers asked children between four and seven years old to make several drawings of adults. ■ When they drew frontal views of these subjects, the sizes of the heads was markedly enlarged.●**However, when the children drew rear views of the adults, the size of the heads was not nearly so exaggerated.** The researchers suggest that children draw bigger heads when they know that they must leave room for facial details. Therefore, the distorted head size in children's drawings is a form of planning ahead and not an indication of a poor sense of scale.

6. It has been observed that periods of maximum rainfall occur in both the northern and southern hemispheres at about the same time. This phenomenon cannot be adequately explained on a climatological basis, but meteors may offer a plausible explanation. When the earth encounters a swarm of meteors, each meteor striking the upper layers of the atmosphere is vaporized by frictional heat. The resulting debris is a fine smoke or powder. ■ This "stardust" then floats down into the lower atmosphere, where such dust readily serves as nuclei on which ice crystals or raindrops can form.●**Confirmation that this phenomenon actually occurs is found in the observed fact that increases in world rainfall typically come about a month after major meteor systems are encountered in space.** This delay allows time for the dust to settle through the upper atmosphere. ■ Furthermore, proof that meteors actually create dust clouds can be seen in the fact that large meteors sometimes leave visible traces of dust. ■ In a few witnessed cases, dust has remained visible for over an hour. In one extreme case—

the great meteor that broke up in the sky over Siberia in 1908—the dust cloud traveled all around the world before disappearing.

7. Circumstantial evidence is evidence not drawn from the direct observation of a fact. If, for example, there is evidence that a piece of rock embedded in a wrapped chocolate bar is the same kind of rock found in the vicinity of a candy factory, and that rock of this type is found in few other places, then there is circumstantial evidence to suggest that the stone somehow got into the piece of chocolate during manufacture. ■ It suggests that the candy-maker was negligent even though there is no eyewitness or direct evidence of any kind. ■ Despite a popular tendency to look down on the quality of circumstantial evidence, it is of great usefulness if there is enough of it and if it is properly interpreted.⬤**Each piece of circumstantial evidence, taken singly, may mean little.** However, a whole chain of circumstances can be as conclusive as direct evidence. ■

8. The model most generally accepted by geophysicists today envisages Earth as composed of three main concentric spheres. The deep heart of the planet is essentially a huge ball of molten iron, about 4,000 miles (6,400 kilometers) in diameter. The physical properties of this great ball are mostly unknown. The incredible pressure at the core would crush matter into a strange, dense substance unlike any known liquid. ■ Surrounding the molten metal core and reaching almost to the surface is the earth's great inner shell, 2,000 miles (3,200 kilometers) thick, known as the mantle. ■ The mantle seems to be, paradoxically, both rigid and plastic at the same time. ■ Above the mantle lies the thin crust of the earth. ⬤**This, too, is divided into layers.** Its lower level is a shell of basaltic material similar to the black rock in lava. Topmost of all stand the granite continents. Our great landmasses are, curiously, the lightest of the materials that compose the earth.

9. Alternative history is generally classified as a type of science fiction, but it also bears some resemblance to historical fiction. This type of writing describes an imaginary world that is identical to our own world up to a certain point in history. ■ At that point, the two worlds diverge. ■ Something happens in the imaginary world that never happened in ours, and after that, this world follows a different direction.⬤**For example, Harry Turtledove, one of the top writers in this field, has written several books about a world in which the South won the U.S. Civil War and a book about a world in which the Spanish Armada conquered England.** Some alternative histories suppose that a certain technology had been introduced earlier into the world's history than actually happened. ■ What if the computer had been invented in Victorian times? Many readers find these stories interesting because of the way they stimulate the imagination and get people thinking about the phenomenon of cause and effect in history.

10. In the early nineteenth century, the United States was still an overwhelmingly rural nation. ■ Shrewd showmen saw that there was a fortune to be made in taking shows to the people. ■ By 1820 there were some 30 small "mud show" circuses (so named because of the treacherously muddy roads and fields over which their wagons had to travel).⬤**The number of shows increased rapidly after the first "Big Top" circus tent was introduced in 1826.** This enabled circuses to perform in rain or shine. ■ Like circuses today, early nineteenth-century circuses featured performing elephants, tigers, and lions, bareback riders,

acrobats, trapeze and high wire artists, circus bands, and, of course, clowns. It was not until after the Civil War, however, that circuses became huge three-ring spectacles involving hundreds of performers.

11. When a mammal is young, it looks much like a smaller form of an adult. However, animals that undergo metamorphosis develop quite differently. ■ The young of these animals, which are called larvae, look very little like the mature forms and have a very different way of life. ■ Take the example of butterflies and caterpillars, which are the larval form of butterflies.⬤**Butterflies have two pairs of wings and six legs and feed on the nectar of flowers.** Caterpillars, on the other hand, are wingless, have many more than six legs, and feed on leaves. ■ To become adults, the larvae must radically change their forms.

12. To accomplish this change, a larva must go through the process of metamorphosis. It does this in the second stage of life, called the pupa stage. When they are ready to pupate, caterpillars settle in sheltered positions. Some spin a cocoon around themselves. The caterpillar then sheds its old skin and grows a protective pupal skin. ■ Inside this skin, the body of the caterpillar gradually transforms itself. ■ The wing buds, which were under the caterpillar's skin, grow into wings. ■ When the change is complete, the pupal skin splits open and the butterfly emerges.⬤**At first, it is damp and its wings are curled up.** Soon it dries out, its wings unfurl, and it flies off. Now it is ready to mate and to lay eggs that will develop into larvae.

13. It is believed that the first migrants to come to the New World were hunters who arrived by way of the only link between the hemispheres, the Siberian-Alaskan land bridge. ■ This strip of land remained above water until about 10,000 years ago.⬤**More recent arrivals no doubt took the same route, crossing on winter ice.** These migrants unquestionably brought with them the skills to make weapons, fur clothing, and shelters against the bitter cold. ■ It seems safe to assume that they also brought myths and folktales from the Old World. But which myths and which folktales? ■

14. Among myths, the most impressive candidate for Old World origin is the story of the Earth Diver. ■ This is the story of a group of water creatures who take turns diving into the depths of the sea, trying to find a piece of solid land.⬤**The animals magically enlarge this piece of solid land until it becomes the earth.** The duck, the turtle, the muskrat, the seal, the crawfish, or some other animal, depending on who is telling the story, finally succeeds, but it has to dive so deep that by the time it returns to the surface, it is half-drowned or dead. ■ However, in its claws or in its mouth, the other animals find a bit of mud. ■ Not every Native American tribe has a creation myth, but of those that do, the Earth Diver is one of the most common. It is found in all regions of the New World except in the Southwestern United States and the Arctic regions. In the Old World, the story is told in many locations in northern Asia, among some aboriginal Australian groups, and in the south Pacific Islands.

15. ■ Lawn tennis is a comparatively modern modification of the ancient game of court tennis. Major Walter C. Wingfield thought that something like court tennis might be played outdoors on the grass, and in 1873 he introduced his new game under the name *Sphairistike* at a lawn party in Wales.⬤**It was an immediate success and spread rapidly, but the original name quickly disappeared.** Players and spectators soon began to call the new

game "lawn tennis." ■ In 1874 a woman named Mary Outerbridge returned to New York with the basic equipment of the game, which she had obtained from a British Army store in Bermuda. ■ The first game of lawn tennis in the United States was played on the grounds of the Staten Island Cricket and Baseball Club in 1874.

16. The game went on in a haphazard fashion for a number of years. In 1879, standard equipment, rules, and measurements for the court were instituted. ■ A year later, the U.S. lawn Tennis Association was formed. ■ International matches for the Davis Cup began in 1900.⬤**They were played at Chestnut Hill, Massachusetts, between British and American players.** The home team won these first championship matches. ■

17. Photosynthesis is the process by which plants capture the sun's energy to convert water and carbon dioxide into sugars to fuel their growth.⬤**This process cannot take place without chlorophyll.** Chlorophyll is so essential to the life of plants that it forms almost instantly in seedlings when they come in contact with sunlight. ■ A green pigment, chlorophyll is responsible for the green coloring of plants. ■ But what turns the leaves of deciduous plants the brilliant reds and oranges and golds of autumn? ■

18. Trees do not manufacture new, colored pigments for fall. Orange, red, yellow, and other colored pigments are present in leaves throughout the spring and summer. However, they are hidden by the far greater amount of green chlorophyll. When the days grow shorter and the temperatures fall, leaves somehow sense the coming of fall. ■ They form an "abscission layer." ■ This layer is a barrier of tissue at the base of each leaf stalk.⬤**It prevents nourishment from reaching the leaf and, conversely, prevents sugar created in the leaf from reaching the rest of the tree.** Thus, sugar builds up in the leaf, causing the chlorophyll to break down. ■ The orange, red, yellow, and brown pigments now predominate, giving the leaves their vibrant autumn colors.

19. Prairie dogs are among the most sociable wild animals of North America. At one time, they thrived nearly everywhere on the semi-arid lands of the West. Native Americans even used prairie dog colonies as landmarks on the relatively featureless plains. Prairie dogs are members of the squirrel family. They are probably called "dogs" because they make a "yip" noise when they are alarmed that sounds a little like the bark of a small dog. This alarm sound was at one time thought to be a simple warning and expression of fear, meaning something like "Yikes! Watch out!" Biology professor Con Slobodchikoff of Northern Arizona University has been studying the alarm calls of the Gunnison prairie dog that lives in Arizona for twenty years. He has discovered remarkable levels of complexity in prairie dog calls. ■ First, he discovered that the call for aerial predators, such as eagles or hawks, was different from the call for terrestrial predators or intruders, such as coyotes and humans.⬤**Then he learned that there were prairie dog yips for specific predators.** For example, there was a distinctive yip for a red-tailed hawk and a different one for a golden eagle. ■ There was one for coyotes, one for foxes, one for domestic dogs, and one for human beings. ■ These sounds were all so distinctive that the differences could be heard with the human ear.

20. By recording prairie dog calls as sonograms and then observing the sonograms on a computer, even more subtle distinctions could be discovered. ■ In one experiment, Professor Slobodchikoff learned that prairie dogs had different sounds for people who wore blue shirts, those who wore yellow shirts, and those who wore green shirts. ■ Even more amazingly, prairie dogs' sounds distinguished between a human who was carrying a gun and one who wasn't. ■ Another experiment showed that prairie dogs could create cries for dangers they had never encountered before.⬤**When shown the silhouettes of European ferrets and of Australian dingoes, the prairie dogs made sounds unlike those that they made for any familiar predators.**

21. The first motel (the term comes from a combination of the words *motor* and *hotel*) to appear in the United States was the Motel Inn of San Luis Obispo, California, in 1925. ■ This kind of lodging quickly became popular at a time when more and more people were traveling by car rather than by railroad. ■ Train travelers generally wanted to stay in downtown areas near the railroad stations, and so that's where most hotels were located.⬤**Motels, in contrast, appealed to motorists, and so they were located along highways, often at the edge of town.** When motorists first began traveling long distances by car, they usually stayed at auto camps or tourist courts. ■ These were generally clusters of cabins, often quite crude. Motels, however, were usually single buildings of connected rooms whose doors faced a parking lot or a common area. Typically one would find a "T" or "L" or "U" shaped structure that included rooms, an attached manager's office, and perhaps a small diner. Postwar motels often featured eye-catching neon signs that employed the pop culture themes of the day, ranging from Western imagery, such as cowboys, to "futuristic" images of flying saucers or depictions of atoms.

22. The story of the motel business from the 1920's to about 1960 is one of uninterrupted growth. Motels became common sights on the U.S. highway system that pre-dated the Interstate Highway System. ■ They clustered along transcontinental highways, such as Routes 40 and 66, and along the north-south routes that ran up and down both the east and west coasts. ■ The motel business was one of the few industries that was not hurt by the economic Depression of the 1930's.⬤**In fact, their cheap rates attracted travelers without much money.** However, in the 1960's, the Interstate Highway System allowed drivers to bypass the smaller roads on which motels were built. ■ At about the same time, large motel-hotel chains began to cut into the business of the small, family-owned motel.

Lesson 8: Completing Summaries and Charts
(Remember, the order in which you list the points is not important, only that you list the three correct points. Notes for the paragraphs will vary. These are given just as examples.)

Exercise 8.1
Passage 1
Paragraph 1 economic resources = property resources (land & capital) and labor & entrepreneurial skills
Paragraph 2 land = all natural resources   capital = tools to produce goods
Paragraph 3 labor = all skills that produce goods except entrepreneurial skills
Paragraph 4 all econ. resources are limited
• E
• F
• B

Passage 2
Paragraph 1 _West Side Story_ based on Shakespeare's _Romeo and Juliet_
Paragraph 2 Bernstein, Sondheim, & Robbins
Paragraph 3 success & awards for play
Paragraph 4 classic movie also successful
• D
• B
• C

Passage 3
Paragraph 1 babies can see but don't have adult ability
Paragraph 2 eye, brain, eye muscles develop
Paragraph 3 parts of eye mature
Paragraph 4 babies detect motion, have other basic abilities
Paragraph 5 newborn vision limited, but at 4 months much better
• B
• D
• E

Passage 4
Paragraph 1 clipper ships fast, beautiful 1840's–50's
Paragraph 2 Chinese tea trade, California gold created need for clippers
Paragraph 3 everything possible done to make fast; sails, etc.
Paragraph 4 sails, rigging, crew, etc. gave clippers speed
Paragraph 5 many records set
Paragraph 6 British tea clippers
Paragraph 7 faded away by 1860; steam ships doomed them
• A
• F
• D

Passage 5
Paragraph 1 Georgia O'Keeffe important artist
Paragraph 2 art school
Paragraph 3 commercial art, teaching, married Stieglitz
Paragraph 4 distinctive style of painting
Paragraph 5 style changed when went to Southwest
Paragraph 6 O'Keeffe's later years
• E
• B
• C

Exercise 8.2
(The order in which you list points is not important.)

Passage 1

Homology	Analogy
• C	• A
• D	• E
• F	

Passage 2

European (Western) Dragons	Asian (Eastern) Dragons
• D	• B
• E	• C
• F	• I
• H	

Passage 3

Luther Burbank	George Washington Carver
• A	• C
• B	• F
• E	• H
• G	

Passage 4

Radiation Fog	Advection Fog
• C	• B
• E	• D
	• F

Passage 5

Primary Cooperation	Secondary Cooperation
• B	• C
• E	• G
• H	

Tertiary Cooperation
• A
• F

Reading Review Test

Noise Pollution

Answer Explanation
1. A The word _routinely_ means "regularly, habitually."
2. B The phrase is a reference to the list of "factors (that) contribute to problems of growing noise levels."
3. D The author says that "secondhand noise" (noise made by others) is no more damaging physically to us than noise made by ourselves. "Secondhand noise is generally more troubling, however, because it is put into the environment by others, without our consent."
4. B The author defines a _commons_ as something that "belongs not to an individual person or a group, but to everyone." A factory does _not_ fit this description, since it is owned by an individual or a business.
5. A The author compares people who interfere with "others' use and enjoyment of a commons" by comparing it to someone who acts "like a bully in a schoolyard." Being bullied in the schoolyard is another negative experience.
6. C _Transient_ means "temporary, passing, momentary."
7. C Choice A contradicts the original sentence. It says that it is hard to measure individual sounds, but the original sentence says we _can_ measure them. There is really no reason to believe that B is true. Nothing in the original sentence indicates that louder sounds are harder to measure. The idea of choice D is also not contained in the original sentence. There is no indication that multiple sounds are more damaging than individual sounds. Choice C best summarizes the idea of the original sentence.
8. B The word _thrilling_ means "exciting, stimulating."
9. D The author says in paragraph 7 that "The actual loudness of a sound is only one component of the negative effect noise pollution has on human beings. Other factors that have to be considered are the time and place, the duration, the source of the sound . . ." There is _no_ mention of the negative effects of a combination of sounds.
10. C The author says "Most people would not be bothered by the sound of a 21-gun salute on a special occasion."
11. The missing sentence is introduced by the phrase, "On the contrary," indicating that it will be in contrast with one of the marked sentences. The main idea of the new sentence is that people must use a commons responsibly. It is in contrast to the idea of the previous sentence, which says that they do not have the right to cause as much noise pollution as they please.

The air into which secondhand noise is emitted and on which it travels is "a commons." ■ It belongs not to an individual person or a group, but to everyone. ■ People, businesses, and organizations, therefore, do not have unlimited rights to broadcast noise as they please, as if the effects of noise were limited only to their private property. ⊛**On the contrary, they have an obligation to use the commons in ways that are compatible with or do not detract from other uses.** Those that disregard the obligation to not interfere with others' use and enjoyment of the commons by producing noise pollution are, in many ways, acting like a bully in a schoolyard. ■ Although they may do so unknowingly, they disregard the rights of others and claim for themselves rights that are not theirs.

12. Noise pollution: A, C, F; **air pollution:** B, D.
Choice A is related to noise pollution. In paragraph 6, the author says, "Noise is transient; once the pollution stops, the environment is free of it." Choice B is related to air pollution. The author says in paragraph 6, "We can measure the amount of chemicals and other pollutants introduced into the air." In the same paragraph, the author says, "The definition of noise pollution itself is highly subjective," so C is a characteristic of noise pollution. D is a characteristic of air pollution, as the author points out in paragraph 6. "Scientists can estimate how much material can be introduced into the air before harm is done. The same is true of water pollution and soil pollution." E is not related to either form of pollution. Nowhere in the passage does the author mention ways to reduce noise pollution or air pollution. In paragraph 7, the author says, "Other factors that have to be considered are the time and place, the duration, the source of the sound, and even the mood of the affected person." Therefore, point F is characteristic of noise pollution.

In A New Light: LEDs

13. C   *Remarkably* means "amazingly, surprisingly, extraordinarily."

14. A   In paragraph 2, the author mentions all of these problems with fluorescent bulbs *except* the need to replace them often. "The harsh color isn't as pleasing as the warmer glow of incandescent lamps. Besides, they have a tendency to flicker on and off and to produce an annoying buzz."

15. A   Paragraph 3 says, "Different types of materials result in light of different colors."

16. A   The reference is to "white-light-emitting diodes (WLEDs)" in the previous sentence.

17. D   The author says that "Shuji Nakamura discovered that, by using layers of gallium nitride, he could create a powerful blue LED." (Other engineers later used his blue LED to create white LEDs.)

18. B   In paragraph 3, the author says that red and green LEDs have been used for many years. In paragraph 5, the author explains how the development of the blue LED led to the development of the white LED. Therefore, the most recent of these types of LEDs to be developed was the white LED.

19. C   In paragraph 5, the author gives two ways in which blue LEDs could be used to create white LEDs. One way involves "a chemical coating similar to that inside a fluorescent bulb that converts the blue light to white."

20. A   The author says, "it will still be some time before WLEDs are commonly used in homes. WLEDs are currently only twice as energy efficient as incandescent. They are also very expensive. But researchers believe that they can create WLEDs that are ten times as efficient and one thousand times as long-lasting as incandescent, making them cost-effective." If WLEDs were cost-effective now, we can assume that more people would use them to light their homes.

21. B   The author says that, today, most lighting in developing countries is provided by kerosene. The author mentions the problems with kerosene (cost, pollution, danger of fires, etc.) to show why it would be advantageous to switch from kerosene to LED lighting.

22. B   In paragraph 6, the author states, "Energy to light these efficient LEDs can be provided by batteries that are charged by pedal-driven generators, by hydroelectricity from rivers or streams, by wind-powered generators, or by solar energy." So while energy to power the LEDs may come *indirectly* from the energy of the sun, water power, or a human-powered generator, it comes *directly* from batteries.

23. C   The word *conventional* means "standard, usual, customary, normal."

24. D   The author says that "LEDs could revolutionize lighting as the cell phone has revolutionized communication in places where land telephone lines are unavailable."

25.   The new sentence is in contrast with the previous sentence (the word *But* tells you this). The previous sentence explains how incandescent lights produce light. The new sentence explains how much of the energy used in incandescent bulbs is wasted. The word *this* in the sentence that follows also is a link to the missing sentence because it refers to the phrase *95% of the energy.*

At the end of the 1800's, Thomas Edison introduced the incandescent light bulb and changed the world. Remarkably, the incandescent bulb used today has changed little in over a hundred years. ■ A glass bulb is filled with an inert gas such as argon. Inside the bulb, electricity passes through a metal filament. ■ Because of resistance, the filament becomes so hot that it glows.⊛**But 95% of the energy goes to produce heat and is basically wasted.** Given that 20% of the world's electricity is used to power lights, this is an enormous amount of wasted energy. ■

26. F, C, E   Choice F summarizes the information in paragraph 3, Choice C summarizes paragraphs 4 and 5, and choice E summarizes paragraph 6. Choices A and B are only details in the passage, and choice D contradicts information that is given in the passage. The author says in paragraph 3, "Engineers say that they are significantly more efficient than either incandescent or fluorescent lights."

27. D   In paragraph 1, the author says, "at the time, no one knew that these paintings would one day be considered masterpieces. The paintings and the painters were virtually unknown at the time and would remain that way for several years."

28. A   *Virtually* means "almost, nearly."

29. B   According to paragraph 2, "Leroy wrote that this piece *(Impression: Sunset)*, and in fact most of the pieces in the show looked like 'impressions'—a term for a preliminary, unfinished sketch made before a painting is done."

30. A   *Derision* means "ridicule or mockery."

31. B   Choice A changes the meaning of the original sentence by stating that it was the core of values that held together the Impressionists. Instead, it was the group's spirit of rebellion and independence that held them together. Choice C also changes the meaning of the original sentence. It indicates that the Impressionists were at first held together by a shared set of techniques and standards but later rebelled. In fact, the Impressionists had different techniques and standards but were held together by their independent spirit. Choice D incorrectly states that the Impressionists' values differed, but that their techniques and standards gave them an independent spirit. Choice B is the best summary of the original sentence.

32. C   Paragraph 4 states, "Many Impressionist paintings feature pleasant scenes of urban life, celebrating the leisure time that the Industrial Revolution had won for the middle class, as shown in Renoir's luminous painting *Luncheon of the Boating Party.*"

33. C   The author says in paragraph 5, "The Impressionists delighted in painting landscapes (except for Edgar Degas, who preferred painting indoor scenes, and Mary Cassatt, who mainly painted portraits of mothers and children)."

34. D   The author says, "Traditional painters generally made preliminary sketches outside but worked on the paintings themselves in their studios."

35. A   The quotation marks around the word *rules* indicate that the author does not really think of this as a true rule. The author also says that this rule was only followed by a few of the Impressionists and for only a short time, also indicating that this was not a strict rule.

36. B   *Spot* means, in this sentence, "identify, recognize."

37. D   The reference is to the last (most recent) layer of paint.

38. The phrase *this play of light* connects with the idea that the Impressionists' landscapes sparkle with light, which is mentioned in the previous sentence.

The Impressionists delighted in painting landscapes (except for Edgar Degas, who preferred painting indoor scenes, and Mary Cassatt, who painted portraits of mothers and children). ■ Traditional painters, too, painted landscapes, but their landscapes tended to be somber and dark. ■ The Impressionists' landscapes sparkle with light. (■) **This play of light can be seen in Claude Monet's paintings** *Water Lilies, Green Harmony,* **and** *The Bridge at Argenteuil.* Impressionists insisted that their works be "true to nature." ■ When they painted landscapes, they carried their paints and canvases outdoors in order to capture the ever-changing light. Traditional painters generally made preliminary sketches outside but worked on the paintings themselves in their studios.

39. Impressionist painters: A, C, E, I; **traditional painters:** B, D, G.

Choice A is a characteristic of Impressionist painters. In paragraph 6, the author says, " 'Classic' Impressionist paintings are often easy to spot because of the techniques used by the painters." Choice B relates to traditional painters. Paragraph 4 says, "Traditional painters tended to paint rather serious scenes from history and mythology." Choice C relates to the Impressionists. In paragraph 6, the author says, "These techniques created paintings that seemed strange and unfinished to the general public when they were first painted, but are much loved in our time." Choice D is characteristic of the traditional painters. Paragraph 5 says, "Traditional painters, too, painted landscapes, but their landscapes tended to be somber and dark." Choice E is related to Impressionists. Paragraph 4 says, "Many Impressionist paintings feature pleasant scenes of urban life, celebrating the leisure time that the Industrial Revolution had won for the middle class . . ." Choice F does not apply to either group of painters. At the time, some people *thought* that the Impressionists' paintings looked unfinished, but this was not true. Choice G is characteristic of traditional painters. Paragraph 6 says, "While traditional painters paid attention to details, Impressionists valued overall effect." Choice H does not relate to either of the two groups. Choice I is a characteristic of the Impressionists. Paragraph 5 says, "The Impressionists' landscapes sparkle with light."

Reading Tutorial: Vocabulary Building

Vocabulary Exercise 1

2. (C) acrid	10. (C) agile
3. (A) allotting	11. (A) arid
4. (A) ailment	12. (B) aversion
5. (B) astute	13. (B) astonishing
6. (B) arduous	14. (A) apt
7. (A) abandon	15. (C) artificial
8. (B) affluent	16. (A) accommodating
9. (C) appraise	

Vocabulary Exercise 2

1. (C) bloom	9. (C) benevolent
2. (C) balmy	10. (C) blow up
3. (A) barter	11. (A) brilliant
4. (C) blundered	12. (B) brisk
5. (B) bland	13. (C) blunt
6. (B) brittle	14. (C) belligerent
7. (A) banned	15. (C) boomed
8. (B) barren	

Vocabulary Exercise 3

1. (C) calamities	9. (C) clusters
2. (A) casual	10. (A) cling
3. (B) cite	11. (B) commerce
4. (B) classified	12. (A) colossal
5. (B) Caustic	13. (C) commodity
6. (C) carve	14. (C) candid
7. (A) commenced	15. (A) clog
8. (C) cautious	16. (B) clues

Vocabulary Exercise 4

1. (C) compulsory	10. (B) complement
2. (C) congregate	11. (B) courteously
3. (A) concise	12. (B) coping with
4. (B) cozy	13. (A) covert
5. (C) convenient	14. (A) conventional
6. (B) crooked	15. (B) cosmopolitan
7. (B) craving	16. (C) critical
8. (A) concrete	17. (A) conflict
9. (C) conspicuous	18. (C) constantly

Vocabulary Exercise 5

1. (A) dazzling
2. (A) divulge
3. (B) delicate
4. (A) device
5. (B) dwindled
6. (C) discarded
7. (A) daring
8. (B) dot
9. (C) delightful
10. (A) durable
11. (C) dispute
12. (B) damp
13. (A) drawbacks
14. (C) drowsy
15. (A) dubious
16. (B) disperse
17. (B) draws
18. (A) dusk
19. (A) domestic
20. (C) drowsy
21. (C) debris

Vocabulary Exercise 6

1. (B) ensued
2. (B) eerie
3. (C) era
4. (B) entice
5. (A) an exhilarating
6. (C) fastening
7. (C) eligible
8. (C) ferocious
9. (A) emit
10. (C) fatigued
11. (C) flaw
12. (B) fragrant
13. (A) evade
14. (C) a flimsy
15. (C) fuses
16. (A) fee
17. (A) forged
18. (A) elude
19. (A) forage
20. (B) fuzzy

Vocabulary Exercise 7

1. (C) hoist
2. (B) grueling
3. (B) harness
4. (A) glitters
5. (A) gala
6. (C) hasty
7. (A) hampered
8. (B) gentle
9. (C) gullible
10. (A) hazardous
11. (C) gap
12. (C) grade
13. (A) foes
14. (B) hazy
15. (B) harsh
16. (B) gregarious

Vocabulary Exercise 8

1. (C) ideal
2. (C) implement
3. (A) intense
4. (C) infamous
5. (C) inhibit
6. (A) illusion
7. (B) indifferent
8. (C) key
9. (C) infinitesimal
10. (B) jolly
11. (A) knack
12. (B) impairs
13. (A) indigenous
14. (C) keen
15. (C) an imaginary
16. (B) inexorable
17. (C) innocuous

Vocabulary Exercise 9

1. (C) mythical
2. (C) lucrative
3. (C) lull
4. (A) lucid
5. (B) mends
6. (B) most memorable
7. (B) minute
8. (A) lurid
9. (B) lack
10. (A) legendary
11. (A) linking
12. (A) mushroomed
13. (B) leisurely

Vocabulary Exercise 10

1. (A) ominous
2. (B) outstanding
3. (C) ornamental
4. (B) overcome
5. (B) obscure
6. (C) obsolete
7. (C) outgoing
8. (A) outlook
9. (B) overwhelming
10. (C) overall
11. (B) overcast
12. (C) negligible
13. (A) nightmarish
14. (C) overlook

Vocabulary Exercise 11

1. (C) precious
2. (B) profound
3. (B) pressing
4. (A) precisely
5. (C) Particles
6. (C) pounces
7. (B) penetrate
8. (A) puzzling
9. (A) profusely
10. (B) pungent
11. (C) prosper
12. (A) plush
13. (B) prudent
14. (C) pulverized
15. (C) prevalent
16. (B) portion
17. (A) pivotal
18. (C) paramount

Vocabulary Exercise 12

1. (A) recklessly
2. (A) rehearse
3. (C) recede
4. (C) rugged
5. (B) refuge
6. (C) raze
7. (A) remote
8. (C) range
9. (C) quaint
10. (A) raw
11. (C) quests
12. (A) remarkably
13. (B) rural
14. (A) risky
15. (B) routes
16. (A) recounts

Vocabulary Exercise 13

1. (A) scale
2. (C) shy
3. (B) seasoned
4. (B) shunned
5. (C) scrapped
6. (C) salvaged
7. (B) sluggish
8. (A) sound
9. (B) severed
10. (A) sheer
11. (C) signifies
12. (B) shredded
13. (B) simulate
14. (C) shimmering
15. (B) slice

Vocabulary Exercise 14

1. (B) spells
2. (B) steep
3. (C) stages
4. (B) sway
5. (C) spawn
6. (B) summit
7. (C) spectacular
8. (C) swiftest
9. (B) spoiling
10. (B) sturdy
11. (B) subsequently
12. (A) stable
13. (B) stages
14. (C) sow
15. (A) spot
16. (B) specimen
17. (C) spot
18. (B) spirited
19. (A) standard
20. (C) strident
21. (B) sundry

Vocabulary Exercise 15

1. (C) tart
2. (A) tedious
3. (C) tampered with
4. (C) thrilling
5. (C) tug
6. (A) tempting
7. (B) thoroughfare
8. (C) toxic
9. (B) torrents
10. (A) thrives
11. (A) traits
12. (A) tales
13. (B) timid
14. (B) tough
15. (A) tangled
16. (A) toppled
17. (C) thaw
18. (B) tranquil

Vocabulary Exercise 16

1. (C) uniformly
2. (B) venomous
3. (A) urges
4. (A) vividly
5. (A) vessel
6. (C) a vigorous
7. (A) vicinity
8. (B) underlying
9. (C) vital
10. (A) vain
11. (B) utensil
12. (A) a vast
13. (C) upkeep
14. (C) unraveled
15. (A) vanish
16. (C) vexing
17. (A) vie with

Vocabulary Exercise 17

1. (C) warp
2. (B) wholesome
3. (B) yields
4. (C) wary
5. (A) wares
6. (C) witty
7. (A) wage
8. (C) wisely
9. (A) wake
10. (B) whiff
11. (C) wrinkles
12. (A) widespread
13. (C) zone
14. (B) well-to-do
15. (A) woes

Section 2: Guide to Listening

(The TOEFL iBT does not use the letters A, B, C, and D for the multiple-choice items. However, in these answer keys, *A* corresponds to the first answer choice, *B* to the second, *C* to the third, and *D* to the fourth.)

Preview Test

Answer	Explanation

1. B The student gets some basic information from the professor about the research paper that she must write for her geology class. The student then discusses a possible topic for that paper (predicting earthquakes through animal behavior) with the professor.

2. C The student says, "Professor Dixon? I'm Brenda Pierce. From your Geology 210 class . . . ?" Her questioning tone of voice indicates that she is not sure if Professor Dixon recognizes her. (Professor Dixon says that it is a large class.)

3. A The professor asks, "Did you oversleep? That's one of the problems with an eight o'clock class. I almost overslept myself a couple of times." This indicates that the professor assumes (believes) that the student missed class because she got up too late.

4. D The student says, "I saw this show on television about earthquakes, and it said that in uh, China, I think it was, they *did* predict an earthquake because of the way animals were acting."

5. B The student worries that the professor thinks her topic is not a good one. However, the professor says, ". . . just because this theory hasn't been proven doesn't mean you couldn't write a perfectly good paper about this topic . . . on the notion that animals can predict earthquakes. Why not? It could be pretty interesting. But to do a good job, you . . . you'll need to look at some serious studies in the scientific journals . . ."

6. D The professor says that the taiga is ". . . also called the 'boreal forest.' "

7. B The professor says, "This sub-zone—well, if you like variety, you're not going to feel happy here. You can travel for miles and see only half a dozen species of trees. In a few days, we'll be talking about the tropical rain forest; now *that's* where you'll see variety." The professor is emphasizing that there are very few species of trees in the closed forest by comparing it with tropical rain forests, where there are many species.

8. B, C, A The professor says that the closed forest, choice B, has "bigger needle-leaf trees growing closer together." In the mixed forest, choice C, "The trees are bigger still here, and you'll start seeing some broad-leafed trees, deciduous trees. You'll see larch, aspen, especially along rivers and creeks, in addition to needle-leaf trees." In the open forest,

choice A, "The only trees here are needle-leaf trees—you know, evergreen trees, what we call coniferous trees. These trees tend to be small and far apart."

9. B, D, E The professor mentions the trees' dark green color (which absorbs the sun's heat), their conical shape (which prevents too much snow from accumulating on their branches), and the fact that they are "evergreen" trees (which allows them to start photosynthesizing right away in the spring) as adaptations to the cold. There is no mention of their bark or of their root systems.

10. B According to the professor, "There's one thing all these predators have in common, the ones that live there all year round . . . they all have thick, warm fur coats . . ."

11. C The professor says, ". . . only young moose are at risk of being attacked. The adult moose is the biggest, strongest animal found in the taiga, so a predator would have to be feeling pretty desperate to take on one of these."

12. C, D, B, A According to Professor Speed, Professor Longdell, who invented the case study method, "insisted that it was based on a system used by Chinese philosophers thousands of years ago." Professor Longdell first began using the case study method at Harvard School of Law in the 1870's. It was first used at Columbia University Law School "a couple of years after that." It was not used at Harvard School of Business until "probably about 1910, 1912, something like that."

13. D Professor Speed explains exhibits this way: "Exhibits . . . those are documents, statistical documents, that explain the situation. They might be, oh, spreadsheets, sales reports, umm, marketing projections, anything like that."

14. B The best answer is B; the professor is not *exactly* sure when case study was first used at Harvard Business School. That's why he says, ". . . When was it? Uh, probably about 1910, 1912, something like that . . ." Notice that choice A is not correct because, although he does ask a question ("When was it?"), he does not ask the class, he asks himself.

15. A Professor Speed says that the case study method is used in many fields of study. "For example, my wife . . . she teaches over at the School of Education . . . she uses cases to train teachers."

16.

	Yes	No
Analyze the business situation and exhibits	✓	
Role-play	✓	
Run a computer simulation		✓
Give a presentation and write a report	✓	
Visit a real business and attend a meeting		✓

The first phrase should be marked **Yes** because it *is* part of the process of case study. Professor Speed says that ". . . you have to analyze the situation, the data . . . Then you have to make decisions about how to solve these problems." The second phrase should also be marked **Yes** because the professor says, ". . . solving the problem usually involves role-playing, taking on the roles of decision-makers at the firm." The third phrase should be marked **No.** Computer simulation is *another* method of studying business; it is not part of the case study method. The fourth phrase should be marked **Yes.** When Professor Speed is asked by a student how grades are calculated, Professor Speed tells him, "You give a presentation, an oral presentation . . . and then you write a report as well. You get a grade, a group grade, on the presentation and the report." The last phrase should be marked **No.** Professor Speed does not mention that students will be visiting real businesses or attending meetings as part of the case study process.

17. A, D Choice A is correct because Professor Speed says, "That's the beauty of this method. It teaches teamwork and cooperation." Choice D is also a correct answer because a student asks the professor, "So *that's* why we study cases? I mean, because managers need to be able to make decisions . . . and solve problems?" and the professor responds, "Exactly . . . well, that's a big part of it, anyway."

18. B The presenter introduces the topic of Venus by saying, "Okay, to start off, I'm going to tell you what people, what they used to think about Venus." He goes on to explain several old beliefs about the planet.

19. A, D Choice A is correct. The presenter explains that, in the distant past, people thought that the object we now know as Venus was once thought to be two stars, Phosphorus, the morning star, and Hesperus, the evening star. Choice D is also correct. The speaker says, "a lot of people believed, for some reason, that there were these creatures on Venus who were superior to us, almost perfect beings, like angels or something."

20.

	Similarity	Difference
Their ages	✓	
The directions in which they spin around their axes		✓
Their atmospheric pressures		✓
The presence of volcanoes	✓	
Their sizes	✓	

The first phrase is a **similarity.** The presenter says, "Venus is about the same size as Earth." The second phrase should be considered a **difference** between the two planets. The presenter says, "All the planets of the solar system turn on their axis in the same direction as they orbit the Sun. All except Venus, of course!" The third phrase is also a **difference.** According to the presenter, the atmosphere on Venus is "really thick . . . so thick, it's like being at the bottom of an ocean on Earth." The fourth phrase should be considered a **similarity.** The presenter says that the space probe Magellan "found out that there are all these volcanoes on Venus, just like there are on Earth." The last phrase should likewise be considered a **similarity** because the presenter says that "Venus is about the same size as Earth."

21. B Choice A *is* true, so it is not the right answer. On Earth, a day lasts 24 hours, but a day on Venus lasts 243 Earth days. Choice B is *not* true and is the best answer. A year on Venus lasts 225 Earth days, but an Earth year last 365 Earth days. Choice C is true. A year on Venus lasts 225 Earth days, but a day on Venus lasts 243 Earth days. Choice D is also true. According to the speaker, a day on Venus is longer than a day on any planet in the solar system, including giant gas planets such as Jupiter.

22. A, D, C, B The presenter says that "The first one to go there, the first probe to go there successfully was Mariner 2 in, uh, 1962," so choice A should be listed first. Choice D should be placed in the second box. According to the presenter, the Soviet probe Venera 4 was sent to Venus in 1967. The presenter says Choice C, Venus Pioneer, was launched in 1978. Choice B, Magellan, should be placed in the last box because this probe went to Venus in 1990. However, although Magellan should be listed last, it is mentioned first in the presentation.

23. C The presenter says, "Well, Caroline will be giving the next report, which is about the third planet, and since we all live here, that should be pretty interesting." Since Caroline's presentation is about the planet where we all live, it must be about the Earth.

Lesson 9: Main-Topic and Main-Purpose Questions

Exercise 9.1
1. C   **3.** C   **4.** A   **5.** A
2. B

Exercise 9.2
1. D   **4.** D   **6.** A   **8.** B
2. B   **5.** C   **7.** C   **9.** D
3. A

Lesson 10: Factual, Negative Factual, and Inference Questions

Exercise 10.1
1. A   **7.** A   **13.** A   **19.** A
2. D   **8.** B, C   **14.** B   **20.** C
3. C   **9.** D   **15.** B, D   **21.** A, B
4. B   **10.** B   **16.** D   **22.** D
5. C   **11.** C   **17.** D
6. D   **12.** A, D **18.** D

Exercise 10.2
1. A, C   **12.** D   **23.** D   **34.** B
2. B   **13.** A   **24.** A, D   **35.** B
3. C   **14.** A   **25.** B   **36.** A
4. B   **15.** B   **26.** A   **37.** B
5. A, D   **16.** B   **27.** B   **38.** D
6. D   **17.** A, C   **28.** D   **39.** B, C
7. A   **18.** C   **29.** C, D   **40.** A
8. C   **19.** D   **30.** A   **41.** D
9. A   **20.** B   **31.** C   **42.** C
10. A, D, E **21.** B, D   **32.** D
11. B   **22.** C   **33.** C

Lesson 11: Purpose, Method, and Attitude Questions

Exercise 11.1
1. D 3. B 5. C 6. A
2. A 4. A

Exercise 11.2
1. C 5. D 8. A 11. B
2. C 6. B 9. C 12. D
3. D 7. C 10. A 13. B
4. A

Lesson 12: Replay Questions

Exercise 12.1
1. T 4. T 7. T 10. F
2. F 5. F 8. F 11. T
3. T 6. T 9. T 12. F

Exercise 12.2
1. A 5. D 8. C 11. D
2. A 6. A 9. A 12. C
3. B 7. D 10. C 13. B
4. B

Exercise 12.3
1. D 5. C 9. A 13. B
2. B 6. B 10. B 14. B
3. D 7. D 11. A 15. C
4. A 8. C 12. D

Lesson 13: Ordering and Matching Questions

Exercise 13.1
1. C, D, A, B 6. A, D, B, C 11. B, C, A
2. B, A, C 7. A, C, B 12. A, B, C
3. C, A, B 8. B, A, C 13. C, A, D, B
4. B, D, C, A 9. D, B, A, C
5. C, B, A 10. D, C, A, B

Lesson 14: Completing Charts

Exercise 14.1

1.

	Yes	No
Plentiful parking is provided in large parking lots.		✓
Residents can walk easily to work or shopping areas.	✓	
Residences, shops, and offices are all found on the same block.	✓	
Communities are located only in large urban centers.		✓
Streets are generally laid out in a grid pattern.	✓	

2.

	Yes	No
Housing is less expensive in New Urban communities than in typical suburbs.		✓
There is less crime in New Urban communities.	✓	
Most New Urban communities are conveniently located close to large suburban shopping malls.		✓
Residents of New Urban communities get more exercise.	✓	
Most houses in New Urban communities feature garages that allow direct access to the house.		✓
There is less air pollution in New Urban communities.	✓	

3.

	Myth	Reality
It created the first democratic society in England.	✓	
It confirmed the rights of the English barons.		✓
It established the first British Parliament.	✓	
It established courts in which citizens were tried by their peers.	✓	
It was signed by King John himself.		✓

4.

	Yes	No
Tend to be found in horizontal caves with small entrances	✓	
Contain only herbivore fossils		✓
May have had both herbivores and carnivores living in them		✓
Usually have a greater variety of fossils than natural traps	✓	
Generally contain well-preserved fossils		✓

5.

	Yes	No
This cave was discovered by professional palaeontologists.		✓
Animals that fell in here died from the impact of the fall.		✓
Its entrance was covered by plants.	✓	
This cave features the fossil bones of a previously unknown giant cat.		✓
This cave contains a greater variety of fossils than most natural traps.	✓	

6.

	Ptolemaic System	Copernican System
This system is also known as the "heliocentric system."		✓
"Epicycles" were used to help explain this system.	✓	
This system became part of the medieval system of belief.	✓	
This system was disproved by the discovery of the phases of Venus.	✓	
This system provided a good picture of the solar system but not of the universe.		✓
According to this system, music was generated by the movement of crystal spheres.	✓	

7.

	Component		
	A	B	C
A consumer visits an Internet site to get more information about tires.			✓
A man feels a bicycle will make his daughter happy.	✓		
A customer buys groceries at the store.		✓	
An investor studies the market for art before buying a painting.			✓
A woman orders a sandwich and a drink at a fast-food restaurant.		✓	

8.

	Value-expressive function	Ego-defensive function
May involve a product that protects a consumer from some threat		✓
May involve a product that consumers believe will make them more popular	✓	
May involve a product that consumers believe will make people dislike them	✓	
May involve a product that is harmful to the consumer who buys it		✓

Listening Review Test

Answer	Explanation
1. B	Scott tells Professor Calhoun, "I've decided, uh, I'm going to drop your biochemistry class."
2. D	Scott says that Professor Delaney has advised him to drop one class. Professor Calhoun says, "With all due respect to Doctor Delaney, I couldn't agree with him less." This means that she respects Professor Delaney but completely disagrees with his advice.
3. A	Professor Calhoun agrees that the unit on atomic structure, etc., was difficult, but she says, ". . . here's the good news! That's as hard as it gets! It's all downhill from there!" She means that the rest of the course will be easier.
4. D	Professor Calhoun suggests that Scott get tutoring (private instruction) from her teaching assistant, Peter Kim.
5. C	Professor Calhoun encourages Scott to stay in the class. She tells him that she thinks he can pass the class if he gets a little help. She says, "You're going to do just fine!"
6. A	Stanley asks Martha why she has come to the library, and she tells him that she has been "using the *Encyclopedia of Art,* looking up some terms for my art history class."
7. C	Stanley has lost some index cards with his research notes written on them.
8. B	In a surprised tone of voice, Martha asks Stanley, "You really like to get a jump on things, don't you?" *To get a jump on things* means "to get an early start."
9. C	Stanley says, "The, uh, book stacks . . . that's what they call the main part of the library, where most of the books are shelved."
10. A	Stanley thinks that his note cards are probably in the periodicals room (where journals and magazines are kept), and he says, "Let me run up to the periodicals room and check." After he finds his notes, he and Martha will probably go to a coffee shop on Williams Street.
11. B, C, E	Choice B is correct because the professor says one sign of writing readiness is "making random marks on the page, sometimes accompanied by drawings." Choice C is also correct. The professor says, "Another sign of writing readiness . . . they ask adults to help them write something by guiding their hands." Choice E is correct because the professor says, "Some kids produce symbols that look more like printing, but with *invented letters.*" Choice A is NOT correct. The professor suggests that children build up their hand muscles by using scissors and modeling clay, but this is not given as a sign of writing readiness. Choice D is not correct because this is a sign of the symbolic stage, not of writing readiness.
12. C	According to the professor, "Many experts divide the process into more stages."
13. B, A, D, C	The professor says, "In this system, the first stage is the symbolic stage." Later she says, "The next stage of writing is called the phonemic stage." Then she says, "After this comes the transitional stage." Finally she says, "Okay, the fourth stage is called the conventional stage."

14. B   The professor says, "It's easier for kids to learn to write in, say, Finnish, or Spanish, which are more or less phonetic languages."

15. C   Choice A would likely be produced by a child in the writing readiness phase. Choice B includes only the most dominant sounds but does not involve separate words. This was probably written by a child at the phonemic stage. Choice D involves only some minor spelling mistakes and represents a child at the conventional stage. Choice C, the best answer, is a transition between phonemic and conventional. It involves separate words, and the writer makes an effort to record all the sounds in the words.

16. B, C   The professor emphasizes two points about teaching writing skills: that "writing activities should be *fun*" and that "communication should be the main focus for writing."

17. D   This lecture provides a basic description of double stars.

18. C   According to the professor, "Most astronomers think about a quarter of all stars are binary stars." She also says that "some astronomers estimate as many as 75% of all stars will turn out to be binary stars."

19. A   A *comes* is the dimmer star in a double star. It is the Latin word for *companion.* (The brighter star is called the *primary.*)

20. C   Mizar-Alcor is a "double-double star," according to the professor, because both Mizar and Alcor are binary stars.

21. B   The professor compares a double star having stars of contrasting colors to "two jewels of different colors lying on a piece of black velvet."

22. C, B, A   Albireo is given as an example of a double star in which the two stars appear to be of two different colors. Algol is given as an example of an eclipsing binary, in which one star sometimes blocks the light from the other star. The professor says that Mizar-Alcor is "one of those optical pairs I was talking about."

23. C   The professor says that the method he uses to classify SBUs is called the BCG method because it was developed by the *Boston Consulting Group.* It is also called the "Boston Box" and the "Growth-Share Matrix." It is NOT called the General Electric/Shell method, which is another system for analyzing a product portfolio.

24. C   The professor says that "SBU #3's shoes aren't selling all that well. This SBU is called a *problem child.*"

25. D   The professor implies that the term *cash cow* is used because this type of SBU provides "a dependable flow of 'milk'" (meaning *profit*) for a company.

26. B   A marketing manager would be most pleased by a move from a "dog" to a "cash cow" because a dog is both low-growth and low-market-share whereas a cash cow is low-growth but high-market-share, and a cash cow brings in substantial profits.

27.

	Yes	No
Increase market share in an SBU and turn a cash cow into a star	✓	
Reduce investment in an SBU and collect short-term profits	✓	
Buy a well-performing SBU from another company, creating a new star		✓
Sell a poorly performing SBU and get rid of a dog	✓	
Raise prices on an SBU's product and change a problem child to a cash cow		✓

The first choice should be marked **Yes.** This is the strategy Langfield-Smith calls **building.** The second choice should also be marked **Yes.** This is the strategy Langfield-Smith calls **harvesting.** The professor doesn't list buying a star as one of Langfield-Smith's strategies, so you should mark the third choice **No.** The fourth choice, which Langfield Smith calls **divesting,** should be marked **Yes.** However, the professor does not give raising prices on an SBU as one of Langfield-Smith's strategies, so the last choice should be marked **No.**

28. A   He says that, "In my opinion, though, dogs may have a place in a portfolio."

29. B, C   We know that humans became aware of the humpback whale song in 1968, so choice A is not correct, and we know that Roger Payne discovered that humpbacks sang, so choice D is not correct. The professor says, "We still aren't exactly sure how they produce the sounds," so B is a good choice. Choice C is also a good choice. A student says, "I'd like to know what these songs mean" and the professor responds, "Well, you're not the only one who would like to know that!" There are some theories, but apparently no one definitely knows the meaning of the whales' songs.

30.

	Low-frequency sound	High-frequency sound
Travels a long distance	✓	
Probably carries a lot of information		✓
Has a simple structure	✓	
Is generally considered the "song" of the humpback whale		✓

The low-frequency sounds can be heard from at least 100 kilometers away, so you should check **low-frequency** for the first choice. The high-frequency sounds "seem to contain a lot of information," so you should check **high-frequency** for the second choice. The low-frequency sound has "a relatively simple structure," so you should check **low-frequency** for the third choice. The high-frequency sounds are "what we generally think of when we think of humpbacks' songs," so you should check **high-frequency** for the fourth choice.

31. C, D,   The professor says that "The most basic unit of
A, B   humpback music is a single sound, or **element.**"
Elements are arranged into patterns called
phrases, consisting of three or four elements. A
collection of phrases is called a **theme.** There are
seven or eight themes in a **song.**

32. C   The professor says that a song lasts from ten to
twenty minutes.

33. D   The professor says that the whales generally only
sing during their winter breeding season, which is
spent in warm waters, and that they sing more at
night than during the day.

34. B   The professor indicates that no one knows for sure
what the songs of the whales mean. Therefore, she
says that the student's theory (that whale songs are
a form of oral history) might be correct.

Listening Tutorial: Note Taking

Note-taking Exercise 1
(Answers will vary. Any understandable abbreviation is a
good answer.)
 1. bus orgs
 2. sole prop   s. prop   s p'shp
 3. pt'ship ptner'shp
 4. corp
 5. lmtd lia co, l.l.c.
 6. advant.
 7. corp tx
 8. s. agnt
 9. respon'ty   respon   resp
10. leg docs lgl docus
11. dist. leg. ent.
12. artif pers.
13. st'hlders   stkhldrs
14. prof prft
15. invstmnts   invests
16. dble tx'tion
17. exec
18. brd of drctrs   brd of direcs   bd. dirs b.o.d.
19. pop
20. hyb

Note-taking Exercise 2
 1. business organizations
 2. sole proprietorship
 3. partnership
 4. corporation
 5. limited liability company
 6. advantage
 7. corporate tax
 8. sole agent
 9. responsibility
10. legal documents
11. distinct legal entities
12. artificial persons
13. stockholders
14. profit
15. investments
16. double taxation
17. executive
18. board of directors
19. popular
20. hybrid

Note-taking Exercise 3
(Answers will vary. Any understandable notes are good
answers.)
 1. Topic: most comm forms of bus structs (bus orgs)
 2. 1st : sole p'ship most comm & simplest
 3. Not much diff sole p'ship & pt'shp excpt pt'shp owned by
    > 1 pers
 4. Some pt'ships: silent parts who inv $ in co but not invlv'd
    w/ mg'ment decis.
 5. Corps are <u>distinc lgl ent'ies</u> artif. pers
 6. Most shr'holders don't attnd, give votes top corp offcrs =
    voting by proxy

 7. Howev, d-to-d ops of corp perf'd by exec offcrs + corp
    br'cracy
 8. BTW, CEO often chrmn of brd + top exec offcr
 9. LLC = hyb org combines best of pt'shp + best of corp

Note-taking Exercise 4
(Answers will vary. It is not necessary to reconstruct the sentences word for word.)
 1. Today we're going to talk about the most common forms
    of business structures, the most common forms of busi-
    ness organizations.
 2. So first, let's discuss the sole proprietorship . . . did you
    know it's the most common form of business organiza-
    tion? Also the simplest.
 3. Basically, there's not much difference between a sole pro-
    prietorship and a partnership except that a partnership is
    owned by more than one person.
 4. In some partnerships, there are *silent partners,* partners
    who invest money in the company but have nothing to
    do with management decisions.
 5. Corporations are (this is an important concept) distinct
    legal entities. They're even called "artificial persons."
 6. Most shareholders don't bother to attend, and often give
    their votes, assign their votes, to the top corporate offi-
    cers. This is called *voting by proxy.*
 7. The day-to-day operations of the corporation are per-
    formed by the executive officers and by the corporate
    bureaucracy.
 8. By the way, the CEO is often the chairman of the board as
    well as being the top executive officer.
 9. An L.L.C., as it's called, is a hybrid organization that com-
    bines some of the best features of a partnership and
    those of a corporation.

Note-taking Exercise 5
(Yes/No answers will vary.)
Sample Notes
Topic: most comm forms of bus structs (bus orgs)
        In past, 3 forms:
        1. S. p'ship
        2. pt'ship
        3. corp.
Now,   4. lmtd lia co.
 1. <u>S. P'ship</u>
    most common & simplest
    1 owner: boss
        start up @ "moment of decision" to start business
            (Pl Samuelson's example of tthpaste)
        Advantage: Txed @ pers inc. rate (< corp rate)
 2. <u>Pt'sthip</u>
    pt'shp ≈ S. p'ship excpt pt'shp owned by > 1 pers
    Tx advant of pt'ship = that of s. p'ship
    Liability: Ea part. can be "sole agnt" for pt'ship
        (e.g. prob of 2 partners both buyng "widgets")
        1 prtnr liab not only for self but for all prtnrs
    Usu, parts. share mgmt but . . . Some pt'ships: silent
        prtnrs who inv $ in co but not invlv'd w/ mg'ment
 3. <u>Corp</u>
    Most complex   most expensive (artic of
        incorp'tion) but most big co's corps
    Limited liability: Corps are <u>distinc lgl ent'ies</u> artif. pers
        Corp does bus under its own name owners
        (st'holders) can only lose invest, not pers prop
    Txation: Corps have to pay txs & so do stckhldrs on
        div'dends: dble txation
    Structure: 3 el'mts
        1. <u>stckhlders</u>: ultim. contrl mtgs. 1ce a yr.
            BUT usu. only biggest stckhldrs

Most stckhldrs don't attnd, give votes top corp
offcrs = voting by proxy

2. <u>Brd of drctrs</u> elec. by stckhldrs makes maj decis
appt CEO sets policy
3. Howev, D-to-d ops of corp done by perf'd by exec
offcrs + corp br'cracy
BTW, CEO often chrmn of brd + top exec offcr
4. <u>LLC</u> incre'ly pop for smaller bus.
LLC = hyb org combines best of pt'shp + best
of corp elim's dble txation

Note-taking Exercise 6

1. T
2. Limited liability company
3. F
4. there is no separate tax on the sole proprietorship (or it is taxed at personal income rates, which are lower)
5. the owner is liable for all the company's debts
6. a partnership is owned by more than one person
7. F
8. F
9. T
10. "artificial persons"
11. T
12. F
13. F
14. T
15. partnership   corporation

Section 3: Guide to Speaking

The Independent Speaking Task

Exercise: Scoring the Response

Response 1   Score: __4__

Comments: The speaker gives an automatic response using clear pronunciation and intonation. The response includes important details about the event, and a listener has little problem understanding her response. Although there are some hesitations, the speaker generally uses grammar and vocabulary appropriately.

Response 2   Score: __2__

Comments: The intonation and pronunciation is unclear—especially the pronunciation of word endings—and this requires very close listening to understand the response. There are a number of repetitions and some grammatical problems. The focus changes from *I* to *you* to *we*, for example. The response is hesitant and choppy and there are a couple of long pauses. While this response mentions that the test is important, the speaker doesn't clearly state whether taking the test or passing the test was the most important to him or if he passed and was accepted to the university. The ideas and the connection between details are not clear.

Response 3   Score: __3__

Comments: While some of the ideas are not fully developed, this is a clear, fluid response. The speaker provides some support for her answer, and the connections between the ideas are generally clear. There are minor problems with intonation and pronunciation, and there are some needless repetitions.

Independent Speaking Preview Test

1. Answers will vary, but successful answers should provide a description of an influential person and reasons why that person has had an influence on the speaker's life.

2. Answers will vary. The speaker should state whether he or she favors a Pass/Fail system or a letter-grade system and give reasons why.

Lesson 15: Personal Preference Task

Exercise 15.1

Answers will vary. The following are given as examples.

2. I think the most interesting discussion I've ever heard was a university panel discussion about the future of my country.
3. I believe that the finest restaurant I've ever eaten at is a restaurant at the Blue House Hotel in Istanbul called the Garden Restaurant.
4. In my opinion, the most important leader in history was Simon Bolivar.
5. The best known monument in my country, Thailand, is probably Wat Arun, the "Temple of the Dawn."
7. The best idea I have ever heard is the use of hydrogen in place of gasoline as fuel.
8. The most important invention, in my opinion, is the invention of the printing press.
9. The most difficult problem in my country, I think, is a lack of good roads.
11. On a nice day, my favorite place to study is under a tree in the area outside the main library.
12. My favorite kind of food is pizza.
13. My favorite singer is the Malaysian singer Jasmine Leong.
15. I like to go to the Web site "How Stuff Works." One reasons I enjoy it is that it explains a lot of things that I don't understand very well, so it is a good place to do research. Another reason is that the English on this Web site is fairly easy to understand.
16. When I was a child, traditional dancing was my favorite activity. There were several reasons for this. One is that dancing is good exercise. Another is that I enjoyed learning about the culture of my country.
17. The most interesting class I ever took was a general science course that I took in high school because the teacher was excellent and I learned a lot about the basics of science. Also, it got me interested in science and technology, and later I decided to become a chemical engineer.

Exercise 15.2

Answers will vary. The following are given as examples.

2. This question asks me to name a traditional or popular food in my country and to explain why it is symbolic of my country. I should choose some food that is unique to my country and is usually eaten on special occasions.
3. This question is asking me to name some special skill (or talent) I have. I could, for example, mention my talent for organization and explain how it has helped me in school, at work, and in other situations.

Exercise 15.3

2. Answers will vary, but a good outline could include the following:
   Topic (name of food)
       Descrip: how taste, wht look like, whn served
       Reasons why symbolic
           (unique to my country, e.g.)
           (served on nat'l holidays. e.g.)
3. Answers will vary, but a good outline for this prompt could include the following:
   Topic (name of skill)
       Descrip of skill
       Reasons why useful

(helped me in school, e.g.)
(helped me get a job e.g.)

Exercise 15.4

2. Answers will vary, but a good response for this prompt will follow the outline in Question 2, Exercise **15.3.** It will clearly state the name of the food that the speaker thinks is symbolic of his/her country and give a brief description of the food. It will give several reasons why this food is important in the speaker's home country.

3. Answers will vary, but a successful response will follow the outline in Question 3, Exercise **15.3.** It will name the skill that the person thinks is important, describe the skill, and give several reasons why this is a helpful skill to have.

Exercise 15.5

1. Answers will vary, but this response should begin by stating the gift that the speaker would give and then give a brief description of this gift. The response should also include reasons why this gift is unique or symbolic.

2. Answers will vary, but the speaker should first say which job he or she would most like to have and give a brief description of it. The speaker should then explain why this position is ideal or give examples of ways in which this job would benefit him or her.

3. Answers will vary, but the speaker should clearly state which of the world's problems he or she thinks is especially challenging and then give a brief description of that problem. The speaker should then give reasons why he or she would choose this problem to solve.

Lesson 16: Paired Choice Task

Exercise 16.1

Answers will vary. The following are given as examples.

2. In my opinion, it's better to take a train or other public transportation.

3. Personally, I feel it is more fun to have dinner at a friend's house.

4. I think showering is better.

5. I believe studying abroad is a better choice for me.

7. I'd rather be rich than famous.

8. I prefer studying at the library because there are too many distractions at home.

9. I enjoy going jogging more than working out at the gym.

11. I agree with the idea that cell phones have actually made it more difficult to communicate with people, not easier.

12. I agree with the people who think that nurses should make as much money as doctors.

14. Generally, I agree with those people who think that a library is the most important feature of a university, but I think that the quality of the faculty is also very important.

15. On the whole, I think that watching a movie at a cinema is a more rewarding experience, but sometimes it's more convenient to watch a video at home.

17. Some people like to travel with large groups of people, but I prefer traveling by myself because I like to make my own decisions about what to do and where to go.

18. Some people enjoy living in a small town. However, I find life in a big city more interesting.

20. There are several reasons why I think students should be required to perform some community service. First, it gives them an opportunity to pay back the community for the education they have received. Second, it teaches them about the importance of helping other people.

21. It is not always important to make quick decisions because people need more time to get information in order to make good decisions.

23. I agree with the people who think watching TV is mostly a waste of time. There are a few good shows but most of them are ridiculous. For example, those "reality shows" and most television comedies are silly and uninteresting.

24. There are some disadvantages to using credit cards, such as the high interest rate that credit card companies charge.

Exercise 16.2

Answers will vary. The following are given as examples.

2. This prompt asks if teachers need special training or if a teacher just has to know the subject matter. If I support the idea that a teacher must study education, I must give reasons why I think this is true. If I support the other point of view, I could give examples of teachers I have had who were experts in their field but had no training in educational methods.

3. This prompt asks me to support or not support the concept of school uniforms. If I support school uniforms, I could give several reasons why I think they are a good idea. For example, I could say that students who wear uniforms don't have to compete with other students to see who can buy the latest fashions. If I choose the negative side of this argument, I could say that children express themselves through clothing and that choosing their clothes in the morning is good practice for their working life.

Exercise 16.3

2. Answers will vary. If the speaker chooses to support the idea that a teacher needs special training, the outline could include the following:

Main point (teachers must be trained)
    Brief description of teacher training
    *Reason why teachers <u>don't</u> need training . . .
<u>But:</u> *I <u>do</u> think teachers need training*
        Why?   teaching requires special skills
                  not all experts can communicate

If the speaker chooses to support the opposite idea—that teachers don't need special training—the outline should include the following:

Main point (teachers don't req. training or certif)
    Basic description of experts who don't need special training
    *Reason why teachers do need training . . .
        <u>But:</u> *I don't think teachers need training*
         Why? most experts have taught people in on-the-job situations
               + the knowledge, not the teaching techniques, is most important

3. Answers will vary. Speakers who support uniforms in school could include the following in their outline:

Main point: *I agree w/ idea of schl uni*
    Basic description of wht it means to wear uni to schl
    *Reason why S's <u>don't</u> need uniforms . . .
    <u>But:</u> *it is best to wear uniforms:*
        Reasons: e.g., cheaper for parents
                e.g., S's don't have to compete for most fashionable clthes

Speakers who don't support uniforms in school could include the following:

Main point: *I agree w/ idea of schl uni*
    Basic description of wht it means to wear uni to schl
*One reason why S's <u>should</u> wear uniforms . . .
<u>But:</u> *Uniforms have disadvant:*
        Reasons: e.g., they encourage S's to behave the same, think the same
                e.g., S's will need to choose their clothes when have jobs

*These points are not necessary to make but can often strengthen your response. This is called "admitting the opposition."

Exercise 16.4

Answers will vary. The following are given as guidelines.

2. Speakers who favor the idea that teachers with special knowledge must be trained in teaching techniques should state this in the introduction. The speaker should then give a brief description of teacher training in general. The speaker may then want to "admit the opposition" and give a reason why teachers *don't* need training, but then give stronger reasons why teachers *do* need special training. For example, the speaker might say that, no matter how much the person knows about his her field, teaching is a special skill that requires training.

   Speakers who oppose the idea that teachers with special knowledge must be trained in teaching techniques should state this in the introduction. The speaker should then give a brief description of teacher training in general. The speaker may then want to "admit the opposition" and give a reason why teachers *do* need training, but then give stronger reasons why teachers *do not* need special training. For example, the speaker might say that experts who have a lot to teach students will not go into teaching because they don't want to spend years getting a degree in education.

3. Speakers who support the idea of school uniforms should state this in the first line of the response. They may give one point that opposes school uniforms and then two or three reasons to support them. The speaker may mention, for example, that it is cheaper and easier for parents to dress their children for school if students wear the same uniform every day.

   Speakers who are against the idea of school uniforms should state this in the first line of the response. They may give one point that supports school uniforms and then two or three reasons to oppose them. The speaker may mention, for example, that clothing is a common way for young people to express their individuality.

Exercise 16.5

Answers will vary. The following are given as guidelines

1. Speakers in favor of small schools should state this in their introduction and give a definition of what they consider a small school to be. They should then list several advantages of a small school, such as the stronger sense of community that comes when you know many teachers and students personally.

   Speakers in favor of large schools should state this in their introduction and give a definition of what they consider a large university to be. They should then give several reasons why it is advantageous to attend a large university. They might say, for example, that a large school can afford a better library and better facilities. They might mention that large schools are generally more famous than small ones, which can be important when looking for a job.

2. Speakers who support the idea that all technological changes are good should explain this in the first sentence. They should then discuss what they mean when they say technological changes are good. Speakers should then give reasons why they think this statement is true. They might mention examples of technology that have had a positive impact, such as the development of antibiotic drugs and satellite communications.

   Speakers who are against the idea that all technological changes are good should explain this in the first sentence.

They should discuss what they mean when they say technological changes are not good. Speakers should provide examples of technology that has had bad results. They might mention, for example, that gasoline-burning engines cause global warming and air pollution.

3. Speakers who like the idea of working at home should explain that in the first line of their response. They should describe what it is like to work at home as opposed to working in an office. They should give some reasons why they favor working at home. They might say, for example, that it is convenient and comfortable, and that they don't have to waste time and money traveling to their offices.

   Speakers who don't agree with the idea of working at home should explain that in the first line of their response. They should describe what it is like to work at home as opposed to working in an office. They should give some reasons why they favor working in an office rather than at home. For example, they might say that working together builds teamwork and that a worker learns from interacting with his or her co-workers.

The Integrated Speaking Task

Exercise: Scoring the Response

Response 1   Score: __3__
Comments: The response fully answers the question and the speaker adequately supports her answer with relevant details. The speech is generally clear, but there are some pronunciation problems and the speaker hesitates a lot, requiring some listener effort.

Response 2   Score: __1__
Comments: The response provides some basic information from the reading, but little or no information from the conversation. The response does not answer the question (about the female speaker's opinion of the parking regulations). Instead, the speaker gives her own opinion of the parking response. Pronunciation and intonation problems make it difficult for the listener to understand.

Response 3   Score: __4__
Comments: The speaker clearly understood the reading and speaking and is able to use the information to answer the questions and provide details. The relationship between the ideas is clear and coherent, and the response is fluent and easily understood.

Integrated Speaking Preview Test

Task 3

Answers will vary, but a successful response summarizes the key points of the plagiarism policy. It should provide a definition of plagiarism and mention the system of punishing students who plagiarize. The response should give the man's opinion of this policy: he approves of it but wishes that it had been better publicized in the past. That's because in the past he unknowingly violated this policy by using part of a paper from one class in another class without his instructors' permission.

Task 4

Answers will vary but should include the following elements:
   First, the speaker should provide a summary of the main ideas in the reading. The response should offer a brief definition of camouflage and note that animals use camouflage for protection. The speaker should explain that humans expect camouflaged animals to appear dull and unnoticeable, but not all camouflaged animals look that way.
   The speaker should then report the main idea of the lecture. The lecture describes an animal that *does* appear

camouflaged to us, the sloth. The sloth's dull colors and slow movements allow it to blend in with its surroundings. The lecturer then mentions a second animal, the morpho butterfly. This animal has bright, colorful wings and *does not* appear camouflaged to humans. It is, however, camouflaged from its predators. They see the flying morphos as flashes of blue sky against trees.

Task 5

Answers will vary. The speaker should describe Lucy's problem. (She is very tired in the afternoon and recently fell asleep during a class.) The speaker should then mention the man's solutions. The man first suggests that Lucy drink some coffee. She says coffee from the vending machine tastes bad and coffee from the shop downtown is too expensive; also, it makes her nervous. The man then suggests that she stop by her dorm between classes and rest. Lucy says she hasn't taken a nap since she was quite young. The man says she doesn't have to sleep, just relax, and that she will feel better.

The speaker must next give his/her opinion about the two solutions, and provide reasons. If the speaker chooses the "coffee solution," he/she must give good reasons why Lucy should have coffee in the afternoon. However, since Lucy doesn't like coffee and it makes her nervous, it is probably easier to support the idea that she should rest in her room for a short time between classes.

Task 6

A good response for this question involves a summary of the main idea and a mention of some of the details in this lecture. The speaker should indicate that the professor finds "dialect" and "language" difficult to explain. The speaker should define what the professor means by the term "dialect" (forms of a language that can be understood by people who speak other forms of that language (such as Jamaican English and Indian English). The speaker should also mention dialects that do *not* fit this description (Chinese dialects, for example). The speaker should give the professor's definition of languages: a language cannot be understood by those who do not speak that language. However, the professor again gives exceptions to this definition, such as Danish and Norwegian. The professor says that sometimes a dialect is considered a language because of national pride.

Lesson 17: Announcement/Discussion Task

Exercise 17.1

Answers and notes will vary. The following are given as examples.

Task A

2. The professor says that the sound of ringing phones is distracting.
3. Students must either turn off their cell phones or leave them at home.
4. The professor wrote the memo because four or five cell phones rang in his class last week.
5. The woman thinks those students are thoughtless. The man agrees that they are rude.
6. The woman thinks that students should be allowed to turn off the ring and set the phone to vibrate because there might be an emergency.
7. The man doesn't agree with the woman. He agrees with the professor that it is distracting to see students handling their phones during class. He thinks students can go for an hour without their phones.

Task B

Sample notes on reading

Lib. Amnesty Prog
Wk. of Nov. 28–Dec. 2, return bks etc to main library & sci lib, bus lib, etc.
    No fees!   No ?'s asked
        Help restore collection

Sample notes on conversation

M: This a break . . .
F: ?
M: 5 overdue bks from sci lib   chckd out last Spr. forgot return by Sept cldn't afford
F: How much a day?
M: 25¢ / day/ bk   5 bks = $1.25/day   a lot!
F: Prog ends Fri
M: Return this eve. not able grad if not return lib mat'l, pay fines

8. The topic of this announcement is the Library Amnesty Program.
9. If students return library materials this week, they don't have to pay fees and don't have to answer questions.
10. This program helps the library by helping it restore its collection.
11. The man thinks this is a good announcement.
12. The man feels this way because he owes a lot of money on the overdue books and because students are not allowed to graduate until they have returned overdue materials and paid library fines.
13. The man is going to return his overdue books this evening.

Task C

Sample Notes on reading

Bulletin Brd outside Comp Sci Dept: now rsvrd for official Dept notices & mssges apprvd by Dept
    Current mssges will be removed & new ones must be stamped by exec sec before posting

Sample notes on conversation

M: Not good—wanted to put up mssge abt rmmate
F: Other bullet brd or campus paper
M: Want to room w/ comp sci major—some1 to talk to abt comps.
F: Just say in ad looking for computer person
    But . . . bullet brd so crowded w/ mssges abt rmmates, study grps etc, that not find real bulletins from Dept
M: True, & many mssges from long ago

14. This announcement is about a new policy regarding the bulletin board located outside the office of the Computer Science Department.
15. Only official department notices and messages approved by the department can go on the bulletin board in the future.
16. All messages on the board on January 9 will be removed.
17. In the future, all messages on the board must be approved by the executive secretary.
18. The man is unhappy with the announcement.
19. He is unhappy because he can't put the message that he is looking for a roommate on the Computer Science Department bulletin board.
20. The woman tells the man that he should use other bulletin boards on campus or put an ad in the campus newspaper.
21. The man particularly wants to use this bulletin board because he wants to room with another computer science major.
22. The man and the woman agree that the bulletin board is crowded and there are many outdated messages on the board.

Task D
<u>Sample notes on reading</u>
Fall Film Fest
2nd annual FFF Oct. 21-23
    Shown @ Curtiss Thea in S. Union Bldg & Uptown Thea
    24 top indep & loc films
        Loc flmmkrs give pres & wkshps
    Tickets @ Curt. Thea   See Mon paper or go on-line
<u>Sample notes on conversation</u>
F: Go FFF last yr?
M: Yes, but hated evry mov.   not mke sense,
F: Some don't mke sense, some deprssing   but not all
M: Saw 3-4 all confus or deprssing
F: So—not want go this yr?
23. The announcement is about a film festival.
24. The festival will feature <u>24 top independent and local films.</u> Also, local filmmakers will <u>give presentations and workshops.</u>
25. The woman isn't interested in the festival because she doesn't like independent films.
26. She feels this way because she attended last year's festival and found the films confusing and boring.
27. He finds some independent movies confusing and boring too, but not all of them.

Exercise 17.2
Answers will vary. The following notes are given as examples.

Task A
<u>Sample notes on reading</u>
Experiment. Particpnts Needed
Psych exprmnt re sleep diffic.
20 F, 20 M
    Eligibility
    Must be stud, 18-24
    "   have prob slpg
    "   spend 1 night/wk in Psych Slp Lab for 4 wks
    "   non-smoker, good hlth
Complete questionnaire, intervw before begin
Partic: $150   psych stu 1 cred-hr   Lrn techniq. to slp better
<u>Sample notes on conversation</u>
F: (happy abt experiment)
M: Dangerous?
F: Not med exper. or drugs   but think pysch exper harmless   take part in 2 or 3
M: ?
F: Good way get $ & cred hrs
M: Have trouble slping?
F: Yes, 3-4 nights/wk   not slp till midnight   maybe lrn how slp better?

Task B
<u>Sample notes on reading</u>
Summer Intern Fair
    Purp of fair to provide oppor to mt w/ reps for 40+ companies etc.
seeking students to fill internships 1 volunt. & commun service positions during summer
<u>Sample notes on conversation</u>
M: I'm going intrnshp fair Sat . . .
F: ?   You want to do volunt wk this summer?
M: Not all volunt   some internships—& most intrnshps paid
F: Not paid much . . .
M: Sister intern at ad agency—paid OK—good experience   lk good on resume   help her find job at NY ad agency
F: Going to be lifegrd this summer—not lk good on resume but fun

Task C
<u>Sample notes on reading</u>
Call for auditions
    Pub. audit. for G.B. Shaw comedy "Heartbrk Hse"
    Audit open to everyone roles avail for actors of all ages
        no prior exper
<u>Sample notes on conversation</u>
F: Thght had to be Thea Arts major to try out . . .
M: Thinking abt trying out?
F: Yes . . . was in play in high schl . . . 1 of Shaw's plays . . . like Shaw
M: But you only have little expernce . . .
F: Says no prior expernce required   if not get part, wrk on costumes, sets, etc.

Task D
<u>Sample notes on reading</u>
Stress Mngement Wkshp
Final Exam wk stressful
        can cause fatigue lower resist to illness
        can hurt perform. during exam
Wkshp: will teach you to handle stress
            exercise & eat right
            monitor stress level
            stay cool & calm
<u>Sample notes on reading</u>
F: Y're signing up for wrkshp?
M: Maybe will help . . .
F: But you seem to handle stress well . . .
M: When taking chem. test, bad anxiety   barely finish exam
F: Maybe shld go
    notice says will teach you to exer & eat hlthy   but no time to do that during final exam wk
M: Mostly want to learn to deal w/ strss during exams

Exercise 17.3
Answers will vary. The following responses are given as examples.

Task A
The announcement is a request for participants in a psychology experiment. The researcher is looking for students who have problems sleeping. The woman is excited and wants to take part in the experiment. The man doesn't like the idea of being an experimental participant and worries that it might be dangerous. She says she wouldn't take part in medical experiments but that she thinks these psychological experiments are not dangerous. For her, it is a good way to get extra money and credit hours. He asks her if she has trouble sleeping, and she says yes, she has trouble sleeping three or four nights a week and hopes to learn some techniques for falling asleep.

Task B
The notice announces a Summer Internship Fair. Companies, foundations, and government agencies are looking for interns and volunteers. The two students discuss the notice. The man says that he will attend the fair and seems enthusiastic about it. The woman asks him if he wants to be a volunteer this summer. He tells her that not all the positions are volunteer positions, some are paid internships. He says that an internship provides good experience and looks good on a résumé. He gives the example of his sister who got a job at a New York advertising agency because of her experience as an intern.

Task C
The topic of the announcement is a call for auditions for the play "Heartbreak House" by George Bernard Shaw. The announcement says this is one of Shaw's finest plays.

The woman says that she thought roles in the play were only for Theater Arts majors and she is excited about trying out for the play. She says she was in a play in high school—it was also a Shaw play. The man says that the woman does not have much experience as an actor, but she points out that the notice says that no previous experience is needed. She says that if she doesn't get a part in the play, she might work on sets or costumes.

Task D

The announcement is about Stress Management Workshops offered by a university counseling center. According to the announcement, final exam week is very stressful and anxiety can have negative effects on students.

The man apparently thinks the workshops are a good idea because he plans to sign up for one. He says that he felt very anxious while taking a mid-term exam. He felt ill and could barely finish the test. The woman agrees that perhaps the man should go to one of these workshops. However, she says that the workshops teach students to exercise and eat healthy foods to reduce stress, but there is no time to exercise or prepare meals during finals. The man says that he is mainly interested in learning how to control stress *during* exams.

Lesson 18: General/Specific Task

Answers and notes will vary. The following are given as examples.

Exercise 18.1

Task A

2. According to the lecturer, a numeral system is a system of symbols used to represent quantities.
3. Most numeral systems are decimal systems, also known as base-10 systems.
4. The Arabic numeral system is a base-10 (decimal) system. It originally comes from India.
5. One reason decimal systems are used is that humans have ten fingers. Another reason is that decimal systems are easy to use.
6. The main topic of the lecture is numeral systems that are not base-10.
7. The two primary examples that the professor mentions are the system used by the Yuki Indians (base-8) and the system used by the Sumerians (base 60).
8. The Yukis used a base-8 system because they counted the spaces between their fingers.
9. The Sumerian system had an impact on the way we measure time.
10. According to the professor, the Sumerian system isn't used in other situations today because it is not easy to use in calculations.

Task B

Sample notes on the reading
Dolls useful way learn abt soc.
  Doll mkers use trad materials, skills
  Nat. Amer. dolls
      some to entertain
      "   "   educate
          1. model adult activ, roles, costumes
          2. teach children abt relig.
Sample notes on the discussion
Prof: Wht kind dolls?
S1: From SW?
Pr: Yes, Hopi in New Mex.
S2: Kachina (?) dolls
Pr: Yes—what for?

S1: Play w/?
Pr: No—edu toys—rel. training—teach Hopi children abt spirits (over 200 spirits)

11. The topic of the reading is dolls, especially Native American dolls.
12. Dolls are a good way to learn about society because doll makers use traditional materials and skills.
13. Some dolls are used to amuse children but some are used to educate children.
14. The two types of educational dolls are those that teach about adult activities, roles, and costumes and those that teach about religion.
15. The discussion is about the Kachina dolls of the Hopi.
16. The Kachina dolls are an example of dolls that provide religious training because they teach Hopi children the names of the spirits and the appearance of the spirits.
17. Hopi children need dolls to learn about spirits because there are over 200 spirits.

Task C

Sample notes on the reading
  Oxidation: metals exposed to air & liq (electrolyte)
  Maybe cosmetic problem: discolor metal
  or may cause weakness in metal (corrosion)
Sample notes on the lecture
Rust = iron oxide
    need iron + air + H_2O (esp. H_2O & salt)
Rust = corrosion
    Problems: affects cars, ships, indus equip etc.
    people spend \$ millions to protect, replace rusted equip.

18. The main point of the reading is to describe the process of oxidation.
19. Rust occurs when a metal is exposed to air and a liquid.
20. According to the reading, oxidation may be a cosmetic problem or it may cause weakness in metal.
21. The professor says that rust is iron oxide.
22. The three things needed to get rust are iron, air, and water.
23. According to the reading, the water that causes rust is called an electrolyte.
24. Rust is an example of corrosion because it damages metal.
25. Some examples of things that are affected by rust are cars, ships, and industrial equipment.
26. Rust costs a lot of money. People spend money on protecting material from rust and replacing materials damaged by rust.

Task D

Sample notes on the reading
Since late 19th c. ident twins used in exprmnts
  Esp. by scientists invest. "nature vs. nurture"
  Most useful: ident twins raised apart (same genetics, dif. environ.)
Not many exprmnts in future: after '70, cples not allowed adopt twins separately
Sample notes on the discussion
S1: Wht kind exprmnt?
Prof: Many med exprmnts . . .
S2: Wht kind psych exprmnt?
Pr: 1 was investig. of happiness . . . capacity for happiness
    accord. exprmnt: happiness not related \$ or marital status—80% genetic
S2: ? Doesn't make sense . . .
Pr: Many pychs not like twin rsrch . . .
    "Separated" twins often have contact: as infants or later as teens or adults

27. The reading passage is about experiments done on twins.
28. Scientists are interested in twins to learn about "nurture vs. nature" (genetics vs. environment).
29. There will there not be many more experiments with separated twins because, after 1970, couples were not allowed to adopt twins separately.
30. The professor and the students mainly discuss the psychological experiment performed on twins that measured the capacity for happiness.
31. The experiment on happiness was done on identical twins because they have the same genetic makeup but are raised in different environments.
32. Many psychologists don't like twin research because most separated twins have actually had some contact.

Exercise 18.2
Notes will vary. The following are given as examples.

Task A
Sample notes on the reading
Except humans, birds best builders
   Nest: place for eggs   shelter
   Vary in complexity: some birds no nests
        "   "   simple nests
      Most famil nest: cup-shaped
        "   complex: enclosed: solid, intricate
                            multi rooms
                            house several generations
                            other animals move in later

Sample notes on the lecture
So. Af. bird: hamerkop   huge nest, see from km. away
          8,000 sticks   Sev. generations
                3 rms. 1) sleeping room (soft plants)
                       2) middle room
                       3) lookout post
Once people thght hamerk. brought baby snake to nest
brought food to snake
      thght snake then protected hamerk. like fam. dog
      actually: snakes move into nest after birds abandon

Task B
Sample notes on the reading
Metamorphic rocks: change from 1 type rock → another type
   "parent rock" usu. sedimentary rock
      buried in earth, heat + pressure → changes in min. compos.
& texture
      (not melt) become denser, stronger
         often impurities mixed w/ parent rock
      Because strong, often used as bldg mater'l
Sample notes on the lecture
   Marble: 1 type of metamphic rock
      formed from sediment, rock, limestone
      but limest. softer, more easily broken than mrble
   Pure limest. → white mrble
         impurities make mrble grn, yellow, etc.
Mrble strong, beautiful   used for temples, statues, pub
bldgs, etc

Task C
Sample notes on the reading
Invest jour'nism   rsch, intervws, fact-finding to expose abuse
      became pop 1st decade of 20th c.
Grp called "muckrakers" exposed mny types abuse: pol.
corruption, child labor, etc,
   Fav. target: large corps called "trusts"
   Helped bring abt reforms
Sample notes on the lecture
Ida Tarbell: began reporting 1894

Wrote abt Standard Oil Co—1 of most powerful corps in world
   investig. reporter: 1 of famous "muckrakers"
2 yrs studying Stand Oil: corp rcrds, intervws, meet w/director
      1904 articles abt corp scandals, abuse, unfair pracs.
Made rdrs angry
   Tarbell's wrtg → Congress break up Stand Oil in 1911

Task D
Sample notes on the reading
Early yrs of photog: all photos were monochrm (= black & white)
2 types: 1. gray-scale (really B&W) stark, cold look
         2. sepia   brown in place of gray warmer
Sepia not aged gray-tone photo
   Use silv. sulfide in place of silv iodide → brown tones
   Silv sulf more stable, last 150 yrs ∴ all old photos sepia
Sample notes on the lecture
Prof: showing 2 monochrom photos, both street scenes in Bos.
S1: 2nd photo looks older
Pr: Same age, but 2nd one does lk older
S1: 1st photo, light harsher, more contrast
      2nd has brownish tint
Pr: 2 photos develop. w/ diff processes—will show diff processes in
dark rm today

Exercise 18.3
Answers will vary. The following responses are given as examples.

Task A
According to the reading, except for people, birds are the best builders. Birds lay their eggs in nests and use nests for shelter. The most complex kind is the enclosed nest.

The professor says that the hamerkop bird from South Africa builds a giant enclosed nest. It's a complex nest made of 8,000 sticks. Like other enclosed nests, the hamerkop's nest has multiple rooms: a sleeping room, a middle room, and a lookout post. Enclosed nests often house more than one generation, and this is true of the hamerkop's nest as well.

The reading says that sometimes other animals move into enclosed nests after the birds leave. This led to an interesting story about the hamerkop's nest. People used to think hamerkops kept snakes in their nest for protection. However, these snakes actually move into the nest after the hamerkops leave.

Task B
The reading is about metamorphic rocks. These are rocks that are formed from some other kind of rock, called the "parent rock." The parent rocks are buried in the earth and the heat and pressure change them to metamorphic rock.

The professor gives an example of metamorphic rock called marble. The parent rock for marble is the sedimentary rock limestone. However, marble is harder and stronger than limestone. Marble that comes from pure limestone is white, but impurities make it different colors. Like other metamorphic rocks, marble is strong enough to be used as a building material. For example, it's often used to make public buildings.

Task C
The reading says that investigative reporting involves research, interviewing, and fact-finding. It became popular in the early twentieth century. One group of investigative reporters were called "muckrakers" They investigated many kinds of problems and helped bring about reforms.

ANSWER KEY

The professor talks about one of these "muckrakers" whose name was Ida Tarbell. She investigated the Standard Oil Company. Like other investigative reporters, she did research and interviewed people, even the director of the company. She published articles about the company's abuses in a magazine. These made readers angry. Congress broke up the Standard Oil Company because of her articles.

Task D

According to the reading, early photographs were monochromatic. In other words, they were black-and-white. There were two types of these: gray scale, which has a stark, cold look, and sepia, which has warmer, brown tones. People often believe that sepia photos are just "old" gray-tone photos, but really, a different chemical is used to process sepia pictures.

The professor shows her class two photos. The first one is probably a gray-tone photo because the light is harsher and there is more contrast. The second one is probably sepia because it is warmer and has brownish tones. It also looks older. According to the reading, sepia pictures seem older because sepia photos last longer than gray-tone photos. Most old photos that people see are sepia photos, and that's probably why this photo seems old.

Lesson 19: Problem/Solution Task

Exercise 19.1

Answers will vary. The following are given as examples.

2. The man urges Kathy to get some new tires.
3. The advisor suggests that the student add another class.
4. David thinks the woman should not sign the lease.
5. The woman tells the man to ask the professor to change his grade.
6. Diane suggests that her friend find a summer job.
7. Thomas urges the woman not to make a quick decision.
8. The dean tells Robert to stay out of trouble in the future.
9. The man thinks his friend should take some tennis lessons.
10. The professor advises the student to do a little more research.

Exercise 19.2

Answers will vary. The following are given as examples.

2. I believe that Elizabeth should follow the man's second suggestion.
3. I think that the woman ought to follow her doctor's original advice.
4. In my opinion, the student should do what the dean suggested first.
5. I agree that Fred should get a good lawyer.
6. I believe that Dana should listen to the advice that her roommate gave her.
7. I agree with the suggestion that the man rewrite his paper.
8. I think the suggestion that the woman study early in the morning is a good one.
9. I also recommend that the man try out for the swim team.
10. In my opinion, Tim should not drop out of school.

Exercise 19.3

Notes and answers will vary. These are given as examples.

Task A

Sample notes on conversation

M: *smoker: pack a day—interested in speed skating   out of breath easily*
   tried quit before, not able

F: *95% of people who quit w/out a program return to smoking*
M: *Hypnosis . . . heard was best way to quit*
F: *Hypnosis not as simple & painless as man say*
   clinic's Smoke Stoppers program not use hypo . . .
   uses "nico. repl'mnt sys": gum, etc.
   + techniques for first few wks   + support grp
M: *Wants to try hypno . . .*
F: *can try but expensive   Hlth Center's programs are free*

2. He is trying to solve this problem now because he has gotten interested in speed-skating recently.
3. He has he tried to solve this problem in the past by trying to quit smoking on his own.
4. The nurse says that 95% of people who quit without a program start smoking again.
5. He wants to try hypnosis because he has heard that this is the best way to quit.
6. The nurse suggests that the man take part in the clinic's Smoke Stoppers program.
7. One advantage of the nurse's solution is that it is free.
8. I recommend that the man follow the nurse's suggestion and join the Smoke Stoppers program because it is free and it uses "nicotine replacement."

Task B

Sample notes on conversation

F: *Get tickets for play?*
M: *Not take check*
F: *?*
M: *Not have right ID*
F: *?   Stud. ID?*
M: *wanted 2 forms pic ID*
F: *drvr's license?*
M: *Not have   had one when 16 but no car on campus   walk or bike   lic expire*
F: *Can get official state ID   less expensive, not need take tests*
M: *Where?*
F: *Bureau Motor Vehic.—but suggest get license; may need to drive sometime*
M: *Will think abt   need to get $ from ATM for tickets now.*

9. The man's problem is that he wanted to cash a check but the box office wanted two forms of picture ID.
10. He is having this problem because his driver's license has expired.
11. The woman first suggests that the man get an official state ID.
12. If he follows this advice, there are two advantages: it is cheaper than getting a driver's license and he doesn't have to take any tests.
13. The woman's second suggestion is that he renew his driver's license.
14. The advantage of following her second suggestion is that he can drive a car if he needs to.
15. I would get my driver's license renewed because, as the woman says, you never know when you might need to drive somewhere.

Task C

Sample notes on conversation

Prof: *Grades on unit tests good but not lab rprts*
S: *Lab not going well . . . lab prtnr Robert's fault*
Pr: *?*
S: *went hgh schl together; asked to be lab prtnr 1st day   no talent in lab   not measure chems   breaks things   burned self*
   worst thing: not help with lab reports
      new lab prtnr?

Pr: Not know ... maybe, but other stu used to prtnrs
　　but can talk to Rob't if want　ask be more careful
　　　　　　　　help w/ lab rprt
S: Something needs to be done ...

16. The student is having a problem with <u>her grades on lab reports.</u>
17. She is having a problem because her lab partner Robert is not careful or helpful.
18. The worst problem, according to the student, is that <u>her lab partner doesn't help with the lab reports.</u>
19. To solve her problem, the student proposes <u>that the professor assign her another lab partner.</u>
20. The professor reacts to this proposal by saying that the other students are used to the lab partners that they have.
21. She offers to talk to Robert and tell him to be more careful and to help with the report.
22. In this situation, I would ask the professor to talk to Robert about the problem. I would also probably talk to Robert myself.

Task D
<u>Sample notes on conversation</u>
M: Have situation ...
F: ?
M: Friend Jack in Mex. ... Jack has pet rat (mouse, actually) Samson—taking care of ... has wheel in cage ... last night whl was making noise ... put in shoebox ... chewed thru cardboard ... disappeared
F: Search apt?
M: Not there ... small apt ... escaped ...
F: Wht do?
M: Maybe go pet store, replace Samson with look-alike mouse Can't tell 1 mse from another ...
F: Can't! ... dishonest ... have to call Jack in Mex ...
M: Guess right, but ruin trip ... Jack attached to Samson ...

23. He is taking care of his friend's pet mouse and it has disappeared.
24. The noise of the mouse's exercise wheel was disturbing his sleep. He put the mouse in a shoebox to stop the noise, and the mouse chewed through the cardboard shoebox.
25. The man's solution is to get a mouse that looks just like Samson and to replace Jack's pet without telling Jack.
26. Karen thinks that the man's plan <u>is dishonest and unfair to Jack.</u>
27. Karen advises the man to call Jack in Mexico and tell him what happened.
28. The man agrees with her that he should call Jack, but says that it will ruin Jack's trip.
29. I would probably call Jack and tell him what happened.
30. I would wait until Jack returned from Mexico and tell him then. Then I would offer to buy Jack another mouse if he wanted me to.

Exercise 19.4
Notes will vary. The following are given as examples.

Task A
<u>Sample notes on conversation</u>
Adv: Heard rumors?
S: Abt dept shutting down?
A: Yes, rumors true　Sept, Central State's Class Lang Dept gone only 20 stu　Univ wanted save $　2-3 depts. closing
S: What _you_ do?
A. Taking posit at Winston College　good Class Lang program
S: Not sure what options are ...

A: Cld change majors　Mod Lang Dept
S: Want M.A. in archaeol.　Class Lang more useful
A: Could transfer Winston Col　will help you
S: Big change　friends
A: Only 40 miles ... see frnds on wkend
S: Maybe ...

Task B
<u>Sample notes on conversation</u>
M: Find place to live next semes?
F: Just signed lease.
M: Don't seem happy ... nice place?
F: Very nice sunny front room, can use for painting ...
M: Wht prob?
F: Too much $ for rent ...
M: Tell landlord you changed mind ...
F: Already have deposit ... could keep $
M: How big apt?
F: Big rm for studio ... bdrm, kitch, lvg rm
M: Get rmmate & you slp in studio
F: Don't know ... like privacy ...
M: If not get depos back, have to share ...

Task C
<u>Sample notes on conversation</u>
Clerk: $352.68—charge?
S: Guess so—textbks so expensive. Wht buy-back policy?
Cl: 50% of new value—abt $175. for these
S: ?　Just ½?
Cl: That's policy　If marked heavily only 25%
S: Wht "heavily" mean?
Cl: Underlining, margin notes, highlighting ...
S: I use hghlghtr to mark imp. txt　study hghlghtd txt for exams
Cl: Cld use pencil—erase after
S: Lot to erase　& rather use hghlghtr
Cl: Some stu mark up then keep bks ...
S: Maybe make good ref bk, but prob. need $ at end of term

Task D
<u>Sample notes on conversation</u>
F: Nervous?
M: Yes, abt. concert tomorrow—50/50 chance of thndrstrms
F: Move indoors ...
M: Alrdy have permis to use gym ... but supposed to be old-fash. concert & ice cream social, won't be same indoors　if have in gym, won't raise much $ for univ orchestra & that purpose of concert
F: Wait until tomor. to decide ...
M: Can't　have to put up posters, etc. abt new location
F: Well, can move this eve or cross fings & hope for best ...

Exercise 19.5
Responses will vary. The following are given as examples.

Task A
The student's advisor tells Stan that the rumors about the Classical Language Department closing down are true. She herself is going to go teach at Winston College. She suggests that Stan change his major. Since he has been taking Spanish courses, she suggests that he major in Modern Languages. However, Stan says that he wants to get his master's degree in archaeology, and classical languages would be better. His advisor then suggests that he transfer to Winston College, and she offers to help him do that. At first, he is concerned about leaving his friends behind. His advisor says that Winston is not that far away, and that he could see his friends on weekends.

I agree with Stan's advisor's second solution. Since Stan wants to study archaeology in graduate school, he should transfer to a nearby school, especially since his advisor will help him.

Task B

Margaret has found an apartment for next semester, but there is a problem. The rent is too high. She liked the sunny front room and thought it would be a perfect place for her to paint, so she signed a lease, but she can't afford it. The man advises Margaret to tell the landlord that she has changed her mind, but she has already given the landlord a deposit. She's afraid he will keep her money. The man then suggests that she sleep in the studio and find a roommate to live in the bedroom. The woman says that she likes her privacy but the man tells her that, if she can't get her deposit back, she'll have to share with a roommate to pay the rent.

I think the best solution is to try the man's second solution. Although Margaret won't have as much privacy as she likes, she will have a nice studio to paint in and she will be able to pay the rent.

Task C

The student is buying textbooks, and they are very expensive. He asks how much the bookstore will buy back these books for. The clerk says that the policy is to give 50% of the new value. However, if the book is heavily marked, the bookstore will only buy back books for 25%. "Heavily marked," according to the clerk, means that there are a lot of underlines, margin notes, or highlighted text. The student says that he studies by marking important text with a highlighter and then just studying highlighted text before a test. The clerk suggests he mark the text with pencil and erase it later, but he says that there would be a lot to erase, and that besides, he likes using a highlighter. The clerk then goes on to say that some students go ahead and mark their texts and then just keep them, suggesting that he could do that too. The student says they might make good reference books but that he'll probably need the money at the end of the semester.

I think the best solution is to mark the books as much as he wants. He will probably only get back 25% of the money he paid, but the most important thing is to do well on the tests.

Task D

The man is nervous about a concert he is planning. There is a 50-50 chance of storms tomorrow, and it is an outdoors concert. The woman suggests that he move it indoors. He has gotten permission to hold the concert in a gym on campus, but he says that it is an old-fashioned concert and ice cream social and that it should be held outdoors if possible. The woman advises him to delay his decision until tomorrow, but he can't because he has to put up posters about the changed location this evening. She says he can either change it tomorrow or hope for the best.

This is a difficult decision, but I think I would take a chance. If it rains, perhaps he can postpone the concert and have it another time, but if he has it indoors, he probably won't make enough money to help the orchestra.

Lesson 20: The Summary Task

Exercise 20.1

Task A

Notes and answers will vary. The following are given as examples.
2. Supermarkets first appeared in the 1930's and were first successful in the 1950's.

3. In the days before supermarkets, most people shopped at small neighborhood stores.
4. After supermarkets appeared, <u>small, family-owned grocery stores mostly disappeared.</u>
5. There are two reasons why supermarkets were successful: <u>lower prices</u> and <u>greater variety.</u>
6. "Economy of scale" means <u>that a company buys so much of a product that they pay lower prices for it.</u>
7. Supermarkets today are facing <u>challenges from "megamarts."</u>
8. The situation faced by supermarkets today is similar to the situation faced by small grocery stores in the 50's because they are being challenged by larger stores that offer lower prices and greater variety.

Task B
Sample notes on lecture
Our Sun: <u>yellow dwarf</u>
Explo. gases   thermonuc. like 1,000's of H. bombs
   Not blow up because gravity
      " collapses " explosions = balance
½ way thru life as yell. dwf
In 5 bill. yrs center get hotter   more explos   expand to orbit Merc.
   <u>red giant</u> Earth too hot for life
   After use up fuel, Sun will lose heat, shrink <u>White dwf</u>
      bill more yrs: lose all ht <u>black dwf</u> Earth cold, dark, lifeless
9. This lecture is mostly about <u>the future of the sun.</u>
10. The Sun consists of <u>exploding gases.</u>
11. The Sun doesn't fly apart because of gravity.
12. The Sun doesn't collapse because of explosions.
13. In five billion years, the Sun's center will <u>get hotter</u> and the Sun will <u>expand.</u>
14. In five billion years, the Earth will be too hot for life.
15. When the Sun uses up most of its fuel, <u>it will shrink.</u>
16. After the Sun burns up all of its fuel, it <u>will lose its heat</u> and the Earth <u>will be cold, dark, and lifeless.</u>
17. The four stages that the sun will pass through are <u>yellow dwarf, red giant, white dwarf,</u> and <u>black dwarf.</u>

Task C
Sample notes on lecture
late 40's, early 50's TV began compete w/ radio & movies
   Prediction: TV wld make radio & TV obsolete
   Didn't happen: media exist side by side
      But: audience habits changed
         e.g. people no longer listen radio serials in eve BUT
         listen to radio music, news esp. when can't watch TV
         (when driving, etc.)
Same true of movies—people used to go 2-3 times a wk, now spec occasion
   Also people like being part of audience, like big screen, sound sys
In fut: maybe new media will replace current (TV, Internt, etc) . . .
but maybe exist side by side)
18. The professor mainly discusses three types of media: <u>television, radio,</u> and <u>movies.</u>
19. Television started to become very popular in the late 1940's and early 1950's.
20. People predicted at that time that television would replace radio and the movies.
21. No, people's prediction about radio and movies was not correct. Radio, movies, and television all exist side by side.
22. After the introduction of television, people did not listen to <u>comedies or dramas</u> on the radio but they listened to <u>music and news.</u> They listened to radio when they couldn't <u>watch TV.</u>

23. After the introduction of television, a night at the movies became a special occasion rather than part of a weekly routine.
24. According to the lecture, many people enjoy going to the movies rather than watching television because <u>they like being part of a big audience</u> and because <u>they like watching the action on a big screen and listening to a good sound system.</u>
25. The professor predicts that if a new method of entertainment and communication appears in the future, it will not replace the current media but will exist alongside them.

Task D
<u>Sample notes on lecture</u>

"Murder mystery" —
  Great Dying   not same as extinct. of dinos 65 million yrs ago
  Grt Dying was 250 mill yr ago   much worse
                    90% of ocean species died
                    75% " land "   "
Causes—large meteor? (like dinos)
      new evidence: molecules of minerals from meteors found
      in rocks from that time
      crater in Austral?
Huge volcanic erupt. Siberia   sea of lava
    dust from meteor, ash from volcano cut off sunlight → plants
    died, no oxy.
    oxy level ↓ to 12% like 6,000 m. mountaintop
  most animal species died out

26. The main topic of this lecture is <u>the "Great Dying."</u>
27. The professor calls this event a "murder mystery" because it involved the death of many species.
28. This event happened <u>250 million</u> years ago. It should not be confused with <u>the extinction of the dinosaurs,</u> which happened <u>65 million</u> years ago.
29. One probable cause of this event was <u>a large meteor hitting the earth.</u>
30. Scientists have found recently found two pieces of evidence indicating this event was caused by a collision: <u>molecules from meteors have been found in rocks from that time</u> and <u>a possible meteor impact crater has been found in Australia.</u>
31. Another possible cause of the event was the eruption of a giant volcano.
32. The direct cause of the event was probably <u>a lack of oxygen.</u>
33. The oxygen level at the time of the Great Dying was similar to <u>the oxygen level on top of a 6,000-meter mountaintop.</u>
34. No. There is some evidence that these theories are true, but the event took place a long time ago, so it is difficult to know for sure.

Exercise 20.2
Notes will vary. The following are given as examples.

Task A
<u>Sample notes on lecture</u>

Topic: psych condition, type depress. called Seasonal Affective
Disorder (SAD)
    only recog. since '85
    starts in autmn, worst in Dec/Jan   gone in sprng
    Light affect brain chem? exact cause ?
        symptoms: depress + fatigue, weight gain etc.
        usually people in 20s   more common ♀ than ♂
Treatment: people sit near bright light (20 X ordin. light)
duplicates Sun

30 min A.M., 30 P.M.
    also: trip to tropics cld cure!

Task B
<u>Sample notes on lecture</u>

Experiment:
  Fractional distillation
    Separ. 2 liqs w/ diff boiling pts
heat water & alcohol   alc boils @ 78° C
            H₂O "   " 100°C
    heat to between 78 & 100   watch thermomtr
      alc → gas
        up column to condenser, cool water arnd condenser
alc. become liq again
          pure H₂O in 1st container
            " alc " 2nd "
  Fract dist very imp.
    use to distll petro   more complic. but same process

Task C
<u>Sample notes on lecture</u>

1900   Nov.3   NYC   1st Nat'l Auto Show
  8000 people   40 auto manu.   like forml soc occas.
Pres of US there: 1st pres to ride car
Auto invent Ger 1880's but merchandising pioneered in US
Almost handmade   undepend. toys for rich
    Steam not pop: explos?
    Gas   "   " : smell, noise
    Elec: safe, quiet
# of manu ↑ 1905: 247
For manu: learn from 1 another
Maybe because 1900 show, US replace Fr as leading car manu in '04

Task D
<u>Sample notes on lecture</u>

If infin # monkey @ typewriters & monkeys type @ random, 1 will
event'ly type perf. copy of Shakespeare's Hamlet. = Infin Monkey
Theorem
Famous: used in math, astron, comp sci, stats etc
        novels, poems, etc even cartoon The Simpsons
Used to illus unlikely events: e.g. poor stu gets good grade
Also illus diff concpts: large #'s coincid, randomness, infin.
How unlikely? ±50 keys on typewrtr
  1 correct letter: 1/50
  2   "   " : 1/2500
  3   "   " : 1/125,000
1st page: 10 bil planets   10 bil monkeys   10 bil yrs
Whole play: incomprehensibly unlikely

Exercise 20.3
Responses will vary. The following are given as examples.

Task A
The lecture concerns a psychological condition—a kind of depression—that's called Seasonal Affective Disorder. It's usually called SAD. This condition has only been known in recent years. It starts in autumn and gets worse in winter. In the spring, it is gone. Possibly less light affects chemicals in the brain, but exactly how it is caused isn't known. The symptoms also include fatigue, weight gain, and so on. More women than men have this condition, and it usually appears when people are in their twenties.

It's easy to treat SAD. People who have it just sit in front of a bright light for a half hour in the morning and a half hour in the evening. This light substitutes for the sun. A trip to some place sunny also cures it.

Task B

This lecture is about an experiment that students will do. It is called fractional distillation. It's used to separate two liquids that have different boiling points. Students must heat alcohol and water together. The alcohol boils at 78°C and the water at 100°. So, the alcohol becomes a gas. It goes up a column and into a condenser. There is cool water running around the condenser that cools the gas and it becomes liquid again. Pretty soon, all the liquid in the first container is water and all the liquid in the second is alcohol. Fractional distillation is very important. It is the same process used to distill petroleum.

Task C

This talk is about the first National Automobile Show, which was in New York City in 1900. Forty car companies were there, and 8,000 people. They were dressed up for a formal social occasion. Even the U.S. president was there—he was the first president to ride in a car. The auto was invented in Germany about twenty years before, but the selling of cars was pioneered in the U.S. The cars were handmade, almost, and were undependable—they were like toys for rich people. Steam cars weren't popular because they might blow up. Gas cars were smelly and loud. People liked electric cars, however, because they were safe and quiet.

The number of companies coming to the National Auto Show went up in the next years. They learned from each other at these shows. Maybe because of the first car show, the United States caught up with the leading car-making country, France, in 1904.

Task D

The lecturer talks about the Infinite Monkey Theorem. This theorem says that if you have an infinite number of monkeys working at typewriters or computers, one of them will eventually write a perfect copy of Shakespeare's play *Hamlet*. This is a famous theory and is used in many fields and it is talked about in poems, books, television shows, and so on.

Sometimes this theorem is used to talk about unlikely events, such as a poor student getting a good grade on a test. But mostly it is used to make people think about concepts such as really big numbers, coincidence, infinity, and so on.

How unlikely is a monkey to type *Hamlet?* A typewriter has 50 keys, so the odds of typing the first letter is one in 50. The odds of typing the first two letters is one in 2,500. The odds of typing the third are one in 125,000. How about the first page? If you have 10 billion planets, and each planet has 10 billion monkeys, it would take 10 billion years just to type the first page. The odds of a monkey typing the whole play are not really comprehensible.

Speaking Review Test

1. Answers will vary. A successful answer should name the event that the speaker thinks is most important and include a brief description of it. The response should explain why the speaker thinks this event is important.
2. Answers will vary. The speaker should begin by stating whether he or she would prefer a trip to the past or the future. If the speaker wants to travel to the past, he or she should explain why and what he/she would like to see or do in the past. If the speaker wants to travel to the future, he/she should explain why and what future action he/she hopes to see.
3. Answers will vary, but should include the following: The response should begin by giving the topic of the announcement (Professor Weng, a microbiology teacher has won an academic award.) The response should then give the woman's opinion. (She is happy that Professor Weng won the prize because she thinks Professor Weng is a good teacher and is doing important research.) The response should also mention that the man is disappointed because he wanted Professor Pottinger to win the award again. He says Professor Pottinger is a great lecturer and an "institution at Colton College." The woman points out that Professor Pottinger has won the award before and that he is retiring, so time off for research is not such a critical issue for him.
4. Answers will vary. The speaker should first give the topic of the reading *(film noir)* and then summarize the reading: *film noir* is a dark, gloomy type of film made in the 1940's and 1950's. These movies are shot in black-and-white and feature a lonely, cynical male character and a *femme fatale*. The speaker should then summarize the lecture: The class will see two examples of *film noir*. One is the 1941 movie *The Maltese Falcon*. This is a typical *film noir* with a tough, cynical male character. The emphasis is on the gloomy atmosphere. The other movie is *Chinatown*. It is not typical of *film noir* because it was not made in the 40's or 50's, and it is in color. However, it has a cynical male character and a gloomy atmosphere, so it is also considered part of the *film noir* genre.
5. Answers will vary, but a good response should include the following: The speaker should first describe Michelle's problem (she needs help designing a Web page for the museum where she works). The response should then discuss the two solutions that the man proposes. He first suggests that she find an Internet site that teaches the basics of Web site design. She says that she would rather work with a person, so he suggests she put a notice on the bulletin board in the computer science department asking for help. The speaker must then decide which of these solutions is best and explain why. Since the woman says that she wants to work person-to-person, it would probably be easier to defend the second solution.
6. Answers will vary. The speaker should begin by giving the topic of the lecture (economic externalities) and give a brief definition of the term (something that happens during production that affects a person or organization but is not reflected in the price). The speaker should mention that an externality can be negative and give an example (pollution) or that it can be positive and give an example (the pollination of crops by bees). Finally, the speaker should mention that some economists think that the government should correct externalities by taxing or regulating negative externalities and awarding positive externalities with subsidies. However, it is very hard to calculate the cost of externalities.

Speaking Tutorial: Building Pronunciation Skills

Exercise 1: Number of Syllables

1. ba sic 2
2. home 1
3. Bra zil 2
4. de cide 2
5. de ci ded 3
6. un der stand 3
7. au tho ri ty 4
8. Ko re a 3
9. pre si dent 3
10. in for ma tion 4

Exercise 2: Syllable Stress

1. lec ture
2. prob lem
3. dis cuss
4. so lu tion
5. pos si bi li ty
6. im por tant
7. com pare
8. si tu a tion

Exercise 3: Stress in Academic Vocabulary

1. <u>mi</u> nor   mi <u>nor</u> i ty
2. <u>val</u> id   val <u>id</u> i ty
3. <u>sta</u> ble   sta <u>bil</u> i ty
4. <u>strat</u> e gy   stra <u>te</u> gic
5. phi <u>los</u> o phy   phi lo <u>soph</u> i cal
6. e <u>con</u> o my   ec o <u>nom</u> ic
7. dis <u>trib</u> ute   dis trib <u>u</u> tion
8. ap <u>ply</u>   ap pli <u>ca</u> tion

Exercise 4: Find the Stressed Syllable

Verbs	Compound *Nouns*	*Nouns*	*Nouns*	*Verbs*
de <u>fine</u>	<u>air</u> port	<u>cred</u> it	<u>pro</u> duce	pro <u>duce</u>
ob <u>tain</u>	<u>soft</u> ware	<u>out</u> come	<u>pro</u> gress	pro <u>gress</u>
pre <u>fer</u>	<u>math</u> test	<u>con</u> cept	<u>con</u> duct	con <u>duct</u>
se <u>lect</u>	<u>health</u> care	<u>of</u> fice	<u>in</u> sult	in <u>sult</u>
com <u>pare</u>	<u>stock</u> mar ket	<u>fac</u> tor	<u>re</u> cord	re <u>cord</u>
as <u>sume</u>	<u>su</u> per mar ket	<u>in</u> put	<u>pre</u> sent	pre <u>sent</u>

Exercise 5: Identify the Stress

se <u>cure</u>	se <u>cur</u> i ty	<u>class</u> ic	<u>class</u> i cal
<u>le</u> gal	le <u>gal</u> i ty	dem <u>oc</u> rac y	dem o <u>crat</u> ic
di <u>verse</u>	di <u>vers</u> i ty	<u>his</u> to ry	his <u>tor</u> ic
e <u>lec</u> tric	e lec <u>tric</u> i ty	ge <u>ol</u> o gy	ge o <u>log</u> i cal
<u>per</u> son al	per son <u>al</u> i ty	pho <u>to</u> gra phy	pho to <u>graph</u> ic
<u>no</u> ti fy	no ti fi <u>ca</u> tion	<u>four</u> <u>teen</u>	<u>for</u> ty
<u>gra</u> du ate	gra du <u>a</u> tion	<u>eigh</u> <u>teen</u>	<u>eigh</u> ty
de <u>fine</u>	de fi <u>ni</u> tion	<u>nine</u> <u>teen</u>	<u>nine</u> ty
<u>re</u> gis ter	reg is <u>tra</u> tion	<u>se</u> ven <u>teen</u>	<u>se</u> ven ty
con <u>gra</u> tu late	con gra tu <u>la</u> tion	<u>fif</u> <u>teen</u>	<u>fif</u> ty

Exercise 6: Producing Word Stress in Context

Well, *edu<u>ca</u>tion* is important to my family and me so . . . I guess . . . the most important day in my life . . . was my *gradu<u>a</u>tion* from Seoul *National University*. I'd always dreamed . . . uh . . . of becoming a *medical* doctor and my degree in *bi<u>ol</u>ogy* was my first step toward that . . . that goal. On my *gradu<u>a</u>tion*, it was a hot day and the *hu<u>mid</u>ity* was high but nobody seemed to . . . notice. Everybody was so excited that they paid no *at<u>ten</u>tion* to the weather . . . even though it took hours to call everyone's name. When the ceremony was over, my family and friends from my *com<u>mun</u>ity* . . . we all went to a restaurant for a *cele<u>bra</u>tion*.

Exercise 7: Listening to Word Stress in a Lecture

<u>mar</u>ble   meta<u>mor</u>phic   <u>lime</u>stone   sedi<u>men</u>tary

Exercise 8: Identifying Stressed and Unstressed Words

1. The <u>problem</u> is her <u>neighbors</u> are <u>noisy</u>.
2. Par<u>ticipants</u> can earn <u>credit</u> and also make <u>money</u>. (Some speakers may stress *earn* and *make*, but that may create too many stresses in this sentence. It really depends on the speaker, how quickly she or he is speaking, and the formality of the situation.)
3. I'd pre<u>fer</u> to <u>work</u> for a <u>company</u>.
4. The an<u>nouncement</u> is about regulations for <u>park</u>ing at the uni<u>ver</u>sity.
5. Her <u>choices</u> are to <u>talk</u> to her <u>neighbors</u> or to <u>move</u>.

Exercise 9: Matching English Rhythm

<u>Stan's</u> trying to make a de<u>cision</u> about <u>college</u> . . . about <u>where</u> to at<u>tend</u> his <u>last</u> se<u>mes</u>ter of college. The <u>problem</u> is . . . that . . . well, his <u>major</u> is <u>classical</u> languages . . . and his uni<u>ver</u>sity is going to <u>close</u> that department at the <u>end</u> of the <u>term</u>.

Exercise 10: English Rhythm in Context

Answers will vary. However, some of the content words that you might have stressed in your response are the following:

ex <u>haus</u> ted   <u>tired</u>   <u>never</u>   <u>sleep</u>   <u>hard</u>
em <u>barr</u> ass ing   <u>bor</u> ing

Exercise 11: Reduced Forms

1. of   7. got to
2. and   8. going to
3. have   9. want to
4. have   10. couple of
5. or   11. ought to
6. have to

Exercise 12: Can or Can't?

1. can't   5. can
2. can't   6. can't
3. can   7. can
4. can't   8. can

Exercise 13: Predicting Thought Groups

Note: Position of pauses may vary.

1. To describe marble,/ first you have to define metamorphic rock./ Metamorphic rock/ is rock that's uh, changed,/ from one kind of rock / to another./ Ummm, marble comes from a softer rock/ that's called limestone,/ which is a sedimentary rock. / Marble is a hard rock. / Marble comes in various colors. / Like other metamorphic rocks, it is so strong / that it is often used for building.
2. Supermarkets have been successful / for two main reasons. The first reason / is that costs are low. / One reason the costs are low / is . . . uh, that supermarkets buy / in huge quantities. / This is called / . . . uh, let's see . . . / economy of scale.

Exercise 14: Listening for Thought Groups

Note: Position of pauses may vary.

She wants to take part ↗
in the experiment. ↘
One reason is ↗
that she can make some extra money. ↘
Another reason is ↗
that she has lots of problems ↗
going to sleep at night. ↘

His sister ↗
got a position as an intern ↗
at an advertising agency ↘
The pay was pretty good, ↗
and besides, ↗
it was good experience for her. ↘
It looks good ↗
on her résumé. ↘

There was a numeral system ↗
that was used by the Yuki Indians ↗
of California ↗
that was base 8. ↘
The Yukis ↗
counted the spaces between their fingers ↗
rather than their fingers themselves. ↘

The announcement is about plagiarism. ↘
What is plagiarism? ↗
According to the announcement, ↗
it is using someone else's words or ideas ↗
as your own ↗
without crediting the other person. ↘

Exercise 15: Listening for the Focus Words
Choice of focus words may differ.

She <u>wants</u> to take part ↗
in the ex<u>per</u>iment. ↘
<u>One</u> reason is ↗
that she can make some extra <u>mon</u>ey. ↘
An<u>oth</u>er reason is ↗
that she has lots of <u>prob</u>lems ↗
going to <u>sleep</u> at night. ↘

His <u>sis</u>ter ↗
got a position as an <u>in</u>tern ↗
at an <u>ad</u>vertising agency. ↘
The <u>pay</u> was pretty good, ↗
and be<u>sides</u>, ↗
it was good ex<u>per</u>ience for her. ↘
It looks <u>good</u> ↗
on her <u>ré</u>sumé. ↘

There was a <u>nu</u>meral system ↗
that was <u>used</u> by the <u>Yu</u>ki Indians ↗
of Cali<u>for</u>nia ↗
that was base <u>8.</u> ↘
The <u>Yu</u>kis ↗
counted the <u>spaces </u>be<u>tween</u> their fingers ↗
rather than their fingers them<u>selves</u>. ↘

The announcement is about <u>pla</u>giarism. ↘
What is <u>pla</u>giarism? ↗
According to the an<u>nounce</u>ment, ↗
it is using someone <u>else's</u> words or ideas ↗
as your <u>own</u> ↗
without <u>cred</u>iting the other person. ↘

Exercise 16: Finding the Focus
My <u>sis</u>ter—
my <u>old</u>er sister—
got a job with an <u>ad</u> agency.
It was a <u>New York</u> ad agency.

He got in trouble for <u>pla</u>giarism.
Well, it wasn't *exactly* plagiarism.
At least, <u>he</u> didn't consider it plagiarism.

The nest of the <u>ham</u>erkop
has at least three <u>rooms</u>.
The <u>high</u>est room
is the <u>sleep</u>ing room
where the female lays her <u>eggs</u>.
When the babies grow <u>up</u>
they move to the <u>mid</u>dle room.

Exercise 17: Putting Thought Groups, Intonation, and Focus Together
Note: Thought groups may be divided up in different ways.
I think I'd prefer living in a <u>dorm</u> ↗ / to living in an a<u>part</u>-
ment ↘. / It's <u>true</u> ↗ / that many apartments are <u>roo</u>my ↗, /
and most <u>dorm</u> rooms ↗ / are kind of <u>cramped</u> ↘, / but there
are <u>oth</u>er reasons why dorm rooms are better ↘. / The <u>first</u> ↗
/ is transpor<u>ta</u>tion ↗. / If I lived off-<u>cam</u>pus ↗, / I'd have to
<u>drive</u> ↗ / and owning a <u>car</u> is ex<u>pen</u>sive. ↘ / So is <u>park</u>ing. ↘.
/ I have heard it can <u>cost</u> ↗ / $100 a se<u>mes</u>ter ↘. / An<u>oth</u>er
reason living in a dorm is better ↗ / is that it is easier to make
<u>friends</u> ↘. / In a<u>part</u>ment buildings, ↗ / people may say he<u>llo</u>
↗ / but they aren't very <u>friend</u>ly ↘. / In <u>dorms</u> ↗ / people

stop and <u>talk</u> ↗ / and are much more <u>so</u>ciable ↘. / Finally, ↗
/ what about <u>meals</u>? ↗ / If I lived in an a<u>part</u>ment ↗, / I'd
have to <u>cook</u> ↘. / On the other hand, ↗ / in a <u>dorm</u> ↗ / meals
are provided ↘. / And that's a re<u>lief</u> ↗, / because <u>frank</u>ly, ↗ /
I'm a <u>ter</u>rible cook ↘. /

Exercise 18: Thought Groups, Intonation, and Focus in Context
Answers will vary.

Exercise 19: Added Sound or Added Syllable?

		Added Sound	Added Syllable
1. add	added		✓
2. park	parked	✓	
3. plan	planned	✓	
4. wait	waited		✓
5. intend	intended		✓
6. apply	applied	✓	
7. decide	decided		✓
8. believe	believed	✓	

Exercise 20: Listening to Present and Past Tense
1. A
2. B   **4.** B   **6.** B
3. A   **5.** B

(Number 2 was probably the most difficult to distinguish. The
/d/ in *believed* links to /ə/ in *the*, and /d/ in *carried* links to
and blends with /s/ in *snakes*.)

Exercise 21: Pronouncing the Past Tense in Context
Answers will vary.

Exercise 22: Saying the –s Ending

	Add Sounds	Add Syllable
1. takes	✓	
2. causes		✓
3. credits	✓	
4. expresses		✓
5. dislikes	✓	
6. explains	✓	
7. fixes		✓
8. thinks	✓	
9. Nancy's	✓	
10. discusses		✓
11. reasons	✓	
12. changes		✓
13. gives	✓	

Exercise 23: Listening to –s Endings in Context
The two <u>students</u> are discussing <u>preferences</u> in housing. They
both <u>prefer</u> living in a <u>dorm</u> to living in an <u>apartment</u>. They
<u>agree</u> that many <u>apartments</u> are roomy, and most dorm
<u>rooms</u> are kind of cramped, but they <u>give</u> some uh, good
<u>reasons</u> why they <u>think</u> that dorm <u>rooms</u> are better. The first
<u>one</u> is that it is easier to make <u>friends</u>. People are more
sociable. Also, a dorm usually <u>provides</u> meals. This is good,
because they are both awful <u>cooks</u>.

Exercise 24: Identifying Voiced and Voiceless Consonants

1. cheering	**7.** fans
2. vast	**8.** bear
3. pat	**9.** girls
4. mob	**10.** dent
5. buzz	**11.** prize
6. tense	**12.** bridges

Exercise 25: /p/ as in <u>p</u>ast vs. /f/ as in <u>f</u>ast
A. 1. peel-peel S 2. copy-coffee D 3. pin-fin D
4. fact-fact S
B. 1. fact 5. feels fine
2. pace 6. pile
3. past 7. fad
4. copy 8. fears

Exercise 26: /ʃ/ as in wa<u>sh</u> vs. /tʃ/ as in wa<u>tch</u>
A. 1. shop-chop D 2. shoes-choose D
3. wish-wish S 4. much-much S
B. 1. shopping 6. chip
2. wash 7. leashes
3. catch 8. shin
4. chose 9. much room
5. share 10. witches

Exercise 27: /v/ as in <u>v</u>erse vs. /w/ as in <u>w</u>orse
A. 1. worse-worse S 2. vial-vial S 3. vest-west D
4. very-wary D
B. 1. vine 4. west
2. verse 5. Vinnie
3. in a while

Exercise 28: /l/ as in <u>l</u>ight vs. /r/ as in <u>r</u>ight
A. 1. late-late S 2. rate-rate S 3. long-wrong D
4. collect-correct D
B. 1. correcting 5. rooms
2. right/wrong 6. clock
3. locks 7. free
4. clouds 8. fry

Exercise 29: /ө/ as in <u>th</u>in vs. /s/ in sin, /f/ in fin, and /t/ in tin
A. 1. think-sink D 2. math-math S 3. tree-tree S
4. both–boat D 5. thought-thought S
B. 1. sink 6. thanks
2. fought 7. boot
3. pass 8. team
4. three 9. thick
5. math 10. free

Exercise 30: /iʸ/ as in h<u>ea</u>t vs. /ɪ/ as in h<u>i</u>t
A. 1. seen-seen S 2. leave-live D 3. still-still S
4. feel-fill D
B. 1. chip 4. heaters
2. fill 5. ship
3. leave

Exercise 31: /eʸ/ as in l<u>a</u>te vs. /ɛ/ as in l<u>e</u>t
A. 1. wait-wet D 2. late-let D 3. men-men S
4. date-debt D
B. 1. debts 4. taste test
2. pepper 5. lace
3. pen

Section 4: Guide to Writing

The Integrated Writing Task

Exercise: Scoring the Response

Response 1 Score: _3_
In this response, the writer mentions some—but not all—of the main ideas from the reading and from the lecture. The first paragraph presents a fairly clear introduction to the topic. In the second paragraph, the writer summarizes several of the main points of the article (although there is at least one factual error: The article does not say that essay tests are easier to grade). The third paragraph attempts to summarize the main points of the lecture, but the summary is not very clear.

There is no successful attempt to integrate ideas from the passage and the lecture There are quite a few grammatical errors, and sometimes these make it difficult to understand the writer's ideas.

Response 2 Score: _2_
Comments: This response is too short to completely cover the topic. The writer tries to give a few ideas from the reading but says little or nothing about the ideas in the lecture. There is no "citation" of ideas (such as "The author says …", "The lecturer mentions …"). There are frequent errors of grammar, spelling (*assay* for *essay*, for example), and mechanics.

Response 3 Score: _3_
The writer mentions some of the ideas from both the lecture and the reading and attempts to contrast the two. In the opening paragraph, the writer says that the lecturer agrees with the article about essay tests but disagrees with the article about the use of objective tests. This shows that the writer understands the main ideas of the lecture and the relationship between the lecture and the article. In the second paragraph, the writer clearly explains the lecturer's position on objective tests (that they can be useful.)

In the third paragraph, the writer tries to paraphrase the lecturer's idea that some students with good writing skills can write good essays about topics that they don't know much about. However, this paraphrase is not very clear. In the fourth paragraph, the writer makes a factual mistake. He says that the lecturer believes "that essay tests should be done at the same time." In fact, the lecturer says that essay tests should be *graded* by the teacher at the same time in order to be fair.

There are some language problems in the essay, but these do not generally interfere with a reader's comprehension.

Integrated Writing Preview Test
Responses for this task will vary, but should include most of the following information:

The main topic of both the talk and the passage is research performed on animals. The author of the reading passage supports it because it reduces human suffering, while the speaker finds it unethical and opposes it.

The author says that it is possible to experiment on animals without being cruel, and that researchers should always make an effort to be humane to animals, using anesthesia and keeping them in clean conditions. The lecturer claims that, in reality, animals are not treated well in research laboratories. They are not adequately anesthetized, and they are sometimes abused.

According to the author, because animals such as chimpanzees are genetically close to humans, there are no real substitutes for animal testing. The lecturer denies this, saying that today there are many ways to avoid animal testing. These include the use of human tissue samples and computer simulations.

The author says that animal testing has been useful again and again throughout history. Some important discoveries, such as Pasteur's germ theory and the invention of penicillin, occurred because of testing on animals. The lecturer says that many of the drugs that were discovered using animal testing may have been discovered by other means. She also says that some drugs might not have been developed at all if they had first been tested on animals. For example, if the drug morphine, which kills pain in humans, had first been tested on cats, it might not have been developed because it stimulates cats.

The author concludes by saying that it is not moral to put the lives of humans in danger when non-humans can be used. On the other hand, the lecturer believes that animals cannot give their consent to be experimented upon, so experimentation on animals is unethical.

Lesson 21: Taking Notes and Planning the Integrated Response

Exercise 21.1

Notes will vary. The following are given as samples.

Task 2

<u>Passage Notes</u>

Sci Fi is FICTION: intel. life only on Earth?

    1,000's of stars, but most stars very different from ours too hot, too big, etc.

    & even stars w/ planets unlikely to have planets w/ conditions like Earth

    maybe too close to star, too far away. etc. unlikely to have just enough H_2O, right atmos., etc.

     even if life, is it intel. life?

     if other intel. life, why not heard from?

        No response to TV/radio signals

<u>Lecture Notes</u>

  Humans like fish in little lake: not think other lakes or fish in world

  400 billions stars in galx if 1 in 1,000 has planets that support life, then there are 400 million of them

Life devel'd on Earth in unfavorable places

  Intelligent life? Carl Sagan, "smart is better" theory intel. helps species survive

    If 1 in a 1,000 worlds w/ life have intel life, then there are 400,000 intel species in our galx

  Why not heard from? Maybe not have same interests, techno.

Humans self-centered if not admit possibil of intel life—like those fish in lake

Task 3

<u>Passage Notes</u>

Gen Australian elect of '22: only 59% of Aus citizens voted

  '24: law make voting in Aus mandatory

  Today 94% of Aus. vote, tho penalties not severe

  Also mandatory: Belg Argent. Greece, etc

     (20% of all democs)

  In countries w/out mandatory voting (e.g., US, UK) only abt 60% vote (≈ Aus in '22)

Why mandatory?

     Thom. Jefferson: gov't gets author. from consent of goverened . . .

     If not vote, not give active consent

    Mandat. voting ? mandatory taxation: gov't depends on taxes

                gov't depend on votes

<u>Lecture Notes</u>

Voter turn-out low in US, UK → discus. of mandat. voting

  True, voting high in Aus, but better to have people who vote well than big turn-out

     If voting not mandatory, those who DO vote are well motivated, well informed

  NOT like taxes: if few people pay taxes, gov't can't operate

     if few people vote, no real effect

If not vote, not give consent BUT are exercising freedm to NOT vote

      perhaps not agree w/ any candid.

      perhaps feel polit process not offer anything

Because you have right to do something doesn't mean you have oblig (e.g. open own business)

Task 4

<u>Passage Notes</u>

11,000 yrs ago, end of Ice Age, conditions good for mammoths plentiful food, strong herds, favorable climate BUT in short time all extinct Why?

3 theories:

  1. "man vs. mammoth" (Paul Martin) Clovis people hunted them to extinction w/dogs, shrp spears

  2. Climate: cold, damp, unchanging climate changed to warm, dry climate → deserts

     no food for mammoths

  3. Disease: brght by humans from Old World maybe by lice, fleas?

     mammoths had no resistance (Ross McPhee)

<u>Lecture Notes</u>

Probs. w/ all 3 theories

1. Mammoths were big, strong, had tusks thick skin & fat hard to kill

  Why wld humans hunt mammoths when smaller anim. around?

  Clovis people few in #, scattered cld only have eaten 10% of mammoths they killed

2. NO sign of infect. in mammoth remains

3. Mammoths endured more severe climate changes, why did this climate change kill them all? And Afric, Ind. elephants survived

Maybe 1 theory right . . . maybe combin. of factors . . . but maybe unknown cause

Task 5

<u>Passage Notes</u>

In '65, Pres. Johnson: "Art precious heritage . . . thru art, reveal to ourselves & others inner vision which guides us as nation."

But . . . more and more diff. for artists to support selves esp. experiment. artists

  In Eur. gov't support for art In U.S. priv + gov't support

However, gov't support stable or drop

In past, great artist supported by patrons

    e.g., da Vinci Tchaikovsky

Today few pple contrib to indiv artists but artists need $ takes time to make art Need gov't grants

Good invest

  Study by Ga. Intitu of Tech: $3 billion invested in art → $134 bil. econ reven

                $24 bil. taxes

<u>Lecture Notes</u>

Spkr an artist himself but NOT agree w/ gov't support of indiv artists

Compare to plumbers; plumbers useful, but no gov't support for plumbers, e.g.

  Not fair to treat plumbers, artists different

  Great artists before gov't grants sold art on mrktplace

  Wht abt unpop artists?

    Produce what want. if can't sell, can get jobs e.g., commerc. artists

             art teachrs

    In past, artists had PRIVATE sponsors, not gov't

  Spkr objts to giving pub $ to one spec grp

  Some artists have corp sponsors; spkr wld not take corp $, but doesn't object to that

Spending $ on arts organizations like ballet may be good invest., but not on indiv. artists

  Some programs to help artists waste $

    e.g., program in Fr: spec. insur. to help artists

everyone connected w/ arts applied, even pple who cut actors' hair

        program had $1 billion euro deficit

    Invstmnts in arts NOT always good

Task 6

Passage Notes

2005 Study: neg. effects of TV outweigh pos. effects

rschrs analyzed stand. test results & TV habits of 1700 chldrn

   childrn 6-7 who watched 3+ hrs of TV/day score sig lower on rdg,

      shrt- term mem. tests

  Another study: chldrn spend more time watching TV doing anything but sleeping

    > time watching TV than in school!

     Replace activ. parents value more: e.g., studying, rdg, sports

    Chldrn watching TV inactive, eat snacks ads for inapprop foods → overwght

Studies show what physch'ists already know: TV harmful, shld be lmtd or elim. from chldrn's lives

Lecture Notes

Spkr not fan of TV, esp. commerc. TV BUT . . . not agree with article . . . or auth's asses. of study

  Difficult to ban TV for kids . . . just go neighbors' hse

Spkr: study mentioned in article says kids 6-7 get lower test scores if watch 3+ hrs/day BUT kids 3-5 who aver 3+ hrs/day score HIGHER on rdg recog. tests than kids who don't

Important to limt time: For All kids for chldrn >2, NO TV

          children 2+, 2hrs. a day (leaves time for play and study)

      Younger kids, edu. TV, little entertainment TV

        Public TV: no commercials

Physical fitness a prob, but not all TV's fault:

  If limit to >2 hrs daily, time for physic. activites

  Teach kids abt nutrition

TV not purely good, purely bad

Exercise 21.2

Notes will vary. The following are given as examples.

Outline for Task 2

Main topic:

Is there intel. life on other planets?

Main idea of the passage:

Sci Fi about UFO's coming Earth, or Earth astron. encountering aliens, but these stories are FICTION: universe a lonely place

Main idea of the lecture:

 Humans like fish in little lake: not think other lakes or fish in world

Key Point 1 + supporting information from the passage:

 1,000's of stars, but most stars very diff. from ours too hot, too big, etc.

Key Point 1+ supporting information from the lecture:

 400 billion stars in galx if 1 in a 1,000 has planets that support life, then 400 million of them

Key Point 2 + supporting information from the passage:

    even if life, is it intell. life?

Key Point 2 + supporting information from the lecture:

 If 1 in a 1,000 worlds w/ life have intel life, then there are 400,000 intel species in our galx

  Life on earth devel'd in unfvorable palces

Carl Sagan, "smart is better" theory intel. helps species survive

Key Point 3+ supporting information from the passage:

    If other intel life, why not heard from?

    broadcast radio/TV into space many yrs—why no response?

Key Point 3 + supporting information from the lecture:

 Maybe other forms of life not same interests, techno.

Conclusion (if any)

    Passage:

No one in space to listen.

    Lecture:

Humans self-centered: we ARE like those fish who don't realize there are other lakes & other fish.

Outline for Task 3

Main topic:

Mandatory voting

Main idea of the passage:

Mandatory voting a good thing

Main idea of the lecture:

Voter turn-out low in US, UK → discus. of mandat. voting

But people should not be required to vote.

Key Point 1 + supporting information from the passage:

Gen Australian elect of '22: only 59% of Aus citizens voted

   '24: law made voting in Aus mandat.

   Today 94% of Aus. vote, tho penalties not severe

Also mandatory: Belg   Argent. Greece, etc

      (20% of all democs)

In countries w/out mandat voting (eg, US, UK) only abt 60% vote (≈ Aus in '22)

Key Point 1 + supporting information from the lecture:

 True, voting high in Aus, but better to have people who vote well than big turn-out

      If voting not mandat those who DO vote are well motiv'd, well informed

Key Point 2 + supporting information from the passage:

    Why mandat?

    Thom. Jeffferson: gov't gets author. from consent of goverened

    If not vote, not give active consent

Key Point 2 + supporting information from the lecture:

If not vote, not give consent BUT are exercising freedm NOT to vote

Key Point 3 + supporting information from the passage:

   Mandat. voting ≈ mandatory taxation: gov't depends on taxes

               gov't depend on votes

Key Point 3 + supporting information from the lecture:

 NOT like taxes: if few people pay taxes, gov't can't operate

          if few people vote, no real effect

Conclusion (if any)

    Passage: No conclusion.

    Lecture:

Because you have right to do something doesn't mean have oblig (eg. open own business)

Outline for Task 4

Main topic:

Reasons for extinct. of mammoths

Main idea of the passage:

  At end of Ice Age, conditions good for mammoths

     plentiful food, strong herds, favorable climate BUT

     in short time all extinct Why? 3 poss. reasons

Main idea of the lecture:

Probs with all 3 theories.

Key Point 1 + supporting information from the passage:

   1. "man vs. mammoth" (Paul Martin) Clovis people hunted them to extinction w/dogs, shrp spears

Key Point 1 + supporting information from the lecture:
Mammoths were big, strong, had tusks thick skin & fat   hard to kill

Why wld humans hunt mammoths when smaller anim. around?
Clovis people few in #, scattered   cld only have eaten 10% of mammoths they supposedly killed

Key Point 2 + supporting information from the passage:
Climate: cold, damp, unchanging changed to warm, dry climate → deserts
no food for mammoths

Key Point 2 + supporting information from the lecture:
Mammoths endured more severe climate changes, why did this climate change kill them all? And Afric, Ind. elephants survived

Key Point 3 + supporting information from the passage:
Disease: brght by humans from Old World maybe by lice, fleas? (Ross McPhee)
mammoths had no resistance

Key Point 3 + supporting information from the lecture:
NO sign of infect. in mammoth remains

Conclusion (if any)
Passage: No conclusion.
Lecture:
Maybe 1 theory right . . . maybe combin. of factors . . . but maybe unknown cause

Outline for Task 5
Main topic:
Gov't support for artists
Main idea of the passage:
In '65, Pres. Johnson: "Art precious heritage . . . thru art, reveal to ourselves & others inner vision which guides us as nation."
Main idea of the lecture:
Spkr an artist himself but NOT agree w/ gov't support for indiv artists
Key Point 1+ supporting information from the passage:
But . . . more and more diffic. for artists to support selves   esp experiment. artists
In Eur. gov't support for art   In U.S. priv + gov't support
However, gov't support stable or drop in U.S.
Key Point 1 + supporting information from the lecture:
Compare to plumbers; plumbers useful, but no gov't support for plumbers, e.g.
Not fair to treat plumbers, artists different
Great U.S. artists before gov't grants   sold art on mrktplace
Key Point 2 + supporting information from the passage:
In past, great artists supported by patrons
e.g., da Vinci Tchaikovsky
Today few pple contrib to indiv artists but artists need $ takes time to make art   Need gov't grants
Key Point 2 + supporting information from the lecture:
In past, artists had PRIVATE sponsors, not gov't
Spkr objts to giving pub $ to one spec grp
Some artists have corp sponsors; spkr wld not, accept but doesn't object to that
Key Point 3 + supporting information from the passage:
Good invest
Study by Ga. Intitu of Tech: $3 billion invested in art → $134 bil econ reven $24 bil taxes
Key Point 3 + supporting information from the lecture:
Spending $ on arts organiz's such as ballet companies may be good invest., but not $ spent on indiv. artists
Some programs to help artists waste $

e.g., program in France: spec. insurance to help artists
everyone connected with arts appled, even pple who cut actors' hair
program had $1 billion euro deficit
Invstmnts in arts NOT always good

Conclusion (if any)
Passage: No conclusion.
Lecture: No conclusion.

Outline for Task 6
Main topic:
Does TV have neg or pos effect on chldrn?
Main idea of the passage:
2005 Study, neg effects of TV outweigh pos. effects
Main idea of the lecture:
Spkr not fan of TV, esp. commerc. TV BUT . . . not agree with article or auth's asses. of study . . .
Difficult to ban TV for kids . . . just go to neighbors' hses
Key Point 1 + supporting information from the passage:
Rschrs analyzed stand. test results & TV habits of 1700 chldrn
childrn 6–7 who watched 3+ hrs of TV/day score sig lower on rdg, & shrt- term mem tests
Key Point 1 + supporting information from the lecture:
Spkr: study mentioned in article says kids 6–7 get lower test scores BUT kids 3–5 who watch a lot of TV scored HIGHER on rdg tests than kids who didn't
Key Point 2 + supporting information from the passage:
Another study: chldrn spend more time watching TV than doing anything but sleeping
> time watching TV than in school!
Replace activ. parents value more: e.g., studying, rdg, sports
Key Point 2 + supporting information from the lecture:
Important to limit time: For All kids   or chldrn >2, NO TV
childrn 2+, 2hrs. a day (leaves time for play and study)
Younger kids, edu. TV, little entertainment TV
Public TV: no commercials
Key Point 3 + supporting information from the passage:
Chldrn watching TV inactive, eat snacks ads for inapprop foods
→ overwght
Key Point 3 + supporting information from the lecture:
Physical fitness a prob, but not all TV's fault: If limit to >2 hrs daily, time for physic. activities   Teach kids abt nutrition
Conclusion (if any)
Passage:
Studies show what physch'ists already know: TV harmful, shld be lmtd or elimin from chldrn's lives
Lecture:
TV not pure good or evil: depends on how used

Lesson 22: Summarizing, Paraphrasing, Citing, and Synthesizing for the Integrated Writing Response

Exercise 22.1
Notes and summaries/paraphrases will vary. The following are given as examples.

Task 2
<u>Notes on the Passage</u>
common systems: parlia. & presid.
Parlia: power concent. in elect assembly

no separ. exec
    P.M. member of parlia & must meet w/ assemb. regularly

Summary/Paraphrase of the Passage

The parliamentary system and the presidential system are two systems of governing democracies. In the parliamentary system, the elected assembly (the parliament) has most of the power. There is no separate executive branch. The prime minister and the other ministers—the cabinet, in other words—are members of the assembly, and must often meet with parliament.

Notes on the Lecture

    Presid. sys. (US) vs. parlia sys (UK)
        Presid. sys: strict separ. of powers
            exec, legis, judic—indep
            Chief exec = president & cabinet NOT part of
            assembly

Summary/Paraphrase of the Lecture

The presidential system is the one used in the United States, while the parliamentary system is used in the U.K. The head executive, called the president, and the president's cabinet are NOT part of the elected assembly. They are part of a separate branch of government.

Task 3

Notes on the Passage

Abt. 6,000 langs. spoken but many by increasingly small # people
Abt ½ endang'd
Cause: rise of Eng. as global lang
        Int'l entertain. e.g. movies, TV, music
        Technology, esp. IT   e.g. 75% of all websites
    Eng = "killer lang," forcing out smaller langs

Summary/Paraphrase of the Passage

Today, about 6,000 languages are spoken around the world. Many of these languages, however, are spoken by fewer and fewer people. Around 50% of all the world's languages are considered endangered. One main reason for this is that the global language English is killing off other languages. Increasingly, English is the language of entertainment, such as movies, television, and music. It is the language of technology, especially of computer technology. Around 75% of all Web sites on the Internet, for example, are in English. English is a "killer language" that is replacing smaller languages.

Notes on the Lecture

True that lang are disap.   Tragedy
    But . . . not fair to put all blame on Eng   also blame regional
    languages
        As a region lang, Eng has hurt lang in Brit Isles, N Amer, Aus,
        etc.
        But so have other regional lang
            1992 study: Hindi (NOT Eng) replace languages in
            India
                Hausa in W. Af
                Swahili in E Af   also Rus, Sp, Arab.
        ± 10 region. lang, not 1 glob lang, = "killer langs"

Summary/Paraphrase of the Lecture

It is true that languages are disappearing. This is indeed a tragedy. But it is not entirely the fault of English. English as a regional language has hurt smaller languages, but English is not the only regional language to have done so. A study done in 1992 indicated that in India, it was the regional language Hindi that replaced smaller languages, not English. Likewise, Hausa in West Africa and Swahili in East Africa have replaced local languages. Russian, Spanish, and Arabic have done the same. Therefore, it is ten or so regional languages—not one global language—that are killing off smaller languages.

Task 4

Notes on the Passage

Accord. environ'ists: need to ↓ depend on fossil fuel, ↑ use renew
energy.
    wind power a promising method   no air pollut, toxic or
    radioact. wastes
    BUT: can't claim no environ. damage   some wind farms
    harm birds
        Worst: California wind farm called Altamont Pass
        5,000 birds/yr   gold eagles, red-tailed hawks, etc.
        No more wind-farms until we can protect birds

Summary/Paraphrase of the Passage

In the opinion of most environmentalists, we must decrease our reliance on fossil fuels and increase our use of renewable energy. Wind energy is a good source of energy since it causes no pollution or dangerous wastes. However, this does not mean that wind farms are completely safe. Some of them kill birds. One example is the enormous wind farm at Altamont Pass, California. Here, over 5,000 birds a year die as a result of the spinning blades of the wind turbines. This includes some rare predatory birds such as golden eagles and red-tailed hawks. Until wind-generated power is safe for birds, no more wind farms should be constructed.

Notes on the Lecture

Article correct: wind power is danger at Altamont Pass   chosen
because constant wind
    Engin. didn't realize was a migration rt.
        BUT Altamont site an exception
    In Denmk, wind ener generates large % of power
        Danish study: wind farm killed only few birds a yr   less
        than aver housecat
            Shld make sure wind farms not in place that
            endangers birds
                Altamont site needs protection for birds or relo-
                cated
        NOT stop building wind farms: better than fos fuels, nuclear

Summary/Paraphrase of the Lecture

The author is correct in saying that the wind farm at Altamont Pass poses a danger to birds. This site was chosen because of the strong winds that blow through the pass, and engineers didn't know that they were building the wind farm on a migratory route. But Altamont Pass is very unusual. Other wind farms have not experienced the same problem with birds. In Denmark, where a great deal of energy is generated by wind, a study was done that showed only a few birds per year were killed by wind farms. This is fewer than the average housecat kills. The Altamont Pass wind farm needs to protect birds or to be relocated, but we should not stop building wind farms because the wind is such a clean, safe source of power. In fact, we should build more.

Task 5

Notes on the Passage

Ltrs to ed of campus paper: from astron'ers: upset because campus, streets too well lit
    difficult to see stars, do experimts
    However, profs of crimonolgy say good lighting stops crime—
    can't ↓ light if want to ↓ crime

Summary/Paraphrase of the Passage

In their letters to the editors of the campus paper, astronomers indicate that they are upset because the campus and the streets of the town are too well lit. This makes it difficult for them to see the stars and to perform their astronomical experiments. This is unfortunate for the astronomers, but according to professors of criminology, good lighting prevents crime. If we reduce the amount of light, we will have a higher crime rate.

<u>Notes on the Lecture</u>
Already said light pollut makes things difficult for astron'ers . . .
*   but . . . does light really ↓ crime? Some studies say yes, equal # say no*
*   Not ask for NO light but for SMART light:*
*   typical unshielded light send 20% light upwards*
*   20% outwards*
*   only 60 % down where needed*
*   By shielding lights, keep streets & campus well lit*
*   but everyone still see stars*

<u>Summary/Paraphrase of the Lecture</u>
The speaker has already said that light pollution makes things hard for astronomers, but is it true that more light on the streets actually prevents crime? Some studies say it does, but others say there is no effect. At any rate, the speaker and his colleagues do not want the campus and streets to be completely dark. They are only requesting SMART lighting. Today's streetlamps send 40% of their light where it is not needed, upwards and out to the sides. If lights are shielded, the streets and the campus can have plenty of light, but it will still be possible for astronomers and in fact for anyone to see the stars at night.

Task 6
<u>Notes on the Passage</u>
Until 50's Protoz consider simple anim.
Some resemble anim: move, eat plnts
Some also resemble plnts: can't move, contain chlorophyll

<u>Summary/Paraphrase of the Passage</u>
Scientists thought up until the 1950's that protozoa were simple forms of animal life. There are resemblances between some types of protozoa and animals. For example, they move about and they eat plants. But other types of protozoa are more similar to plants because they can't move and they contain chlorophyll.

<u>Notes on the Lecture</u>
Prob for biologists: large animals easy to classif as plnts or anim
*   Wht abt protoz?*
*   Since had to be either plnts or anim, were consid anim.*
Linnaean system: used 2-kngdm model, plnt & anim.
*   Protoz ≠ fish, horse, etc. but had to be something, ∴ anim*
*   Bacter ≠ oak trees "   "   "   "   "   "   ∴ plnts*
(Sq pegs, rnd holes)
*   in 50's: brilliant idea: change classif. system!*
1ˢᵗ 1 new kngdm, protoz was put in this
Then 5-kngdm model
Now, 3 domains, 8-15 kngdms
Conclu: If something is difficult to classify, look at classif system—maybe prob is there

<u>Summary/Paraphrase of the Lecture</u>
Protozoa and other microscopic forms of life are problematic for biologists. Unlike larger forms of life, they are hard to classify. At one time, protozoa were believed to be animals. That's in part because the Linnaean system, used to classify all forms of life, had only two kingdoms: animal and plant. Protozoa weren't much like familiar forms of animals, such as fish and horses, but since they had to be classified in one of two kingdoms, they were classified as animals. Bacteria, which were not much like familiar plants such as oak trees, also had to be something, so they were classified as plants. This was like fitting square pegs into round holes. In the 1950's, scientists had a wonderful idea. They decided to change the whole system of classification. At first, one new kingdom was added, and protozoa were put into this new kingdom. Later, there

was a system involving five kingdoms, and today there is a new system involving 3 domains and from 8 to 15 kingdoms. This all indicates that if something is difficult to classify, scientists should examine the system of classification.

Exercise 22.2
Students will cite and synthesize information in various ways. The following are given as examples.

Task 2
The author of the passage tells us that the parliamentary system and the presidential system are two systems of governing democracies. According to the author, in the parliamentary system, the elected assembly (the parliament) has most of the power. There is no separate executive branch. The author says that the prime minister and the other ministers—the cabinet, in other words—are members of the assembly, and must often meet with parliament. The lecturer tells us that the presidential system is the one used in the United States, while the parliamentary system is used in the U.K. She focuses on the presidential system. She says that the head executive, called the president, and the president's cabinet are NOT part of the elected assembly. They are part of a separate branch of government.

Task 3
The passage informs us that today, about 6,000 languages are spoken around the world. Many of these, however, are spoken by fewer and fewer people. Around 50% of all the world's languages are considered endangered. According to the author, one main reason for this is that the global language English is killing off other languages. Increasingly, English is the language of entertainment, such as movies, television, and music. It is the language of technology, especially of computer technology. Around 75% of all Web sites on the Internet, for example, are in English. The author believes that English is a "killer language" that is replacing smaller languages. The lecturer, on the other hand, does not take this view of English. He says that it is true that languages are disappearing. This is truly tragic; however, it is not entirely the fault of English. The speaker agrees that, as a regional language, English has hurt smaller languages, but it is not the only regional language to have done so. The speaker mentions a study done in 1992 indicating that in India, it was the regional language Hindi that replaced smaller languages, not English. Likewise, according to the speaker, Hausa in West Africa and Swahili in East Africa have replaced local languages. Russian, Spanish, and Arabic have done the same. The speaker concludes, therefore, that it is ten or so regional languages—not one global language—that are killing off smaller languages.

Task 4
The passage says that, in the opinion of most environmentalists, we must decrease our reliance on fossil fuels and increase our use of renewable sources of energy. Wind energy, the author believes, is a good source of energy since it causes no pollution or dangerous wastes. But the author points out that this does not mean that wind farms are completely safe. Some of them kill birds. The author gives the example of the enormous wind farm at Altamont Pass, California. Here, over 5,000 birds a year die as a result of the spinning blades of the wind turbines. This includes some rare predatory birds such as golden eagles and red-tailed hawks. Until wind-generated power is safe for birds, the author believes, no more wind farms should be constructed. The speaker agrees that the

author is correct in saying that the wind farm at Altamont Pass poses a danger to birds. He says that this site was chosen because of the strong winds that blow through the pass, and engineers didn't know that they were building the wind farm on a migratory route. But, according to the speaker, Altamont Pass is very unusual. Other wind farms have not experienced the same problem with birds. In Denmark, where a great deal of energy is generated by wind, a study was done that showed only a few birds per year were killed. This is fewer than the average housecat kills. The speaker admits that Altamont Pass Wind Farm needs to protect birds or to be relocated. In contrast to the author's point of view, the speaker says that we should not stop building wind farms because wind energy is a safe, clean source of energy. In fact, we should build more.

Task 5

The author mentions that, in the letters to the editors of the campus paper, astronomers indicate that they are upset because the campus and the streets of the town are too well lit. The astronomers say this makes it difficult for them to see the stars and to perform their astronomical experiments. The author agrees that this is unfortunate, but according to professors of criminology, good lighting prevents crime. If we reduce the amount of light, the author says, we will have a higher crime rate. The speaker, however, disagrees with this point of view. He tells the class that he has already said that light pollution makes things hard for astronomers, but he wonders if it is true that more light on the streets actually prevents crime. According to the speaker, some studies say it does, but others say it is not effective. The speaker goes on to say, however, that he and his colleagues do not want the campus and streets to be completely dark. They are only requesting SMART lighting. He says that today's street lamps send 40% of their light where it is not needed, upwards and out to the sides. If lights are shielded, the professor says, the streets and the campus can have plenty of light. However, it will still be possible for astronomers and in fact for anyone to look up and see the stars at night.

Task 6

According to the passage, scientists thought up until the 1950's that protozoa were simple forms of animal life. Yes, there are resemblances between some types of protozoa and animals. For example, protozoa, like animals, move about and they eat plants. But, according to the passage, other types of protozoa are more similar to plants because they can't move and they contain chlorophyll. In the speaker's opinion, protozoa and other microscopic forms of life are problematic for biologists. Unlike larger forms of life, they are hard to classify. At one time, protozoa were believed to be animals. According to the speaker, that's in part because the Linnaean system, used to classify all forms of life, had only two kingdoms: animal and plant. Protozoa weren't much like familiar forms of animals, such as fish and horses, but since they had to be classified in one of two kingdoms, they were classified as animals. Bacteria, which were not much like familiar plants such as oak trees, also had to be something, so they were classified as plants. The speaker believes this was like fitting square pegs into round holes. She points out that in the 1950's, scientists had a wonderful idea. They decided to change the whole system of classification. At first, one new kingdom was added, and protozoa were put into this new kingdom. Later there was a system involving five kingdoms, and today there is a new system involving 3 domains and from 8 to 15 kingdoms. The speaker concludes that if something is difficult to classify, scientists should examine the system of classification.

Lesson 23: Writing the Integrated Response

Exercise 23.1

Responses will vary. The following are given as examples.

Task 1

The subject of both the passage and the lecture is a treaty regulating economic activity in Antarctica. The author of the passage explains that a 1991 treaty created a "natural reserve." All economic activities except tourism and fishing were banned. In the author's opinion, this treaty should be changed to allow for the exploration and extraction of oil and gas resources. The professor, however, feels that the ban on development in Antarctica is useful and that the treaty should not be altered.

The author says that Antarctica is an immense continent, but that only the coastal areas support life. This means that the interior could be safely developed. However, the lecturer points out that it is from these coastal regions that gas and oil would have to be shipped. She reminds the class that these waters are very dangerous for ships because of the vast number of icebergs, and mentions the terrible danger that an oil spill would pose for animals that live in the coastal regions, such as whales and penguins.

The author says that, while conditions in Antarctica would make it difficult to extract oil and gas, conditions were also difficult in Alaska and in the North Sea. In those places, however, the difficulties were overcome and these sites became valuable sources of oil. Today, and in the future, technology for extracting oil is better than it was when oil was taken from Alaska and the North Sea. The lecturer, though, has a different point of view. She says that people who have not been in Antarctica (and she has worked at a research base there) do not truly understand how difficult conditions there are. She doesn't believe it will be possible to exploit any oil or gas deposits there.

It will be very expensive to remove oil and gas from Antarctica, the author admits. However, as gas prices go up around the world, it will become economical. The speaker disagrees with this assessment. She feels that it will never be economically feasible to develop oil and gas resources in Antarctica. In her opinion, it would be better to invest this money in developing new sources of energy, such as hydrogen fuel.

In summary, the author thinks that it is not fair for only a scientific elite to control the future of Antarctica, and that the possibility of developing the continent's resources should at least be open to discussion. The speaker rejects this idea. She points out that it was not only scientists who negotiated this treaty—it was also representatives of governments from all over the world. She also believes that it is a good idea to protect the southern continent from exploitation by politicians and international corporations.

Task 2

Both the passage and the lecture discuss the possibility of intelligent life on other planets. The passage says that we have all seen science fiction movies about UFOs coming to Earth, or about astronauts from Earth encountering aliens on other worlds. The author reminds us, though, that these stories are only fiction and that in reality, we may be the only intelligent species in the universe. According to the speaker, however, this point of view is a little like that of fish in a little lake who believe that, because they have never been to other lakes, there are no other fish in the world.

The author says that, while there are thousands of stars in our galaxy, most are quite different from our own sun. They are too big, too small, emit too much radiation, or are unsuitable in some way for life. Even though we know there are planets around other stars, the author says, it is unlikely that they are in just the right position for life to develop. However, the speaker says that in just our own galaxy, there are 400 billion stars. Even if our star is unusual and even if only one star in a thousand has planets that can support life, there will still be 400 million planets that support life. He also reminds us that life on earth has developed under some rather harsh conditions.

Of course, as the author explains, just because a planet has life does not mean that it has intelligent life. Of the millions of species found on earth, there is only one intelligent life form. The speaker says that if only one in a thousand of the 400 million plants that contain life have intelligent life, there are still 400,000 intelligent species in our galaxy. He also mentions the "smart is better" theory of the scientist Carl Sagan. This theory says that, just as tigers evolved the ability to hunt in order to survive, people evolved intelligence in order to survive. Why shouldn't this also be true on other planets?

The author wonders why, if there is life on other planets, we have not been contacted. We have been sending out radio and television signals for many years. Why haven't we gotten a response? The speaker says that aliens may not be interested in contacting us, or they may have developed other forms of technology.

The author concludes by saying that there is no one out there to hear us. The speaker, on the other hand, finds this point of view self-centered, much like that of the fish who didn't realize that there were other lakes and other fish in the world.

Task 3

The author of the passage writes in favor of mandatory voting, while the speaker opposes it.

The author first mentions the fact that, in the general election of 1922, only 59% of Australian voters participated. Shortly after this, Australia required eligible citizens to vote. Today, according to the author, 94% of eligible Australians vote. Voting is also mandatory in Belgium, Argentina, and, in fact, in about 20% of all democratic countries, and all of these have high voter turnout. However, in countries without mandatory voting, such as the United States and the United Kingdom, the percentage of voters participating in elections is much lower. The author counters this argument by saying that it is more important to have people vote well than to have a large voter turnout. In countries where voting is not required by law, the author reminds us, those who do vote are usually well informed and highly motivated.

The author says that a high voter turnout is important because, as Thomas Jefferson said, governments get their authority from the consent of the people they govern. If those people do not vote, they are not actively giving their consent. The speaker admits that this might be true, but says that people who do not vote are exercising a freedom too. They may not like any of the candidates who are running for office or they might not feel as though the system is giving them any real choices. Therefore, they choose not to vote.

The author compares mandatory voting to mandatory taxation. Just as the government depends on taxes, the government depends on votes. The speaker, however, does not agree that this is a valid comparison. If many people do not pay taxes, a government cannot operate properly. However, people's decision not to vote has no real effect on a government.

The author believes that it is beneficial to require people to vote, but the speaker concludes by saying that, just

because one has the right to do something, he or she does not have the obligation to do it. The fact that everyone has the right to open a business, for example, does not mean that everyone must open a business.

Exercise 23.2
Responses will vary. The following are given as examples.
Task 4
The author and the speaker both discuss reasons why mammoths became extinct. The author says that 11,000 years ago, at the end of the Ice Age, conditions were optimal for mammoths. Food was plentiful, the herds were strong, and the climate was favorable. In a short time, however, mammoths all became extinct. The author explains that there are three reasons why that may have happened. The speaker, however, says that there are problems with all three of these theories.

The first theory mentioned by the author is the "man vs. mammoth" theory, which was created by Professor Paul Martin. According to this theory, the Clovis people, who crossed over the land bridge between Asia and Alaska, hunted the mammoths to extinction. They were armed with sharp spears and had the help of their dogs. The speaker, however, disputes this idea. She says that mammoths were huge, powerful animals and with their long tusks, they would have been quite dangerous to hunt. They had thick skin and a thick layer of fat that would have been difficult for the sharpest spear to pierce. There's no reason why the Clovis people would have hunted them when there were smaller, less dangerous animals around. Besides, the Clovis people were small in number and were widely scattered. According to a computer model, they could only have eaten about 10% of the mammoths that they supposedly killed.

Another theory that the author mentions is that mammoths were killed off by the changing climate. The mammoths thrived in the cold, damp, unchanging weather of the Ice Ages. However, at the end of the Ice Ages, the climate became warmer and dryer and the grassy plains became deserts. The vegetation that the mammoths ate disappeared, and therefore, so did the mammoths. The speaker, however, challenges this theory. She states that mammoths had lived through more severe climate changes than this change. Moreover, the African and Indian elephants survived major climate shifts, so why didn't the North American mammoths?

The author mentions a third theory, which was conceived by the scientist Ross McPhee. This theory states that mammoths may have been killed off by an infectious disease brought by humans from the Old World. It might have been carried by insects, such as lice in the humans' hair or fleas on the humans' dogs. It then passed to the elephants and spread from group to group. Because the New World animals had no resistance to the Old World disease, it killed them all off. The problem with this theory, as the speaker points out, is that there is no physical support for it. In none of the remains of mammoths that have been found has there been any sign of an infectious disease.

While the author seems convinced that the mammoths died off for one of these three reasons, the speaker is not so sure. She says that, while it is possible that the mammoths went extinct for one of these reasons, or for a combination of these reasons, it is also possible that the real reason is still unknown.

Task 5
The author of the passage believes in the importance of the arts, and quotes President Johnson to indicate how the arts show our "inner vision." The author believes that the government should support artists. The speaker, on the other hand,

does NOT agree with the idea of public support for individual artists even though he himself is a working artist.

The author states that it is more and more difficult for artists to support themselves financially, especially for experimental artists whose works do not have much commercial appeal. In Europe, the author says, governments commonly provide financial backing for artists. In the United States, that support has been provided by a combination of private and governmental support, but in recent years, governmental support has remained the same or even decreased. The speaker, however, points out that we do not, for example, provide governmental support to plumbers, who certainly provide useful services. He believes it is not fair to support one group and not another. Why should artists be different from plumbers or from anyone else, he wonders. He says that in the past, great American artists supported themselves by selling their works. Today's artists can do the same. Artists who cannot easily sell their art can work as commercial artists or in other jobs related to the arts.

The author tells us that in the past, individual artists such as da Vinci and Tchaikovsky received funding from wealthy patrons. Today, there are few wealthy patrons providing this kind of support for individual artists, but artists still need money to complete projects. The speaker says that he does not object to funding from private sources such as corporations (although he himself would not accept corporate funds). He only objects to government money being spent on any special group, including artists.

The author cites a study done by the Georgia Institute of Technology. This study shows that a few billion dollars invested by the government generated many billions of dollars in economic activity and that the government was more than repaid in taxes. The author concludes that government spending on art is a sound investment. The speaker says that this study dealt only with art organizations, such as ballet companies. Money spent on individual artists probably does not generate much economic activity, in his opinion. He points out that some government programs to help artists actually waste money. He gives the example of the French program that was designed to provide unemployment insurance for artists. Everyone who had a job that was even distantly related to the arts—such as people who cut actors' hair—applied for this insurance, and the program wasted a great deal of money.

In summary, the author believes that money spent on supporting artists is well spent, while the speaker thinks that it is unfair to help one group of people (artists) and that money spent to support artists is sometimes wasted.

Task 6

The topic of both the passage and the lecture is the effects that television watching has on children. The author discusses a study done by the Association of Pediatric and Adolescent Medicine in 2005. According to the author, the study shows that the negative effects of television are stronger than the positive effects. The speaker—who is not a supporter of television, especially commercial television—does not completely agree with the author's view or of her interpretation of the study. For one thing, she says it is almost impossible to ban children from watching television because children will simply watch it somewhere else.

The author of the article says that the study involved 1,700 children. She says that according to the study, children who are from six to seven years old, and who watch a significant amount of TV (more than three hours a day) score lower on standardized reading tests and on short-term memory tests than kids who don't. The speaker, however, refers to the same study. She points out that while older children who watch a lot of TV do badly on standardized tests, the opposite is true of younger children. Kids from three to five who watch a lot of TV actually do better on reading recognition tests than kids who don't watch much TV.

The author cites another study that says children spend more time watching TV than doing anything else but sleeping. According to the author, the average child actually spends more time watching television than attending school. Television watching takes the place of activities that parents put more value on, such as studying, reading, or taking part in athletics. The speaker, however, says that what is important is to monitor the time children spend in front of TVs. Children under the age of two should not watch any TV. Children two and over should be limited to two hours or less per day. This leaves time for other activities. They should be encouraged to watch educational shows and non-commercial television.

The author points out that watching television is a passive activity. Children do not get any physical exercise and they eat snacks as they watch. Television commercials in fact encourage children to eat unhealthy snacks. The speaker admits that physical fitness is a problem for children, but says that this problem is not entirely caused by television viewing. If children are limited to less than two hours of viewing time per day, there is time for exercise and other physical activity. The speaker also says that children should be taught about proper nutrition.

In the conclusion to the passage, the author says that the 2005 study reinforces what child psychiatrists already know: that television harms children and that it should be severely limited or completely cut out of children's lives. The speaker does not take such a harsh view of television. She says that, like many things in life, television has both negative and positive effects and that it should be used intelligently.

Lesson 24: Checking and Editing the Integrated Response

Exercise 24.1
Answers will vary. The following are given as examples.

Paragraph 1
According to the passage, there should not be a mandatory retirement age. The author says that this practice takes valuable workers from the work force. Older workers have the most experience and making them retire wastes their talent. Furthermore, the author says that studies show that older workers can do most jobs as well as younger workers. The lecturer, however, says that if older workers stay at their jobs, then it is not possible for younger workers to get promotions or more responsibility. The speaker also says that, although there are exceptions, many young workers have qualities that employers need, such as concentration, memory, and energy.

Paragraph 2
The speaker says that not many animals can capture the attention of both young and old people like the dinosaur. One of the best known dinosaurs is the animal we used to call the "brontosaurus." Everyone is familiar with this dinosaur. It has appeared in museums, movies, advertisements, even in cartoons such as *The Flintstones*. But recently, this animal has another name. It is now called the "apatosaurus." The speaker believes that we should keep the name "brontosaurus." The author of the article does not agree with this concept. He says that it is not scientific or fair to call this creature a brontosaurus. In 1877, a scientist whose name was Marsh found

the bones of a dinosaur and he <u>named it</u> "apatosaurus." In 1879, another scientist <u>whose</u> name was Cope found the bones of a dinosaur. He <u>believed</u> it was a <u>different</u> species and called it a brontosaurus, but later <u>it</u> was learned that these two animals were <u>the</u> same. <u>An</u> international commission for naming animals has rules that say the name given for the first animal <u>that is discovered is the</u> <u>name</u> that should <u>be</u> <u>used</u>. Therefore<u>,</u> the name <u>"apatosaurus"</u> is really correct.

Paragraph 3
Both the author and the <u>lecturer</u> discuss the same sociological study<u>, a study</u> about online education. The author takes the positive point of view. <u>He cites statistics from the study</u> <u>that show</u> that a high percentage of students think online courses <u>are</u> very <u>effective</u>. The <u>lecturer</u> concentrates <u>on the</u> negative <u>points</u>. He says <u>that</u> even though students think <u>online courses are effective</u>, a higher percentage of students in online <u>courses</u> drop (out) before <u>the end of the course</u> than in "face-to-face" <u>classes</u>. He says students in online classes don't like to study alone and <u>that they</u> feel <u>isolated</u>. But <u>the</u> <u>author</u> says <u>that</u> maybe changes in technology in <u>the</u> future will solve some <u>of today's</u> problems with online classes.

Paragraph 4
<u>The article says that languages are vanishing because English</u> is a killer language. <u>Most</u> magazines<u>,</u> television <u>shows,</u> and <u>Web sites</u> are in <u>English</u>, and this <u>fact</u> kills <u>small</u> languages. <u>On the other hand,</u> the lecturer says that English is not <u>the</u> main reason <u>that languages are vanishing. He says that,</u> while <u>it is true that</u> many <u>magazines</u> and <u>newspapers</u> are in English, <u>this does not compare with the number of those</u> <u>written in the language of the country or region. The same is</u> <u>true of movies and television. The lecturer says that the use of</u> <u>English</u> is penetrating only big <u>cities</u> and <u>places</u> where tourists go, but <u>that the</u> national and regional language <u>pene-</u> <u>trates</u> all <u>parts</u> of a country or region. <u>The lecturer says that</u> <u>English</u> can often coexist with other <u>languages</u>. <u>An example is</u> <u>the use of "Singlish," a form of English spoken in Singapore. It</u> <u>does not pose a danger</u> to other languages in Singapore.

The Independent Writing Tasks

Scoring the Response
Response 1   Score: _2_
This essay has three paragraphs: the opening/thesis paragraph, the body with some supporting ideas, and the conclusion. The writer attempts to follow writing guidelines and makes an effort to organize his/her thoughts and support them with examples. However, there are numerous problems. Much of the thesis statement is taken word for word from the prompt; it should be re-stated. The response lacks solid sentence development and contains many errors in spelling, verb tense, and word usage that make it difficult to understand the writer's ideas.

Response 2   Score: _5_
The writer of this essay acknowledges that there are two sides to the debate on space research, then takes a clear position in support of it. The writer combines clear sentence structure, proper use of grammar and upper-level vocabulary, and numerous examples to support his/her position. The essay shows that the writer is informed about the topic and clearly indicates specific benefits of space research and technology. In addition, the essay is very well organized and coherent.

Response 3   Score: _4_
The essay writer understands the assignment and addresses the topic. The response is generally well organized and offers some examples for the position taken, but sometimes the connections are a little difficult to follow. There is overall unity and coherence. However, the essay contains mistakes in

spelling, punctuation, and grammar. The writer also sometimes chooses inappropriate words and uses words from his/her native language. These errors are distracting but do not obscure the writer's ideas.

Independent Writing Preview Test
Answers will vary, but successful answers should answer if zoos are useful or not. The writer should choose one side and write a clear thesis stating his or her opinion. A good paper will support the writer's point of view with clear reasons and examples.

Lesson 25: Pre-Writing the Independent Response

Exercise 25.1
Answers will vary. The following are given as examples.

Analysis of Task 1
This prompt says that there are two opinions involving basic educational philosophy. Education can emphasize either competition or cooperation. I have to decide which one of these I want to support.

If I choose to support cooperation, I need to show how learning to cooperate will be useful in later life. For example, I could show how it is an advantage to learn how to work with one's colleagues on the job. If, on the other hand, I choose to defend the opposite point of view, I must show the advantages of being a competitive person—in sports, in business, and so on.

Another possibility is to defend neither point of view completely. I might say that a good education should show people that at times they must cooperate well and at times they must be strong competitors.

Analysis of Task 2
For this prompt I must choose a figure from the past that I want to talk to. It could be someone internationally famous, such as Julius Caesar, Simon Bolivar, Abraham Lincoln, or Mahatma Gandhi. Or I could choose to speak to someone who is important to me personally, such as my great-great-grandfather. It will be best if I choose someone I know quite a bit about, and preferably someone in a field that I am interested in. I could choose Pelé or David Beckham because I am interested in football. Or I could choose Lord Keynes or Adam Smith because I am interested in economics. The most important thing is to have good reasons why I want to speak to the person that I choose, and to have some specific questions that I'd like to ask this person.

Analysis of Task 3
For this prompt, I need to decide whether I agree with the idea that when people travel they behave differently from the way they behave at home. It will probably be easier to think of examples and reasons why most people do act somewhat differently when traveling. I can give personal experiences. I can talk about unusual things I have done on trips that I probably wouldn't do at home. I could mention how I eat different foods and wear different clothing when I am on trips. I can also think of some reasons why people behave differently. They want to try new things and experience new cultures. Also, because they are in a new environment, they are not as restricted by the normal rules and regulations that they are used to.

Analysis of Task 4
When writing this essay, I have to show the benefits of either on-campus living or off-campus living. One advantage of dorm living is convenience. Another is that it provides oppor-

tunities for making friends with other students. I could support these concepts with examples from my own life or from the lives of people I have known who have lived in university dormitories. However, if I decide to support the opposite point of view, I would list the advantages of living in an apartment or house. These might include independence and privacy, I suppose. If I choose to take this side, I'll need to think of ways that living in an apartment or house off campus might make someone a better student and better prepared for life after the university.

Analysis of Task 5

I could choose to agree with this statement. If I do, I have to show how taking a wide variety of classes makes a person well-rounded and better informed. I might say that it is fine for graduate students to specialize, but that undergraduates should be generalists with some knowledge of history, science, math, art, and all the other important fields. On the other hand, if I take the opposite point of view, I have to give reasons why it is a good idea to concentrate on only one field of interest. I might say, for example, that for students in scientific and technical fields, there is so much to learn in four years that it is impossible for them to take many elective courses.

Analysis of Task 6

The prompt says that I can fund any one of a variety of city services, but only one. To write this response, I need to decide what kind of service my hometown needs most. For example, if there is a high crime rate, then I could make a good case for funding the police department. It would probably be easy to explain why funding should go to either schools or hospitals because almost any community needs improvements in education and health care.

Exercise 25.2
Notes will vary.

Exercise 25.3
Outlines will vary.

Exercise 25.4
Outlines will vary.

Lesson 26: Giving Opinions and Connecting Ideas in the Independent Response

Exercise 26.1

1. I believe that women should have the right to serve in the military. <u>However/On the other hand,</u> I don't believe that they should be assigned to combat roles.
2. Many actors, rock musicians, and sports stars receive huge amounts of money for the work that they do. <u>For example,</u> a baseball player was recently offered a contract worth over twelve million dollars. <u>Personally,</u> I feel that this is far too much to pay a person who simply provides entertainment.
3. The development of the automobile has had a great impact on people everywhere. <u>Similarly/Likewise,</u> the development of high-speed trains has had an impact on people in many countries, including my home country of France.
4. I used to work in a restaurant when I was in college. I realize what a difficult job restaurant work is. <u>Therefore,</u> whenever I go out to eat, I try to leave a good tip for my waiter or waitress.
5. Many people would agree with the idea that the best use for the open space in our community is to build a shop-

ping center. <u>On the other hand/However,</u> there are other people who feel we should turn this open space into a park.
6. In the United States, people celebrate their independence from Britain on July 4. <u>Likewise/Similarly,</u> we Mexicans celebrate our independence from Spain on September 16.
7. Corporations should do more to reduce air pollution. <u>Furthermore,</u> they should encourage recycling.

Exercise 26.2
Sentences will vary. The following are given as models.
1. Young children have a special talent for language learning; therefore, <u>schools should offer language classes to children at an early age.</u>
2. Some forms of advertising serve a useful purpose; however, <u>other ads are simply irritating.</u>
3. Small classes are the best environment for learning, but <u>sometimes large classes are unavoidable.</u>
4. Some people relax by watching television; personally, <u>I prefer listening to music.</u>
5. Although there are many ways to learn a language, <u>I think the best way is to live in a country where the language is spoken.</u>
6. The use of computers has had a major impact on the banking industry; likewise, <u>it has significantly changed the travel industry.</u>

Exercise 26.3

There are certain people who <u>prefer</u> to take their vacations in the same place. When they return from a vacation, they ask themselves, "When can I go back there again?" <u>On the other hand/However,</u> there are people who <u>would rather</u> visit many places. <u>Moreover/Furthermore,</u> they <u>enjoy</u> doing many different things on their vacations. When they return from a vacation, they ask themselves, "Where can I go and what can I do next?"

My parents are perfect examples of the first kind of people. They always go to a lake in the mountains. They first went there on their honeymoon, and several years later they bought a vacation cabin there. They have gone there two or three times a year for over thirty years. They have made friends with the people who also own cabins there and often get together with them. My mother <u>enjoys</u> sailing and swimming <u>while</u> my father <u>prefers</u> to go fishing. My parents like variety, <u>but</u> they say they can get variety by going to their cabin at different times of the year. They particularly like to go there in the autumn when the leaves are changing color.

<u>Personally,</u> I feel it's important to visit different places. Of course, when I was a child, I went to my parents' cabin with them for my vacation, <u>but</u> when I got older, I began to want to travel to many different places. I <u>enjoy</u> skiing; <u>however,</u> the ski resorts in my country are very crowded and expensive. I <u>would rather</u> go skiing in Switzerland or in Canada. My favorite subject at the university was ancient history; <u>therefore,</u> I like to visit historic places. Several years ago, I traveled to Angkor Wat in Cambodia with my uncle and aunt. I also want to visit the pyramids in Egypt; <u>furthermore/moreover,</u> I'd like to see Machu Picchu in Peru.

My parents believe that you can never get to know a place too well. I understand their point of view. <u>However,</u> I find that going to strange places is more exciting. I don't want to go to the same place twice <u>because</u> the world is so huge and exciting.

Exercise 26.4

Responses will vary. The following are given as examples.

2. I would choose to live in London. Although I have never visited this city, I have heard that it is one of the world's most exciting cities. One reason I would like to live there is because it is an international city. There are people from every country on the globe living there, and I think I would enjoy that cosmopolitan atmosphere. Moreover, I would like to live there because of its culture. In my opinion, London has some of the best museums, theaters, and concert halls in the world. Finally, I would like to live there because I believe it would be the best place for me to learn English.

3. I believe that many people learn from their failures in school, in business, and in life. In college, the only class I ever did badly in was a calculus class. I did so badly that I had to repeat the class. However, the second time I took the class, I knew what to expect. I knew what the tests would be like. Therefore, I got one of the best scores in the class. Here's another example. In the late 1970's, my father and my uncle opened an electrical appliance business. The business was not successful and they had to sell it for almost no profit. However, in the 1990's, they opened a store that rented videotapes. This business was a great success and when they sold it after about ten years, they made a very good profit. My father always said that it was the lessons that he learned from his first, unsuccessful business that made his second business a success.

    On the other hand, there are some people who give up after failing again and again. A friend of mine was in a band. The band tried to get jobs playing music in clubs and they tried to record a CD, but they didn't have any luck. After being rejected so many times, the band broke up and my friend gave up music.

    In my opinion, for most people, mistakes and failures represent one of the best ways to learn to improve. However, for some people, repeated failure leads to discouragement.

4. I used to watch the daily news on television, but these days I read the paper on the way to work and I also read the news on the Internet, so I seldom watch television news anymore. Today, I mostly enjoy watching television to relax and escape from reality after a day at work. Therefore, I usually watch comedies. Comedies don't require much thought. You can just sit back and relax and enjoy the jokes, and you don't even need to watch every week in order to keep up with the action.

5. I would probably choose to attend a top university in another country. Certainly there are some good reasons to attend a good university in your own country. You do not miss your family and friends so much. Moreover, there is no language barrier or culture barrier to overcome. However, in my opinion, you can learn a lot more by studying abroad. Not only do you learn about your subject, but you also learn about another culture. I believe that studying abroad will be particularly valuable for me because I plan to study medicine. Information on some of the most up-to-date medical procedures may not be available at the university in my country.

Lesson 27: Writing the Independent Response

Exercise 27.1

Responses will vary.

Exercise 27.2

Responses will vary.

Lesson 28: Checking and Editing the Independent Response

Exercise 28.1

Answers will vary. The following are given as examples.

Paragraph 1

Technology has had a major impact on many fields. Nowadays, we can't even imagine business, communication, or travel without computers. I want to discuss the impact of computers on education. Modern technology has made life easier for students and professors. If a student wants to contact a professor, it's simple. The student can send the professor an e-mail rather than go to his or her office. Moreover, many universities have created special networks for students in order to make the process of studying easier for them. Students can enter this kind of network by using their passwords and identification numbers. There are many categories a student can choose to enter, such as "student tools" or "assignment box," which contains homework assignments. It is also possible to access the university library to do research. Computers also give students the opportunity to gather information about various topics from the Internet. This is one of the easiest ways for students to do research. Computers can also help students, especially those from other countries, to stay in touch with their friends and family at home. Personally, I could not study in the USA if I were not in contact with people at home, because I am not only a student but also a manager in my family's business. Therefore, I must stay in touch with my assistants.

Paragraph 2

Some people believe that it is impossible to fall in love with someone "at first sight." On the other hand, there are other people who believe that you recognize a person that you love immediately. I know it is possible to fall in love at first sight because this happened to my wife and me.

Paragraph 3

If you are ever in Thailand in the month of May, I suggest that you go to the Rocket Festival. It is held every year in a small town called Yasothon about 500 kilometers from Bangkok. This two-day festival is well known in Thailand. It marks the beginning of the rice-growing season. The festival opens with a parade of women performing a Bang Fai Dance. They dance around the villagers and they carry colorful rockets in the shape of river snakes. Villagers construct gigantic homemade rockets and fire them into the sky to "ensure" plentiful rainfall during the rice-planting season. The farmers believe that if the spirit is pleased by their actions, he will deliver the rains necessary for a good rice harvest. People from all over Thailand and tourists from all over the world join the local people in celebrating. First, a single rocket is launched to foretell the next season's rains. The higher it goes, the better the rains will be. Then the rocket competition begins with one rule—the rocket that goes highest is the winner of the game. If a rocket fails to take off or explodes, the owner is thrown into the mud. The Rocket Festival is spectacular and provides a great opportunity to have fun. However, if you go, you need to be careful. Both villagers and tourists are sometimes injured or even killed by rockets that go out of control.

Paragraph 4

When I was a small child I lived in the town of Sendai, the biggest city in the northern part of Japan. My grandmother lived in Tokyo, which is in the central part of Japan. While I was living in Sendai, I often went to see my grandmother, but it took five hours to get to Tokyo by local train. About twenty-five years ago, the <u>high-speed</u> express train called the "Shinkansen" <u>was built, connecting Sendai and Tokyo.</u> For me personally, this was <u>the</u> most <u>important</u> development in transportation. It now <u>takes</u> only <u>an</u> hour and <u>a</u> half to travel to Tokyo from Sendai. The trip <u>became</u> very easy. It also <u>had</u> a great impact on Sendai. <u>Economic</u> development there increased. <u>On</u> the negative side, prices for housing and other things went up. <u>On</u> the whole, however, this development was <u>very beneficial</u> for the city.

Paragraph 5

I'm from Korea. Once, Koreans had large families. <u>Three generations lived together</u> (grandparents-parents-children). They were almost all farmers, so they preferred large numbers of <u>children. Today,</u> Korea has <u>developed</u> and <u>changed</u> from an <u>agricultural society to an industrial one.</u> Many people <u>have</u> moved from rural areas to urban ones <u>because</u> their <u>jobs are</u> in the <u>cities.</u> For example, my husband went to Seoul in 2000 for his college. He <u>left</u> his parents and lived alone. <u>After graduation,</u> he got a job <u>in</u> Seoul. At that time we worked together. After we <u>were married,</u> we lived <u>in</u> Seoul. Of course, his parents <u>wanted</u> us to live <u>with them</u> as Koreans <u>traditionally</u> do, but <u>there were no</u> jobs in the <u>area where they live.</u> For me, I think <u>these</u> changes <u>in</u> society are natural and reasonable.

Paragraph 6

Today you can <u>often hear</u> people arguing about the advantages of computer <u>games.</u> There are millions of <u>different</u> computer games today. <u>Sometimes</u> computer games <u>are</u> so attractive that young people, and not <u>only</u> young people, <u>spend hours</u> and even days in front of <u>their computers.</u> And of <u>course,</u> if you spend too much <u>time playing</u> computer games, you can <u>hurt</u> your <u>eyes and</u> your physical <u>condition,</u> and you can <u>isolate</u> yourself from <u>society. You</u> may <u>also</u> have <u>problems</u> communicating with other people.

Paragraph 7

When I first <u>came</u> to the <u>United States,</u> I was only 17 years old, and I <u>had</u> never been away from <u>home. I came</u> here for one year. I lived with <u>an American family</u> in <u>a suburb of New Orleans.</u> I went to high school there. Imagine how difficult <u>it was</u> for me on <u>the</u> first day of school. I didn't know where <u>to go or what to do.</u> I <u>spoke</u> only a little <u>English. But</u> I was very fortunate. The daughter of my host <u>family's</u> neighbors <u>recognized</u> me, and she did everything <u>to help</u> me. Not only <u>did she help me</u> talk with the principal of the school, <u>but she also</u> introduced me to the teacher of my first class. She even ate lunch with me. I <u>still</u> remember her kindness!

Writing Review Test

Answers will vary.

Writing Tutorial: Written Grammar

Grammar Exercise 1

F	2.	We heard a lecture by Professor Taylor, who is chairman of the history department.
F	3.	Thomas Edison invented the light bulb and the phonograph, but not the telephone.
C	4.	
RU	5.	Seals appear clumsy on the land, but they are able to move short distances faster than most people can run.
F	6.	You can't get to the island from here without a boat.
C	7.	
RU	8.	A barometer is a device used to measure atmospheric pressure.

F	9.	Sometimes cloth is made by blending natural fibers and synthetic fibers, such as rayon and cotton.
F	10.	Professor Roberts bought a car in Rome, then sold it in Amsterdam after her vacation.
RU	11.	Technical climbing means mountain climbing without special equipment. It shouldn't be attempted without training.
RU	12.	Almost 92% of people get married. Over one third of these marriages end in divorce, but half of all divorced people choose to get married a second time.

Grammar Exercise 2.1

2. A battery is a device that provides electricity by chemical means.

3. In May, the university will finish building a new wing of the library where rare books will be stored.

4. The melting point is the temperature at which a solid changes to a liquid.

5. A keystone species is a species of plants or animals whose absence has a major effect on an ecological system.

6. Active stocks are stocks that are frequently bought and sold.

7. There are many varieties of snakes, most of which are harmless to humans.

8. Charlotte Gilman's best-known book is *Women and Economics,* in which she urges women to become financially independent.

Grammar Exercise 2.2

C	2.	
X	3.	which
C	4.	
X	5.	whose
X	6.	which chemists use
X	7.	for which it was
X	8.	which

Grammar Exercise 3.1

2. Although parrots are tropical birds, they can live in temperate or even cold climates.

3. Advertising has had an enormous effect on American life since it is so widespread in the United States.

4. As a wave moves toward shore its shape is changed by its collision with the shallow sea bottom.

5. When added to a liquid, antifreeze lowers the freezing temperature of that liquid.

6. While most bamboo blooms every year, there are some species that flower only two or three times a century.

7. Once granted by the Patent Office, a patent becomes the inventor's property.

Grammar Exercise 3.2

X	1.	Despite
X	2.	because
X	3.	People
C	4.	
C	5.	
C	6.	
X	7.	Because

Grammar Exercise 4.1
1. annually
2. simple
3. food   rainy
4. severity
5. Generally   simple
6. industry   products
7. relieve
8. scholarly   immigration
9. easy
10. tropical   ability
11. automatically
12. lose   rapidly
13. ripen
14. beautiful
15. distinction   perfectly

Grammar Exercise 4.2
X	1. intellectual
C	2.
X	3. analyzes
X	4. dances
X	5. weight
X	6. well
X	7. reaction
C	8.
X	9. harden

Grammar Exercise 5.1
2. was founded
3. have used
4. will fly
5. were made
6. wrote
7. is suited
8. have revolutionized

Grammar Exercise 5.2
X	2. was
X	3. was
X	4. took
C	5.
X	6. worn
X	7. were chosen
X	8. study
C	9.
X	10. are played
C	11.
X	12. is
X	13. were produced.
X	14. is used

Grammar Exercise 6.1
2. Anyone working under conditions that cause a heavy loss of perspiration can suffer heat exhaustion.
3. A mosquito filled with blood is carrying twice its own body weight.
4. A delta is a more or less triangular area of sediments deposited at the mouth of a river.
5. Natural resources provide the raw materials used to produce finished goods.
6. In this part of the campus there are several buildings dating from the 1790's.
7. A filter placed in front of a camera lens changes the color of the light that reaches the film.

Grammar Exercise 6.2
X	2. mixed
X	3. grown
C	4.
C	5.
X	6. crushed
C	7.
C	8.
X	9. Receiving
X	10. stimulating

Grammar Exercise 7
X	1. it
C	2.
X	3. its
X	4. their
X	5. those
X	6. its
X	7. our
X	8. that
X	9. their
C	10.
X	11. their
X	12. they

Grammar Exercise 8.1
2. human
3. children
4. automobile
5. thousands
6. appliances

Grammar Exercise 8.2
X	1. feet
X	2. kinds
X	3. farm
X	4. medicine
X	5. trees
X	6. percent
C	7.
X	8. 500-page
X	9. women
X	10. sunlight

Practice Test 1

(The TOEFL iBT does not use the letters A, B, C, and D for the multiple-choice items. However, in these answer keys, *A* corresponds to the first answer choice, *B* to the second, *C* to the third, and *D* to the fourth.)

Reading

Bioluminescence

Answer	Explanation
1. D	Paragraph 1 says, "The only groups that do not display bioluminescence are freshwater fish, mammals, birds, reptiles, amphibians, and leafy plants."
2. B	According to paragraph 2, bioluminescence "compares favorably in (energy) efficiency with fluorescent lighting."
3. A	*Eerie* means "strange, unusual, mysterious."
4. C	Choice C is best because paragraph 3 says that the phenomenon of "milky seas" (caused by the disturbance of dinoflagellates) occurs when a ship moves through tropical waters at night. Tropical waters are close to the equator and would there-

fore be warm. Choice A is not inferable; although the passage says the phenomenon is "particularly common" in the Indian Ocean, it must also happen in other tropical waters. Choice B is also not inferable. Dinoflagellates glow when disturbed (as by a ship). They do not blink on and off. Choice D is not inferable because nothing in the paragraph tells us that the dinoflagellates are destroyed by the passing of the ship. They are simply disturbed and therefore glow.

5. B   *The wake of a ship* is the track of waves and white water left behind as a ship moves through the water.

6. B   Choice B best summarizes and simplifies the original sentence. Choice A mistakenly says that the shark's bioluminescence attracts small fish, which then attract large predatory fish. In fact, the shark's bioluminescence itself attracts the large predators. Choice C mistakenly says that the shark uses bioluminescence to frighten off large predatory fish. In fact, it attracts the large predators with a bioluminescent patch that resembles a fish and then attacks the predators. Choice D is not the best answer. It is generally true that large predators such as sharks are attracted by the sight of small fish, but this does not summarize the information in the original sentence.

7. C   According to the passage, "Some squids use luminous fluids to confuse and escape from predators in the same way that other squids use their dark ink." Choice A is incorrect because most people do *not* have experience with squids' fluids of any type. Choice B is incorrect; the bobtail squid is given as an example of a creature that uses its bioluminescence to camouflage (hide) it at night, not as an example of a squid that confuses its enemies with glowing fluids. Choice D is wrong; no information is given about the chemical composition of the squids' fluids.

8. A   According to paragraph 4, "It is widely believed that many of the creatures that live in the dark depths of the ocean developed the ability to produce light simply as a way to see around them." The author then supports this idea by pointing out that, unsurprisingly, deep-sea creatures mainly use blue and green light, which best penetrates water.

9. D   The word *obscure* means "unclear or unknown."

10. D   The phrase *these organisms* refers to the species that, millions of years ago, developed bioluminescence to remove oxygen from their immediate environment.

11. B   There is *no* mention in paragraph 6 that bioluminescence can be used to light houses. (However, it is mentioned in the same paragraph that scientists are studying bioluminescence in order to build lamps that work in a similar way.)

12. The new sentence should be inserted at the third black square in the passage:

In some species, the role of bioluminescence is obvious. Fireflies and marine fireworms use their light to attract mates. The anglerfish uses a dangling luminous organ to attract prey to come within striking distance. The cookie cutter shark utilizes a bioluminescent patch on its underbelly to appear as a small fish to lure large predatory fish such as tuna and mackerel and when these fish try to consume the "small fish," they are

attacked by the shark. The bobtail squid uses its bioluminescence as nighttime camouflage. When viewed from below, it's spots of light blend in with the light of the stars and the Moon. Some squids use luminous fluids to confuse and escape from predators in the same way that other squids use their dark ink. ■ It is widely believed that many of the creatures that live in the dark depths of the ocean developed the ability to produce light simply as a way to see around them. ■ Most deep-sea creatures produce blue and green light, and unsurprisingly, the light of those colors has the most powerful penetrating power in water.■**For some reason, however, bioluminescence is not common in the unending darkness of caves.** The only cave-dwelling creature capable of generating light is a New Zealand glowworm. ■

The word *however* in the missing sentence links it to the previous sentences. Those sentences explain how deep-sea creatures use bioluminescence to light their dark environment. On the contrary, few creatures that live in dark caves use bioluminescence, so the word *however* is used to talk about cave creatures. *Cave-dwelling* in the next sentence is also a link to the mention of caves in the missing sentence.

13. A, C, F   Choice A is correct because it correctly summarizes paragraph 6. Choice B is incorrect. Fireflies still use bioluminescence to attract mates, according to information in paragraph 4. Choice C is a good answer. It summarizes the information in paragraph 3. Choice D is not correct. The passage says that there was a time when there was less oxygen in the air, but does not say that bioluminescence caused this. Choice E is true but is only a detail in the passage. Choice F correctly summarizes paragraphs 4 and 5.

Modern Times

Answer   **Explanation**

14. A   Paragraph 1 explains, "the film's main concerns are those of millions of people at the time: unemployment, poverty, and economic oppression."

15. C   In paragraph 1 the author says, "Chaplin was motivated to make the film by a journalist who, while interviewing him, happened to describe working conditions in industrial Detroit."

16. B   *Gags* are "jokes or funny situations."

17. C   Paragraph 2 says, "While there is no dialogue, there is music and sound effects, such as the roar of machinery and the scream of factory whistles."

18. C   Paragraph 3 indicates that "Only about one-third of *Modern Times* takes place inside a futuristic factory." Two-thirds of the movie must, therefore, take place outside the factory.

19. B   The word *This* refers to the scene in which the Tramp is strapped onto the assembly line and the automatic feeding machine throws food at him.

20. A   The word *nightmarish* means "terrifying, frightening." (A *nightmare* is a bad dream.)

21. D   The fact that the Tramp "loses his mind" when the speed of the assembly line is increased (paragraph 3), that the attendants who take him away are wearing white coats (paragraph 3), and that the doctor dismisses him by telling him to take it easy (paragraph 4) all indicate that the Tramp is taken to a mental hospital.

22. B   The doctor tells the Tramp to "Take it easy and avoid excitement," but for the rest of the film the

Tramp has a series of adventures and problems (paragraph 4).

23. D   In this context, *stock* means "standard, typical." When the author says that *Modern Times* has a stock ending, he means that this ending was used in other Chaplin films.

24. A   Paragraph 5 begins, "Clearly, *Modern Times* has its flaws . . ." *Flaws* are imperfections, so it is obvious that *Modern Times* is not a perfect film.

25. The new sentence should be inserted at the third black square in the passage:

Chaplin not only starred in *Modern Times* but also wrote the script and the music and directed and produced it. It was the last movie in which Chaplin played the "Little Tramp," a popular character he had first created in 1915. The Little Tramp is a simple, kind wanderer with a small mustache, a Derby hat, baggy pants, and a cane. He falls into many misfortunes but always maintains a sweet, sad optimism. *Modern Times* was also Chaplin's final silent movie. "Talkies" had appeared nine years earlier but Chaplin's humor was mostly based on body language and visual gags. ■ However, it is somewhat deceptive to call *Modern Times* a silent film. ■ While there is no dialogue, there is music and sound effects, such as the roar of machinery and the scream of factory whistles.■**The voice of the brutal factory owner is also heard coming through a giant two-way television screen (many years before television was actually invented).** In *Modern Times,* the world of sound is the noisy world of technology, although the Tramp, a symbol of humanity, is silent. ■

The second marked sentence says that, while there is no dialogue, there is music and sound effects, and gives some examples of sound effects. The missing sentence should be placed at the third black square because it gives further examples of sounds that are heard in the "silent" movie.

26. B, C,   Choice A is only a detail, a piece of background
E   information. Choice B is correct. It summarizes the information in paragraphs 3 and 4. Choice C summarizes the most important idea in paragraph 2. Choice D contains some incorrect information. The passage does not say that the Tramp marries the orphan (although in real life, Chaplin was married to the actress who played the orphan). Choice E correctly summarizes paragraph 5. Choice F is a detail from paragraph 2.

Balloon-Frame Houses

Answer   **Explanation**
27. A   In this context, *domestic* means residential, related to houses. (In some cases *domestic* refers to one's home country and is the opposite of *international*.)
28. A   *The other* refers to a second factor, the shortage of labor. (The first factor was the abundance of wood.)
29. D   According to paragraph 3, "while constructing houses in Fort Dearborn, Illinois, Augustine Taylor . . . invented a new method of building that utilized a framework of lightweight lumber. This was the birth of the balloon-frame house."
30. C   Builders of traditional homes did not require nails because "Wooden pegs were used instead of iron nails" (paragraph 2).
31. D   *Balloon-frame houses* was at first a term given by critics to this type of house. These skeptics said

that because the houses were made of such lightweight material, they would blow away like balloons in the wind (paragraph 4).

32. A   *Scorn* means "disapproval, mockery." People show *scorn* by criticizing and laughing at something they don't like.

33. C   The main point of the sentence is that, because of falling prices, a bag of nails in the United States cost less than the tax on a bag of nails in Europe. Choice C best summarizes this idea. Choice A is incorrect because it does not compare the cost of U.S. nails with the tax on European nails; it compares the taxes on nails in general to taxes in general. Choice B is wrong; the author does not say taxes on European nails were increasing, but that prices for nails in the U.S. were falling. Choice D is also wrong; nail makers in the U.S. dropped prices not because of declining taxes but because of better technology.

34. A   The word *mushrooming* means "growing rapidly, expanding quickly."

35. C   Paragraph 6 states, "The downside of balloon-frame houses was that they were made almost exclusively of flammable materials. Chicago rapidly became a city of wood. That fact came back to haunt the city on a hot, terrible night in 1871." The fact that the use of *flammable* (easily burnable) materials caused a problem in Chicago indicates that the problem was a disastrous fire. (Note: The phrase *came back to haunt* means that some mistake in the past caused problems later.)

36. C   The company sold building kits that included wood, parts, and building plans for people to build their own balloon-frame houses (paragraph 7).

37. B   The author gives information about both the smallest, cheapest house sold by the company and the biggest, nicest, most expensive house to show the full range of housing sold by the company.

38. The new sentence should be inserted at the first black square in the passage:

Two factors made building different in North America. One was an abundance of wood. Wood was used at a rate impossible to match in a mostly deforested Europe. The other was the fact that labor was scarce in most communities.■**In particular, there was a lack of trained artisans.** European houses built in the traditional timber-frame style used heavy cut stone. ■ That took a huge toll in labor. ■ Another key feature of European houses was the use of heavy timbers fitted with complex joints. ■ Wooden pegs were used instead of iron nails. This type of home construction was time-consuming and required a team of expert carpenters and other workers with specialized tools. Fundamentally, it was the same method of building homes that had been used in Europe since medieval times.

The sentence before the first marked sentence says that labor was scarce in North America. The missing sentence clarifies this with specific information, saying that there was especially a lack of trained artisans (skilled workers).

39. Timber-Frame Houses: C, F, G;
Balloon-Frame Houses: A, D, E, H
Choice A should be listed under balloon-frame houses because, according to paragraph 7, the reasonable prices for this kind of house allowed many U.S. workers to own their own homes. Choice B is not a characteristic of either

building style because timber-frame houses required a team of skilled workers, while balloon-frame houses required one or two unskilled workers (paragraphs 2 and 3). Choice C belongs under timber-frame houses because, according to paragraph 2, timber-frame houses were built basically in the same way houses had been built in Europe since medieval times. Choice D is a characteristic of balloon-frame houses because, according to paragraph 5, balloon-frame housing was made possible by improvements in sawmill technology and nail-making technology. Choice E should be listed under balloon-frame houses because this type of housing changed home building from a specialized craft to an industry (paragraph 3). Choice F should be considered a characteristic of timber-frame houses because constructing this form of housing was time-consuming and required a lot of skilled laborers. Choice G should also be listed as a characteristic of timber-frame houses because, according to paragraph 2, this type of house was built of heavy timbers and cut stone. Choice H should be listed under balloon-frame houses. Paragraph 6 says that another advantage of balloon-frame houses was their mobility, and many Chicagoans in the nineteenth century moved their houses from place to place. Finally, Choice I should not be listed under either type of housing. Timber-frame housing was replaced as the dominant type by balloon-frame housing in the 1830's, but balloon-frame housing was dominant only until the 1940's.

Listening

Answer	Explanation

1. B　　Ted tells the professor, "I'm working on the campus newspaper and . . . and I need to get over there right after class for a meeting . . ."

2. A　　Ted's intonation when he says, "I don't know what to say" indicates that he is surprised that Professor Jacobs is asking him to take part in the reading. "I don't know what to say" might indicate confusion (Choice D) but Ted is not upset; he is happy and flattered (pleased) to be asked.

3. A　　Ted says, "I'd really like to read the first two or three chapters of this novel I've been working on . . ."

4. B　　Ted thought that Professor Jacobs didn't like his poem *Northern Lights* because the professor didn't say much about it when Ted read it in class. However, the Professor says that he "quite liked it," but he *"wanted to hear what the other students in class thought of it."* Therefore, we can infer that choice B is correct; the professor sometimes doesn't express his feelings about his students' work in class.

5. C　　Professor Jacobs says, "Drop by my office sometime this week and we'll figure out which poems you should read."

6. A　　Dana tells Ms. Fong, "I really have no money for living expenses, so, uh, that's why I'm hoping to land a part-time job . . ."

7. D　　Ms. Fong explains that there are two types of work-study jobs, needs-based and merit-based, and that needs-based positions "are the ones funded by the government." Therefore, merit-based positions must not receive government funding.

8. D　　When Ms. Fong mentions the tour-guide job, Dana says "Really? Wow, that sounds fabulous." She does *not* want a job in a cafeteria (A) and Ms. Fong does not suggest that she work either as a receptionist (B) or as a lab technician (C).

9. C　　Ms. Fong says, "The first step is to fill out the financial aid forms I mentioned."

10. A　　Ms. Fong tells Dana not to give up on the position, which means to not stop trying to get the job. She says "we really encourage job-sharing—two students working one position."

11. B, A, C　　The professor says that the Inuit of Northern Alaska, where driftwood (wood brought to the shore by waves) was plentiful, built winter houses of wood. In North Central Canada and on Greenland, the Inuit built the snow houses that are called igloos in English. In Labrador in northeastern Canada, the Inuit built winter houses made of stone and earth supported by whalebones.

12. B　　This information about the isolation of the Inuit of Greenland is not directly relevant to the topic of the lecture (igloos). It is additional information about these people that the professor finds interesting.

13. A　　Since the Inuit word *igloo* means *house*, it could be used to refer to a summer house or any other kind of house.

14.

	Yes	No
Build a framework to support the igloo from inside		✓
Cut blocks of hardened snow with a knife	✓	
Dig an entrance tunnel	✓	
Stand on top of the igloo in order to compress the snow and make it stronger		✓
Melt snow on the interior surface of the igloo with lamps and then let the water re-freeze.	✓	

An igloo is the only type of traditional dome-shaped house built *without* interior support, so the first phrase should be marked **No.** The professor says that Inuit "used knives made of bone or ivory to cut wind-packed snow into blocks," so the second phrase should be marked **Yes.** The third phrase should be marked **Yes** because, according to the professor, "the entrance tunnel to the igloo was dug out so that it was lower than the igloo floor." The professor claims that an igloo was strong enough to support the weight of a man standing on top of it, but this would not have been part of the normal construction process; therefore, the fourth phrase should be marked **No.** The Inuit used a lamp to melt a little of the interior of the igloo and then let the water refreeze, forming a layer of ice. This made the igloo stronger. The fifth phrase should therefore be marked **Yes.**

15. B, E　　According to the professor, the Inuit "held dances and wrestling matches and their famous singing competitions in these larger igloos," so answers A, C, and D are all true. There was *no* mention in the lecture that larger igloos were used as multi-family houses (although the lecture does say that five or more families lived in igloos built in clusters, in several small igloos built close together). There is no mention of using igloos for storage.

16. D　　The professor says that in the 1950's, the Inuit began living in permanent housing and "only used igloos when they went on overnight hunting trips."

17. D   Professor Fuller says that Albert Einstein said faster-than-light travel was impossible, and then she says, "Who am I to argue with Einstein?" This expression means that she agrees with Einstein.

18. A   Professor Fuller says, "Then you fire intense bursts of laser beams at the sails."

19. C   According to Professor Fuller, what is required to travel to the stars is "some revolutionary drive system that requires little or no fuel."

20. C, D, A, B   The speculation stage involves dreaming up ideas for a new technology; the science stage involves testing these ideas with experiments; the technology stage involves building the technology; and the application stage involves putting the technology to use.

21. A, D   According to Professor Fuller, most of the "extra-solar" planets discovered so far are gas giants similar to Jupiter, and a few of them are small planets very close to their stars.

22. B   When she says "I don't think I'd pack my bags and head for the spaceport any time soon," she is joking since there are no passenger spaceports now, but what she really means is that flight to other stars will not occur in the near future.

23. A, C   The professor says that when Photorealism began "in the sixties and seventies, art was dominated by Minimalism and Conceptual Art, which were very *non*-representational types of art, very abstract . . ."

24. B   According to the professor, Audrey Flack "worked with an airbrush and she used acrylic paints," so choices A and D *are* given in the lecture. The professor also says that Audrey Flack "made a slide from the photo and projected the picture onto her canvas" so choice C is mentioned in the lecture. There is no mention that Flack used a computer.

25. A, B   She quotes two Photorealist painters (Chuck Close and Richard Estes) talking about the subjects of their paintings, and she gives specific examples of the subjects of some Photorealist paintings (for example, a gas station, an elderly man waiting at a bus stop, and an old, closed-down drive-in movie. (A drive-in movie is an outdoor movie theater where people watched the movie from their cars. This kind of movie theater was especially popular in the U.S. in the 1950's and 1960's.)

26. C   The professor says that Estes painted urban scenes reflected in large plate-glass windows. Only choice C qualifies as an urban scene reflected in glass.

27. D   The professor describes one of Hanson's sculptures as being so lifelike that people would try to ask the statue questions. She emphasizes the extreme realism of his works.

28.

	Yes	No
They feature three-dimensional optical illusions.		✓
Their subjects are ordinary people and scenes.	✓	
They are often painted in bright colors.	✓	
They may be either representational or non-representational.		✓
They show great attention to detail.	✓	

The professor mentions a school of art from the eighteenth century called *trompe l'oeil* that has some similarities to Photorealism. However, *trompe l'oeil* paintings feature optical illusions, such as figures that seem to be three-dimensional, while Photorealism was not concerned with optical illusions. Therefore, the first sentence should be marked **No.** The professor says that Photorealists "always painted ordinary, everyday, banal (boring) subjects," so the second sentence should be marked **Yes.** The professor also mentions that "most Photorealist paintings tend to be bright and colorful," so the third sentence should be marked **Yes.** All Photorealist works were representational, unlike the non-representational works of Minimalists and Conceptual Artists, so the fourth sentence should be marked **No.** The professor says that Photorealists "portrayed their subjects down to the smallest detail, and so their paintings look like photographs," and so the fifth sentence should be marked **Yes.**

29. B, C   The professor says that "By far the most damage is done to vehicles and . . . farmers' crops."

30. C   There is no mention in the article that dancing was ever used to prevent hail. In fourteenth-century Europe, church bells, pots and pans, and cannons were used. Cannons continued to be used in wine-producing areas through the nineteenth century, and in the Soviet Union in the 1950's, cannons shooting silver iodide into the air were used to try to reduce the size of hailstones. Cannons, therefore, have been used most recently.

31. B   A student asked the professor if people are often hurt by hailstones. When the professor says "Hmmm, well, it doesn't . . . it doesn't really seem like it to me," he really means that he doesn't think people are often injured, but he is not absolutely sure.

32. B   The professor says a hailstone "looks . . . like an onion cut in half—lots of layers." He is therefore comparing the internal structure of a hailstone to that of an onion.

33. A   One student says, "The hailstorm I was caught in was in April, maybe early May, so I'd guess spring," and the professor agrees that the student has guessed correctly.

34.

	Yes	No
Hailstones become so heavy that they fall to the ground.	✓	
Water droplets are lifted into the cold region of a thundercloud and freeze.	✓	
Tornado clouds circulate ice crystals inside of thunderclouds.		✓
Droplets are lifted into the cloud again and again, adding more ice.	✓	
A mass of fast-moving warm air hits a slower-moving mass of cold air.		✓

The professor says that, as the final step of hail formation, "the hailstone gets so heavy that the updrafts can't lift it anymore, so it drops out of the cloud and . . . bingo, you've got hail!" Therefore, you should mark the first sentence **Yes.** You should also mark the second sentence **Yes.** The professor says, "One of these updrafts picks up the droplet and lifts it high into the cloud, where the air is cold, and it freezes." Although hail is sometimes associated with tornadoes, tornado winds are not involved in the formation of hailstones, so you should mark the third sentence **No.** According to the professor, the process of being lifted back into the cold part of the clouds by updrafts "happens again and again. With each trip above and below the freezing level, the hailstone adds another layer of ice." Therefore, the fourth sentence should be marked **Yes.** There is no mention in the lecture that hail is formed by the collision of a fast-moving warm front and a slow-moving cold front, so the fifth sentence should be marked **No.**

Speaking

Independent Speaking Tasks

Answers for these two tasks will vary.

Integrated Speaking Tasks

Answers for these tasks will vary, but should include the following:

3. The woman agrees with the notice. The notice says that the university believes students need at least four terms of language instruction because the world is now more globalized and students need another language to communicate internationally. She says that people need a language to understand another culture and to work and travel abroad. The notice urges students with high levels of language ability to study an additional language, and she plans to follow this advice and study a European language.

4. Both the *Columbia* and the *Hindenburg* are lighter-than-air craft. The blimp *Columbia* is a non-rigid airship. Blimps are much smaller than zeppelins, and they have no internal structure. Because they are filled with helium, they are safer than zeppelins. Blimps like the *Columbia* are often used as platforms for cameras at sporting events and for advertising.

   The German zeppelin *Hindenburg* was a rigid airship. It had an internal aluminum frame. It was huge, about 250 meters in length, and was used to carry passengers. The *Hindenburg* was filled with flammable hydrogen and was destroyed by an explosion and fire in 1937. This disaster ended the age of zeppelins.

5. Diane's problem is that she would like to go see her sister in Boston during Spring Break. However, she didn't make an airline reservation in advance, and now she can't afford the fare. She doesn't want to drive because buying gas would be expensive and the drive would be tiring.

   Mike suggests two solutions: using the Ride Board or taking a train. Test-takers who chose the first solution should mention that she could find someone to do some of the driving and to share the cost of gasoline. She could also either take her car or go in another person's car.

   Test-takers who chose the second solution should mention that she could relax or study on the train, and that it is a little bit cheaper than flying.

6. Lantana plants need insects to visit their flowers to spread their pollen. Insects need the nectar that fertile plants produce for food. The lantana plant uses color to direct insects to flowers full of nectar and pollen. On the first day a lantana flower blooms, the flower is yellow and it is fertile and ready for a visit from an insect. On the second day the flower is orange and there is less pollen and nectar. On the third it is red and there is no pollen or nectar at all. Insects know this and visit the yellow plants much more often than they visit orange or yellow flowers. This system helps the plant because it does not have to try to keep pollen and nectar in all of its flowers. It helps the insect because it does not have to spend time visiting all the flowers.

Writing

Integrated Writing Task

Responses for this task will vary, but should include the following:

The main point of the article is that unnecessary risk-taking is illogical, and in its extreme forms, pathological (caused by mental illness). The speaker, however, believes that risk-taking is sometimes necessary and can even be beneficial.

The article states that there is a "universal risk-taking personality." In other words, some people take risks in all aspects of their lives. The speaker disagrees with this idea. He says that some people take risks in one area of their lives but not in others. He gives the example of an investment banker who makes safe investments but who risks his life by racing motorcycles on weekends.

The article says people who take extreme risks are motivated by suicidal tendencies. However, the speaker thinks that most people who take risks believe that nothing terrible will happen to them. He gives the example of motorcycle racers who never think they will be involved in accidents.

The article says that there is no reward for taking risks. The speaker contradicts this idea as well. He says that for some people, there are physical rewards that come from chemicals such as adrenaline that are released when someone takes risks. There may also be psychological rewards. According to research studies, risk-takers tend to be more confident and more successful financially and socially.

Practice Test 2

Reading

Lichens

Answer	Explanation
1. C	The author emphasizes in Paragraph 1 that lichens can live in many environments and gives examples (tropical rain forests, hot springs, mountain tops, deserts, the Arctic, Antarctica, etc.). It is true that lichens grow in cold places (choice A), such as Antarctica, but they also grow in hot places such as tropical rain forests and hot springs. It is true that lichens grow in remote places (B), but they also grow in cities. And it is true that lichens grow on rocks (D), but they also grow on other surfaces such as farmers' fenceposts.
2. B	The word *secrete* means "produce," especially, "to produce a liquid."
3. C	Paragraph 2 says that lichens contribute to the process of weathering, which creates soil. "This property enables lichens to be pioneers," according to the article, "beginning the process of soil formation that allows mosses, ferns, and other plants to later take root."
4. A	Choice A best summarizes the sentence. The original sentence says that many people associate

lichens with mosses, but that mosses are green while lichens appear in many colors. Choice B incorrectly says that many people are familiar with mosses but not with lichens. Choice C incorrectly states that green lichens are a type of moss. Choice D incorrectly says that the two types of plants are difficult to distinguish.

5. C Paragraph 3 says that acids from lichens can be used as dyes (A). Some lichens can be used as antibiotics (B). Oils from lichens are used in perfumes (D). There is no mention that lichens are used as human food (C), so this is the best answer.

6. A The word *tangled* means *twisted* or *tied in knots*.

7. D Paragraph 5 tells us that symbiosis is a relationship in which "the two types of organisms live together to the benefit of both." In choice A, the mistletoe benefits, but the oak tree does not. In choice B, the remoras benefit, but there is no evidence that the sharks do. In choice C, the tiger benefits, but the grass is not affected. In choice D, both the protozoa and the termites benefit because both receive nourishment, so this is the best answer.

8. D Paragraph 5 explains that the fungi "protects the tender algae from direct sunlight . . ." Therefore, direct sunlight must be damaging to the algae.

9. B The reference is to one organism. The sentence means that for hundreds of years people thought that this double organism was a single organism.

10. C The best answer is C because the author says that ". . . if they are classified as separate species, these fungal species that cannot live alone seem rather strange." There is no information in the passage to support choice A. Choice B is incorrect; the algae make the food for the fungi. Choice D is also incorrect; paragraph 6 says that the fungi "can be placed in known families of fungi but are unlike any species that live independently."

11. B The word *splendid* means "excellent, very good."

12. The new sentence should be inserted at the fourth black square in the passage:

Lichens are a partnership of two or more types of plants, a fungus and a type of algae. ■ If you look at the lichen body through a magnifying glass, you will see that it is made up of a tangled mass of fungal strands called hyphae. ■ In the upper layer of these hyphae grow colonies of another type of plant. ■ These are most commonly green algae but are sometimes blue-green algae.(■)**A few enterprising lichens contain both.**

The word *both* refers to green algae and blue-green algae. You may have thought that *both* refers to "a fungus and a type of algae" in the first sentence, but *all* algae consist of a fungus and an algae, not just "a few enterprising lichens."

13. Fungi: A, D, E; **Algae:** B, F

Choice A is a characteristic of fungi. Paragraph 5 says "The fungus inserts threads . . . to anchor the plant in place." Choice B is a characteristic of algae. Paragraph 6 says "The algal components . . . are recognizable as species that grow alone." Neither fungus nor algae produces carbon dioxide, so choice C should not be listed. Choice D should be listed as a characteristic of fungi because paragraph 5 says that "The fungus provides moisture and minerals for the plant." Choice E is also a characteristic of fungi. Paragraph 6 says that "The fungal components . . . cannot live apart from their partners."

Choice F is characteristic of algae. Paragraph 5 says that "The algae contain chlorophyll and synthesize sugar from carbon dioxide and sunlight."

The Rosetta Stone

Answer	Explanation
14. D	Paragraph 1 tells us that "The priests of the king wrote a short history of the king's family, described his accomplishments, and explained his future plans. Choice C, "To present information about the current ruler of Egypt, Ptolemy V," best summarizes this idea.
15. C	The word *incursions* means "invasions, attacks, raids."
16. A	The passage states, "This message was written on stone tablets in demotic Egyptian for the common people, in Egyptian hieroglyphs for the priests, and in Greek for the ruling class. Thus, it was written in two languages but in three scripts." The three scripts must have been the demotic alphabet, the hieroglyphic alphabet, and the Greek alphabet. Since Greek is obviously one of the languages, this means that demotic Egyptian and the form of Egyptian used by the priest must have been basically the same language written in different scripts.
17. B	There are two common uses of quotation marks in a passage. One is to report the exact words that someone spoke or wrote. The other is to indicate that, although something is called an *X*, it is not really an *X* (The child's "house" was made of blankets draped over chairs.) The author uses quotations in the second way. The French were not really on an extended (long) vacation in Egypt. They were trapped there because the British had destroyed their fleet (ships) and they couldn't get back to France.
18. C	The passage says that "French military engineers strengthened existing defensive positions. In the port town of Rosetta (now known as El-Rashid), the French were rebuilding an old fort when Captain Pierre-François Bouchard discovered an irregularly shaped slab made of dark granite." Since Bouchard was rebuilding a fort (a strong military position), he was most probably a military engineer.
19. D	According to the passage, people are often mistaken about the type of stone that the Rosetta Stone is made of. The passage says the stone is an "irregularly shaped slab made of dark granite (often misidentified as basalt) with three types of writings on it." (Granite and basalt are types of stone.)
20. A	*Bands* are lines or rows.
21. A	The author writes, "some scholars even believed that hieroglyphs were not really an alphabet at all but were merely decorations." If the hieroglyphs were only decorations, then they could never be translated.
22. B	In paragraph 5, the author lists the three assumptions made by Champollion in order to translate the hieroglyphs. The second assumption was that "Hieroglyphics served not only as symbols of words and ideas (ideograms) but also as symbols of spoken sounds." Therefore, choice A is one of assumptions that Champollion used to make the translation. Champollion's third assumption was that "Certain hieroglyphs enclosed in ovals were

phonetic transcriptions of pharaohs' names." Choice C, therefore, is one of Champollion's assumptions. Champollion's first assumption was that "The Coptic Egyptian language, still spoken by a small group of Egyptians, was the final stage of the ancient Egyptian language. Champollion could consult with experts on Coptic Egyptian to learn about Ptolemaic Egyptian." Choice D is one of Champollion's assumptions. Only Choice B—that the three messages did not have exactly the same message—was not given in the paragraph. (In fact, he must have assumed that the three messages did have exactly the same meaning.)

23. D The phrase *the rest* refers to the rest of the hiero-glyphs on the Rosetta Stone.

24. C The main point of paragraph 6 is that Egypt wants the British Museum to return the Rosetta Stone to the land where it came from. The author empha-sizes this point by quoting an expert in this field, the archaeologist and government official Zahi Hawass.

25. The new sentence should be inserted at the second black square in the passage:

> It was through the Rosetta Stone that scholars learned how to read Egyptian hieroglyphs. The hieroglyphic alphabet, one of the earliest writing systems ever developed, had been used by the Egyptians for 3,500 years.(■)**Hieroglyphic script is mostly pictorial, images of natural and man-made objects.** However, it is far more complex than simple picture writing and contains thou-sands of symbols. ■ After Egypt was conquered by the Romans, Latin became the dominant language and by the fourth century A.D., no one could understand the symbols. ■ Before the Rosetta Stone was discovered, some scholars even believed that hieroglyphs were not really an alphabet but were merely decorations.

The words *However* and *it* in the second marked sentence are the keys to the correct placement of the missing sen-tence. The second sentence says, "*However,* while *it* is pic-torial, it is more complex than simple picture writing." The word *it* in the second sentence connects to the phrase *hieroglyphic script* in the missing sentence. The missing sentence says that hieroglyphics is mainly picto-rial, using images of natural and man-made things as symbols. The next sentence says that, while the hiero-glyphic script is pictorial, it is more complex than simple picture writing. This sentence is in partial contrast with the missing sentence and therefore the word *However* connects these two sentences.

26. B, E, There is no information in the passage about the
   F   British Museum's response to Egypt's request for the return of the Rosetta Stone, so choice A is not a good answer. Choice B summarizes the points made in paragraphs 4 and 5 and is one of the main points of the passage. Choice C is not true. According to paragraph 2, the Rosetta Stone was made of dark granite, a type of stone. Choice D is a detail provided in paragraph 2, but it is not a main idea of the passage and does not belong in the summary. Choice E is a summary of paragraphs 2 and 3 and is a main point in the passage. Choice F summarizes paragraph 6 and belongs in this sum-mary outline.

Transient Lunar Phenomena

Answer	Explanation

27. D Choice D is best because this passage mainly involves a description of a phenomenon (TLP) and possible explanations of it.

28. C The word *fleeting* means "short-lived, quickly pass-ing, transient."

29. A The phrase *this mechanism* refers to the fact that light hitting a reflective surface such as the surface of a satellite or a car's windshield, can cause a flash (a brief, intense display of light).

30. A The author mentions Gervase because he saw a TLP many years before the era of artificial satel-lites. This weakens the theory of Raste and Maley because they believe that TLP are actually caused by the reflection of light from satellites.

31. B The author says, "Grant claimed in an interview that he had seen flocks of red and white birds, herds of 'diminutive bison,' and strange beavers that walked on their hind legs. Not only that, but he claimed even to have seen people with bat-like wings who had built towers and pyramids beneath the domes." The use of the phrase *not only that* and the word *even* (which is often used to give a surprising or extreme example) tells us that the author finds the people with bat-like wings and their buildings the *most* unbelievable of Grant's strange sightings. (Although, in truth, they are all pretty unbelievable.)

32. A Choice A gives the essential information in the original sentence. Choice B mentions the fact that both trained and amateur scientists watched the moon from 1968 to 1972. This information is not part of the original sentence. (The word *trained* in the original sentence means "aimed at.") Choice C says that more TLP actually occurred from 1968 to 1972; the original sentence simply says that more TLP were *seen* during that period because more people were looking at the moon then. Choice D is correct as far as it goes, but does not include an essential idea from the original sentence (that more TLP were observed from 1968 to 1972 than in any other period).

33. C This choice is best because the author says "Though many sightings were dubious, some were highly plausible because they were made by inde-pendent observers at different locations."

34. B Bonnie Buratti used "photographs of the moon taken by the U.S. lunar mapping satellite *Clementine* and indeed, these images confirmed the presence of a reddish cloud obscuring part of the crater."

35. D The word *stray* means "undirected, uncontrolled, on the loose." (*Stray* dogs are dogs without a mas-ter that wander around on their own.)

36. C According to the passage, *thermal cracking* occurs as a result of a sudden change in temperature. ("A rock heats up in the intense sunlight. Suddenly, when the sun sets, the temperature drops, and the stone cracks.") The only example of this among the four choices is C. (The cool glass is suddenly warmed up by hot water.)

37. D The paragraph tells us that "The rocks might also be shattered by 'moonquakes,' seismic activity on the Moon (choice A) or by meteors (choice C).

Thermal cracking (choice B) is also given as a possible reason why lunar rocks crack. There is no mention that gas pressure can cause rocks to crack. (However, the pressure of gases trapped beneath the surface of the Moon may be the cause of the "billowing clouds" sometimes seen on the moon.)

38. The new sentence should be inserted at the first black square in the passage:

And what about the billowing clouds?(■)**Many observers once thought that they were caused by lunar volcanoes, but today the moon is believed to have been geologically inactive for billions of years.** The most commonly held belief today is that they are caused by pockets of gas trapped beneath the lunar surface. ■ The clouds may be caused by the rapid escape of these gases, which kicks up clouds of dust. ■ The pockets of gas may be freed by moonquakes or the pockets may be punctured by meteors. ■

The first sentence in the paragraph asks what causes the billowing clouds. The rest of the paragraph discusses today's theory. Logically, the best place to put the missing sentence—which discusses what people in the past thought was the cause of the clouds—is between the introductory question and the rest of the paragraph.

39. Theories that explain why TLP do *not* exist: B, E; **theories that explain why TLP *do* exist:** C, D, F

Choice A is *not* mentioned in the passage at all. Choice B is mentioned in paragraph 1 as a theory of Raste and Maley to explain why TLP do *not* exist. Choice C is given in paragraph 4 as a theory of Zito to explain why TLP *do* exist. Choice D is given in paragraph 4 as a possible reason why TLP *do* exist. Choice E is given in paragraph 1 as an explanation of why TLP do *not* exist. Choice F is mentioned in paragraph 2 as a theory (although a very unlikely theory)—of why TLP *do* exist.

Listening

Answer	Explanation
1. C	Janet tells Allen, "I'm running for re-election for the seat on the Student Council that belongs to the School of Business. But you can't vote for me, because you're in the School of Engineering."
2. C	Students vote for a representative from their own school, for president, and for vice-president (a total of three).
3. A, D	It's clear that Janet is currently a member of the Student Council because she says that she is running "for re-election." She also says "I'm thinking that next year, I'll try to get elected president."
4. A	Janet says, ". . . the most important thing is—the Council gets to decide how to spend your money. Fifteen dollars from each student's fees goes into the Student Council's general fund."
5. B	The idiom *don't push your luck* means "you've been lucky so far—don't try to get anything else." In other words, Allen means, "You're lucky to get me to agree to vote tomorrow—don't try to get me to go to the debate tonight too."
6. D	Alison asks Tony to be part of a "focus group." A focus group helps companies determine whether to market a product or not, or which version of a product to market. This would therefore most likely be a topic in a marketing class.
7. A	Alison tells Tony, " . . . when you come in the classroom tomorrow, Professor Marquez will give you a

little card that tells you your vital information: your age, your occupation, how much education you have, that sort of thing . . . and that's the role you play when you're pretending to be in this focus group."

8. C   According to Alison, an experiential focus group helps decide which of several versions of a product to market. In Hollywood, focus groups help film companies decide which version of a movie to release, so Hollywood focus groups must be experiential focus groups.

9. D   According to Alison, "Professor Marquez says that . . . that the chemistry, the, uh, interaction between the moderator and the focus group is key in making sure a focus group goes well." Professor Marquez will probably concentrate on this interaction during the classroom activity.

10. B   Tony says that he is free the following day but does not definitely agree to be part of the activity until he learns that the flavor of ice cream that he will be testing the next day will be mint chocolate chip. Then he enthusiastically says, "That settles it . . . I'm in" meaning that now he is definitely willing to take part. He must enjoy this flavor of ice cream.

11. C   The lecturer says, "After a while, Stowe and her husband moved back to New England, to Brunswick, Maine. He encouraged her to write a book that showed the evils of slavery. So, Stowe wrote *Uncle Tom's Cabin* . . ."

12. C, A, D, B   *Uncle Tom's Cabin* was first published as a newspaper serial (in other words, a small part was published every day) in the *National Era* newspaper in 1851. The next year, in 1852, it was published as a book and became very popular. According to the lecture, plays based on the books ("Tom Shows") appeared "soon after the book was published." The movie came much later, in 1927.

13. B   Charles Dickens is given as an example of a great writer of that age who also wrote about some characters in a sentimental way. The professor gives the character of Little Nell in the book *The Old Curiosity Shop* as an example.

14. B, D   According to the professor, this scene was part of George Aiken's play but did not appear in the book. It was also a part of the 1927 movie, which may be why "this scene sticks in people's minds" (is remembered).

15.

	Yes	No
It is not strong enough in its criticism of slavery.	✓	
It treats its characters too sentimentally.	✓	
It is not based on the author's firsthand experiences.	✓	
It is difficult for modern readers to understand.		✓
It is far too long and repetitive.		✓

The first choice should be checked **Yes.** The professor says, " . . . some Northern Abolitionists thought that it didn't go far enough, that it painted too soft a picture of slavery." The second choice should also be checked **Yes.** According to the professor, "Another criticism is that Stowe's treatment of her characters is overly sentimental, overly emotional." The third choice should be checked **Yes** as well. According to the professor, "that's one of the criticisms that Southerners directed at her—that she had no firsthand knowledge of slavery, of life in the South, because she'd never spent time there." The fourth and the fifth choices should be checked **No.** The professor does not mention these criticisms in her lecture.

16. D   The professor advises the students to read *Uncle Tom's Cabin* "cover to cover"—in other words, to read every page. (She is talking about reading the novel, not their textbook, choice B, which contains only short selections from the novel.

17. D, B, C, A   According to the professor, all glaciers start with *ordinary snow.* When ordinary snow melts and refreezes several times, it becomes *névé,* a compressed form of snow. If *névé* lasts for a year, it becomes even more compressed and forms a compact form of ice called *firn.* Firn, buried under more and more snow and ice, finally becomes *glacial ice.*

18. C, D   According to the lecture, continental glaciers are today found only in Greenland and Antarctica.

19. B, C   A glacier may follow a V-shaped creek path down a mountainside, but the rocks that it picks up on the way "round out the bottom of the valley, and the V-shaped stream bed becomes U-shaped." Therefore, choice A is *not* correct and choice C *is* correct. Also, according to the lecture, "because they are rigid, glaciers don't take sharp corners very well, so their downhill paths are generally gonna be a series of gentle curves." Therefore, choice B *is* correct and choice D is not.

20. A   Choice D, continental glacier, is not correct. The lecturer tells us that a continental glacier is much larger than a valley glacier. Valley glaciers flow together to form piedmont glaciers, so piedmont glaciers must be bigger than valley glaciers. However, tributary glaciers flow into valley glaciers, and therefore, must be the smallest type of glacier.

21.

	Valley Glaciers	Continental Glaciers
Today cover about 10% of the world's land surface.		✓
Flow together to form piedmont glaciers.	✓	
As they recede, seem to flow uphill.	✓	
About 11,000 years ago, covered 30% of the world's land surface.		✓
As they grow, seem to flow outwards in all directions.		✓

Choice A is a characteristic of continental glaciers. The professor says that the two continental glaciers in existence today, in Greenland and Antarctica, cover 10% of the earth's land surface. Valley glaciers flow together to form piedmont glaciers, so choice B is a characteristic of valley glaciers. So is choice C; the professor says that "When they recede, valley glaciers seem to be moving

uphill . . . What's really happening is that they are melting faster than they are adding new materials." Choice D is a characteristic of continental glaciers. During the last Ice Age, around 11,000 years ago, continental glaciers covered much of the northern hemisphere and about 30% of the land surface of the earth. Choice D is also a characteristic of continental glaciers. The professor says "a continental glacier moves out in all directions from the glacier's central point."

22. A   The danger mentioned by the professor is that global warming may cause glaciers to melt and that this will cause the level of oceans to rise.

23. C   This passage mainly deals with the four stages of the business cycle.

24. B   The professor says that these terms are the ones most commonly used these days, implying that, in the past, other terms were more common.

25.

	Yes	No
They vary in length from cycle to cycle.	✓	
They are measured from the peak of economic activity to the trough, the lowest point of economic activity.		✓
They vary in intensity from cycle to cycle.	✓	
They have involved deeper recessions in recent years because of globalization.		✓
They are sometimes called *fluctuations* because they are irregular.	✓	

The first choice should be checked **Yes.** The professor says "no business cycle is exactly the same. They vary in length, for example." The second choice is not a valid choice. Cycles are measured from peak to peak, according to the professor, not from peak to trough. Check **No.** Choice C, however, should be checked **Yes** because, when a student asks the professor about this, he says, "You're right, they do vary in intensity." You should check **No** for the fourth choice. Some economists in the 1990's thought that globalization prevented downturns in business in the U.S.—which turned out to be false—but there is no indication in the lecture that globalization makes recessions worse. The last choice is also mentioned in the lecture. The professor says, "In fact, they are so irregular in length that some economists prefer to talk about business *fluctuations* rather than a business cycle." Check the last choice **Yes.**

26. A, B   One depression occurred in the 1870's and one, the Great Depression, occurred during the 1930's.

27. D   According to the professor, "What they usually do is, the government . . . the Central Bank, really . . . manipulates the money supply."

28. A   The professor says, "Today, though, it's no longer considered a valid theory. Still, you have to admit, it's an interesting one."

29. A   The professor says that most people think of science fiction as a contemporary type of film but in fact, some of the earliest films were science fiction films. She gives as an example George Méliès's film *A Voyage to the Moon.*

30. D   According to the lecture, the 1926 film *Metropolis* ". . . was set a hundred years in the future, in the year 2026."

31. C   The professor says that the movie *Them!* was about giant ants that had been affected by radiation from nuclear weapon tests. She says that there were many other movies about "big bugs" (insects) that had been radiated.

32. A, C   The professor tells the class that her favorite movie, *Forbidden Planet,* is "based on William Shakespeare's play *The Tempest.* It also makes use of ideas from the theories of the famous psychologist Sigmund Freud."

33. B   What the professor finds interesting about *ET* is that, unlike most movies about visitors from space, this one features a friendly, smart, likeable alien.

34. B   The professor says, "Then, uh, unfortunately, we just have time for a few quick scenes from my favorite, *Forbidden Planet.*" She is sorry that they won't have time to watch more of the movie *Forbidden Planet.*

Speaking

Independent Speaking Tasks
Answers for these two tasks will vary.

Integrated Speaking Tasks
Answers for these tasks will vary, but should include the following:

3. The woman thinks this is a great program. The man agrees that it is a good program for her, but says that it doesn't help him. That's because it affects only first-year students, and he is a second-year student. The woman mentions that he can buy a low-cost laptop computer through this program, but he says that he already bought one last year. He does agree that laptop computers are important for students.

4. The reading discusses the general concept of utopian communities. According to the reading, some people in the nineteenth century believed they could reform society by creating cooperative communities. The reading gives the general characteristics of a utopian community: (1) They were isolated from the surrounding communities. (2) They had experimental societies. (3) They usually lasted only a short time.

The speaker looks at one specific example of a utopian community, Brook Farm. Brook Farm was the most famous of utopian communities. It fit the general characteristics of a utopian community. For one thing, it was isolated geographically. Although the location today is in suburban Boston, at the time it was founded it was in the countryside. It had an unusual economic structure. People who lived there traded 300 days of work a year for their room and board. Also, there was equality of the sexes, which was unusual at that time. Brook Farm, like most utopian communities, lasted only a short time. It closed after six years as a result of financial problems, disease, and a fire.

5. Nancy's problem is that she has noisy neighbors and cannot study or sleep at home. (They are musicians and they practice their music at home.) She has spoken to her neighbors several times but they continue to make noise. The man suggests that she contact the police, but Nancy says she doesn't really like that idea. Besides, they are not the only neighbors in her building who are noisy. The man then suggests that she move, perhaps to his building, which is quieter.

Test-takers who think the first solution is best might point out that these noisy neighbors should be taught a lesson, that they might not be so noisy in the future if Nancy called the police. They might also say that, since Nancy is not the one who is causing the problem, she is not the one who should have to move.

Test-takers who support the second idea might point out that this might be a good option because she does not want to get her neighbors in trouble with the police. Because her building is noisy in general, she might be better off moving to a quieter location such as the man's building, where she could study and sleep.

6. Before 1953, hurricanes did not have names. After that, the storms were given female names. Beginning in 1979, male and female names began to alternate. No names begin with the letters Q, U, X, Y, and Z, so there are only twenty-one names in each list. There are six lists of names that are used over and over. However, when a storm is very bad, its name is retired and another name is added to the list for that year. If there are ever more than twenty-one named storms in one year, then hurricanes are named after Greek letters.

Writing

Integrated Writing Task
Responses for this task will vary, but should include the following:

The main point of the article is that eco-tourism is a positive form of development. On the other hand, the speaker says that, like all forms of development, eco-tourism has good points and bad points.

The article says that eco-tourism blocks the development of other types of development, such as logging and manufacturing. The speaker agrees that eco-tourist development may be better than other types of development, including the development of facilities for ordinary tourists. However, she says that there is development, especially road-building, in sensitive areas.

The article says that an area that is visited by eco-tourists is a resource and that both the government and the local population will be interested in preserving it. The speaker points out that just because an area is protected does not mean that it is not exploited, and that roads make exploitation easier.

In the article, the author explains that eco-tourism provides jobs and better conditions for the locals. The speaker says that yes, jobs are provided, but they are generally very poor jobs, and sometimes people from outside the area take the better jobs. Also, there is the problem of "cultural pollution." Isolated people are brought too quickly into the world of western technology.

In summary, the article emphasizes only the positive side of eco-tourism, saying that everyone benefits, but the speaker points out that eco-tourism also has its negative aspects.

Independent Writing Task
Responses will vary.